Options Theory and Trading

A Step-by-Step Guide to Control Risk and Generate Profits

RON IANIERI

WILEY

John Wiley & Sons, Inc.

Published by John Wiley & Sons, Inc., Hoboken, New Jersey.
Published simultaneously in Canada.

For general information on our other products and services or for technical support, please contact our Customer Care Department within the United States at (800) 762-2974, outside the United States at (317) 572-3993 or fax (317) 572-4002.

Wiley also publishes its books in a variety of electronic formats. Some content that appears in print may not be available in electronic books. For more information about Wiley products, visit our web site at www.wiley.com.

Library of Congress Cataloging-in-Publication Data

Ianieri, Ron, 1964–
  Options theory and trading : a step-by-step guide to control risk and generate profits / Ron Ianieri.
      p.   cm. – (Wiley trading series)
  Includes index.
  ISBN 978-0-470-45578-4 (cloth)
1. Stock options.   2. Portfolio management.   3. Risk management.   4. Options (Finance)
I. Title.
  HG6042.I36   2009
  332.63′2283–dc22

                                                                              2009004113

Printed in the United States of America

10 9 8 7 6 5 4 3 2 1

To my family and friends

Contents

Preface   xi

Acknowledgments   xv

PART I   Understanding Terms and Theory   1

CHAPTER 1   Options Basics and Terms   3

Calls and Puts   4
Classes and Series   5
In the Money, Out of the Money, and At the Money   7
Premium and Time Decay   9
Intrinsic versus Extrinsic Value   9
Volatility   12

CHAPTER 2   Calls and Puts   15

Call Options   15
Put Options   16

CHAPTER 3   Option Theory   19

Option Pricing Models   20
Fundamentals of Pricing Models   21
Types of Pricing Models   25
Inputs of the Options Pricing Model   32
Outputs of the Pricing Model   39

CHAPTER 4   Option Theory and the Greeks   **41**

Delta   42
Gamma   52
Vega   57
Theta   68
Second-Tier Greeks   80

CHAPTER 5   Synthetic Positions   **85**

Defining Synthetics   86
Synthetic Stock   88
Synthetic Call   96
Synthetic Put   106

PART II   Basic Strategies   **117**

CHAPTER 6   Introduction to Trading Strategies   **119**

Directional Trading Strategies   119
In-the-Money, Out-of-the-Money, and At-the-Money Options   123
Leverage and Risk   128

CHAPTER 7   Covered Call/Buy-Write Strategy   **131**

Foundations of the Strategy   131
Performance in Different Scenarios   135
Lean   138
Rolling the Position   139
Examples   141
Covered Call/Buy-Write Synopsis   146

CHAPTER 8   The Covered Put/Sell-Write Strategy **147**

Reviewing Selling Short   147
Foundations of the Strategy   148
Performance in Different Scenarios   151
Lean   154
Rolling the Position   157

Examples 157
Covered Put/Sell-Write Synopsis 163

CHAPTER 9   The Protective Put Strategy 165

Foundations of the Strategy 165
Performance in Different Scenarios 166
Lean 168
When to Use the Protective Put Strategy 170
Examples 172
Protective Put Synopsis 177

**CHAPTER 10 The Synthetic Put/Protective
          Call Strategy** 179

Foundations of the Strategy 179
Performance in Different Scenarios 181
Lean 183
When to Use the Protective Call Strategy 184
Examples 187
Synthetic Put Synopsis 191

CHAPTER 11 The Collar Strategy 193

Foundations of the Strategy 193
Performance in Different Scenarios 194
Lean 197
Examples 199
Collar Synopsis 204

**PART III Advanced Strategies: Spread Trading,
          Straddles, and Strangles** 207

CHAPTER 12 Vertical Spreads 209

Construction of a Vertical Spread 210
Value and the Vertical Spread 211
Spread Prices Fluctuate 217

Factors that Affect Spread Pricing 218

Rolling the Position 218

Time Decay and Volatility Trading Opportunities 220

An Imaginary Spread Scenario 222

Recap with Special Insights 224

Examples 225

Bull Spread Synopsis 230

Bear Spread Synopsis 231

CHAPTER 13 Time Spreads 233

Construction of the Time Spread 233

Behavior of the Spread 234

Effects of Stock Price on the Time Spread 236

Effects of Volatility on the Time Spread 237

Buyer Risk and Reward 244

Seller Risk and Reward 245

Rolling the Position 246

Concluding Thoughts 249

Examples 249

Time Spread Synopsis 253

CHAPTER 14 The Stock Replacement/Covered Call Strategy (Diagonal Spread) 255

When to Use the Diagonal Spread 257

Rolling the Position 259

Conclusion 259

CHAPTER 15 Straddles 261

What Is a Straddle? 261

Straddle Scenarios 262

How It Works 262

Factors that Affect Straddle Prices 263

Risks and Rewards 266

Break-Even, Maximum Reward, and Maximum Risk 267

Conclusion 271

Examples   271
Long Straddle Synopsis   276
Short Straddle Synopsis   277

CHAPTER 16 Strangles   **279**

What Is a Strangle?   280
Strangle Scenarios   281
How It Works   281
Factors that Affect Strangle Prices   282
Risks and Rewards   285
Break-Even, Maximum Reward, and Maximum Risk   285
Conclusion   289
Examples   289
Long Strangle Synopsis   294
Short Strangle Synopsis   294

PART IV   Combination Strategies   **297**

CHAPTER 17 The Butterfly   **299**

Constructing the Butterfly   299
Why Use Butterflies?   301
Butterfly and Synthetic Positions   303
What Will a Butterfly Cost?   305
Butterfly and the Greeks   307
Iron Butterfly   309
Long Iron Butterfly   312
Using the Butterfly   312
Long Butterfly Synopsis   313
Short Butterfly Synopsis   314

CHAPTER 18 The Condor   **315**

Long Condor   315
Short Condor   316
Why Use Condors?   317
How It Works   320

Condors versus Butterflies   321
Condors and the Greeks   323
Iron Condors   326
How Do We Use Condors?   330
Long Condor Synopsis   331
Short Condor Synopsis   332

Conclusion   335

Appendix: Five Trading Sheets   337

About the Author   343

Index   345

Preface

Over the last several years, more and more investors have taken on the responsibility of managing their own investments and retirement accounts. The numbers of those doing so is steadily increasing for a variety of reasons. Investing your own money is not an impossible task but requires a conscious commitment to that endeavor. Private investors can make profitable investment decisions if they are willing to dedicate the time and effort necessary to learn how to invest wisely.

Options Theory and Trading is designed to help you, as an investor, take a more proactive approach to managing your money and controlling your financial future. Its aim is to help you learn how to use options to protect your portfolio, manage risk, and enhance returns. Keep in mind that no one cares more about your money than you do. So it makes sense that you, more than anyone else, should know where your money is and how it is performing.

As diligent investors, we rely on research, analysis, and experience to turn the odds in our favor. Having access to the right information is often the key factor to an investor's long-term success in the market. To be successful in any endeavor, you must know what to do, and how and when to do it.

My goal in *Options Theory and Trading* is to give you the key information needed to excel in the financial markets. I will discuss the ins and outs of options, and how they can significantly improve your returns and dramatically reduce risk. My job is to educate you in the field of option investing just as I have educated many professional traders and active private investors.

Options, when used smartly and correctly, can greatly enhance your profits. The leverage in options, again when used correctly, can help small accounts trade like big accounts without the normally associated risks. And in times of financial turmoil, when the markets are constantly trading down, options can keep you from catastrophic losses. Options are life insurance policies for your portfolio and, when used in a judicious manner, can be an investor's best friend.

Used appropriately, options can serve as valuable additions to an investor's arsenal of effective investment and hedging vehicles. A proper understanding of option strategies will completely change how you invest. That understanding will show you how to increase profits and reduce risk while limiting the amount of capital you put at stake.

As we move forward into a future where world economies are becoming more and more globalized, we are finding that the effects of one economy directly affect all. This results in an environment of increasing volatility in the financial markets and a greater risk of market corrections endangering the savings of individual investors around the world. Investors' only hope for stabilizing the growth of their investments may well depend on their acceptance and use of options.

Over the course of my 20-plus years in the options market, I have read many books on options. Some have been general but oversimplified; others have been very specific but too technical. During those years, I have also trained many professional traders and, recently, many individual investors. I learned many valuable lessons about how people learn and how instructors teach. From those experiences, I have made some interesting observations concerning education in the field of options.

One observation is that many option instructors—by far the large majority I have encountered—have trouble being easy to understand and still completely thorough in the depth of their teachings. Easy to understand should not mean that important but difficult topics are omitted. It does mean that those difficult topics must be broken down into understandable pieces. That is what will happen in this book.

Another observation is that options are constantly taught backward. Option theory is taught last as an "advanced topic" while the strategies based on that theory are taught first. These topics should be taught the other way around. Logically, option theory should be, and needs to be, first in instruction...before the strategies. Option theory is the foundation on which strategies should be built. Those who do not understand the theory first never fully understand options. If you do not fully understand options, then you cannot truly understand the strategies based on options. And those who do not understand their positions in all market situations are not around for too long.

The topics of option theory are the cornerstones, the foundations of understanding an option. Having investors truly understand options and their uses is my goal. When investors understand options, they are able to select the optimal strategy on a consistent basis and to construct that strategy in the most cost-efficient way. Understanding options helps when things do not go the way you thought they would. Remember, we all have losing trades from time to time. Understanding options allows you to be in a position to cut losses quickly. Understanding will let you know where your risks are before you put on the trade and will give you the tools to counter those risks.

Options are a more sophisticated product than their underlying instruments, such as stocks. As they are more sophisticated, there are many more topics and concepts to master in order to use their power properly. With options, as with any other highly technical vehicle, a solid foundation is the key to understanding.

The ability to truly understand the options you are trading is critical to consistent profitability in all markets: up, down, and sideways. So, when I designed my option trading course for the professional floor trader, I built it in a way that forced students to learn in a logical step-by-step way. Individual investors also can use this method to understand options.

In this book, I present basic option theory and strategy in the same manner and specifically following the same order that I use in my options classes to retail and professional traders, As you move through the book, a logical progression of topics will become evident. This logical progression will enable you to learn in a way that leads to a quicker understanding of options and, in turn, quicker understanding in your option use. I know many people who trade options. Some win, but many lose. Those who truly understand options are those who win, making money consistently and with less risk.

Having said all that, let me add a caveat. Understand that just reading this one book will not make you an expert. Just as you cannot read one book on golf and expect to be in a class with Tiger Woods or any pro, reading my book is by no means the end of your learning process. In fact, it is my hope that this is just the beginning of your option education. *Options Theory and Trading* should provide a strong foundation for your understanding of options. But you will need to read more, take classes, practice paper trading, and continue your education; in other words, you must take the steps necessary to be proficient not just in understanding options but in using them to safeguard your financial future.

Acknowledgments

To Think or Swim (www.thinkorswim.com), for allowing me to use their charts and graphs to illustrate this book.

To my friend John Person of nationalfutures.com, for the inspiration and gentle kick in the butt I needed to get this book started.

To John Wiley & Sons, especially Meg Freeborn and Kevin Commins, who made my next-to-impossible transition from trader to author as smooth as possible, considering who they had to work with: me. One book down, two more to go. Thanks, guys.

To my partner and friend Brett Fogle, in appreciation for the tireless hours of work and personal sacrifices it took to make the dream a reality.

To my parents, in appreciation of the love, support, and encouragement they have given me not only through this process but through life itself... not to mention the tireless hours of editing and proofing. Thanks, Mom and Dad.

To my son Christopher, who sacrificed potential quality time with his dad during the time it mattered most without a whimper or complaint. I could never ask for a better son than you. I am proud and honored to be your father.

Finally, and most especially, to my wife, Sherry, whose undying and unwavering love, loyalty, devotion, and friendship made this book and everything else that's good in my life possible. When no one else believed in me, you did. You deserve much better than me. I hope to live up to all you deserve in a husband and a friend.

PART I

Understanding Terms and Theory

A s with any field of study, an understanding of the vocabulary and special terms used is essential. Options use a special language. Specific terms that you should master are noted in italics. Learning the language of options is the first step in learning how to use them.

Continuing the development of our foundation toward option understanding, we devote time to the study of the two types of options, the call and the put, and their unique risk/rewards for the investor.

From there, we move on to option theory with special emphasis on the pricing model, the Greeks, and synthetic positions.

The pricing model gives you an overview of those components that contribute to the price of options; the Greeks provide the tools necessary to manage risk; and the synthetic positions set the groundwork for the versatility of option use.

CHAPTER 1

Options Basics and Terms

An *option* is a traded security that is a *derivative product*, a product whose value is based on or derived from the price of something else. A *stock option* is based on, among other things, the price of the underlying stock. Options also exist on other traded securities, such as currencies, commodities, bonds, indexes, and interest rates.

A distinguishing factor of an option is that it is a *depreciating asset*; that is, it has a limited life. It has to be used before the date on which it expires. As time goes by, the option loses value as it moves closer to its expiration date.

When we speak of options in terms of volume, we refer to *contracts*. Each stock option contract is equivalent to 100 shares of stock. When we talk about two contracts, we are talking about 200 shares; 10 contracts, 1,000 shares; 75 contracts, 7,500 shares; and so on.

It is important to understand the *dollar cost* of options before actually trading them. When an option is quoted at $1.00 per contract, the investor must realize that the $1.00 represents a price of $1.00 per share, not per contract. Remember that each contract represents 100 shares. This means that if you buy one option contract at a quoted price of $1.00, your total cost would be $100.00 (1 contract × $1.00 per share × 100 shares per contract). If you buy 10 contracts for $1.00 per contract, your total cost will be $1,000.00. Use the following formula when calculating total dollar cost of the option, and review Table 1.1.

$$\text{Total Dollar Cost of Trade} = \text{Number of Contracts} \times \text{Price per Contract} \times 100$$

TABLE 1.1 Option Dollar Costs ($1.00 Quoted Price of Option)

Number of Contracts	×	Price per Contract	×	100 (Shares per Contract)	=	Dollar Cost of Trade
1		$1.00		100		$100.00
5		$1.00		500		$500.00
10		$1.00		1000		$1,000.00

Option contracts are literally a sales agreement between two parties. The two parties are the *buyer* (or holder) and the *seller* (or writer). When you buy an option contract, you are considered *long the option*. When you sell an option contract, you are considered *short the option*. This, of course, is assuming you have no previous position in that option.

In an option contract, although it seems as if the buyer and seller must be tied together, they are not. You see, the buyer doesn't really buy from the seller and the seller doesn't really sell to the buyer. In reality, an organization called the *Options Clearing Corporation* (OCC) steps in between the two sides. The OCC buys from the seller and sells to the buyer. This makes the OCC neutral, and it allows both the buyer and the seller to trade out of a position without involving the other party.

CALLS AND PUTS

There are two types of options, a *call option* and a *put option*.

1. A call option gives the buyer the right, but not the obligation, to buy a specific security at a specific price by a specific date. It is a way of locking in the purchase price of the stock for a period of time.

2. A put option gives the buyer the right, but not the obligation, to sell a specific security at a specific price by a specific date. It is a way of locking in the sales price of a stock for a period of time.

The specific date is known as the contract's *expiration date*. On or prior to the expiration date, the holder of the option contract has the right to exercise the option; that is, the option holder can trade out of the position at any time up to expiration in the open market.

The term *exercise* stands for the process by which the buyer of an option converts the option to a long stock position in the case of a call or a short stock position in the case of a put. Buyers of options exercise.

The term *assign* or *assignment* refers to the process by which the seller of an option is notified of the buyer's intention to exercise.

The *strike price* or *exercise price* is the price at which the holder has the right, but not the obligation, to buy (for a call) or sell (for a put), the underlying security. Strike prices are quoted in dollars; for example, May 50 calls means May $50.00 strike calls.

A *long position* is defined as any position that theoretically will increase in value, should the price of the underlying security increase. Likewise, the position theoretically will decrease in value, should the underlying security decrease. The buying of stock, the buying of a call, or the sale of a put all constitute establishment of long positions since they all represent ways that will benefit the position owner from an increasing stock price

A *short position* is defined as any position that theoretically will increase in value, should the price of the underlying security decrease. Similarly, the position theoretically will decrease in value, should the underlying security increase. The selling of stock, the selling of a call, or the buying of a put establishes a short position where all will benefit from a decrease in the underlying stock price.

CLASSES AND SERIES

The *option class* identifies the specific underlying security the option is written on. The *option series* describes the expiration month and strike price. As an example, let's use the Microsoft (MSFT) May 65 calls. MSFT is the option class (identifies the security). May 65 call is the option series. May is the expiration month, and 65 is the strike price. All segments of this option are represented by symbols. The underlying stock, month, and price have a special code.

All stocks and options are identified by *symbols*. Each stock has a specific symbol. For example, stock symbol HD = Home Depot, while MSFT = Microsoft. Options have symbols too. These symbols are standardized for all exchange-traded (listed) options. Most stock symbols match their ticker symbol. For options of the New York Stock Exchange (NYSE) and American Stock Exchange (AMEX), the option's symbol is always the same as the ticker symbol. The exceptions are the stocks of the NASDAQ. The stock symbol for NASDAQ stocks consists of four letters. Option-class symbols are limited to three letters. Symbols for NASDAQ-traded options are close to the ticket symbol but include the letter Q (to signal NASDAQ). For example, consider the computer maker Dell; its ticker symbol is DELL and

TABLE 1.2 Month Symbols

Month	Calls	Puts
January	A	M
February	B	N
March	C	O
April	D	P
May	E	Q
June	F	R
July	G	S
August	H	T
September	I	U
October	J	V
November	K	W
December	L	X

its option symbol is DLQ. The ticker symbol for Intel is INTC and its option symbol is INQ.

Another exception for the ticker symbol use is with LEAPS. Options in different years receive different class symbols to overcome the limitation of the expiration month symbol, which does not take into account the same month existing in different years. The month symbol remains the same but the class symbol changes to signify the different year.

After the option-class symbol, a different letter identifies each specific month's call or put. Table 1.2 shows which letters coincide with which month's calls and puts.

The strike price symbol (shown in Table 1.3) follows the month symbol. A letter represents each different strike price. These strike prices are also standardized for all listed options.

We are using the basics to introduce the decoding of option symbols. However, since there is a wide range of potential strike prices and a limited

TABLE 1.3 Strike Prices (Basics)

A = 5	H = 40	O = 75	V = 12.5
B = 10	I = 45	P = 80	W = 17.5
C = 15	J = 50	Q = 85	X = 22.5
D = 20	K = 55	R = 90	Y = not assigned
E = 25	L = 60	S = 95	Z = not assigned
F = 30	M = 65	T = 100	
G = 35	N = 70	U = 7.5	

number of letters, each letter represents more than one strike price. This fact creates the need for a bit of guesswork, but nothing too complicated when you are familiar with the basics. For instance, the letter A represents a $5 strike price but can also represent $105. The value of the stock should guide you to the meaning of the letter used. If a stock is listed for $95, the A is $105 rather than $5. When in doubt, you can go to the Option Clearing Corporation web site (www.optionsclearing.com) for a detailed explanation of the symbols.

Using Tables 1.2 and 1.3, let's decode the symbol HD GF: "HD" is the stock symbol that represents Home Depot. "G" signifies a call option with a July expiration date. "F" indicates a strike price of $30. This means that the buyer of this option has the right to purchase 100 shares of HD between now and July expiration at a price of $30 per share.

In the case of the symbol PG US, "PG" stands for the stock Procter & Gamble. The "U" signifies a put with an expiration date in September. Finally, the "S" stands for a strike price of $95. This means that the buyer of this option has the right, but not the obligation, to sell 100 shares of Procter & Gamble between now and September expiration for a price of $95 per share.

Though exceptions do exist in option symbols, when decoding, it generally helps to remember that the last letter in the group refers to strike price and the letter right before it refers to the expiration months (puts and calls).

IN THE MONEY, OUT OF THE MONEY, AND AT THE MONEY

An option can be described by the proximity of its strike price to the stock's price. An option can either be *in the money* (ITM), *out of the money* (OTM), *or at the money* (ATM). It is necessary to understand how calls and puts can be ITM, OTM, and ATM and the characteristics each carries.

At the Money

An at-the-money (ATM) option is described as an option whose exercise price or strike price is approximately equal to the current price of the underlying stock. For instance, if Microsoft (MSFT) is trading at $65.00, then the January $65.00 call would be an example of an at-the-money call option. Similarly, the January $65.00 put would be an example of an at-the-money put option.

In the Money

An in-the-money call (ITM) option is described as a call whose strike (exercise) price is lower than the current price of the underlying. An in-the-money put is a put whose strike (exercise) price is higher than the current price of the underlying (i.e., an option that could be exercised immediately for a cash credit if the option buyer wanted to exercise the option).

Using our Microsoft example, an in-the-money call option would be any listed call option with a strike price below $65.00 (the price of the stock). So, the MSFT January 60 call option would be an example of an in-the-money call. That is because at any time prior to the expiration date, you could exercise the option and profit from the difference in value: in this case $5.00 ($65.00 stock price – $60.00 call option strike price = $5.00). You could exercise your right to buy the stock at $60 and then sell it at the market price of $65, realizing a $5 gain. In other words, the option is $5.00 in the money.

Again, using our Microsoft example, an in-the-money put option would be any listed put option with a strike price above $65.00 (the price of the stock). The MSFT January 70 put option would be an example of an in-the-money put. It is in the money because at any time prior to the expiration date, you could exercise the option and profit from the difference in value: in this case $5.00 ($70.00 put option strike price – $65.00 stock price = $5.00). You can sell for a guaranteed $70 stock that you can purchase for $65. In other words, the option is $5.00 in the money.

Out of the Money

An out-of-the-money (OTM) call is described as a call whose strike price (exercise price) is higher than the current price of the underlying. Thus, the entire premium of an out-of-the-money call option consists only of extrinsic value. There is no intrinsic value in an out-of-the-money call because the option's strike price is higher than the current stock price. For example, if you chose to exercise the MSFT January 70 call while the stock was trading at $65.00, you would essentially be choosing to buy the stock for $70.00 when the stock is trading at $65.00 in the open market. This action would result in a $5.00 loss. Obviously, you wouldn't do that.

An out-of-the-money put has a strike (exercise) price that is lower than the current price of the underlying. Thus, the entire premium of an out-of-the-money put option consists only of extrinsic value. There is no intrinsic value in an out-of-the-money put because the option's strike price is lower than the current stock price. For example, if you chose to exercise the MSFT January 60 put while the stock was trading at $65.00, you would be choosing to sell the stock at $60.00 when the stock is trading at $65.00 in

TABLE 1.4 ITM, OTM, and ATM Call Determination Calculation

Strike	<, >, or =	Stock Price	Determination
55	<	65	ITM
60	<	65	ITM
65	=	65	ATM
70	>	65	OTM
75	>	65	OTM

the open market. This action would result in a $5.00 loss. This is another trade you would not want to do.

Review the ATM, ITM, and OTM option determinations by studying Table 1.4.

PREMIUM AND TIME DECAY

Premium is the total amount of money (price) you pay for an option. If the Microsoft (MSFT) May 65 calls cost you $1.50, then the $1.50 is the amount of the premium of the option. The total price of an option (premium) consists of two components: intrinsic value and extrinsic value. Be advised that many in the industry, particularly traders, use the term *premium* to represent only the extrinsic value. I mention this to help you avoid confusion about this in the future.

INTRINSIC VERSUS EXTRINSIC VALUE

Intrinsic value is the amount by which an option is in the money. In the case of a call, the intrinsic value is equal to the current stock price minus the strike price. In the case of a put, the intrinsic value is equal to the strike price minus the current stock price. **Only in-the-money options have intrinsic value.** Out-of-the-money options have no intrinsic value. For example, with MSFT trading at $65.00 the MSFT January 60 calls have $5.00 of intrinsic value. If the MSFT January 60 calls trade at $5.70, then $5.00 of that premium would be intrinsic value. At the same time, the MSFT January 70 put will also have $5.00 of intrinsic value. So, if the MSFT January 70 puts trade for $5.70, then $5.00 of that premium would be intrinsic value.

Extrinsic value is defined as the price of an option less its intrinsic value. In the case of out-of-the-money options, the entire price of the option consists only of extrinsic value. Extrinsic value is made up of several components, the largest being volatility. In the examples given, if the MSFT January 60 calls were trading at $5.70 and $5.00 of that was intrinsic value, then the remainder ($0.70) is extrinsic value. The same also holds true for the January 70 puts. If they were trading at $5.70 and $5.00 of that was intrinsic value, then the rest ($0.70) is extrinsic value.

When we discuss *parity* in terms of options, we say that parity is the amount by which an option is in the money. Parity refers to the option price trading in unison with the stock price. **Parity and intrinsic value are closely related.** When we say that an option is trading at parity, we mean that the option's premium consists only of its intrinsic value. Remember, only ITM options can have intrinsic value; thus only ITM options can be said to be trading for parity. For call options, we can use a simple formula to decide whether an option is trading at parity. If the strike price plus the option price is equal to the current stock price, then the call is said to be trading at parity. A call is trading at parity when: strike price + option price = stock price.

For example, if Microsoft was trading at $53.00 and the January 50 calls were trading at $3.00, then the January 50 calls are said to be trading at parity. Adding the strike price (50) to the option price (3) equals the stock price (53). Under the same guidelines, the January 45 call would be trading at parity if it was trading at $8.00. The strike price of the call (45) plus the price of the call ($8) would be equal to the current stock price ($53). So parity for the January 50 calls is $3.00 while parity for the January 45 calls is $8.00.

A put option is said to be trading at parity when the strike price minus the option price is equal to the stock price. Just as with the call, any put trading with only intrinsic value and no extrinsic value is said to be trading at parity (with the stock). This means that only ITM puts can ever be trading at parity. A put is trading at parity when: strike price – option price = stock price.

For example, if IBM was trading at $71.00 and the May 75 puts were trading at $4.00, then the May 75 puts are said to be trading at parity. The strike price ($75.00) minus the option price ($4.00) would equal the stock price ($71.00). Under the same guidelines, the May 80 put would be trading at parity if it was trading at $9.00. The strike price of the put (80) minus the price of the put ($9.00) would be equal to the current stock price ($71). Therefore, parity for the May 80 puts is $9.00 while parity for the May 75 puts is $4.00.

Now, when an option, call, or put is trading for more than parity, the amount (in dollars) over parity is called *premium over parity*. Thus, this term is synonymous with *extrinsic value*, which was discussed earlier. For example, with Microsoft stock trading at $53.00 and the January 50 calls

TABLE 1.5 Intrinsic and Extrinsic Values of Calls (Stock Price $65)

Strike Price	Option Price	Status	Intrinsic Value	Extrinsic Value
50	15.10	ITM	15.00	.10
55	10.30	ITM	10.00	.30
60	5.70	ITM	5.00	.70
65	**1.50**	**ATM**	**0**	**1.50**
70	.75	OTM	0	.75
75	.35	OTM	0	.35
80	.15	OTM	0	.15

trading at $3.50, we would say that the calls are trading at $0.50 over parity. The $0.50 of the option's value over the $3.00 of parity would be the premium over parity or *extrinsic value*.

Table 1.5 (calls) and Table 1.6 (puts) show examples of several options broken down into their total price, amount of intrinsic value, and extrinsic value. When we discuss the different strategies later in the book, you will realize that understanding the amounts and the ratio of the amounts of intrinsic and extrinsic values to each other provides valuable insight in determining which options are best to use in certain strategies. Knowing particular pricing characteristics becomes very important when constructing the optimal strategy for the specific investing or trading opportunity identified.

Any discussion of the term *extrinsic value* would be incomplete without mentioning the term *time decay*. Options are considered a wasting asset due to the fact that they have a time limit attached to them (they expire at a point in time in the future). Time decay, or theta, is defined as the rate by which an option's extrinsic value (the amount of premium over parity) decays over the life of the contract. The concept of time decay is discussed in greater depth when we discuss the Greeks (Chapter 4).

TABLE 1.6 Intrinsic and Extrinsic Values of Puts (Stock Price $65)

Strike Price	Option Price	Status	Intrinsic Value	Extrinsic Value
50	.10	OTM	0	.10
55	.30	OTM	0	.30
60	.70	OTM	0	.70
65	**1.50**	**ATM**	**0**	**1.50**
70	5.70	ITM	5.00	.70
75	10.30	ITM	10.00	.30
80	15.10	ITM	15.00	.10

VOLATILITY

Volatility is defined as the degree to which the price of a stock or other underlying instrument tends to move, or fluctuate, over a period of time. A stock that has a wide trading range (moves around a lot) is said to have a high volatility. A stock that has a narrow trading range (does not move around much) is said to have a low volatility. It is important to note that volatility is a relative term. This means that high and low volatility are determined by the volatility relative to each specific underlying security. A volatility of 100 is not high in a stock that normally averages a 130 volatility level. A 30 volatility level is not low for a stock that normally averages a 15 volatility level.

Volatility is important because it has the single biggest effect on the amount of extrinsic value in an option's price. **When volatility goes up (increases), the extrinsic value of both calls and puts increases.** This makes all the option prices more expensive. The reason is quite simple. As volatility increases and the potential range of the stock expands, the uncertainty of where the stock will finish at expiration increases, thereby increasing the amount of extrinsic value.

When volatility goes down (decreases), the extrinsic value of both calls and puts decreases. This makes all of the option prices less expensive. The reasoning here is that as volatility decreases and the potential range of the stock tightens, there is less uncertainty of where the stock may finish, thus decreasing the extrinsic value of the option.

In Table 1.7 and Table 1.8, notice the comparison between similar options on fictitious XYZ Corp. at two different volatility levels. It is very important that you recognize the difference in value of the same option (calls or puts) at differing volatilities. One of the biggest mistakes a newbie in the options market can make is not understanding the contribution of volatilities to option price. Many first-timers coming from the stock market do

TABLE 1.7   Option Call Prices at 30 VOL and 70 VOL (Stock Price $65.50)

Strike Price	Call Price 30 Volatility	Call Price 70 Volatility
50	$15.60	$16.60
55	$10.70	$12.70
60	$6.38	$9.45
65	$3.13	$6.80
70	$1.21	$4.77
75	$0.38	$3.27
80	$0.09	$2.16

TABLE 1.8 Option Put Prices at 30 VOL and 70 VOL (Stock Price $65.50)

Strike Price	Put Price 30 Volatility	Put Price 70 Volatility
50	$0.01	$0.97
55	$0.12	$2.09
60	$0.74	$3.80
65	$2.47	$6.15
70	$5.56	$9.11
75	$9.75	$12.60
80	$14.50	$16.50

not realize that unlike stock prices, which ultimately are guided by one thing—movement of supply and demand—**option prices are guided by three things: movement of stock price, movement of volatility, and passage of time.**

Implied volatility, which you will hear much about, is a value derived by the option pricing model from the option's price. It indicates what the market's perception of the volatility of the stock or underlying will be during the future life of the contract. A stock that has a wide trading range (moves around a lot) is said to have a high volatility. A stock that has a narrow trading range (does not move around much) is said to have a low volatility.

The importance of volatility is that it has the single biggest effect on the amount of extrinsic value in an option's price. When volatility goes up (increases), the extrinsic value of both calls and puts increases. This makes all the option prices more expensive. When volatility goes down (decreases), the extrinsic value of both calls and puts decreases. This makes all of the option prices less expensive.

CHAPTER 2

Calls and Puts

N ow that you have a basic understanding of terms, the next step is a more comprehensive understanding of calls and puts. Calls and puts are the options you will use naked or in combination with stock or other options to formulate strategies for making money, protecting what you already have, or doing both. Using calls and puts requires a specific understanding of their use as related to profit potential and risks.

CALL OPTIONS

As stated, a call option is a contract between two parties (a buyer and a seller) whereby the buyer acquires the right, but not the obligation, to purchase a specified stock or other underlying instrument at a predetermined price on or prior to a specified date. The seller of a call option assumes the obligation of delivering the stock or other underlying instrument to the buyer should the buyer wish to exercise the option. The call is known as a *long instrument*, which means the buyer profits from the stock going up and the seller hopes the stock goes down or remains the same.

For the buyer of a call to profit, the stock must move above the strike price plus the amount of money spent to purchase the option. This point, known as the *break-even point*, is calculated by adding the strike price of the call to its premium. The buyer hopes the stock price exceeds the break-even point to ensure a profitable trade by expiration. Now, this does not mean that the buyer must have the stock exceed the break-even point to be profitable. If the stock rises quickly, the buyer could see a profit before expiration.

The buyer of the call has limited risk and unlimited potential gain. The buyer's risk is limited only to the amount of money spent in purchasing the call. Risk is limited due to the fact that the buyer has no obligation, only rights. If buyers choose to do nothing, then their only loss could be the amount spent purchasing the call. The unlimited potential gain comes from the stock's upside growth potential. **The seller, however, has limited potential gain and unlimited potential loss**. The seller can gain only what is collected for the sale of the call. The seller's unlimited risk comes from the combination of the possibility of the rise of the stock's price during the life of the contract and the fact that, as the seller of an option, he or she has no rights, just obligations. Sellers must comply with the terms of the contract if buyers decide to exercise their rights.

The seller is obligated to deliver the stock to the buyer at the strike price regardless of the stock's prevailing market price. That is why the seller receives a premium for the sale; it is compensation for taking on this risk.

For example, if a seller sold the Microsoft (MSFT) January 65 call for $2.00, he is giving the buyer the right to buy 100 shares (per contract) of MSFT from him for $65.00 per share at any time until the option expires.

If MSFT rallies and trades up to $75.00, the seller would realize a $10.00 loss less the amount received for the sale of the option ($2.00). The loss occurs because the seller must deliver the stock for $65.00, missing out on the $75.00 he could get on the market.

Meanwhile, the buyer would realize a $10.00 profit less the amount she paid for the option ($2.00). She gets the MSFT assigned to her for $65.00 and can sell it on the market for $75.00.

If MSFT were to trade down to $55.00, the seller would realize a $2.00 profit (the amount of money he was paid by the buyer). Meanwhile, the buyer would lose only what she paid for the option ($2.00).

Notice the difference in profit potential between the purchasing of the option and the selling of the option. Also, it is important to note the unlimited potential risk inherent in the sale of an option compared to the fixed risk of an option purchase.

PUT OPTIONS

A put option is a contract between two parties (a buyer and a seller) whereby the buyer acquires the right, but not the obligation, to sell a specified stock or other underlying instrument at a specified price by a specified date. The seller of a put option assumes the obligation of taking delivery of the stock or other underlying instrument from the buyer, should the buyer wish to exercise the option. The put is known as a *short instrument*, which means that the buyer profits from the stock going down.

For the buyer of a put to profit, the stock must move below the strike price plus the amount of money spent to purchase the option. This point is known as the *break-even point* and is calculated by subtracting the price of the put from the put's strike price. The buyer hopes the stock price proceeds below the break-even point to ensure a profitable trade by expiration. Now, this does not mean that the buyer must have the stock move below the break-even point to be profitable. If the stock drops quickly, the buyer could see a profit before expiration.

The buyer of the put has limited risk and unlimited potential gain. Risk is limited only to the amount of money spent in purchasing the put. The unlimited potential gain comes from the stocks' unlimited downside potential. **The seller, however, has limited potential gain and unlimited potential loss**. The seller can gain only what he or she paid for the put. The unlimited risk comes from the stock price's ability to decline during the life of the contract.

For the seller to profit, the stock must not move below the strike price plus the amount of money received for the sale of the option. This point is known as the break-even point and is calculated by adding the call's strike price to the option's premium. Obviously, the buyer hopes that the stock price exceeds the break-even point.

For example, you buy the MSFT January 65 put for $2.00 because you think Microsoft is going to go down. This option gives you the right, but not the obligation, to sell the stock at $65.00. In order to obtain this right, you had to spend $2.00. In order for you to make money, the stock would have to trade down below $63.00 by expiration. This is because the stock has to trade down below the strike plus the cost of the option. If the stock traded down to $60.00, you would make $5.00 because you have the right to sell it at $65.00. However, because you paid $2.00 for the put, you must subtract that from your $5.00 profit for a total profit of $3.00. You have just made $3.00 on a $2.00 investment. Not a bad return.

For example, if a seller sold the MSFT January 65 put for $2.00, he is giving the buyer the right to sell 100 shares (per contract) of MSFT to him at $65.00 per share at any time until the option expires. If MSFT declines and trades down to $55.00, the seller would realize a $10.00 loss less the amount he received for the sale of the option ($2.00), for a net loss of $8.00.

Meanwhile, the buyer would realize a $10.00 profit less the amount she paid for the option ($2.00), for a net gain of $8.00 per contract. If MSFT were to trade up to $75.00, the seller would realize a $2.00 profit (the amount of money she was paid from the buyer). Meanwhile, the buyer would lose only what she paid for the option ($2.00).

The seller is obligated to take delivery of the stock from the buyer at the strike price regardless of the current market price of the stock. This is why the seller receives a premium for the sale. Note that there is a difference in the profit potential between purchasing the option as opposed to selling the option. Last, it is important to note the unlimited potential risk inherent in the sale of an option, compared to the fixed risk of an option purchase.

The definitions and concepts contained in this and the previous chapter are the building blocks of the option strategies to be discussed. It is of vital importance that you review these concepts and definitions several times to gain a clear understanding of them.

CHAPTER 3

Option Theory

I n Chapters 1 and 2 we discussed the cost of the option. That cost determines our ability to make money using options. How is the cost of an option determined? In comparison to stock pricing, option pricing seems arbitrary. Stock pricing appears concrete, attached to a company with assets and subject to supply and demand and the public's perception of value based on those assets and their value.

From an investor's point of view, a stock is attached to a company. But options are one step removed from the stock: The option is attached to a stock, which is attached to a company.

Each of the elements in that point of view has a value. The basis of trading any security centers on the idea of value, and options are no different. They have a value, and how that value is determined is the basis of whether they are a good deal or good value for the investor.

The theoretical value of an option can be determined using a variety of techniques called *models*. These models, developed by quantitative analysts, can predict how the value of the option will change in the face of changing conditions. Therefore, the risks associated with trading and owning options can be understood and managed with some degree of precision compared to some other investments.

Value determination and changes in value are the keys to managing risk and getting a good deal. The determination of value tells us whether we are getting a good deal, whether we are buying something low or selling it high. The determination of the value of an option is based on a complex algorithm known as the option pricing model.

OPTION PRICING MODELS

An *option pricing model* calculates the values of different options. The models—and there are many of them—involve complex, convoluted, and abstract math. When we talk about an option pricing model, we are talking some very sophisticated algorithms that probably are beyond the mathematical ability of most investors.

Fear not, however, for the ability to understand the math is not what is important. Understanding how the model does what it does, and why it does what it does, is the important issue. What we need to know is what goes into each model, what comes out of it, and what weakness certain models display. It is important to know not only what the model offers in terms of price determination but also what it discerns in terms of calculating an option's sensitivity to changing variables.

Even without mathematical understanding, we can know what an option is, how it is priced, how it is going to react, and its overall nature. It is important for you to understand how each model calculates value. The method itself offers a glimpse of the option's nature. Once you understand the nature of the option, it will be that much easier to understand how the option will function, how it will react, where it will be at risk, and where it will be profitable. In order to begin our exploration into the nature of options, there are a few things we need to know about the model.

First, you need to know that the term *option pricing model* refers to one of several different pricing models, each with its own mathematical algorithms. Again, we don't need to get into the high-end mathematics, but we do need to know how the models differ from each other. Differences in the models could lead to a difference in pricing in varying situations. Recognizing differences also can lead to identifying a weakness, flaw, or disadvantage in a specific model. Understanding that weakness or flaw means knowing which model may be more accurate at certain times and in certain ways. You need to know which model was used to determine the value of an option and recognize its advantages and disadvantages for your needs: accurate valuation.

I break the discussion of the pricing model into four sections:

1. *The fundamentals of all pricing models.* What they share and the basics upon which they were established.
2. *The types of pricing models.* The evolution of the various models as an answer to a flaw or lack in an earlier model.
3. *Inputs into the models.* What variables must be addressed to arrive at a determination of value.
4. *The outputs (Greeks).* What the output numbers and probabilities mean to our investment strategy (see Chapter 4).

You can understand anything best by studying its nature. The foundation of the price of options is generated by the pricing models. So, to some extent, we need to understand the fundamentals of the pricing models in order to understand the nature of options.

Therefore, we are going to talk about some of the pricing model concepts, discussing concepts that are inherent in all of the models. Bear in mind that all the models are connected. They are related. How? They start at the same place—setting up a probability model to predict an expected value of an option. And they all end up at the same place—with a theoretical value, a value that determines an option's worth. They start from the same place (probability), and try to get to the same place (value determination).

Let's begin our talk about the fundamentals of the option pricing models.

FUNDAMENTALS OF PRICING MODELS

Where does the pricing model start? Where does it begin? Basically, it all begins with a theory called the *random walk theory*.

The random walk theory states that a stock moves independently and unpredictably in either direction, with no barriers. There is nothing that gets in the way of the stock being able to go wherever it wants to go, however it wants to go there. Further, the theory states that a stock's next movement is independent of its last movement. Each successive movement is not influenced by the last. Understand that the random walk theory goes against the idea that technical analysis has any basis in fact.

After a series of movements, the random walk theory generates a normal distribution or bell curve. A *normal distribution* or *bell curve* represents a theoretical frequency distribution of measurements. In a normal distribution, scores are concentrated near the mean and decrease in frequency as the distance from the mean increases.

As you can see in Figure 3.1, we have the random walk theory on the left-hand side. It almost looks like one of those little kids' games where you put the ball in the top, and it works its way down the pyramid of pegs, hitting different pegs as it zigzags its way to the bottom.

In random walk theory, the ball has a 50–50 chance of going either way off the first peg that it hits. And when it hits the next peg, it again has a 50–50 chance of going in either direction with nothing obstructing it. If we were to put something to block off access between two of those pegs, then obviously the random walk theory would be affected, because we would be preventing the ball from going where it wants to go freely and independently. Unimpeded, the ball will make its way to the bottom, where

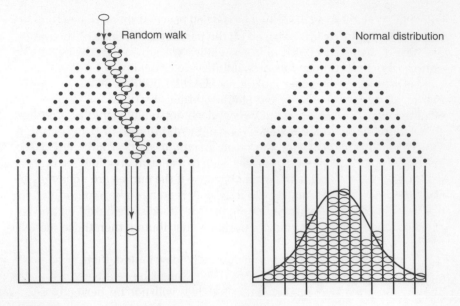

FIGURE 3.1   Random Walk and Normal Distribution

it will come to rest in a specific section. If a series of balls are allowed to fall, not all will find their way into that one section at the bottom. Because of the odds, those balls should fill up the areas at the bottom in a specific pattern. They will create a normal distribution.

The right-hand side of Figure 3.1 displays a distribution pattern. This pattern is referred to as normal distribution—normal outcomes. Some may recognize the pattern as the bell curve. The formal definition of a normal distribution is complicated; however, for our purposes, it is simply a measure of dispersion around the mean, or the average. That is a very simple definition, but it is adequate for our use.

Our market system functions under the random walk theory. It is supposedly designed to allow stocks to move and flow independently and freely in any direction at any given time. According to the random walk theory, stocks will zigzag their way to a potential outcome. From random walk, we are led to the bell curve.

The bell curve is a normal distribution. The bell curve demonstrates that among a certain number of samples, there is a normal outcome. Normal distribution points out the normal outcome among a variety of possible outcomes. For our purposes in option pricing, the bell curve answers the question of what is the normal outcome (or percentage chance) of the stock finishing at a specific price. The pricing model takes a look at all the different places where the stock can finish and adds the chances of the stock finishing there as described by the bell curve. It then creates theoretical option values or prices based on the percentage chance of the option finishing in the money (with value) by expiration. Obviously, the bell curve or normal distribution and its probabilities are critical to option pricing.

Let's take a little closer look at normal distributions. What you see in Figure 3.2 are two separate but similar normal distributions charts. The term *normal distribution* (*bell curve*) does not really signify the perfect shape of the bell. What it signifies is a family of different distributions that are evenly dispersed around the mean. *Evenly dispersed* indicates that a bell curve must be symmetrical (each side of a central dividing line is identical to the other). That is important because if the curves are not symmetrical, they are not a normal distribution; this is going to be a major distinction later because the majority of the pricing models are based on normal distributions. If stock returns are normally distributed, then these models will work perfectly.

However, if stock returns aren't normally distributed, then these models are not going to be very accurate. They might be relatively accurate. They might even be very accurate, but they will not be perfectly accurate. And in certain instances, that can hurt you. Later we are going to talk about what those instances are and how we can adjust for them. But for right now, a normal distribution is any family of distributions that is symmetrical.

Normal distributions are broken down by the bell curve into three standard deviations: three to the right and three to the left. A standard deviation (distance from the mean) is a statistical measure that tells you how tightly a group of examples in a sample are clustered around the average or mean. A standard deviation is a measure of spread or dispersion.

Since there is only a 100 percent chance of anything happening, the bell curve encompasses all of the possibilities—all the possible outcomes.

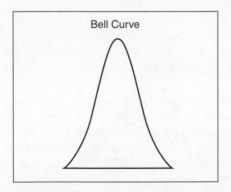 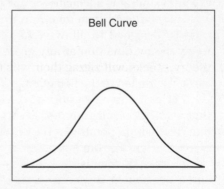

FIGURE 3.2   Two Normal Distributions

The curve gives the percentage chance of potential outcomes occurring. Obviously, there is a mean or average that is core to the distribution model of the bell curve. However, what we are most concerned with seeing when we look at normal distribution (the bell curve) is how the distribution is dispersed, creating our probabilities.

Figure 3.3 shows a bell curve. The curve is broken down into three different shades: white, gray, and black. Under each shaded region, at the very bottom, you see percentages. Each of the regions represents a different standard deviation from the mean.

Standard deviation tells you to what degree your potential variables are spread out away from the mean. White signifies all potential outcomes that fall within 1 standard deviation from the mean. Gray signifies all potential outcomes that fall 2 standard deviations from the mean. Black signifies all potential outcomes that fall 3 standard deviations away from the mean.

When we look at the bell curve in Figure 3.3, we know that everything that is 1 standard deviation plus or minus from the mean (white) occurs 68.4 percent of the time: The potential outcome falls in that white area 68.4 percent of the time. That is 1 standard deviation from the mean (represented by heavy black line in middle). The area in gray shows a movement of 2 standard deviations from the mean. The chance that a move of 2 standard deviations will occur is 13.5 percent to the downside and 13.5 percent to the upside, which together is a 27 percent chance. So, you have a 68.4

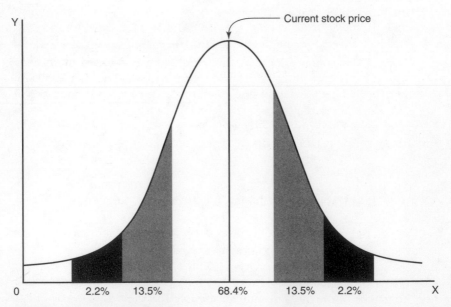

FIGURE 3.3 Bell Curve

percent chance of potential outcomes landing plus or minus 1 standard deviation off the average. And from there you have a 27 percent chance of potential outcomes landing 2 standard deviations, plus or minus, away from the mean. Finally, you have the black area, which is a movement of 3 standard deviations from the mean. That will occur 4.4 percent of the time. In a normal distribution that is symmetrical, that 4.4 percent is evenly distributed—2.2 percent to the left, or downside, and 2.2 percent to the right, or upside.

Look back at Figure 3.1 showing random walk and normal distribution. When you look at the normal distribution, do you see that little ball all the way on the left-hand side by itself? That represents the day that the stock has a dramatic movement, most likely a news-related gap opening. Remember, on most days, stocks fluctuate only a little bit. That limited fluctuation occurs in the white area and happens 68.4 percent of the time. However, that little ball way over to the far side by its lonesome, that is the day when something really good/bad happens and that only occurs 2.2 percent of the time.

Let's review the similarities of the different pricing models so far. All pricing models are related in that they all:

- Are probability models.
- Seek to determine a theoretical value that indicates what an option should be worth.
- Are based on normal distribution (bell curve dispersion around the mean).

Many of the option pricing models are formulated based on an error or a weakness in a previous model or due to unexpected market evolution. The models have had to evolve and change as a result of the way that pricing of the trading markets has evolved. Models have had to adapt to the different ways things are priced, the different ways things happen, and the different variables that affect the prices of options at different times.

TYPES OF PRICING MODELS

So, we will talk about the pricing models by giving a brief overview of several selected models, discussing their strengths and weaknesses. This will make it possible for you to see an evolution as these models try to compensate for the ever-changing market environment. It is important to remember the names of the most prominent models and their unique advantages and disadvantages.

One of the earliest models was the Monte Carlo simulation method. Credit for inventing this method often goes to Stanislaw Ulam, a Polish-born mathematician who worked for John von Neumann on the Manhattan Project in the United States during World War II. Ulam is known primarily for designing the hydrogen bomb with Edward Teller in 1951. He invented the Monte Carlo method in 1946 while pondering the probabilities of winning a card game of solitaire.

The Monte Carlo method was extremely accurate but incredibly slow. Back when models were first being auditioned for their use in option pricing, computers simply were not powerful enough to warrant the use of the Monte Carlo simulation. It was not possible to get all of the many calculations done fast enough to suit the requirements of traders who needed instant answers. Delays caused by the extended waiting periods cost traders money, which was unacceptable.

When you observe the prices of options from the different pricing models, you will notice that all the models value the first-, second-, and third-month options pretty closely. Users found that a penny more accuracy was not worth the wait of 20 or 30 more seconds to get results, especially when the results were so similar to other models. In summary, the Monte Carlo simulation method, while extraordinarily accurate, was just too complex and just too slow.

Black-Scholes Model

The first notable option pricing model is the granddaddy of them all and has been the basis for many subsequent models. The *Black-Scholes model* is probably the best-known and most popular option pricing model. Formulated in 1973 by Fisher Black and Myron Scholes, this model won them the Nobel Prize in Economics in 1997.

While an award winner, the Black-Scholes had its flaws. The Black-Scholes model originally was supposed to calculate the price of European-style options. European options do not allow for early exercise as do American-style options. European-style options are very much like futures in this way. The main problem with the Black-Scholes model is that it does not account for (price) the ability of early exercise of American options. It does not account for exercising early to collect interest rate or the dividend. Further, as you go out over time, the model loses integrity. Since the original version, the Black-Scholes model has been modified to adjust for this deficiency. (This adaptation is known as the modified Black-Scholes model.)

After the Black-Scholes model came out and its weaknesses were identified, Cox, Ross, and Rubenstein developed the binomial model. The binomial model was based on the same precepts as the Black-Scholes model.

Obviously, the intent was to develop a model that was very similar to the Black-Scholes in its speed and accuracy but adjusted for early exercise and for better integrity out over time. That is what the binomial model does. To this day, probably more people use the Cox, Ross, and Rubenstein binomial model than the Black-Scholes model.

Binomial Model

The *binomial model* is what is called a lattice model (see Figure 3.4). It breaks down time until expiration into a series of intervals or steps. Then a tree of stock prices is produced moving forward from the present to expiration. At each step, it is assumed that the stock price will move either up or down.

The model assumed that a stock will move either up or down, from one level up to the next or down to the next, continuing the pattern until you can see it form a two-branch type tree (binomial tree).

Where the model did account for early exercise and where it did have better integrity over time, it was missing something: the fact that most of the time, stocks *do not* move. It assumed that at every level a stock either moves up or down to the next level. It only recognized two choices. It did

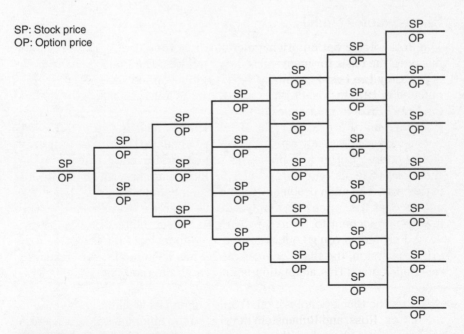

FIGURE 3.4 Binomial Model

not fully account for a stock's major tendency to stay still (stagnant). Not properly pricing this lack of movement is an obvious flaw, because studies show that most stocks make their major movements during only a couple months out of the year. Most stocks are dormant most months.

Trinomial Model

The response to that omission in the binomial model was the creation of the *trinomial model.* Instead of having two choices and a two-branch tree, the trinomial had three choices and a three-branch tree, as seen in Figure 3.5.

From each step, the next step could either be up a level, down a level, or straight across sideways at the same level, which happens much more often than not. In this way, the trinomial model was able to account for a

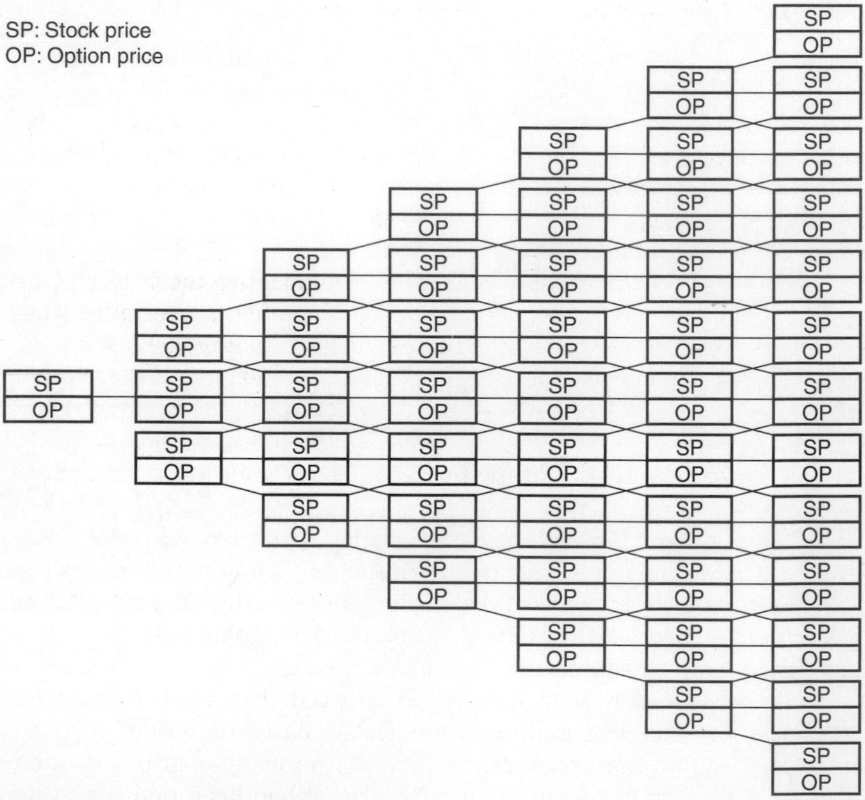

FIGURE 3.5 Trinomial Model

stock not moving. How does this difference between the binomial and the trinomial model affect us?

A little later we are going to talk about volatility and something called a volatility smile. The smile occurs when the implied volatility of options with the same underlying asset and expiring on the same day and across the various strike prices forms a curve in the shape of a smile when graphed. The binomial model does not account for the volatility smile, which exists in almost all options. However, the trinomial model does. How? The trinomial model accepts the fact that a stock can stay still; stocks do not have to move either up or down; they also can move sideways. The binomial model, by its nature, does not take that fact into consideration. While the binomial model improved on the Black-Scholes model by properly pricing the value of early expiration, it failed to see the volatility smile. The trinomial model takes into consideration that next step, the possibility that the stock will not move, and thus accounts for the volatility smile.

Adaptive Mesh Model

One of my favorite models is an extension of the trinomial model called the adaptive mesh model. (See Figure 3.6.) The *adaptive mesh model* takes the three branches of the trinomial and adds some twigs. It adds more avenues or time intervals for the stock to move than the trinomial model. Basically the adaptive mesh model is as quick as the binomial model, more accurate than the trinomial model, and takes into account everything those models do, including the volatility smile.

However, because it has more nodes, the adaptive mesh model becomes much more accurate and stays more accurate out over time while the others lose some of their integrity. Of course, each model loses a different amount of integrity at a different rate. The adaptive mesh model, however, combines all the best elements of all the previous models, including the ability to price the volatility smile, as the trinomial did. It is more accurate, and the integrity of the model stays together much farther out in time.

As I said before, these models were made a while ago. And as the markets evolve, these models have had to evolve and adapt to different situations. One thing about some of the earlier models is that they based their pricing on the fact that they felt stock returns were going to fit into a normal distribution—that bell curve we talked about.

However, as time went by, studies showed that stock returns did not follow a normal distribution. If models are based on normal distributions, and we find that stock returns are not normally distributed, there is a flaw. The flaw had to do with a factor that had been omitted in the pricing model's calculations. That factor was the conditions that affected

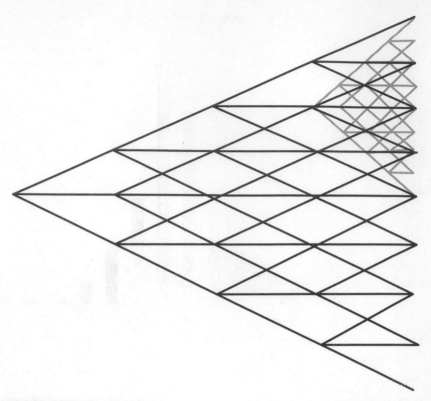

FIGURE 3.6 Adaptive Mesh

distribution of the stock. Observe the bell curves of the NASDAQ (Figure 3.7) and the Standard & Poor's (S&P) (Figure 3.8), and you can easily see that the results do not fit the shape of "normal distribution."

The models were missing conditions called *skewness* and *kurtosis*. We are going to discuss more about skewness and kurtosis a little later when we talk about inputs of the model. But the fact of the matter is, if we are using a model that is based on a normal distribution to get prices for something that does not follow a normal distribution, then we are using a model that is not perfectly fit for the job. If we need a model that can find prices in a distribution that is not normal, we cannot use a model that is based on a normal distribution. Stock returns come to us as a log-normal distribution; they do not come to us as a normal distribution. A model that takes that fact into account was needed.

Instead of a symmetrical bell curve normal distribution, stock movements show log-normal distributions, as shown in Figure 3.9.

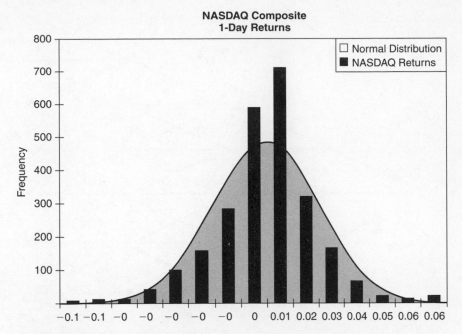

FIGURE 3.7 Nasdaq/Bell Curve

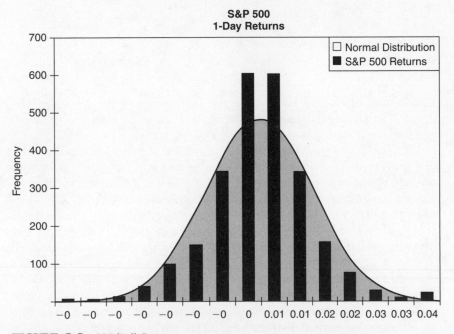

FIGURE 3.8 S&P/Bell Curve

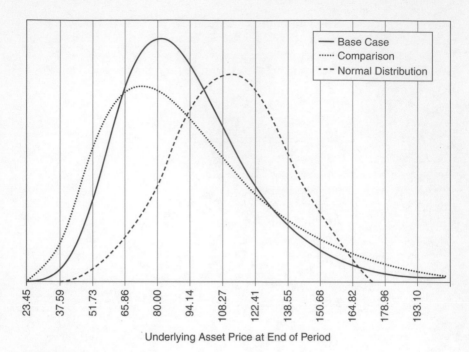

FIGURE 3.9 Log-Normal Stock Price Distribution

Lo and behold, the VSK (volatility, skewness, and kurtosis) model was formulated. The VSK model allows for an adjustment of prices, or price changes, because of skewness and kurtosis. This model is basically a derivative of the Black-Scholes model adjusted to take into account skewness and kurtosis because stock returns are not normally distributed.

It is important to note that there are many other pricing models out there; all have their own unique strengths and weaknesses. It is imperative that you always know what model you are using. Also, when using any model to price options, be aware of its potential weaknesses in order to adjust for potential discrepancies in pricing.

INPUTS OF THE OPTIONS PRICING MODEL

No matter which model is being used, all pricing models need inputs. In order for any of the pricing models to produce the theoretical value of an option, some factors need to be put into the model. The models base their output value on variables that you input. Let's talk about the inputs of the option pricing model so you understand how the price of an option is calculated. Note that you will not have to calculate the value of an option yourself. Online brokerage firms offer a platform that will do it for you in real time. Nevertheless, you should be aware of the inputs that contribute to that value.

Stock Price

One of the major inputs is the *stock price*. Before the value of a certain option can be determined—whether it is a call or a put—it is necessary to know where the stock is because the stock price is going to affect that option price. A stock price must be put into the model. When inputting the stock price (one of the most heavily weighted factors in option price determination), the current stock price is used.

It is important to note that *current stock price* does not specifically mean the last sale. Traders/investors may use their knowledge of the market to lean toward the price of the bid (if the stock looks heavy) or the price of the offer (if the stock looks light) in order to predict the stock's next move or expected direction. Proper anticipation of potential stock movements can lead to better entry and exit prices for investors.

Volatility

As important as stock price is to an option's price, *volatility* is just as important. There are several different types or definitions of volatility. For the purposes of pricing model inputs, we want to concentrate on *forecast volatility*, which is our personal volatility estimate. That is what we feel will be the volatility level for a specific period of time in the future. That specific time should coincide with the length of time to expiration of the particular option of interest.

Obviously, using a volatility estimate for the next two months would not be adequate in pricing a nine-month option. For proper or reasonable accuracy, we need to consider what we feel the volatility level will be for the whole nine-month period, not just two. Several models are designed to help you properly estimate what future volatility is most likely to be. The use of these volatility estimators can be quite helpful.

Now, regardless of how we choose to estimate or calculate our forecast volatility, we need to come up with a specific volatility level that we will plug into the model to enable the model to do its calculations and return the all-important theoretical value. Therefore, the accuracy of this approximated volatility speculation is critical to the legitimacy of the pricing and, in turn, directly affects the profit potential of the trade.

Strike Price

Another important input is the *strike price*, (the fixed price at which the owner of an option can purchase, in the case of a call, or sell, in the case of a put, the underlying security or commodity). Which strike are we talking about? Are we talking about an option with a strike price of 20, of 30, or of 70? Different strike prices refer to different options and thus to different option values. The strike price value is important in determining the amount of intrinsic value that will reside in the option.

Interest Rate and Dividend

Two other input components of the model are *interest rate* and *dividend*. Together, they combine to form what is called *cost of carry*. An option's price is based on the stock's price. Anything that can directly affect the stock's price will affect the option's price indirectly and has to be accounted for in the model. How does the interest rate affect the stock price? When you buy the stock, you will no longer receive interest. Think about it. You have money in your account. While that cash is in the account, it collects interest.

When you use that cash to buy stock, you are no longer gaining interest at a specific rate. That fact indirectly affects the return you can expect from your stock purchase. You are already losing the interest you could have earned. The stock will have to outperform that interest rate just to break even. So, in essence, lost interest is a cost of stock ownership. In theory, anything that affects the price of the stock purchase indirectly affects the price of the option.

On the other side, when you sell stock, you receive money into your account for that sale, and that money will gain some interest because it's sitting in an account as cash.

As a rule of thumb, when interest rates rise, the prices of calls increase while the prices of puts decrease. As rates rise, the value of being short stock increases due to fact that the money you receive into your account from the sale of the stock gains a new, higher interest rate payment. Buying calls allows investors to short the stock in a protected manner.

When rates drop, put values increase and call values decrease. Since you will be paid less interest on money that you have in your account when rates are lower, buying stock with your money does not hurt you as much because you are not really missing out on interest being paid to you. Investors' ability to buy a put allows for the purchase of the stock in a protected manner. The ownership of puts becomes more valuable, thus the puts price rises.

Dividends are the other piece of our two-headed cost-of-carry monster. Carry cost consists of interest and dividend. Why is dividend an input of the model? Dividend, in fact, directly affects the price of the stock. The value of any stock is basically the value of all the company's assets minus liabilities. If that company were to take money out of its cash account and hand it to all its shareholders, as it does with a dividend that stock will now be worth less by the amount of the dividend paid. Cash is an asset. If the company pays out a dividend, it is decreasing its total assets; therefore, the company stock commands a lower value. For example, let's imagine that Company XYZ decides to pay out a dividend in the sum of $400,000. Prior to the payment of the dividend, the company used to have $400,000 in cash. Now it has $0 in cash. Everything else remains the same. We didn't take that $400,000 and invest it in machinery or anything. We took that $400,000 and just gave it to the shareholders. The value of the company has decreased by $400,000 so the stock should be down by $400,000 divided by the amount of shares outstanding. That's why it is said that on the day a stock goes ex-dividend, the stock should be, in theory, down the amount of the dividend paid. Although dividends might not really have an effect directly on the option, they have a direct effect on the stock. Since the stock price has a direct effect on the option price, you must pay attention to cost of carry.

Kurtosis and Skewness

Now to the more difficult inputs: kurtosis and skewness. Not every model requires or even allows for these two inputs. They are found in some of the newer pricing models because long after the development of most of the option pricing models, it was found that stock returns did not behave in a normal distribution. The models based on a normal distribution—the majority of the models—did not account for the fact that stock returns are not normally distributed but are log-normally distributed. How do we adjust for this? Simple, use skewness and kurtosis. Let's look at kurtosis first.

Kurtosis is a measurement of the fattening of the wings in a bell curve. Let's step back for a second. Remember that when we looked at the bell curve, we said that most of the events would fall in the middle. The bell curve is broken up into three standard deviations. The first standard deviation in either direction from the mean accounts for 68.4 percent of the possible scenarios. In other words, 68.4 percent of the time, stocks will stay in between the line drawn by 1 standard deviation in each direction. A second standard deviation move shows that only 13.5 percent of the potential outcomes fall 2 standard deviations beyond the center in either direction. And the third standard deviation in any one direction accounts for only 2.2 percent of the potential outcomes (see Figure 3.10).

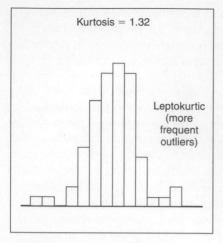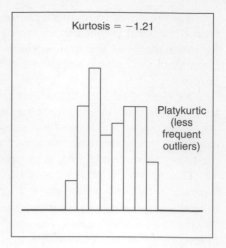

FIGURE 3.10 Kurtosis Chart

The likelihood of an event falling within 3 standard deviations is 99.7 percent of the time, or roughly 369 out of 370. In theory then, a stock should see a movement larger than 3 standard deviations only 0.3 percent of the time, or once in 370 days. That is what the bell curve tells us mathematically. However, it has been well documented that this is not correct. The frequency can be much more often.

During one nine-month period, on six separate days Dell Computer (I was a specialist in Dell options) had a one-day movement larger than 3 standard deviations. You heard it right: six times in nine months! According to the bell curve, that type of event should have happened roughly over nine years, not nine months.

What does this say? It is telling us that the bell curve—the normal distribution—for some reason is not properly accounting for the way stocks actually deliver returns. As we said earlier, studies have shown that stock returns are not normally distributed. So, somehow we had to account for all of these additional samples landing outside of 3 standard deviations. What could we do? We fatten up the wings on either side. How do we fatten them up? By using kurtosis.

In order to fatten up or increase the chances of a stock having a move of more than 3 standard deviations, we must increase the percentage chance located in the wings. Increasing the percentage chance in the wings has to affect the percentage chance somewhere else in the bell curve. This is because a bell curve cannot add up to more than 100 percent.

If we're going to increase the percentage chance of a move of more than 3 standard deviations, we must decrease the percentage chance of the stock moving 1 standard deviation or decrease the chance of it moving 2 standard deviations, or some combination of the two to maintain 100 percent.

We have to balance the percentage chance to a total of 100 percent. If we increase the wings by 5 percent, we have to take away that additional 5 percent chance from something else. Once we have adjusted the percentage chance to either 1 or 2 standard deviations (or combination thereof), the total percentage chance of an event is back in line.

This may seem complicated, but this is what kurtosis is. This is how kurtosis is used to mutate the bell curve to adjust for the fact that stock returns are log-normally distributed, not normally distributed.

It is necessary to take a measure of a stock's kurtosis and account for it in the pricing of the options. A model was needed to allow for the kurtosis adjustment. The *VSK model* was developed to do just that. Kurtosis can be calculated and measured historically, which will allow for comparison to previous time periods.

The VSK model proved to be extraordinarily accurate in its pricing of options for stocks that were very volatile. Therefore, for growth stocks that had high volatilities back in the Internet-crazed days, having a model that understood kurtosis was very important, especially for pricing options with longer expirations (out months). Today, any stock with high volatilities and prone to radical movements should be put into the VSK model to allow for the input of kurtosis in the pricing model.

Skew tells us which way or direction these log-normally distributed returns lean. While kurtosis talks about the fattening of the tails and by how much, skew talks about equality in the size of the two tails. We do not have to adjust both tails equally. A stock showing a tendency toward more frequent upside 3-plus standard deviation movements is said to have a positive skew; a stock with more frequent downside movements is said to have a negative skew. (See Figure 3.11.)

When we are looking at the bell curve, if we notice that we are having more 3-plus standard deviation events to the upside then to the downside, we may want to increase the upside tail more than the downside tail. This means that the stock has a tendency toward more frequent large upside movements than large downside movements. In this case, instead of increasing the percentage chance of both outliers equally, skewness allocates a higher amount to the upside than to the downside.

In this way, the concept of skewness will fatten the upside tail more than it fattens the downside tail. Skewness is linked to the difference in frequency between the large upside movements and the large downside

Normal Distribution (No Skew)

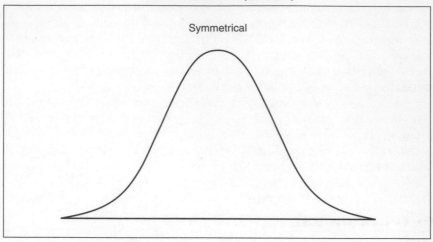

Symmetrical

Skew

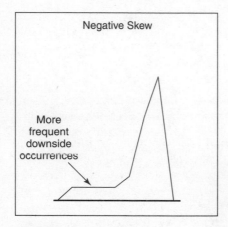

Negative Skew

More
frequent
downside
occurrences

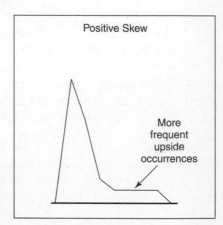

Positive Skew

More
frequent
upside
occurrences

FIGURE 3.11 Skewness

movements. Skew allows us to quantify this relationship and then adjust the fatness of the two tails accordingly.

Skew, like kurtosis, can be calculated and measured historically for comparison with previous time periods. So, when using a VSK model, you can calculate a stock's historic skew and kurtosis to help you determine where they run normally and use this to help determine whether the current conditions are high or low. This will help you determine whether the current volatility smile is trading too peaked or too flat.

While some of these inputs are weighted more heavily in an option's price than others, it is critical to realize that they are all important. It is said that you can only get out as good as you put in, and this is true with the option-pricing model as well. The better and more accurate your inputs, the better and more accurate your outputs will be.

As I've mentioned, online brokerage platforms input these variables and calculate the theoretical value by the option pricing model based on these inputs automatically and in real time. Thus, all you need to do is obtain a general understanding of the concept in order to better understand how an option derives its price.

OUTPUTS OF THE PRICING MODEL

As important and possibly even more important as the inputs to the model are the outputs. The most notable output of the pricing models is theoretical value. *Theoretical value* is the expected value of the option as calculated by the option pricing model based on the inputs provided by the user. Obviously, we all know the importance of obtaining an accurate theoretical value. All trades are based on it.

But another output of the pricing model unfortunately often is overlooked by the individual investor. This output is more commonly known as the Greeks. What is a Greek? A *Greek* is a measure of an option's sensitivity to a certain variable. The Greeks are statistical references that are calculated by the option pricing model. They not only identify an option's sensitivity to a number of critical variables, they actually quantify them as well. Therefore, not only do the Greeks tell you what might hurt your position or portfolio; they tell you exactly how much it will hurt at different levels. The Greeks are discussed in detail in Chapter 4.

Option Theory and the Greeks

The Greeks give us an insight into the nature of options by showing us how an option will behave and respond to different stimuli during the course of its life. There are several different Greeks, some a little more popular, some better known, and some more important than others. The Greeks are a risk measurement tool. They tell what will happen to your option as it is affected by stock price, interest movements, time, and volatility.

Let us identify some of the Greeks. First, we have *delta*, which is known as the first derivative. Delta tells us how much an options price will change with a movement in the underlying stock price.

Next, we have *gamma*, the second derivative. It is considered the delta of the delta. Gamma tells us how much the option's delta will change with a $1.00 movement in the stock.

Theta stands for time decay and tells us the rate at which an option's price will decay on a daily basis.

And finally, there is *vega*, which tells the option's price change in relation to a one-tick movement of implied volatility. Vega is a measure of the option's volatility sensitivity.

The Greeks allow investors to objectively calculate changes in the value of the option contracts with changes in the factors that affect the value of stock options. Having a number to calculate these changes gives traders the ability to hedge their portfolio, or construct positions with specific risk/reward profiles. This is why the Greeks are important.

DELTA

Delta, the first of our Greeks, is considered the first derivative. Although it has several different definitions, in general, delta explains or measures the price movement of an option with a $1.00 movement in the stock. That is the generic description. Delta has three definitions: percent chance, percent change, and hedge ratio. All are of equal importance; none is ahead of the other.

If we are looking at a 50-delta option and the stock moves $1.00, the option should move $0.50. If we are looking at a 30-delta option and the stock moves $1, we are looking at a $0.30 move. This movement demonstrates delta's definition of *percent change*. Delta describes the percent the option price moves with a stock price move. A 40-delta option will move 40 percent of what the stock just moved. That is percent change.

Delta is also defined as *percent chance*. A 50-delta option has a 50 percent chance of finishing in the money. A 30-delta option has a 30 percent chance of finishing in the money. Delta as percent chance describes the chance in terms of percentage of an option finishing in the money.

Delta's last definition is that of *hedge ratio*. Remember we talked about options being the perfect hedge. In any situation we could sell a number of deltas through options to perfectly hedge the delta risk of our stock. If we were long 800 shares of stock (or 800 deltas, as each share of stock is equal to 1 delta) and wanted to hedge our position, we could buy some puts to hedge that position. The question is: How many puts? The answer is in delta's definition of hedge ratio. Hedge ratio tells us how many puts we need to buy to become delta neutral.

Let's look at an example. With the 800 deltas (1 share of stock equals 1 delta; thus 1 option contract has a maximum of 100 deltas) from the 800 shares of stock, we will look at, for instance, a 40 delta put. The 800 long delta position from the stock divided by the 40 deltas of the put will equal 20. That is how many puts we would need to buy: 20. Thus, if we bought 20 of the 40 delta puts, we would be short 800 deltas, and that would perfectly hedge our long 800 delta from the stock.

We can also use calls to hedge our long stock delta. It is important to know that hedging long stock positions with calls does not give us as complete a hedge as puts. Puts provide full downside protection, protecting your position down to zero. Calls provide only a limited downside protection, limited to the amount of money you received from the sale of the calls.

 Back to our example. If we were long 800 shares of stock and we were looking at a 50-delta call, we would sell 16 of them. Why? Because the 50 deltas of the calls, multiplied by 16 calls, will give us short 800 deltas. The short 800 total delta from the 16 calls we sold will perfectly hedge the long 800 delta from our long 800 share stock position. Make sense?

It also works the other way. If we bought ten 50-delta calls, we would have acquired 500 long deltas. In order to delta hedge our position, we should sell 500 shares of stock. Remember, 1 share of stock equals 1 delta. Selling 500 shares of stock will perfectly hedge our long-500 delta position from the calls we purchased.

Delta of Calls

Calls are a long instrument so calls have long delta. Obviously, calls with different strike prices and different expiration months will have different deltas. When trading calls, buyers of calls acquire long delta positions while sellers of calls acquire short delta positions. **It is important to remember that call deltas are positive.**

Any call whose strike price is lower than the current stock price is considered an in-the-money (ITM) call and will have a delta above 60. The deeper in the money you go, or the lower price strike price you look at, the higher the deltas will be until they finally approach 100 (+100). (See Figure 4.1.)

Any call whose strike price is equal to or close to the current stock price is known as an at-the-money (ATM) call and will have deltas right around 50 (+50). (See Figure 4.2.)

Any call whose strike price is higher than the current stock price is said to be an out-of-the-money (OTM) call and will have deltas less than 40. The farther out of the money you go, the lower the deltas will be until finally reaching zero. (See Figure 4.3.)

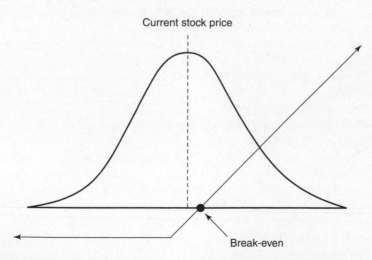

FIGURE 4.1 Bell Curve ITM Call

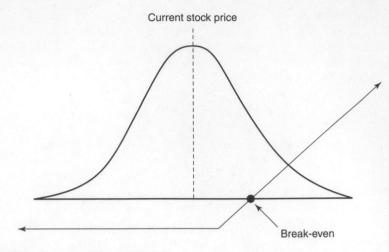

FIGURE 4.2   Bell Curve ATM Call

Delta of Puts

Puts are a short instrument so puts have short deltas. Obviously, puts with different strike prices and different expiration months will have different deltas. When trading puts, buyers of puts acquire short delta positions while sellers of puts acquire long delta positions. **It is important to remember that put deltas are negative.**

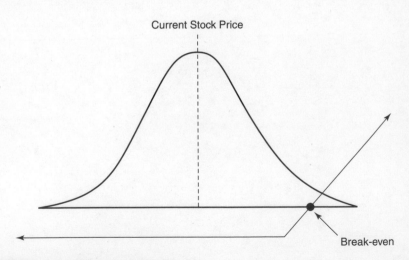

FIGURE 4.3   Bell Curve OTM Call

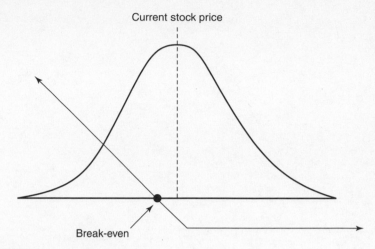

FIGURE 4.4 Bell Curve ITM Put

Any put whose strike price is higher than the current stock price is considered to be an in-the-money (ITM) put and will have a delta above 60. The deeper in the money you go, or the higher-priced strike price you look at, the higher the deltas will be until they finally approach 100 (−100). (See Figure 4.4.)

Any put whose strike price is equal to or close to the current stock price is known as an at-the-money (ATM) put and will have deltas right around 50 (−50). (See Figure 4.5.)

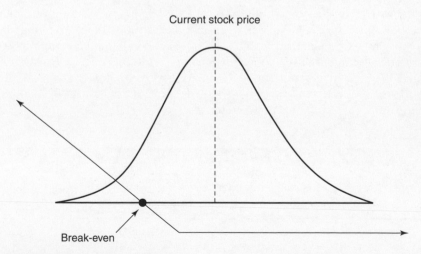

FIGURE 4.5 Bell Curve ATM Put

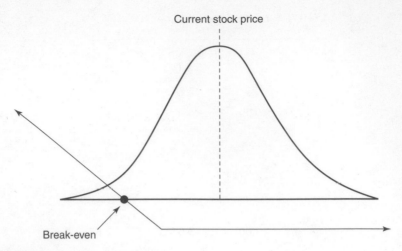

FIGURE 4.6 Bell Curve OTM Put

Any put whose strike price is higher than the current stock price is said to be an out-of-the-money (OTM) put and will have deltas less than 40. The farther out of the money you go, the lower the deltas will be until finally reaching zero. (See Figure 4.6.)

Delta Connection

An extremely important delta connection exists between a call and its corresponding put. First, what does *corresponding* mean? *Corresponding* refers to two options, one a put, the other a call, in the same month with the same strike price. For instance, the January 20 call's corresponding put is the January 20 put. The May 90 call's corresponding put is the May 90 put. The corresponding call of the July 60 put is the July 60 call. The important thing to remember is that when looking at the deltas of a call and its corresponding put, the sum of the absolute value of a call plus the absolute value of its corresponding put equal 100. (See Table 4.1.)

 KEY POINT

The absolute value of a call delta plus the absolute value its corresponding put delta equals approximately 100.

Let us try a few samples to see how that works. What we have in Table 4.1 is an excerpt from a real trading sheet. Find the deltas of the calls and

TABLE 4.1	Delta Call–Put Connection as Seen on Trading Sheet 1		
JUL	60.00	1.49	3.86
		38	−62
JUL	65.00	0.42	7.81
		15	−86
JUL	70.00	0.09	12.5
		4	−97
JUL	75.00	0.01	17.5
		1	−100
JUL	80.00	0.00	22.5
		0	−100
OCT	50.00	8.97	1.21
		81	−19
OCT	55.00	5.67	2.88
		64	−36
OCT	60.00	3.31	5.50
		46	−54
OCT	65.00	1.77	8.97
		30	−71
OCT	70.00	0.89	13.1
		18	−83
OCT	75.00	0.42	17.6
		10	−92

puts (they are directly under the prices). Look to see if the absolute value of a call and its corresponding put will equal approximately 100.

Look at the July 60 calls with a delta of +38. Now look at the put. The July 60 put delta is −62. The absolute value of −62 is 62. And 62 plus 38 is 100.

Try another one. Look at the October 50 calls, which are a +81 delta. The Oct 50 puts are a −19 delta. The absolute value of −19 is 19. Eighty-one plus 19 equals 100.

Do another one. Look at the October 60 put, which is a −54 delta. Its absolute value is 54 deltas. The October 60 call has a +46 delta. The absolute value of 54 added to the absolute value of 46 equals 100.

While this connection holds true overwhelmingly, you will encounter some cases where the total is 100-101-102 and even rarely 103. You will find some examples on Table 4.1. The reasons range from rounding errors to inefficiency of the pricing model. We said that their calculations in some models lose integrity over time. However, as a guide for determining the cost of corresponding options, generally the total for a put and call option of the same strike is 100.

Position Delta

Position delta is defined as the total delta of your position. It is calculated as the sum of all the deltas of the stock position, plus the deltas of all the calls and of all the puts in that single stock. The puts and calls could be all over the board. You could have many strikes where you are long 20 calls and short 15 puts.

This strike, you are long 100 calls. That strike, you are short 40 puts. And this other strike, you are long 100 puts. When we talk about position delta, we take the net total of all the deltas of the puts, all the deltas of the calls, and all the deltas we have in the stock and add them together.

When we do that, we will get one number, one delta number (plus or minus), and that is our position delta. Position delta tells us that if our overall position is long 1,000 deltas and the stock goes up $1.00, we will make $1,000. If we are long 1,000 deltas and the stock goes up $0.50, we will make $500. If we are short 500 deltas and the stock goes up $1.00, we will lose $500. If we are short 1,000 deltas and the stock goes up $1.00, we will lose $1,000. That is what position delta is (the aggregate total of all the delta of our position in a stock) and what it tells us (the dollar amount we stand to gain or lose with a movement of the stock). (See Figure 4.7.)

You may create a position that has no delta, a position called *delta neutral*. That means you have eliminated your position's sensitivity to stock

TODAY'S TRADE ACTIVITY								
▽ Working Orders								
	▼ Time Placed	Spread	Side		Qty	Symbol	Exp	Strike	Type
▷ Filled Orders: 9 orders, 9 fills								
▷ Cancelled Orders								

POSITION STATEMENT									
▷			Delta	Gamma		Theta			Vega
▽ AAPL			295.98	24.21		−72.63			6.94
	Days	Qty	Delta	SPC	Exp	Strike		Mark	Mark Ch..
STK ◉		0	.00					87.10	+1.75
OPT ◉		+10	−66.50	100	JAN 09	70	P	.415	−.125
◉		−10	−763.44	100	JAN 09	80	C	8.825	+1.175
◉		−10	237.85	100	JAN 09	80	P	1.72	−.47
◉		+30	1246.10	100	JAN 09	90	C	2.905	+.505
◉	14	−20	−261.85	100	JAN 09	100	C	.635	+.085
◉		−10	−247.68	100	JAN 09	110	C	3.15	+.24
SELECTED TOTALS			N/A						
	Overall Totals		295.98	24.21		−72.63			6.94

FIGURE 4.7 Position Chart with Delta Position
Source: Courtesy of TOS

movement. You might wonder how you will make money doing that. Remember, options allow you to make money in many more ways than a stock does. You might have an opportunity to try to collect decay. In the course of doing that, you do not want to double your bet by having a delta position on also.

Therefore, you neutralize your delta, become delta neutral, and just play your decay. Or you might have a volatility position on. You might be making a bet that volatility is going to go up or go down. If so, you would hate to double down on that bet by having a delta position that can work against your volatility position. For that reason, you eliminate your delta position by becoming delta neutral. That way, if the stock goes up or if the stock goes down, it does not matter. Your focus is on whether volatility goes up or down without the worry of a delta position.

Take a look at the delta table (Table 4.2). These are the deltas of the calls that I took off the trading sheet with a stock price of $65.50 and 30 volatility. We will use this chart to observe the effect of time on delta (also called trumpification).

First, observe the vertical look of delta in these calls. What I mean by that is, just look at June. As you can see, with the stock price at $65.50, you have some strikes (the 50s, the 55s, and the 60s) that are in the money. The 65s are at the money, and the 70s, 75s, and 80s are out of money.

We previously said that any in-the-money option will have a delta approaching 100—or at least higher than 60; the 50s, 55s, and 60s do have this delta. You can see that as you go deeper in the money, or lower in strike price, the deltas increase. Our at the money was going to have a delta of 50 or so, which our 65s do have.

Our out-of-the-money options were going to have deltas less than 50, and those deltas would decrease as we go farther out of the money, meaning up higher in strike prices, which the 75s and 80s do have. Our table supports the theory of the delta of calls.

TABLE 4.2 Delta Chart Calls, 30 Volatility, Stock Price $65.50

Strike Price	June	July	October	January
50	100	99	94	90
55	100	95	85	81
60	91	81	72	70
65	56	56	57	58
70	18	30	41	46
75	3	13	28	35
80	0	4	18	26

Time Effect on Delta

As individual investors, most of us will be engaging in longer-term positions as opposed to short-term trading, such as day trading. For this reason, the effects of time on your position, specifically delta, will be of great value. Positions change over time: That is a fact. We need to know how they change. For the record, time affects in-the-money calls, at-the-money calls, and out-of-the-money calls differently. Let's take a quick look at each one.

In-the-money call deltas for the same strike are lower with more time to expiration. Look at any in-the-money strike in the delta chart: 50, 55, 60. Notice as you go out in time, the deltas decrease. That is because with more time, there is more chance of the stock finishing at a price where the strike is out of the money. There is a greater potential range of the stock due to the longer period of time.

Out-of-the-money call deltas for the same strike are higher with more time to expiration. Look at any out-of-the-money strike in the delta chart: 75, 80. Notice that as you go out in time, the deltas increase. That is because with more time, there is more chance of the stock finishing at a price where the strike is in the money. Due to the longer period of time, there is a greater potential range of the stock.

At-the-money deltas remain the same. Time expands the potential range of the stock in both directions away from the middle. Thus, something in the middle with a 50–50 chance of expiring in the money will remain a 50–50 chance if the potential range of the stock is simply expanded in both directions.

This same effect on delta can be seen when volatility rises, because time and volatility are connected. Volatility is an annualized number, which indicates that time and volatility are intertwined. For purposes of the effects on delta, higher volatility levels expand the potential range of the stock the same way more time increases potential stock range. This effect is known as trumpification (see Figure 4.8).

Trumpification is defined as a delta effect caused by time and/or volatility movement in which the deltas of in-the-money options decrease toward 50, the deltas of out-of-the-money options increase toward 50, and the deltas of at-the-money options hold steady around 50. Trumpification is important because it shows how an option's delta changes as the option approaches expiration. Many investors new to options are unaware that their position can change even though the stock does not move. Those changes can create unexpected losses. Understanding trumpification will prepare you to understand changes made by time and volatility without stock price movement.

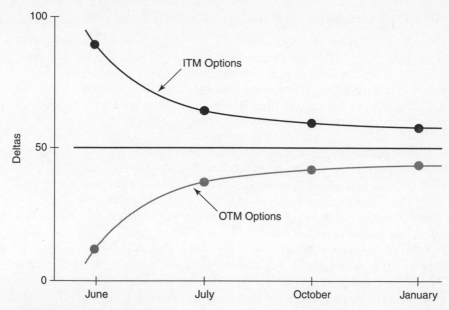

FIGURE 4.8 Trumpification

Delta and Volatility

We saw the effect of the movements of stock and the movement of time; but what about the effect of volatility? Remember that time movement created trumpification. The definition of trumpification is the effect on delta caused by time and/or volatility that increases the deltas of out-of-the-money options and decreases the deltas of in-the-money options, pushing them all toward 50. So, by definition, we should be able to see this effect with a change in volatility.

Let's take a look at the effect of a volatility movement on our deltas. Table 4.2 showed the deltas of all the calls listed by month and strike with the stock trading at $65.50 with 30 volatility. When we looked before, we saw the range of deltas in each month listed. June had a high of 100 deltas to a low of 0 deltas at a 30 volatility. Compare that with the call chart with a volatility of 70 (Table 4.3).

Look at the range of deltas in June at 70 volatility: a high of 96 deltas to a low of 12 deltas. Look at your range in July: a high of 88 deltas to a low of 26 deltas. Continue to notice the range of the next months' deltas, and go back and compare them to the chart run at 30 volatility (Table 4.2). To really notice the change in the delta range from 30 volatility to 70

TABLE 4.3 Delta Chart Calls, 70 Volatility, Stock Price $65.50

Strike Price	June	July	October	January
50	96	88	80	78
55	88	79	74	73
60	74	69	67	68
65	55	57	60	63
70	37	46	54	58
75	23	35	47	53
80	12	26	42	49

volatility, look at January and compare both volatility levels head to head. Under 30 volatility, the range is 90 to 26. Compare this to the range at 70 volatility. At 70 volatility, the range is only 78 to 49. Look how tight all those deltas are under the 70 volatility table, strangled around that at-the-money strike. Notice how tight they are. That is trumpification as caused by volatility.

Why do you want to know trumpification? Because if you understand trumpification, you understand how time and volatility affect the deltas of your option positions.

If you are long some in-the-money calls and volatility is up big in your stock, you would know immediately that your overall delta position has decreased because of trumpification. How does this affect your money position? You will have been prepared for this because you know that trumpification affects in-the-money calls by decreasing their deltas. Although you cannot control the changing of the delta due to the movement of volatility, you will have been prepared for the possibility and not surprised by it. So, you already have a better understanding of your position because you know what is going to happen to your deltas.

Depending on where your option deltas are located (in the money, at the money, or out of the money), you will know what volatility's increase will do to your delta position and what a volatility decrease will do. Here lies the importance of trumpification: knowing how your overall delta position will change with changes in volatility and the movement of time so you can be prepared to take the appropriate action.

GAMMA

Next we are going to take a look at *gamma*, the second derivative. The thing to remember about gamma is that it is the delta of the delta. It measures how much the delta changes with a movement in the stock. Therefore, it is called the second derivative. Delta measures how much an option's price changes with a movement in the stock. Gamma measures how much delta moves, so obviously, delta and gamma are connected.

Deltas are not fixed. They are determined by where the stock is, and as the stock moves, deltas move. How do we quantify the amount by which our deltas are going to change? Gamma tells us that.

However, delta and gamma differ in a very important way: calculation. Delta is calculated for each and every different individual call and put. But gamma is calculated by strike price. Gamma does not differentiate between calls and puts; it only focuses on strike price.

Gamma knows the strike, not the call or put of that strike. It does not acknowledge the difference between the August 50 call and the August 50 put. It views them both the same: the August 50 strike. This means that corresponding calls and puts have the same, identical gamma value. This is a very important concept for later.

There are two types of gamma: *long gamma* and *short gamma*. How do you acquire gamma? Any time you buy an option, any option, whether it is a call or a put, you acquire long gamma. Any time you sell an option, call or put, you gain short gamma. **Simply stated, you obtain long gamma by buying an option; you obtain short gamma by selling an option.**

Time affects gamma. Gamma increases as expiration approaches. As time goes by, an option's gamma value increases because gamma is highest in the front month at the money. Let us take a look at that.

Look at the gamma chart (Table 4.4). These gamma values are taken straight from your trading sheets. These are the calculated gamma values with the stock at $67.50 and with volatility of 30. Both the 65 and 70 strikes are roughly at the money. As we look at the month of June and we look vertically at gamma, we see that gamma is the highest when it is at the money. The 65 and 70 strikes have the highest gamma.

TABLE 4.4 Gamma Chart, Volatility 30, Stock $65.50

Strike Price	June	July	October	January
50	0	.1	.7	.9
55	.1	.8	1.5	1.5
60	1.8	2.8	2.4	2.0
65	7.2	5.0	3.0	2.3
70	7.7	5.2	3.2	2.4
75	2.8	3.7	2.9	2.3
80	.4	1.8	2.3	2.1

The gamma values decrease as you move away from the at-the-money strikes in either direction. We have identified the 65 and 70 as at the money. Look at the 60 strike. You will see a decrease in the gamma value from the 65 and 70 strikes. Now look at the 55 strike and notice even more of a decrease. Let us turn our attention to the upside. June 75's gamma value is lower than the 70 strike gamma value. The June 80 gamma value is even lower than that. So, when we are looking at gamma vertically—that is, in a single month—we must remember that gamma is the highest at the money and decreases as we move away from the at the money in either direction, whether we go further in the money or further out of the money.

KEY POINT

In either direction, gamma values decrease away from its highest point, which is located at the money.

Now, how does gamma behave over time? Let us look at gamma horizontally or out over the months at the same strike price. First, let's look at the 70 strike. The June 70 strike gamma value is 7.7. Meanwhile, the July 70 gamma value is 5.2, which is less than the June 70 gamma value. The October 70 gamma value is even less than the July gamma. Finally, the progression continues into January, where the gamma value is the lowest of any of the months.

Take another strike as an example. Look at the 65 strike from month to month and compare the results. In June, the gamma value of the 70 strike is 7.2. It decreases in July to 5.0 and decreases even further to a 3.0 gamma value in October. It has even more of a drop out in January. As you can see, the gamma decreases when we look at it horizontally (i.e., at a single, specific strike out across time). The lesson learned from this observation is that gamma is highest in the front month, at the money.

You may notice something odd when looking at Table 4.4: The June 50 gamma value is lower than the January 50 gamma. As you can see, the difference is minuscule, but it is true. That is because the January 50 calls are so deep in the money they are acting like stock, and stock does not have gamma. When you talk about very deep in-the-money options, you might actually see an increase in gamma values over time.

You see it a little in the 55 strike also. Why? Because in the front months, the very deep in-the-money options are trading at parity to the stock. Parity, as you know, means equal to. These options trade at parity because there is so little time left until expiration. These options are so deep in the money that the pricing model feels that the current implied volatility of the stock is not enough to threaten that the strike will not finish in the money by expiration. In July, there is more time, so the July 55 strike is a little more of an option (not as high a delta) than the June 55 strike. Thus, the July 55 strikes have a little more gamma.

The same exception holds when you get way out of the money. When you get way out of the money, as in the 80 strike, these options are valueless. They are so far out of the money that the option model is saying that, under the current volatility and with such little time left, there is no way for that option to finish in the money by expiration. The options are no longer viable. They are worthless. Since the option (June 80) is worthless and no longer a viable option, it can't have gamma. Because the July 80s have a little more time left before expiration, they are a somewhat more of an option. They still have a chance. Thus, they have a little more gamma.

When you are looking horizontally at the deep in the moneys and the out of the moneys, you will notice the gamma probably increases slightly out over those times. **However, the rule of thumb is that gamma is highest front month at the money and decreases when you move vertically in either direction away from the strike; gamma decreases out over time except for deep in-the-money options and way out-of-the-money options.**

Like delta, gamma also can have a position effect. That means that there is a gamma for every single different option strike. If you have a position of multiple options series under the same stock, each one of those options will be subtracting from or adding to the gamma of the total position. Look at the position statement in Figure 4.9. Notice that the positions are listed for gamma and delta, which we have already discussed, and vega and theta, which we discuss later.

If you took a net option position for each strike under an individual stock and multiplied it by the gamma of the strike, you would get a gamma position for each strike price in which you have open contracts. From there, you can add together all the gammas from all the different strikes to give you a total position gamma. The two types of gamma, long and short, affect your delta position differently. Some traders believe that long gamma is good gamma and short gamma is bad gamma. This perception is totally untrue.

Gamma is neither a good nor a bad thing; it is simply long or short. You must be able to apply or trade both long and short gamma just as easily because different conditions require different types of gamma positions. Some feel that long gamma is easier to trade, and it normally is. However, we know that selling options is the right side of the trade between 75 and 80 percent of the time, so being comfortable with trading short gamma is very important. It is important to favor neither and know both equally well.

TODAY'S TRADE ACTIVITY									
▽ Working Orders									
▼ Time Placed	Spread	Side		Qty	Symbol		Exp	Strike	Type
▷ Filled Orders: 9 orders, 9 fills									
▷ Cancelled Orders									

POSITION STATEMENT									
▷			Delta		Gamma		Theta		Vega
▽ AAPL			295.98		24.21		−72.63		6.94
	Days	Qty	Delta	SPC	Exp	Strike		Mark	Mark Ch..
STK ◉		0	.00					87.10	+1.75
OPT ◉		+10	−66.50	100	JAN 09	70	P	.415	−.125
◉		−10	−763.44	100	JAN 09	80	C	8.825	+1.175
◉		−10	237.85	100	JAN 09	80	P	1.72	−.47
◉		+30	1246.10	100	JAN 09	90	C	2.905	+.505
◉	14	−20	−261.85	100	JAN 09	100	C	.635	+.085
◉		−10	−247.68	100	JAN 09	110	C	3.15	+.24
SELECTED TOTALS			N/A						
Overall Totals			295.98		24.21		−72.63		6.94

FIGURE 4.9 Gamma Position from TOS
Source: Courtesy of TOS

Long Gamma Trading

First, let's talk about *long gamma* and how it affects your delta position. When you are long gamma and the stock increases in value, your delta position increases by the amount of your gamma position per $1 move in the stock. If the stock were to go down, your delta position would decrease by the amount of your gamma position per $1 movement in the stock. Simply put, if the stock went up and you were long gamma, your delta would increase. If the stock went down and you were long gamma, your delta would decrease.

Short Gamma Trading

Now let us talk about *short gamma*. Short gamma behaves in an opposite way from long gamma. If you are short gamma and the stock goes up, your delta position would decrease. If you were short gamma and the stock goes down, your delta position would increase.

Make sure that you are fully comfortable with both the long and the short gamma effect on delta. Make sure that you understand both equally well and always remember: **There is no good gamma, and there is no bad gamma. There is only long gamma and short gamma, and both will affect your profitability.**

VEGA

Before we begin our discussion of vega, let us review all the things we should understand about volatility. We fully realize volatility's importance in option pricing. We recognize the way that implied volatility looks and is used vertically and horizontally. We know how volatility affects the price of an option and how it affects delta and gamma. We understand the importance of the concept that when volatility increases, the value of all options increase and when volatility decreases, the price of all options decrease . . . but by how much?

Now we want to quantify that understanding with a number. That is where vega comes in. Vega is the output of the pricing model, or Greek, that provides us with that number.

Vega tells us the dollar change in the price of an option per a one-tick movement in implied volatility. Exactly how much does an option's price change? What exact dollar amount change occurs with a one-tick movement in volatility? That is what vega measures. Vega is also used to calculate expected changes in option price based on anticipated changes in volatility. So vega gives two important pieces of information: It not only tells you where something will trade when volatility moves, but it gives you a general idea of what your option is going to do based on a set of potential risks that you might encounter.

Let us explore a possible real-life scenario. You have an option that has been trading at 40 volatility. You understand that it could very easily trade down to 35 volatility. What does that move mean in dollars and cents? Vega lets you know the dollar amount you have at risk; it gives you the exact dollar amount you could lose. Vega is a very important tool for risk management because it puts an actual dollar amount on the change of your option's price per a one-tick movement in volatility.

How does vega work? Let's use an example. In our hypothetical scenario, we have purchased the July 70 call for a price of $3.00 at an implied volatility of 40 and a vega of 9.2 cents, which we will round to 9.0 cents for this example. Now, if implied volatility increased to 41, the option's price would increase to $3.09.

Remember, vega measures the change in an options price per a one-tick movement in volatility. So, with volatility increasing one tick to 41, the option will increase in value by 9 cents. If implied volatility were to decrease one tick down to 39, the price of the option will decrease by 9 cents for a new value of $2.91. It is important to realize that movements in implied volatility are not restricted to just one tick at a time. In order to calculate an implied volatility movement of more than one tick, you simply calculate the difference between where implied volatility is and where it was. Next, take that difference and multiply it by the option vega. Then add or subtract that amount to the old theoretical value to create the new theoretical value.

For instance, recall the particulars of our previous example: The July 70 call is worth $3.00 at 40 volatility with a vega of 9 cents. If implied volatility were to increase five ticks to 45 volatility, you could calculate the new theoretical value at this new volatility level (45). First, note that there is a five-tick volatility difference (original 40, new 45). Take that five-tick difference and multiply it by the 9-cent vega. This equals $0.45 (5 × .09). Now add this to the original theoretical value of $3.00, and you come up with a new theoretical value of $3.45 at an implied volatility of 45. Remember, if volatility decreases rather than increases, we would use the same calculation except we would subtract from our original theoretical value instead of add to it. So, in our previous example, if the volatility decreased five ticks down to 35 volatility, we would still multiply the vega (9 cents) by the change in volatility, which is five ticks (40 − 35), and that will again equal 45 cents. This time, however, we are dealing with a decrease in volatility, so we subtract 45 cents from $3.00, giving us a value of $2.55. This will be the new theoretical value of the July 70 call at 35 volatility.

As a rule of thumb, if we are looking at an increase in volatility, we will be increasing the value of the option. If we are looking at a decrease in volatility, then we will be decreasing the value of the option. Using this concept, we can also calculate the volatility in regard to a change in theoretical value. The previous few paragraphs showed you how to use vega to determine the new theoretical value of an option with a set and known volatility change. Now we will use vega to determine the implied volatility level at which an option is trading.

Again, there is a formula to follow for this calculation. Using our previous example once more, we first take the difference of the two theoretical values. The original theoretical value in our scenario was $3.00, which we know to be 40 volatility.

Let's say that the July 70 call is now trading at $3.18 (all other things being equal), which is an increase in price. The difference in price is 18 cents. We take this difference ($0.18) and divide it by the options vega ($.09) to solve for volatility. When we do this, we come up with two volatility ticks. We now take those two ticks and add them to our original implied volatility of 40. Since we are looking at an increase in option price, we know we must be dealing with an increase in implied volatility. From our calculation, we know we are dealing with a two-tick increase in the implied volatility. With the option now trading at $3.18, the new implied volatility level must be 42. We know that the price of options can decrease as well as increase. So, in a situation where the option price decreases below the original theoretical value ($3.00 in this case), we use the same calculation method we just used

TABLE 4.5 Vega Chart

Strike Price	June	July	October	January
50	0	.001	.035	.080
55	0	.013	.076	.129
60	.011	.047	.123	.174
65	.050	.087	.156	.205
70	.053	.092	.164	.215
75	.018	.063	.149	.207
80	.003	.030	.120	.186

to find the volatility level except we subtract the volatility ticks from our original volatility.

Vega's importance is huge. Volatility is what separates the option product from all the other products. What separates options from stocks is that you can trade the volatility. Let's take a closer look at vega to see how it works (Table 4.5).

Vega is the dollar amount in cents. So when you see something that has a 5 vega, it means a 5-cent vega. Take a look at the month of July and focus on the 70 strike. The 70 strike is roughly at the money. In fact, both the 65 and 70 strikes are roughly at the money because the stock is located in between the two at $67.50.

We see that the 65 and 70 strike vega prices are similar. However, when we move down in strike but continue looking at July, we see that the July 60 vega is less than the July 65 and 70 strikes and that the July 55 vega is even less than the July 60 vega. Looking in the other direction, toward the higher strikes, we see that the July 75 vega is lower than the July 65 and 70 strike vega. The July 80 strike vega is even lower than the July 75 strike vega.

When observing vega's behavior vertically along all the strikes in the same month as we did when we viewed gamma, we see vega is highest at the money and decreases as you move away from the at-the-money strike in either direction.

Let me say that again: Vega is highest at the money and decreases as you move away from the at-the-money strike in either direction. That is vega's vertical look: highest at the money, decreasing as we move in either direction away from the at-the-money strike. Vertically, vega is similar to gamma in appearance.

Remember, gamma is also highest at the money. As you move away from the at-the-money strike in either direction, gamma decreases.

However, there is a difference between vega and gamma when viewed on the charts. We see it when we look at vega horizontally, or across the same strike from month to month. Remember we spoke about gamma being highest in the front month and decreasing as we went out over time. Vega presents the opposite picture; vega *increases* as we go out over time.

Let's take a look at vega across the same strike but out from month to month. Focus your attention on the June 65 strike, with a 5-cent vega, as the starting point. Bounce out to the July 65 strike and see that it has an 8.7-cent vega. Move a little farther out to the October 65 strike and see a 15.6-cent vega and finally, in the January 65 strike, a 20.5-cent vega. When we look horizontally, vega is highest in the out months and lowest in the front months. This demonstrates that as we go out over time, vega increases. This is the opposite behavior from gamma, which decreases as you go out over time. It is important to note two salient points about vega: Vega is highest at the money and decreases as you move in either direction away from the at-the-money strike, and vega is highest in the out months and lower in the front months.

All these options, as you can see on Table 4.5, have a different vega number. When vega increases one tick, each option is going to change differently based on the size of each individual option's vega value. If you were to take volatility up one tick across the board, all these options would change in price differently. The June 65 strike would increase by 5 cents, the July 75 strike by 6.3 cents, the October 60's would be up 12.3 cents, and January 70's would be up a whopping 21.5 cents. If volatility were to increase one tick across the board, the result would lead to overpricing the out-month options in relation to the front months. This is why there is a volatility smile and a volatility tilt.

Volatility Smile

In a perfect world, the volatility levels of all strikes in the same month should be the same. After all, if we are looking at all options that expire in the same month—May, for instance—we know that there can be only one volatility that the stock can trade at between now and May expiration. Thus, all the strikes with May expiration should all be the same volatility—theoretically.

However, theory is not necessarily reality. In reality, the strikes under the same expiration month are almost never the same. In fact, they are almost always different. This volatility "skew" is called the *volatility smile*. A volatility smile can be seen in almost every month of every option product in the financial industry. To identify this smile, all you need do is go into a single expiration month and look for a situation of different strikes in that single month trading at different levels.

Let's look at a volatility smile situation. In Table 4.6, you can see the volatility smile that exists in each individual month.

TABLE 4.6 Volatility Smile Chart

Strike Price	June	July	October	January
50	54	52	50	46
55	50	49	47	43
60	47	46	44	40
65	45	44	42	39
70	47	46	44	40
75	50	49	47	43
80	54	52	50	46

First, look at the front month (June) calls. Look at the at-the-money strike. As you can see, the volatility level of the June 65 call is 45. Now as you scan further in the money (60 strike) and out of the money (70 strike), you see that the volatility level of these two strikes has increased to 47.

Continuing further in the money, the 55 strike and then the 50 strike, we see the volatility level increasing to 50 in the 55 strike and finally to 54 in the 50 strike. As we look toward the out-of-the-money strikes, we see the same effect. As we head further out to the 75 strike and then the 80 strike, we see the volatility levels rising again. The volatility level rises to 50 in the 75 strike and finally the volatility level rises to 54 in the 80 strike.

This pattern holds true in the other months as well. In the financial markets, of course, nothing holds true under every situation, but the volatility smile holds true much more often than not. Looking in the other months, we see that the same pattern exists. The pattern can be summarized in a general rule of thumb. Mind you, this is not a law; it is not a black-and-white rule. However, most volatility smiles start with the at-the-money strike as the lowest in any given month. From there, the volatility level rises as you move further in the money and as you move further out of the money.

The reason for this is a little complicated and an advanced topic. With that said, there are a few answers to this question. For those of you who are math hounds, the volatility smile exists because it has been shown through empirical data that stock returns are not normally distributed but log-normally distributed. For those of you who are more risk and reward based, the volatility smile exists due to risk and reward reasons. When you sell options, you can gain only what you sell the option for. A cheap option, therefore, does not offer enough reward for the accepted risk. So, these options trade at higher volatilities to keep the prices higher to help balance the risk with more appropriate reward.

Again, the reason behind the existence of the smile is an advanced topic. At this level, the beginner level, it is enough to know that the

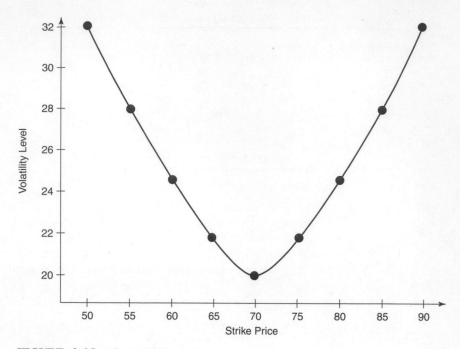

FIGURE 4.10 The Volatility Smile

smile exists, it can be identified, and there are legitimate reasons for its existence.

If you were to graph any of the months from the volatility chart (Table 4.6), you would see the smile (Figure 4.10).

Volatility Tilt

The *volatility tilt* can be seen in a stock where different expiration months are trading at different volatility levels. This can be observed simply by going to the at-the-money strike and looking at the current implied volatility from month to month across the same strike (Table 4.7).

A stock trading with a normal volatility tilt is one whose options have the front month at a higher level of implied volatility. From there, the second month trades at a lower implied volatility than the first month but higher than the third month. The third will trade at a higher implied volatility than the fourth month. The fourth month will trade at the lowest implied volatility on the board. This is known as a decreasing tilt (Figure 4.11).

If a stock has leaps, however, the first January leap will obviously be trading at a lower implied volatility level than the fourth month, and the

TABLE 4.7 Volatility Tilt Chart (Monthly Implied Volatility)

Strike Price	June	July	October	January
50	54	52	50	46
55	50	49	47	43
60	47	46	44	40
65	45	44	42	39
70	47	46	44	40
75	50	49	47	43
80	54	52	50	46

second January leap will then trade at the lowest implied volatility on the board. As a rule of thumb, a decreasing level of implied volatility as you look out over time creates volatility tilts.

The level of implied volatility will be lower the more time there is to expiration. Remember that when looking at the option board, mathematical relationships exist between months, between strikes, between calls and their corresponding puts, and between synthetic positions and their actual counterparts.

You can use vega to move implied volatility proportionally, thus keeping the horizontal relationships in line. With lower relative vega values in

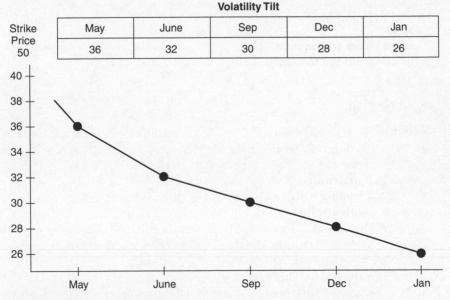

Volatility Tilt

Strike Price 50	May	June	Sep	Dec	Jan
	36	32	30	28	26

FIGURE 4.11 Decreasing Tilt

the front month, you might move June up 10 ticks in implied volatility while only moving July up 4 volatility ticks.

Further, you may move October up just 2 ticks and January up only 1 volatility tick. Why? Because each change of a single volatility tick affects these options differently. In times of dramatically increased volatility, such as a surprise news event, the volatility of the front two months (in this example June and July) will be up dramatically, but the outer months, (October and January) might not be up much at all. October might be up 2 or 3 ticks, January might move up 1 or 2 ticks if at all, yet June might be up 10 to 15 ticks and July might be up 8 to10 ticks. That is how the tilts are developed. You have to move implied volatility more or less in some strikes due to the sensitivity differences between the strikes. But you still have to keep the option's mathematical relationships in line. It is vega that is responsible for the formation of volatility smiles and tilts. This concept is important to note because you will be dealing with volatility smiles and tilts in every option class you trade.

It is also very important to note that when engaged in a strategy that uses more than one option, such as a spread (vertical spread or time spread), straddle, strangle, condor, or butterfly, you must first make sure that all of the options are calculated at the same volatility level in order to calculate the actual volatility level of the entire trade.

You might think doing so presents a dilemma since we have just shown how the volatility smile and the volatility tilt creates situations where practically all options on the board will trade at different implied volatility levels. The smile will make all the options in a given month trade at different volatility levels while the volatility tilt will make all the different months trade at different volatility levels.

How can we adjust the volatility levels of different options to make them uniform?

The answer: Use vega to adjust one of the options either up or down, to the volatility level of the other option. How do you do that? Another example will help clarify things. We will do a vertical spread with two strikes trading at two different volatility levels. Let's establish the pertinent information about the components of this vertical spread.

We Buy:	We Sell:
Strike: July 60	Strike: July 65
Price: $3.00	Price: $1.50
Vega: 4.5	Vega: 8.5
Volatility: 46	Volatility: 44

We can easily see what the implied volatility level is for each individual option. But we are looking for the volatility of the spread itself.

Unfortunately, we can't take the average of the two volatilities of the two options because calculating the average implies that the two options are weighted equally. Obviously, the different vegas show that the options are not evenly weighted in terms of volatility sensitivity. We need to equalize the two different volatility levels.

That means we must adjust one option's volatility so that both options are at the same volatility. To do that with this example, we need to move the volatility level of one option up or down to the volatility level of the other. This adjusting or moving of volatility will create a change in the theoretical value of the option being adjusted. How can we do that? We use the vega.

The first step is to decide which option to keep at a fixed volatility level and which to change. Fortunately, it does not matter which option you choose. If you adjust the option properly, either one work. In our example, we take the July 60 call and determine its value at a 44 volatility, moving it down to an equal volatility with the July 65 calls. Or we figure out the value of the July 65 calls at a 46 volatility, moving them up to the level of the July 60 calls. The goal here is to have both options calculated for the same fixed volatility. If you want to lower the 60s or raise the 65s, fine, either action will give the same results—equal volatilities.

Let's say we choose to move the July 60 calls down two ticks from 46 volatility to 44 volatility, making them equal in volatility to the July 65 calls. This will create a fixed implied volatility at 44. The first thing is to determine the theoretical value of the July 60 calls at a volatility two ticks lower. To do this, we must take the vega of the July 60 calls, which is 4.5. That means, for every one-tick decrease in volatility, that option is going to decrease 4.5 cents. We have a theoretical value for the July 60 calls of $3.00 at 46 volatility and we know that that option is going to decrease 4.5 cents per tick. We want to take it down two ticks to the 44 level. That means we want to take 9 cents (4.5 vega times a two-tick volatility movement) from the price of this option. Now, instead of being worth $3.00 at 46 volatility, this option is worth $2.91 at 44 volatility. Meanwhile we do not need to touch our July 65 calls because they are already calculated for 44 volatility.

We have now adjusted our July 60 calls to 44 volatility at which level the theoretical value is $2.91. Our July 65 calls are worth $1.50, also at 44 volatility. We can now take the new theoretical value of the July 60 calls, which is $2.91, and subtract the value of the July 65 calls, which is $1.50. In a spread, we are buying one option and selling another, so the price of the spread is the difference in price between the two options. Now we have the new theoretical value of our spread as $1.41 at 44 volatility.

Does that mean that is what we traded the spread for? No, it's just telling you that at 44 volatility, this spread is worth $1.41. If you did trade the spread at this price and you bought it, then you own the spread at 44 volatility. If you sold it for $1.41, then you sold the spread at 44 volatility. Now we need to know what the vega of the spread is. Because a spread involves the purchase of one option against the sale of another option, we must use subtraction in our calculation.

The vega of the spread will be equal to the difference between the vega of the two options. In this case, the spread vega will equal −4.0 cents (−8.5 + 4.5). This means that when we calculate the new volatility, it will have to be subtracted from our fixed volatility.

An obvious question arises here. How do you know whether this vega is going to be a positive vega and added to our calculated, fixed volatility or a negative one and subtracted from our calculated, fixed volatility? Easy, you just look at which option you are long and which option you are short in your spread. In this case, we are long the July 60 calls with a 4.5-cent vega. This makes us long 4.5 vega. We are short the July 65 calls with an 8.5-cent vega, making us short 8.5 vega. When we combine the two, we are overall short 4.0 vega.

As volatility decreases, this spread will widen and increase in value, so, as owners, we will profit. As volatility increases, this spread tightens, thereby decreasing in value; as owners, we will lose money. Now that we know for certain the exact theoretical value of the spread ($1.41) and that the spread trades at $1.61, we can discover what volatility level that represents.

The spread is trading 20 cents higher than the $1.41 value at 44 volatility. Our next step is to divide that difference in price by the spread's vega, which is −4.0 cents. This will tell us the difference in volatility ticks of the two spread prices.

Remember, vega tells you how much the price will change with a one-tick movement in volatility. In this case, a 20-cent difference in price divided by a negative 4-cent-per-tick vega will give us a difference of 5 volatility ticks. Because we are dealing with a price increase in the spread from $1.41 at 44 volatility to $1.61 at an unknown volatility, we must subtract this 5-tick volatility increase from the 44 volatility and come up with a 39 volatility for the spread trading at $1.61. If we were dealing with a price decrease in the spread, we would have added to our known 44 volatility.

Let's try it the other way to see what happens. Instead of moving the volatility of the July 60 calls down to the volatility of the July 65 calls, we'll move the 65 calls volatility up to the volatility of the 60 calls. How do we do it? Use the same process as before.

We know the July 65 calls are theoretically worth $1.50 at 44 with an 8.5-cent vega. We will now move them up to a 46 volatility to make them even with the July 60 calls. To do this we increase the volatility two ticks. This will increase the theoretical value of the July 65 calls by 17 cents

(2 volatility ticks times an 8.5-cent vega). This will create a new theoretical value in the July 65 calls of $1.67 at a 46 volatility. From there we can calculate an accurate theoretical value of the spread at 46 volatility because both options are set for the same volatility. At 46 volatility, the spread will be worth $1.33.

Now that we know for certain the exact theoretical value of the spread ($1.33) at an exact volatility (46) with an exact vega (−4.0 cents), we can calculate an exact volatility for the spread trading at any price.

Going back to our example price of $1.61, let's see if we come up with the same volatility level as we did when we changed the July 60 calls. First, we take the difference in price between the two spreads, which is 28 cents ($1.61 − $1.33). We then divide that 28 cents by the spreads vega of (−4.0 cents), which gives us a negative (−) 7 volatility ticks. We then subtract those 7 volatility ticks from our known volatility of 46 and wind up with a 39 volatility for the spread worth $1.61.

This matches up exactly with our first calculation, as it should. As stated before, it does not matter which option you choose to change; they will both work in similar fashion.

The key concept to remember is that when you are dealing with spreads, you have to use the vega of each option to make sure that the theoretical value of the individual option components of the spread is based on a similar volatility.

You cannot compare an option where the volatility component is a 42 with another option that has a volatility component of 48. For comparison, volatility levels must be identical.

So, your rule of thumb for volatility calculation is:

1. Equalize the individual option volatility to a fixed level using vega.
2. Calculate the difference in spread prices.
3. Calculate the vega of the spread.
4. Divide the spread price difference by the spread vega.
5. Add or subtract value (from step 4) to or from fixed volatility level as determined by the positive or negative vega value of the spread.

When you are dealing with a spread, you take the difference of the theoretical prices because you are buying one option and selling the other. You have to remember that when you are trading a straddle or strangle, you are doing the same thing in both options, either buying both or selling both. Therefore, you don't take the difference between the vega in a straddle or strangle. You still calculate the same fixed volatility level for both options by moving one up or the other down using their vega. That will give you a theoretical value of that straddle or strangle at that same volatility level.

To get the vega of that straddle or strangle, you must add the vega of the two together, not subtract one from the other as you would in a spread.

Remember: With the spread, you are buying one option and selling the other; that is why you have to take the difference of the options' vega. In a straddle or strangle, you are either buying both options or selling both options so you have to add the vega amounts together to get the vega of the whole straddle or strangle.

When comparing volatility between options at different volatility levels, first you must adjust one of the option's volatility levels to match the volatility level of the other using the vega of the options.

THETA

The last of the major Greeks is theta. *Theta* measures an option's rate of decay over time. When we study theta, we must have a clear understanding of time and value.

First, we have to remember that options possess two types of value: intrinsic and extrinsic value. We have spoken about value before several times. Theta does not have any effect on an option's intrinsic value. Intrinsic value does not decay or erode over time. Theta affects an option's extrinsic value, the amount of money over and above parity, the amount of money over and above intrinsic value. Theta affects only the extrinsic value of an option.

Next, note that every option has a limited life. The life of an option is the number of days that it exists. No matter what option we look at, it has a limited life. When we look at a six-month option, we know that after six months, that option is going to end. It will no longer exist. The key here is to remember that an option is a wasting asset.

We say that an option is a wasting asset because its value wastes away as time goes by, until the time that the option expires. Theta measures that rate of decay. **Theta is time decay, the measurement of the rate at which an option is going to decay over the course of its life.** That measurement is expressed in a number, an amount of money.

Theta measures the decay in money that takes places during an option's life, as shown in Table 4.8.

If we are dealing with an out-month option with 160 days until expiration, then theta will measure that specific option's rate of decay. If it is a front-month option that has 20 days, theta will measure how fast the extrinsic value of that option will decay on a daily basis until expiration.

So, if we know that there is $1.00 worth of extrinsic value in an option that has 20 more days of life, we would want to know at what rate that

TABLE 4.8 Theta Chart

Strike Price	June	July	October	January
50	0	.007	.006	.005
55	.013	.013	.010	.007
60	.041	.033	.019	.011
65	.059	.042	.026	.018
70	.055	.038	.024	.016
75	.028	.024	.017	.009
80	.018	.020	.011	.006

$1.00 will decay over the 20 days. Theta measures that on a daily basis. An option does not decay at an even rate. It does not decay linearly. An option decays at a nonlinear rate. What does that mean? Let's use an example to explain nonlinear rate.

Remember our earlier example where we were long an option that had $1.00 worth of extrinsic value and 20 days until expiration. *Nonlinear* means you cannot just take that $1.00, divide it by 20 days, and decide that the option will decay at $0.05 a day. Nonlinear time decay does not work like that. As an option gets closer to expiration, it decays more rapidly on a daily basis. Instead of decaying at $0.05 a day each of the 20 days, on day 1 that option might decay only 1 cent and then increase that decay amount daily continually into expiration.

For example, the option may decay .015 cents on day 3, but the last few days it might be decaying .05 cents, .06 cents, or even more. The decay rate is nonlinear. Let's take a look at a time decay curve in Figure 4.12 and see what we mean by nonlinear decay.

At the top chart, we have extrinsic value, or the time value, on the left-hand side. Across the bottom, we see the months to expiration. As you can see, the decay rate picks up dramatically as we head into expiration, or timeline zero.

Early in the option's life, five months out (while there are still five months to go before expiration), you can see that the curve is almost a flat line. There is just a slight downgrade. The option, at this time, does not seem to be really decaying.

However, once the option hits the 60-day mark (two months until expiration), it starts to feel the effects of decay significantly. A month out (30 days), the slope is starting to increase considerably. Finally, as you can see, all of the remaining extrinsic value, whatever is left, bleeds out in the last couple of days of the option's life.

The bottom chart shows you a close-up of the last two-month section of the top chart. Down at the bottom of the chart, we have the timeline, the

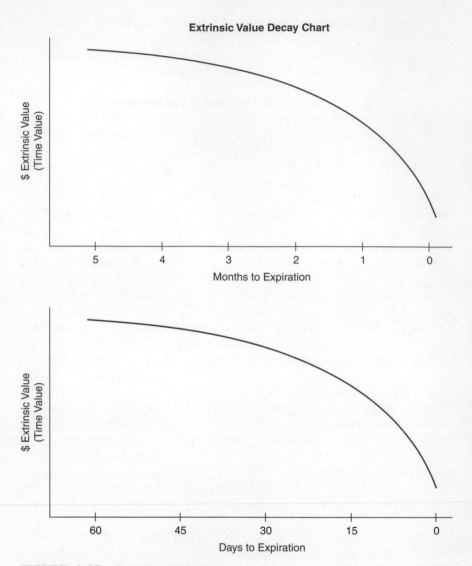

FIGURE 4.12 Time Decay Curves

x-axis, which represents the number of days until expiration. To the left, we have the *y-axis*, which shows the extrinsic value, or time value.

Again, we can see that at the 60-day mark, this option does not seem to reflect major time decay effects. However, as it gets closer and closer to expiration, the decay increases rapidly. It increases and continually increases its daily rate.

Every day that passes, the option is feeling the effects of the decay more and more. Remember that an option's decay is nonlinear. It is not fluid throughout the life of the option. The closer the option gets to expiration, the more rapidly it decays on a daily basis. Every day there is progressively more decay, day after day.

This is why we talk about the fact that if you are going to buy a naked option, or at least an option that has a fair amount of extrinsic value, you want to trade out of that option as soon as the stock, or volatility, produces the movement you have been waiting for.

Moreover, while waiting for an anticipated movement, you must realize that as you wait and time goes by, that option will be decaying, or losing value. The longer you wait, the more the option decays. The more the option decays, the more aggressive movement you will need to offset its time decay just to break even.

This spotlights the idea and importance of selection timing. The better you plan your timing, the more likely your trade will be profitable. Work on your timing. Remember, the longer you wait, the more the option decays. That is why, when buying options, especially those with a good amount of extrinsic value, you have to be reasonably precise in your timing.

We will talk more about timing later when we talk about the purchase of a naked call or a naked put. Right now what you need to know is that options decay at a progressively higher rate every day. You can see that in Table 4.8.

Theta has affects on other components besides the overall dollar value of an option. For instance, time decay, or theta, affects delta. We have previously discussed delta and time's affect on it. So, we know that as time goes by, the delta of an option is going to change. If nothing were to happen at all, all things being equal, the delta of an option is going to change day to day as time passes.

Theta and Delta

Let's take a look at the effect of theta on delta in at-the-money options, in-the-money options, and out-of-the-money options. Theta affects the delta of each of these types of options but does so differently. We don't really need to worry about whether the option is a put or call. Theta's effects will be the same in both calls and puts.

First, let's take a look at an in-the-money option. Imagine we have an option that is $5.00 or so in the money and is 75 deltas with 30 days left to expiration. Now remember what that 75 deltas means. One of the definitions of delta, as you recall, is percentage chance. So, what we are saying here is that this option has a 75 percent chance of finishing in the money at expiration.

What can affect that expectation? Well, the stock could move. Volatility could increase or decrease. Several things can affect that 75 delta (that 75 percent chance of finishing in the money).

Time decay, or theta, is one of them. Remember, the longer time an option has before expiration, the bigger chance there is for a major movement. So, this 75 delta option with 30 days left, with a 75 percent chance of finishing in the money, is going to have a higher percentage chance of finishing in the money after 15 of those days have gone by without anything happening.

At that point this 75 delta option will have even more of a chance of finishing in the money because there is less time for something to happen to knock it out of the money. Therefore, it will now trade with a higher delta, possibly as high as 90.

Why does the delta increase? The delta of in-the-money options increases with the passage of time because as time goes by, there is less time for stock (or volatility) movement to change this in-the-money option to an out-of-the-money option.

At the 30-day mark, this option might be only 75 deltas. However, with 15 days left, the option might be 90 deltas. With only 15 days left, there is a much larger percentage chance that the option will finish in the money; there is much less time for it to not finish in the money. With two days, left this 90-delta option might actually be 98 or 99 deltas, perhaps even 100 deltas.

Theta has influence over delta's definition of percentage chance. Percentage chance in the option's world is predicated by the amount of time left until the end of an option's life. As long as the option exists, there is at least some kind of chance for something to happen. Remember what Yogi Berra said: "It ain't over 'til it's over." The same can be said of options. However, once it is over, at expiration, all in-the-money options will be 100 deltas and convert to stock.

Theta affects the natural progression of delta's movement over time. Theta, or time decay, affects the delta of in-the-money options by increasing their deltas as time passes, with all other things being equal.

Again, it is important to remember that the delta of in-the-money options (both calls and puts) increases with the passage of time. In-the-money call options obtain higher positive deltas (get longer) while in-the-money put options obtain higher negative deltas (get shorter) as theta affects the option.

Out-of-the-money options work the opposite way. Let's take a look at an option that has 30 days to expiration, is $3.00 out of the money, and has maybe a 30 delta. Fifteen days go by, and neither the stock nor the volatility has moved. The option is still $3.00 out of the money. But half of that option's life has gone by without any type of movement that could change its price.

That option will no longer be a 30 delta. Why? Because its percentage chance of finishing in the money has decreased further due to the fact that time has passed with nothing to stimulate an increase in the option's price. Thus, its percentage chance of making that movement, with even less time to do it, is lowered. With only 15 days left, this option may be only a 20-delta option.

Theta, or the passage of time, decreases the delta of out-of-the-money options. The less time the option has to move, the lower its chance of making the move. For an out-of-the-money option, that means its delta has to decrease. So, out-of-the-money call deltas will decrease or become less positive (less long), while out-of-the-money put deltas will decrease or become less negative (less short) as theta affects the option.

Finally, let's talk about at-the-money options. An at-the-money option is a little different from the other two. An at-the-money option, whose delta is around 50, is not going to be affected by the passage of time. Its price may be affected by theta in terms of price erosion, but the option's delta will not be. That is because that option is still on the fence between being in the money and out of the money.

In that sense, nothing has changed. If the stock was trading directly at the option's strike price today, had been trading so 10 days ago, and will still be trading at the strike tomorrow, then the option still has a 50–50 chance of being either in the money or out of the money at expiration.

One cent one way or 1 cent the other is going to make the difference whether that option is in the money or out of the money, and that does not change with the passage of time. In other words, this option's status is going to be a coin toss that will come down to the last second.

If we are looking at the 50 strike and the stock is trading at 50 right on the nose, a movement either up or down 1 cent is going to determine whether this option finishes in or out of the money. And that can happen on the very last stock tick on expiration Friday. Expiration Friday at 3:59 P.M. and that stock might be trading at $50 exactly. If the last tick at 4:00 P.M. is $50.01, the option is in the money and 100 deltas. If the last tick is $49.99, the option is worthless and out of the money with zero deltas.

All of this can happen in a split second; more precisely, at the last moment before the last, closing stock price on expiration Friday. The days leading up to expiration are not as important for an at-the-money option as is the closing stock price at expiration.

So, time is not really going to play a factor on that at-the-money option's delta. Stock movement, not time, will be the deciding factor on delta. Theta is not going to have the same effect on at-the-money options as it will on an in-the-money or an out-of-the-money option. Theta is going to have very little effect on at-the-money options.

So let's review the effect of theta (time decay) on delta.

- *In the money.* The passage of time increases the delta of the in-the-money options whether they are puts or calls. With less time for the option to fall out of the money, the percentage chance of the option staying in the money has to increase. That means the delta will have to increase.
- *Out of the money.* The passage of time, or theta, decreases the deltas of out-of-the-money options, whether they are puts or calls. Why? Because with less time for the option to move from out of the money to in the money, the percentage chance of that option doing it is decreased, thus a lower delta.
- *At the money.* Theta has very little effect on the deltas of at-the-money options, whether they are puts or calls. They are going to stay around 50. Why? Because the stock would need to make a very small movement to make that option become in or out of the money. It doesn't have to move $5 or $6. It might only have to move 1 cent. And that type of movement can happen in one tick at exactly 4:00 P.M. on expiration day. Time doesn't play a big role in the delta of an at-the-money option.

Theta and Gamma

Theta's effect on gamma is not a black-and-white issue. We can't just say that the passage of time increases gamma positions. Nor can we say that the passage of time decreases gamma positions.

Unfortunately, we cannot make a simple blanket statement. We described above how theta affected the deltas of in-the-money, at-the-money, and out-of-the-money options differently; theta is also going to affect gamma positions differently based on where the gamma is located.

Theta has a different gamma effect on different strikes. Its effect will be determined by where (the strike) the gamma is located. Theta affects the gamma of in-the-money options and out-of-the-money options differently than it affects at-the-money options. We saw this in theta's affect on the deltas of options.

Because gamma is a derivative of delta—the first derivative of delta, to be precise—it marks the change in the delta. Therefore, it stands to reason that theta is going to have an effect on gamma also.

When we look at a long gamma position, we first have to check where the long gamma is located. If our long gamma position is located in an in-the-money or out-of-the-money option, the passage of time will work to decrease the size of the gamma position. Let me say that again.

If our long gamma is located or positioned in an in-the-money or out-of-the-money option, all things staying equal, the passage of time will decrease that long gamma position.

We know that the farther the option is either in or out of the money, the quicker those deltas move to 100 or zero, and they move even quicker with the passage of time. At that moment when those deltas are either 100 or zero, they are probably not going to move much, if at all, other things being equal. And because those deltas don't move much, the gamma has to be very small.

The more they don't move and the closer the option gets to expiration, then obviously, the smaller and smaller those gammas get because the deltas are not moving and there is increasingly less time for them to move. So when talking about a long gamma position, if that long gamma is located in an in-the-money or out-of-the-money option, with all other things equal, the passage of time is going to decrease the size of that gamma position.

However, if that long gamma position is located in an at-the-money option, whether it is a call or a put, the passage of time is going to increase that gamma position. The gamma will get larger. We hinted at this when we talked about gamma.

Remember when we were talking about the 50 strike and the stock trading at exactly $50.00. We said that as you get closer to that final closing stock price on expiration day, if the stock is trading directly at the strike price—$50.00—the smallest possible dollar increment move in that stock can and will create the largest delta movement possible. If this stock closed at $50.00 on the nose, the delta of that option will be zero. However, if the stock closed at $50.01, the delta of that option will be 100 for calls.

For puts it is the opposite. If the stock closed at $49.99, then the puts would be 100 negative deltas. The important point here is that a 1-cent stock move at the close on expiration will create a 100-point movement in delta. Delta can go from zero to 100 with a 1-cent movement at the last closing price on expiration Friday.

Keeping that in mind, remember what gamma measures. Gamma measures how much delta changes. At expiration, at that single moment in time, your delta can go from absolute maximum to absolute minimum, or absolute minimum to absolute maximum, with 1 cent.

A 1-cent movement and an option can go from zero to 100 deltas or 100 to zero deltas. How big do you think gamma is at that moment? Gamma has to be gigantic at that moment. So if you are long an at-the-money call or put going into expiration, when gamma is the absolute biggest ever, you will see your long gamma position grow exponentially.

The absolute largest that gamma can ever be occurs at 4:00 P.M. on the close of expiration day in an at-the-money option, whether it is a call or a put. That is the biggest that gamma will ever be, because that is where delta changes the most with the smallest possible movement in the stock. If your gamma position is located in an at-the-money option, it will continue to grow bigger and bigger as we move into the final tick of that stock on expiration Friday. How does theta affect a long gamma position that is located at the money? It increases it, right into the closing bell on expiration Friday.

Theta affects short gamma positions much in the same way as it affects long gamma. Again, it all depends on where your short gamma is located. If your short gamma is located in an in-the-money option or an out-of-the-money option, theta will work to decrease your short gamma position. A short gamma position decreases as time goes by if the gamma is located in in- or out-of-the-money options.

Just like long gamma positions, your short gamma positions located in in- or out-of-the-money options will decrease, all things being equal, as time goes by. The reasoning is the same as it was for why it would decrease in long gamma positions for the in-the-money and out-of-the-money options: There is just less chance that those options are going to change their present in- or out-of-the-money status.

Therefore, their deltas will approach either 100 or zero. With the continued passage of time, those deltas will move less and less, thereby creating smaller and smaller gammas. As for a rule of thumb, we can say that as time goes by, theta decreases the size of gamma in in- and out-of-the-money options. What about the at-the-money option?

The same theory that applies to long gamma positions also applies to short gamma positions. If your short gamma position is located at the money, then that short gamma position will increase in size, all the way into the final tick of the stock on expiration Friday.

In other words, as time goes by and all things being equal, your short gamma position is going to increase in size (get shorter) up until the final closing stock tick on Friday of expiration, for the same exact reasons that it would in a long gamma position.

Remember, gamma measures how much delta changes. At expiration, your delta can go from absolute maximum to absolute minimum, or absolute minimum to absolute maximum with a stock movement as little as 1 cent. A 1-cent stock movement and an option can go from zero to 100 deltas or 100 to zero deltas. How big do you think that gamma is at that moment? Gamma has to be gigantic then.

If you are short gamma in an at-the-money put or call going into the final moments before expiration, you will see your short gamma position grow exponentially. That is the biggest that gamma will ever be, because that is where delta changes the most with the smallest possible movement in the stock.

If your gamma position is located in an at-the-money option, it will continue to grow bigger and bigger as time moves into the final tick of that stock on expiration Friday. As for a rule of thumb, the gamma of an at-the-money option will grow (get larger) as time passes into expiration.

So, let's review and consolidate this concept. What is theta's effect on gamma positions as a whole? It depends on where your gamma position is located. That is the key. How is theta going to affect your position? It depends on where your gamma position is located. If it is in an in-the-money or out-of-the-money option, it is going to decrease the size of whatever gamma position you have, whether long or short. If you have a long gamma position, it is going to get shorter. If you have a short gamma position, it is going to get longer.

Theta is going to decrease your gamma, moving it toward zero. If your gamma position is located in an at-the-money option, whether put or call, whether long or short, the passage of time, or theta, will increase that gamma position. It will make a long gamma position longer, and it will make a short gamma position shorter. It is as simple as that.

Obviously, theta has a real, close working relationship with gamma. That happens since the way you obtain theta is the same way you obtain gamma, by either buying or selling options. In a sense, gamma and theta are two peas in a pod. Where you have one, you have the other. You obtain long gamma by buying options. You obtain short gamma by selling options.

Theta is obtained in the exact same manner. In fact, you cannot have gamma without theta, and you cannot have theta without gamma.

Although they come together and are indeed inseparable, gamma and theta also have an inverse relationship.

It is very simple. Think for a second. You obtain long gamma from purchasing options but, at the same time, that option purchase creates decay, a negative theta.

Why? It is because your option purchase creates a positive gamma position while your premium purchase creates a time-decaying scenario. When you sell an option, however, you create a negative gamma position while your premium sale creates a positive collection scenario. Consider the relationship between gamma and theta. If you own an option, you're going to be long gamma. And if you are long gamma, then you're going to be paying for it. That means you are going to be short theta. If you are short an option, you are going to be short gamma. And if you are short gamma, you are going to be collecting from it. That means you are going to be long theta.

Another little relationship between gamma and theta is this: Where gamma is the highest, theta is the highest and vice versa.

Look at the theta chart (Table 4.9). You should see something that looks very familiar. A theta chart tells you the rate of the decay of each

TABLE 4.9 Theta Chart, Stock $65.00

Strike Price	June	July	October	January
50	0	.007	.006	.005
55	.013	.013	.010	.007
60	.041	.033	.019	.011
65	.059	.042	.026	.018
70	.055	.038	.024	.016
75	.028	.024	.017	.009
80	.018	.020	.011	.006

option. It looks familiar because of its pattern. Compare the theta chart to the gamma chart (Table 4.10), and ask yourself where gamma is the absolute highest.

We already know that gamma is going to be the absolute highest in the front-month, at-the-money strike. Now look on the theta chart and ask where theta is going to be the highest. Coincidently, it also is going to be highest in the front-month at-the-money strike. Let us compare as we move away from the at-the-money strike in either direction. We notice that gamma decreases as we move away from the at-the money strike, and so does theta. When we look at the theta chart, we see that the at-the-money strike is the 65 strike. If we move down to the 60 strike, theta decreases. If we move up to the 70 strike, theta decreases. And as we move progressively out in either direction, the amount of theta continues to decrease, just like gamma.

What about going out over time? We know that when you go out over time, gamma decreases. Let us compare this to theta. Look at the June 65 strike; the theta is almost $0.06. Now let us look at the July 65 strike. The theta value has decreased. The theta in the October 65 strike is lower

TABLE 4.10 Gamma Chart, Stock $65.50

Strike Price	June	July	October	January
50	0	.1	.7	.9
55	.1	.8	1.5	1.5
60	1.8	2.8	2.4	2.0
65	7.2	5.0	3.0	2.3
70	7.7	5.2	3.2	2.4
75	2.8	3.7	2.9	2.3
80	.4	1.8	2.3	2.1

than the July 65 strike, and the January 65 strike is the lowest of the 65 strikes. This shows the time decay curve, an obviously nonlinear function. As you study the chart, you can see that the farther you look out in time, the smaller the theta is.

The theta chart and the gamma chart are going to look identical in their pattern. This is not a coincidence. Why? Because where gamma is the highest, theta is the highest, and vice versa. Theta is always highest front month, at the money. In any given month, as you move away from the at-the-money strike, theta decreases. As you go out over time, across any single month, theta decreases.

A little aberration occurs here. Look at a deep in-the-money strike and a deep out-of-the-money strike: the 50 strike and the 80 strike, for instance. You can see that in the July 80 strike, you actually have a little higher theta than in the June 80 strike. This violates our rule of thumb. The reason is that the June 80 strike is starting to become so far out of the money that it is losing all of its sensitivities. It is becoming worthless and losing its status as an option. You see the same thing when you look at the June 50 strike. The June 50 strike has lost all of its sensitivity.

There is a decrease in theta because the June 50 strike is now stock. It is so deep in the money that it is like stock. It is 100 deltas. There is no more option-related sensitivity in the June 50 strike because it is now considered to be stock.

As you know, stock has no theta. This is why you will sometimes see an increase in theta from a front-month option (such as the June 50) to an outer-month option (such as the July 50). This will occur only in deep in-the-money and far out-of-the-money options near expiration. So, when you see that higher theta, understand what is happening. But even in this situation, the theta chart looks exactly like the pattern of the gamma chart.

Here are some highlights of the important concepts about theta:

- Theta measures an option's rate of decay over time.
- Theta affects an option's extrinsic value.
- Theta's effect on options is nonlinear.
- Theta affects not only an option's price but also its delta and gamma.
- Theta affects the gamma and delta of the three option categories differently.
- Theta (time decay) is a 24/7 happening.
- Theta has a special relationship with gamma that is observable on graphs.
- Theta gives a good idea of what an option will do as time passes.

That is what theta is about.

SECOND-TIER GREEKS

We have discussed all of the front-line Greeks—those major outputs of the pricing model, more commonly referred to as the first-tier Greeks. There are, however, other levels of Greeks. Here we are concerned with the level called the *second-tier Greeks*. These Greeks do not directly measure a stock or an option. They measure, using a number, the change in a first-tier Greek caused by changes in certain variables.

Second-tier Greeks quantify the sensitivities of front-line Greeks to changes to outside factors, such as time and volatility. There are many second-tier Greeks, but I focus on the five that I believe are important for you to know and for your success as an investor/trader.

The second-tier Greeks discussed in this chapter are important because they quantify (using a specific number) a special relationship between two of the major Greeks—a relationship that may affect your positions or portfolio. The effect of one part of the relationship on the other is expressed in numbers.

In the interest of clarity, let's identify the five relationships:

1. *V-delta (V-del)* measures the effect of a change in volatility on delta.
2. *T-delta (T-del)* measures the effect of the passage of time on delta.
3. *V-gamma* measures the effect of a change of volatility on gamma.
4. *T-gamma* measures the effect of the passage of time on gamma.
5. *V-theta* measures the effect of a change in volatility on theta.

V-Delta

The first important relationship is V-delta, which measures the effect of a change in volatility on delta. We have discussed this before. We have also discussed what volatility changes do to the deltas of individual options. V-delta tells you what the change in volatility is going to do to the overall delta of your position or to the overall delta of your entire portfolio.

It is important to understand what V-delta measures and how it measures. V-delta connects volatility and delta. It creates an actual number for us to determine the effects of that relationship: for example, +400, −1,500, +60, −97.

A positive V-delta (V-del) tells you that for each tick volatility moves, your delta position will either increase or decrease by a set amount of deltas. For instance, suppose you have a +500 V-del and volatility is trading at 35.

Your new overall delta position would increase by 500 deltas if volatility went to 36. Meanwhile, if volatility were to go down a tick, to 34, then your position would decrease 500 deltas.

If you had a negative V-del and the volatility went up, your delta position would decrease by the amount of V-del components you had. If you had a negative V-del and volatility went down, then your delta position would decrease by however many V-dels you were short.

This becomes important when a stock has a major volatility move. I am not talking a tick or two. I'm talking a minimum of 10 to 15 ticks, a 20, 30, or 40 percent increase. You have to know what your real delta is at that new volatility level. V-del tells you that.

T-Delta

T-delta (T-del) measures the theta-to-delta relationship. It tells you how your delta position will change (by what amount) with the passage of time. This second-tier Greek is not evaluating a movement in volatility; it is evaluating the effects of the movement of time. How does the movement of time, all things being equal, affect your delta position?

If you are +T-del, it means your delta position gets longer as the days go by. If you are –T-del, then your position—your delta position—gets shorter as the days go by.

You might see the value of V-del but question the value of T-del. How is it important? T-del helps when you are going to be away from your position for a time. We touched on this when we discussed theta. Remember, time decay happens even when the market is not open. When you leave for a long weekend or a vacation, you know where your delta position stands at that time; however, it will not be the same when you get back. T-del tells you what you can expect when you return. Your delta position is going to be different, and potentially vastly different, when you get back. Even if the stock hasn't moved, even if the stock and volatility have not moved, the passage of time, those days gone by, are going to affect your delta position. T-del tells you by exactly how much.

If your T-del is +100, that means that one day from now, with all things being equal, your new delta position is going to be longer by 100 more deltas. Two days go by, 200 long deltas, three days, 300 longer deltas. T-del tells you by how much per day your delta position is going to increase or decrease, all things being equal, and with the only changing variable the passage of time.

V-Gamma

Although V-gamma is not as important as V-del, volatility levels definitely have an effect on your gamma position. You need to understand V-gamma, especially if you are gamma trading. You need to know not only how the movement or changes in implied volatility affect your gamma position, but by how much. As stated before, those of you who are going to be interested in gamma trading need to know what your gamma is at all times under every condition in order to trade it effectively. That gamma level will be affected by changes in implied volatility.

As a rule of thumb, increases in volatility decrease the size of your gamma position.

Whether you are long gamma or short gamma does not matter. An increase in implied volatility will decrease the size of your gamma position.

If you are long gamma and implied volatility increases, you will get shorter gamma. If you are short gamma and implied volatility increases, you will get longer gamma.

V-gamma tells you by what amount gamma is going to change per one tick change in implied volatility. It is as simple as that. Continuing with our rule of thumb, a decrease in implied volatility will increase the size of your gamma position. If you are long gamma and implied volatility decreases, you will get longer gamma. If you are short gamma and implied volatility decreases, you will get shorter gamma.

T-Gamma

T-gamma works in a similar way as V-gamma, except that the T-gamma relationship is evaluating the effect of the passage of time, theta's effect on gamma. T-gamma, like T-delta, tells you what to expect when you are away from your position. You leave knowing the gamma of your position. You return and your gamma position is now different. Remember, time goes by. Whether the market is open or not, the passage of time will have an effect on your gamma position. How? The more time that goes by, the larger your gamma position gets.

The passage of time increases the size of your gamma position. So, if you are long 500 gammas on Thursday afternoon, you might be long 600 gammas when you check them on Monday morning. If you are short 200 gammas the day before the Fourth of July weekend, you may be short 300 gammas when you come back from the holiday weekend.

Beware, there is a slight monkey wrench thrown into T-gamma. I hope some of you have remembered what we talked about in terms of the effect of gamma and theta on gamma.

Theta's effect really depends on where your gamma is located. Theta's effect is different depending on whether gamma is located in in-the-money, out-of-the-money, or at-the-money options. As we approach expiration, both in-the-money and out-of-the-money options start losing their optionness.

As these options near expiration, they either become worthless because they are way out of the money with little or no extrinsic value, or they become stock because they are so far in the money. And we know that something with no extrinsic value has no delta gamma, vega, or theta. And we know that something that is stock has no gamma, vega, or theta.

The lesson here is that as the in-the-money and out-of-the-money options get close to expiration, they will lose gamma. This is contrary to our rule of thumb. There is a point as time progresses when these options will no longer gain gamma but will start to lose gamma. That point in time is near the very end of the option's life. The at-the-money option, however, will continue to gain gammas up until the final minute of its life, provided the stock is still trading at the strike price.

Therefore, you have to be cautious with T-gamma. Not gigantically cautious, but you have to be aware. You also must be aware of the specific location of gamma for V-gamma. You have to know where your gamma position is located and how that option is going to behave as it gets closer to expiration.

Earlier when we examined the appearance of gamma on its chart, you saw gammas in the way out-of-the money and the way in-the-money options decrease a bit as they approached expiration. However, the at-the-money gamma got much bigger; in fact, it exploded. That is the glitch that you must be aware of with gamma. You absolutely must know where your gamma is located. Is it located in an at-the-money option, or is it located farther away from at the money? Is it deep in the money or deep out of the money? Keep that in mind. The purpose of T-gamma is to tell you how the passage of time is going to affect your gamma position no matter where it is located.

V-Theta

The final second-tier Greek that is of special interest to us is V-theta, which measures the effect of a change in volatility on theta. This one is easy. Recall what we know about volatility's affect on option prices: If volatility increases, then option prices—all option prices, both puts and calls—increase. When volatility decreases, the value of all options—both puts and calls—decreases. So, when implied volatility goes up, prices go up; when implied volatility goes down, prices go down.

How does that affect theta, your rate of decay? Volatility affects the prices of options by either increasing the amount of extrinsic value in the option (when volatility increases) or by decreasing the amount of extrinsic value in the option (when volatility decreases).

The more extrinsic value present in that option, the more it has to decay. An option that has $1.25 of extrinsic value with 30 days left to expiration has to decay $1.25 in the remaining 30 days.

However, that same option priced at $1.50 (after an increase in volatility), now has $1.50 worth of decay over the 30 days remaining to expiration. This point demonstrates that the more volatility goes up, the more theta you have in an option. That more expensive option has more to decay. V-theta, or the volatility to theta relationship, basically tells you, with a number, how much your decay is going to change with a movement in implied volatility.

Are these tools critical? In my mind, yes they are. You need to be properly instructed on how different changes in the different influencing factors of option pricing will affect your position, your investment. You need to know your risks!

These second-tier Greeks help you understand what is going to happen or what can happen to your position before it happens, not after. No one should enter a trade without knowing and understanding what the risks are.

The beauty of the second-tier Greeks is they tell you what can happen to your position in an "if" scenario. If volatility goes up, this will happen to your delta. If theta goes down, this is what will happen to your delta. If volatility increases, this is the effect or could be the effect on your gamma position. The passage of time will cause this amount of change in your gamma position. Volatility affects your theta by this amount. All of these scenarios can affect your position, thereby affecting your profit and loss.

Knowledge of the second-tier Greeks prepares you to handle and adjust your position to account for what can happen. And if you can stay prepared, you are going to do much better in trading. That is the particular significance and importance of the second-tier Greeks. They give a concrete expression, a number, to the changes brought on by implied volatility and by the passage of time.

CHAPTER 5

Synthetic
Positions

Average option experts most likely avoid the topic of synthetic positions. Most feel that this topic does not directly correlate to moneymaking so they do not teach it. Unlike those experts, I feel that synthetic positions are a vital topic for everyone serious about learning options the right way and becoming consistent in profiting from their use.

Synthetic positions are an important topic of study for several reasons. First is their importance in morphing positions. If you do not know synthetic positions, you cannot morph. Second is that knowledge of synthetic positions can increase profits by lowering costs and allowing an investor to take advantage of the put/call skew. Finally, and in my mind most important, mastering of synthetics greatly aids in investors' real, true understanding of options themselves. Synthetics show us and define for us the mathematical relationship that exists between a call, its corresponding put, and the stock.

Synthetics, in combination with reverse/conversions, the box, and jelly rolls, actually connect the prices of all options together mathematically. Once you understand this, option theory and pricing become much, much easier.

I have mentioned the components that we will deal with when we develop our strategies. We know that the strategies will use stocks and options. Before we explore the strategies, you should be aware of an element about the combination of stocks and options: synthetics. Synthetics employ stocks and options as partners in special ways. Synthetics are used in rolling and morphing option positions. In addition, synthetics play a role in the construction of many strategies, including the butterfly and the condor.

DEFINING SYNTHETICS

When we talk about the term *synthetic*, we have a particular definition in mind. That definition is: to fabricate and combine separate elements to form a coherent whole. When we apply that definition to options, we mean that by using a combination of stocks and options, we will fabricate an artificial position that is identical to a natural or real position in terms of its risk and reward. What we want to do is to create strategic alternatives for certain types of real positions.

That is one of the unique advantages of options. Traders are given the ability to mimic any natural position by combining stocks with options and options with options.

Think about just plain stock trading, for instance. When you want to take advantage of a rising stock price, what can you do? The *only* thing you can do is to buy the stock. That's it. How else can you take advantage of an anticipated upward movement in the stock?

Conversely, if the stock is going down or if you feel the stock is going to go down, again, there is only one way to take advantage of the situation, and that is to sell the stock.

There are many reasons why you might not be able to do either of those things at any given time: margin requirements, down-tick rules, not enough money in an account, or too much risk. When those reasons prevent taking action, a synthetic position employing options can be a viable alternative.

Options allow us to take advantage of certain potential scenarios in different ways. Options offer us alternatives. They make it possible to synthetically create a position that is identical to another, natural position. That is what we are talking about: creating a position that is identical to another position by using different types of securities.

There are several types of different "synthetic" positions that we can create or re-create through other means. These positions will match the overall risk and reward scenarios of the "real" positions that we are trying to mimic.

- We can re-create a long stock position synthetically by use of a call and its corresponding put.

- We can synthetically create a short stock position by use of a put and its corresponding call.
- We can also synthetically re-create a call by use of the stock and the real call's corresponding put.
- Similarly, we can synthetically re-create a put by use of the stock and the real put's corresponding call.

The different types of synthetic positions that are available include synthetic long stock, synthetic short stock, synthetic long call, synthetic short call, synthetic long put, and synthetic short put. Later you will see how these synthetic positions relate to their real counterparts.

Further, you will see how these two positions, the real and the synthetic, when used together, display a fundamental, mathematical relationship that links all options together under a particular underlying. This relationship is critical to proper option pricing and strategy.

Before we focus our attention on synthetic positions, we must recall a few facts from earlier. First, we must review the meaning of the term *corresponding*. What do we mean by this word? *Corresponding* means options of the same stock, in the same month, and with the same strike price. For example, if we are talking about the January 30 call, its corresponding put is the January 30 put. If we are talking about the May 30 call, the corresponding put is the May 30 put. This also works the other way around. So, if we are talking about the July 60 put, its corresponding call is the July 60 call.

Second, we need to recall concepts from our talk about delta. We have to remember what we said about a call and the delta of its corresponding put. The absolute value of a call's delta plus the absolute value of its corresponding put's delta equals 100 deltas. Likewise, the sum of the absolute value of the delta of a put plus the absolute value of the delta of its corresponding call is going to be 100. This is the basis of *synthetic stock*.

Third, we must also remember our discussion in Chapter 4 of the other Greeks. More specifically, we talked about gamma, vega, and theta being calculated by strike and not by individual call or put. Remember, we stated that gamma, vega, and theta do not differentiate between call and put; they refer only to the strike (strike-based Greeks). We talked about the gamma of a specific strike, the vega of a specific strike, the theta of a specific strike. So, a put and its corresponding call or a call and its corresponding put will have the exact same gamma, vega, and theta. That is also very important. Keep these three facts in mind when we start talking about all the synthetic positions.

SYNTHETIC STOCK

The first synthetic position we will discuss is *synthetic stock*. With the use of calls and their corresponding puts, we can re-create both a long and a short stock position. This synthetic stock position will have the same risk and reward scenario as a position in the regular stock (Figure 5.1).

Long synthetic stock is constructed by purchasing a call and selling its corresponding put in a one-to-one ratio. Now let's construct a synthetic long stock position and a real long stock position, and compare one to the other.

We will compare the two positions, look to see if they are identical, and then look at how they function. That comparison is the best way for us

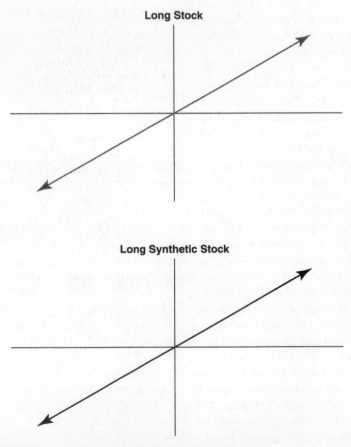

FIGURE 5.1 Long Stock versus Long Synthetic Stock

to see that the synthetic stock position we have created and the real stock position are identical.

Example: Trading Sheet 1

For our example, you will want to refer to trading sheets found in the appendix. Find Trading Sheet 1, and we will create a synthetic long stock position.

Look at the left-hand side of the sheet. The volatility is listed first and should be 30 all the way down the page. Next the long stock position is established when we buy the stock. In this case, the stock price will be $65.50. We make a stock purchase of 100 shares at $65.50. We now have our long stock position for comparison purposes.

The June options are the first group of options that appear on your sheet. Directly below them, you will see (in order) the July, followed by the October and then the January options. For purposes of this exercise, we are going to create a synthetic long stock position using the June 65 calls and puts.

Scan down the sheet until you see the June 65 strike, then skim across to where it matches up underneath the stock price of $65.50. You will see a value there. That value should be $2.04, which is the value of the July 65 calls with the stock priced at $65.50. Next to that is the value of the put, which is $1.48.

According to the formula, in order to create the synthetic long stock position, we have to first buy the call. The call is worth $2.04. So let's purchase the call for $2.04. At the same time, according to the formula, we have to sell the corresponding put in a one-to-one ratio. The put is worth $1.48. So we will sell the put for $1.48. The whole trade is going to cost $0.56. We paid out $2.04 for the call we are buying, and we receive $1.48 for the put we are selling for a difference in cost to us of $0.56.

Now that the two positions are set up, the real long stock position and the synthetic stock position, we may begin our comparison. First, we will talk about the profit and loss of each. Truly, if these two positions are identical, their profit and loss should match identically under similar circumstances. Obviously, in these examples, we are simply comparing the performance of two separate positions and how they profit and lose in the same manner at every price level.

We will start by talking about the profit side. Let's see what happens to our long stock position when the stock goes up. We bought our stock at $65.50. Now if the stock were to trade up to $71.50, we would find that our real stock position had a profit of $6.00.

Let's see how our synthetic long stock position did. First let's look at the call. We purchased the call that we are long at $2.04 with the stock priced at $65.50. Now, with the stock at $71.50, the July 65 call is worth $6.71. This will give us a profit of $4.67.

Now focus your attention on the short July 65 put. We sold the put at $1.48. With the stock now trading up at $71.50, the put is worth only $0.15. Since we sold it at $1.48 and it is now worth $0.15, we have a $1.33 profit in the put. When we combine the profit in the call (+$4.67) with the profit in the put (+$1.33), we have a profit of $6.00 exactly.

Interestingly enough, the profit from the synthetic long stock strategy is exactly the same as the profit we garnered when we bought the real stock at $65.50 and it went to $71.50 (Table 5.1).

From a profit standpoint, our long synthetic stock position has the same exact profit potential as our real long stock position. Now let's take a look at what happens when the stock goes down. How are our two positions affected?

Our positions remain the same as in our previous example. We bought the real stock at $65.50, and to construct its synthetic counterpart, we bought the June 65 calls for $2.04 and sold the June 65 puts at $1.48. Let's take a look at the position when the stock goes down.

Let's say the stock moves down to $61.50. Well, in the actual real stock position, if we bought the stock at $65.50 and it traded down to $61.50, we would have a $4.00 loss. Now let's see what our synthetic long stock position does under the same conditions.

The June 65 call was purchased for $2.04 with the stock at $65.50. With the stock now down at $61.50, the call is worth only $0.49. This represents a loss of $1.55. Meanwhile, the June 65 put that we sold at $1.48 with the stock at $65.50 is now worth $3.94 with the stock at $61.50. This represents a loss on the put in the amount of $2.46. So when we combine the loss from the call (−$1.55) with the loss from the put (−$2.46), we come up with an overall loss of $4.01.

TABLE 5.1 Synthetic Long Stock Profit

Real Long Stock	Synthetic Long Stock
Buy 100 @ $65.50	Buy 1 Jun 65 calls @ 2.04
	Sell 1 Jun 65 puts @ $1.48
Stock trades up to $67.50	**Stock trades up to $67.50**
Positive P&L of $200 (100 shares up $2.00)	Call goes from $2.04 up to $3.34, a $1.30 profit ($130)
	Put goes from $1.48 down to $0.77, a $0.71 profit ($71)
Total P&L = +$200.00	**Total P&L = +$201.00**

TABLE 5.2 Synthetic Long Stock Loss

Real Long Stock	Synthetic Long Stock
Buy 100 @ $65.50	Buy 1 Jun 65 calls @ 2.04
	Sell 1 Jun 65 puts @ $1.48
Stock trades down to $61.50	**Stock trades down to $61.50**
Negative P&L of $400 (100 shares down $4.00)	Call goes from $2.04 down to $0.49, a $1.55 loss ($155)
	Put goes from $1.48 up to $3.94, a $2.46 loss ($246)
Total P&L = –$400.00	**Total P&L = –$401.00**

As you recall, the actual stock would have also lost $4.00. So, on the way down, our synthetic long stock position functioned like our real long stock position. From the standpoint of profit and loss, our synthetic long stock position did exactly what our actual long stock position did. See Table 5.2.

Synthetic short stock is constructed by selling a call and at the same time purchasing its corresponding put in a one-to-one ratio. Now let us construct a synthetic short stock position and a real short stock position and compare one to the other. We will compare those two positions, looking to see if they are identical and at how they function. That comparison is the best way for us to see if the synthetic stock position we have created and the real stock position are the same.

According to the formula, in order to create our synthetic short stock position, we have to first sell the call. Again, we will use the June 65 call and put example as before. The June 65 call is worth $2.04. So let's sell the call at $2.04. At the same time, according to the formula, we have to buy the corresponding put in a one-to-one ratio. The June 65 put is worth $1.48. So we will purchase the put for $1.48. Our whole trade is going to bring in $0.56. We paid out $1.48 for the put we are buying, and we receive $2.04 for the call we are selling for a total credit to us of $0.56. For comparison, we will sell the real stock at $65.50.

Now that the two positions are set up, our real short stock position and our synthetic short stock position, we may begin our comparison. First, we will talk about the profit and loss (P&L) of each. Truly, if these two positions are the same, their P&L should match under similar circumstances.

We start by talking about the profit side. Let's see what happens to our short stock position when the stock goes down. We shorted our real stock at $65.50. Now, if the stock were to trade down to $61.50, we would find that our real stock position had a profit of $4.00. For those of you who do not know how make money from a decrease in stock price, here is a quick explanation on how it works.

To make money from a decrease in stock price, we would need to sell the stock now at a higher price and buy it back later at a lower price. The question is how to sell the stock when we do not own it. We can short (sell short) a stock we do not own by borrowing it from our broker now, selling it at the current price, and buying it back lower at a later time. Then, when we buy it back, we simply return the shares to our broker and pocket the difference.

Now let's see how our synthetic long stock position did. First, let's look at the call. The call that we are short was sold at $2.04 with the stock priced at $65.50. Now, with the stock at $61.50, the July 65 call is worth $0.49. This will give us a profit of $1.55.

Next, focus your attention on our long July 65 put. We bought our put for $1.48. With the stock now trading down at $61.50, the put is now worth $3.94. Since we bought it at $1.48 and it is now worth $3.94, we have a $2.46 profit in the put. When we combine the profit in the call (+$1.55) with the profit in the put (+$2.46), we have a profit of $4.01. In these examples, you may find an "extra" dollar lying around. This is simply a rounding error.

Interestingly enough, the profit from the synthetic short stock strategy (Table 5.3) is the same as the profit we garnered when we sold the real stock at $65.50 and it went down to $61.50. From a profit standpoint, our short synthetic stock position has the same profit potential as our real short stock position. Now let's take a look at what happens when the stock goes up. How are our two positions affected? Again, our positions remain the same as in our previous example. We sold the real stock at $65.50. To construct its synthetic counterpart, we sold the June 65 calls at $2.04 and we bought the June 65 puts for $1.48. Let's take a look at the potential loss scenario of the two strategies to see if that also matches up.

TABLE 5.3 Synthetic Short Stock Profit

Real Short Stock	Synthetic Short Stock
Buy 100 @ $65.50	Buy 1 Jun 65 calls @ 2.04
	Sell 1 Jun 65 puts @ $1.48
Stock trades down to $61.50	**Stock trades down to $61.50**
Negative P&L of $400 (−100 shares down $4.00)	Call goes from $2.04 down to $0.49, a $1.55 profit ($155)
	Put goes from $1.48 up to $3.94, a $2.46 profit ($246)
Total P&L = +$400.00	**Total P&L = +$401.00**

TABLE 5.4 Synthetic Short Stock Loss

Real Short Stock	Synthetic Long Stock
Buy 100 @ $65.50	Buy 1 Jun 65 calls @ 2.04
	Sell 1 Jun 65 puts @ $1.48
Stock trades up to $71.50	**Stock trades up to $71.50**
Negative P&L of $600 (–100 shares up $6.00)	Call goes from $2.04 up to $6.71, a $4.67 loss (–$467)
	Put goes from $1.48 down to $0.15, a $1.33 loss (–$133)
Total P&L = –$600.00	**Total P&L = –$600.00**

Let's say the stock moves up to $71.50. In the real short stock position, if we sold the stock at $65.50 and it traded up to $71.50, we would have a $6.00 loss. Now let's see what our synthetic short stock position does under the same conditions. The June 65 put was purchased for $1.48 with the stock at $65.50. With the stock now down at $71.50, the put is only worth $0.15. This represents a loss of $1.33.

Meanwhile, the June 65 call that we sold at $2.04 with the stock at $65.50 is now worth $6.71 with the stock at $71.50. This represents a loss on the call in the amount of $4.67. So, when we combine the loss from the call (–$1.33), with the loss from the put (–$4.67), we come up with an overall loss of $6.00. As you recall, the actual short stock would have also lost $6.00 (Table 5.4). So, on the way up, our synthetic short stock position functioned exactly like the real short stock position.

 KEY POINT

From the standpoint of profit and loss, our synthetic short stock position did what our actual short stock position did (Figure 5.2).

Try some paper trading. Now that you understand the concept, take a few different strikes, add the corresponding put and the corresponding call together, and create synthetic long stock positions and synthetic short stock positions, then move the stock and take a look. See if the synthetic position matches what the actual stock would have done. You will see a similar loss/profit in each case.

You might wonder how this is possible. How does it work? Why does it work? Let's take a look at the actual construction of the position. What do we know about stock? We know that stock has delta. Actually, it is all delta; that is what stock is: pure delta. Delta is stock. Stock is delta.

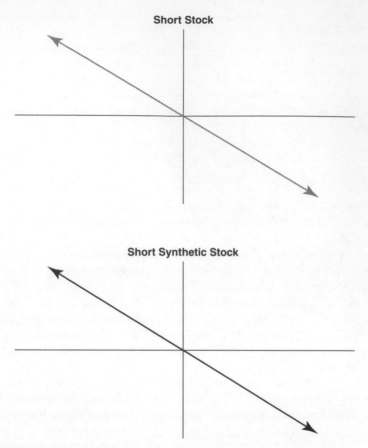

FIGURE 5.2   Short Stock versus Short Synthetic Stock

We also know that a stock does not have gamma, vega, or theta. Unlike stock, options do have gamma, vega, and theta. However, we are using corresponding puts and corresponding calls.

We know that corresponding options have identical gamma, vega, and theta values. So, if the values are identical and we gain positive value when we purchase the call and negative value when we sell the put, then the gamma, vega, and theta will cancel each other out. This will leave the position with no gamma, no vega, and no theta . . . only delta. What other position consists of only delta with no gamma, no vega, and no theta: stock!

So while stock has delta and only delta, our long synthetic stock position has delta and only delta also. Why? Because, when we look at our gamma, vega, and theta positions, we see that they have been canceled out by being long one option and short its corresponding partner in a one-to-one ratio.

Remember one of the facts I told you to always keep in mind: Gamma, vega, and theta are calculated by the strike. They do not differentiate between put and call. So when we look at the strike and we look at a put and the corresponding call from the same strike, the same month, we know that that put and that call have to have the same gamma, the same vega, and the same theta.

Due to the fact we are long one and short the other, every bit of long gamma that we get from the long call is the same amount of short gamma that we acquire from being short the put (or vice versa, depending on whether you are long or short synthetic stock). So, if the call gamma is 2.7, then the put's gamma is also going to be 2.7. If we are long one (+2.7), short the other (−2.7), you combine them, what do you come up with? Zero. Zero gamma.

The same conditions apply to vega. The vega of the put is going to be identical to the vega of its corresponding call. Why? Because vega is determined by strike also, and not by put and call. Vega does not differentiate between put and call. So a put and its corresponding call have the exact same vega. If you are long 5.6 vegas from the long puts, you are at the same time also short 5.6 vegas from the short calls (or vice versa, depending on whether you are long or short synthetic stock). You combine them in a position. How many vegas do you have in your position? Zero vegas.

Finally, the exact same thing happens with theta. Theta is also calculated by strike, not by put and call. So the put and its corresponding call or the call and its corresponding put both have the same theta. If you are long one and short the other, they will also cancel each other out.

When we are synthetic long stock, we are long delta because we are long the call that creates long delta, short a put that creates more long delta. Remember another fact I told you to keep in mind: When you add the absolute value of the delta of a call to the absolute value of its corresponding put, that sum must add up to 100—in this case, 100 long delta in the synthetic long stock position, and 100 long deltas in the actual long stock position. This matches identically. There is no gamma in our synthetic stock position. We showed how the gammas canceled out; there is no vega and no theta, just like there is no gamma, vega, or theta in the actual stock position. This is why they match. All you are left with in the synthetic long stock position is long delta, just as you are left only with long delta in the real long stock position.

The same applies when we are synthetic short stock. When we are synthetic short stock, we are short delta because we are short the call, which creates short delta, and long a put, which creates more short delta.

Remember what I just said about adding the delta of a call and its corresponding put. Use absolute value for both the call and the put; their sum must add up to 100. In this case, there are 100 short deltas in the synthetic short stock position and 100 short deltas in the actual short stock position.

This matches perfectly. There is no gamma in our synthetic stock position. We showed how the gammas canceled out; there is no vega and no theta, just as there is no gamma, vega, or theta in the actual stock position. This is why they match. So, all you are left with in the synthetic short stock position is short delta, just as you are left only with short delta in the real short stock position. That is why the synthetic stock strategy works.

Use your trading sheets and add up a put's delta and its corresponding call's delta. See if it really adds up to 100. Repeat the exercise. The deltas of the calls and their corresponding puts will add up to 100 most times. (We discussed this earlier and explained the possibility of a 100 to 103 total.) Then create a long synthetic stock position by buying the call and selling its corresponding put. Observe how the gammas cancel each other out every time. Watch the vegas and thetas cancel themselves out.

Now move the stock price around and see what happens to that position's profit and loss compared to the real stock. Try some paper trading to better understand the important concept of synthetic stock.

SYNTHETIC CALL

Another type of synthetic position is the synthetic call. The *synthetic call* will behave exactly like its real counterpart. There are two types of synthetic call positions: long synthetic call and short synthetic call. Just as we observed the relationship and likeness between the synthetic stock and its real counterpart, we will do the same for the synthetic call.

First, let's look at the synthetic long call. To establish the synthetic long call, we must purchase the stock and purchase the call's corresponding put in a one-to-one ratio. That ratio means that for every 100 shares of long stock we purchase, we must buy one put. That will create a synthetic long call that will be equivalent to an actual long call position in virtually every way (Figure 5.3).

Let's put together an example for testing purposes. We will set up a synthetic long call position and then compare it to its corresponding actual long call. Once that is done, we will take a look at how each position reacts to stock movements. First, we set up our actual call. For this example, we will use the June 65 calls with the stock at $65.50. With the stock trading at $65.50, the call is worth $2.04. We will buy it at that price. Next we create the synthetic long June 65 call.

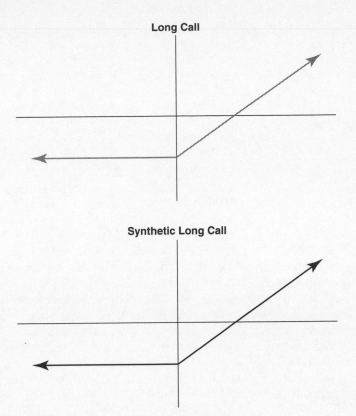

FIGURE 5.3   Long Call versus Synthetic Long Call

Following the previously stated guidelines, we buy the June 65 call's corresponding put, the June 65 put, for $1.48. We then buy the stock at $65.50. We now have our two positions: an actual long call and its equivalent, the synthetic long call. In order to compare the risk/reward scenarios of the two positions, let's first take a look at the profit side of the equation. What happens to our positions if the stock trades up from $65.50 to $71.50? If the stock runs up to $71.50, the actual, real call will be worth $6.71.

Remember, we bought this call for $2.04, so our profit from the actual call with a $6.00 upward movement in the stock is a profit of $4.67.

Now turn your attention to the synthetic long call. We constructed it by purchasing the stock at $65.50 and purchasing the June 65 put for $1.48. When the stock runs up to $71.50, we have made $6.00 in the stock component. Remember we are long the stock in the construction of the long synthetic call position. Our other component, the June 65 put, purchased for $1.48 with the stock at $65.50, is now only worth $0.15 with the stock at

TABLE 5.5 Long Call versus Synthetic Long Call Profit

Real Long Call	Synthetic Long Call
Buy 1 Jun 65 call @ $2.04 with stock $65.50	Buy 100 shares @ $65.50
	Buy 1 Jun 65 puts @ $1.48
Stock trades up to $71.50	**Stock trades up to $71.50 . . . a $6.00 profit ($600)**
Call trades up to $6.71 . . . a profit of +$4.67 ($467)	Put goes from $1.48 down to $0.15 . . . a $1.33 loss (−$133)
Total P&L = +$467.00	**Total P&L = +$467.00**

$71.50. Where we made money in the stock, we lost money in the put. We lost $1.35 in our June 65 put. A profit of $6.00 from the stock minus a loss of $1.35 from our put gives a net profit of $4.65. That is the same profit you would have made if you bought the call itself and the stock moved from $65.50 to $71.50. So, both positions produce an identical profit (Table 5.5).

Let's move on to the loss scenario. What will happen to our positions if the stock trades down? We will now compare what happens to the actual long call versus what happens to our synthetic long call if the stock trades in the inverse direction.

First, let's take a look at the actual long call. Remember, we purchased the June 65 call with the stock trading at $65.50 for $2.04. If the stock were to trade from $65.50 down to $61.50, you can see on your trading sheets that the actual June 65 call is now worth $0.49. We bought it for $2.04 and it's now worth $0.49. Our real call will have lost $1.55 with the stock down $4.00 from $65.50 to $61.50.

The question now is: How did our synthetic long June 65 call do? Our synthetic long call consists of being long the stock and long the June 65 put. First, let's see how our long stock position did. We purchased the stock at $65.50, and now with the stock trading at $61.50, we incur a $4.00 loss in the stock. The stock portion of our synthetic long call is down $4.00.

However, along with purchasing the stock, we also purchased the June 65 put, which was worth $1.48. With the stock down $4.00 to $61.50, our June 65 put will now be worth $3.94. That will give us a profit in the June 65 put.

The profit is $2.46. So, for our total, we lost $4.00 in the stock; but we made $2.46 in the put, giving us a total loss of $1.54. Add in your cost of carry (−$0.01), and the loss in both strategies is a match.

From a profit and loss standpoint, these two positions are similar (Table 5.6). No doubt about it. But, there is one more question that needs answering. What about the risk of the two positions? In order to really be

TABLE 5.6 Long Call versus Synthetic Long Call Loss

Real Long Call	Synthetic Long Call
Buy 1 Jun 65 call @ 2.04 with stock $65.50	Buy 100 @ $65.50
	Buy 1 Jun 65 puts @ $1.48
Stock trades down to $61.50	**Stock trades down to $61.50 . . . a $4.00 loss (–$400)**
Call trades down to $0.49 . . . a $1.55 loss (–$155)	Put goes from $1.48 up to $3.94 . . . a $2.46 profit ($246)
Total P&L = –$155.00	**Total P&L = –$154.00**

identical, the two positions need not only have the same profit and loss scenario, but they also need to have the same risk scenario. How can we compare this? Simple, let's look at our Greek positions.

The Greeks measure a position's sensitivity to outside variables, such a stock movement, volatility movement, and time movement. Our Greek positions will tell the tale. They will tell us if these two positions are truly similar.

Let's begin by taking a look at the delta of these two positions. First, find the delta of our actual June 65 call. If we go to the June 65 calls on our trading sheet and pan across to a stock price of $65.50, we see the delta we're looking for. Just below the theoretical value of the June 65 call ($2.04), we see the delta. The delta is 56. Because the call is a long instrument and we own it, the delta is a long 56 delta.

Next we compare this to the delta of our synthetic long June 65 call. Our synthetic long call consists of being long the stock and long the June 65 put in a one-to-one ratio. Using our trading sheet again, we find that the delta of the June 65 put is 44 deltas.

The put, being a short instrument, will give us negative deltas, as we are long it. So we are short 44 deltas from our long June 65 put position and long 100 deltas from our long stock position. This gives us a total position delta of long 56 deltas (100 – 44), just like the actual June 65 call. So the actual June 65 call delta and the synthetic June 65 call delta are identical.

What about our gamma? Take a look at the trading sheets again. When we look at the June 65 calls with the stock price at $65.50, we see an option price and the deltas. But if you pan all the way over to the far right of your trading sheet, you will see some additional columns, labeled "G" and "V." That "G" column is the gamma value of that strike. Remember, we stated earlier that a call and its corresponding put have the same gamma. So let's take a look at this situation. We are long the June 65 call. Because we are long the call, long an option, we know we will acquire long gamma. What is the gamma of the June 65 call? If you pan over and look under the "G" column next to June 65, you'll see it is 7.2 gammas. So our actual June 65 call position has a long gamma of 7.2.

Does this match our synthetic long June 65 call position? Our synthetic long call position consists of long stock, which has no gamma, and a long June 65 put, which has gamma. Remember we stated that the call and its corresponding put have the same gamma. Our long June 65 put will have the same gamma, 7.2, as the actual long June 65 call. The long June 65 call will give you 7.2 gammas. The long June 65 put, used in the construction of the long synthetic June 65 call, also gives you 7.2 gammas. These two positions, the actual call and its synthetic, both give you 7.2 gammas. They are identical.

What about vega? Vega works much in the same way as gamma. Remember we said gamma, theta, and vega do not differentiate between call and put. They are calculated by strike price, and we are dealing with the same strike here. The real call and its synthetic counterpart are both the June 65 strike. Again, pan over to the far right on the trading sheet along the June 65 strike line and you will see the "V" column. That is your vega value. You will see that the vega for the June 65 strike is 0.05, or 5.0 cents. So the real call has a 5.0-cent vega.

Our synthetic long call position is constructed of long stock (which has no vega) and a long put. As stated by formula, that long put happens to be the June 65 put. The June 65 put, being the corresponding put to the July 65 call, also has a vega of 5.0 cents. So the combination of the long stock and the June 65 put give you a 5.0-cent vega, the same as the actual call.

The delta, gamma, and vega for both our real position and our synthetically constructed equivalent are identical. Theta, also being calculated by strike price, obviously will work the same way. As you can see, all of the Greeks, which are your measurement of risk, are identical between the real call and its synthetic counterpart; and the profit and loss is the same.

The only difference we see is a little bit of money in interest, which is part of your cost to carry and thus part of your calculation. Now we are going to move onto synthetic short call. How do we construct a synthetic short call? Obviously it will be constructed differently from the synthetic long call. The construction of the synthetic short call is to sell the call's corresponding put and sell the stock in a one-to-one ratio. Since we now know the proper construction of a short synthetic call, let's put one together and see how it compares to the actual short call (Figure 5.4).

Our first test is the profit and loss test. For our comparison, let us again use the June 65 call. The actual June 65 call, with stock at $65.50, is worth $2.04. In order to create the actual short June 65 call, we must sell the call.

Since its theoretical value is $2.04 with the stock at $65.50, we are going to sell it at that price. We make the sale at $2.04. Let's take a look and see

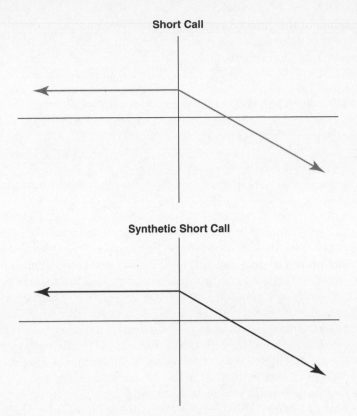

FIGURE 5.4 Short Call versus Synthetic Short Call

what happens to our short call when the stock drops $4.00 down to $61.50. Look at your trading sheet. With the stock price at $61.50, the June 65 call is now worth $0.49. Since we sold the call at $2.04 and it is now worth $0.49, we realize a profit of $1.55. With the $4.00 drop in the stock price we have a profit of $1.55 from selling the actual June 65 call.

Remember, we build the synthetic short call by selling the stock and selling the corresponding put in a one-to-one ratio. To construct this for our example, we first sell the stock at $65.50. By the requirements of the formula, we must also sell the corresponding put in a one-to-one ratio with the stock. With the stock at $65.50, the June 65 put has a theoretical value of $1.48. We therefore sell the put at $1.48. After dropping the stock price from $65.50 down to $61.50, our short stock position nets us a profit of $4.00. The second component of the synthetic short June 65 call is the short June 65 put. When the stock was trading at $65.50, we sold the June 65 put at $1.48. Now, with the stock trading down at $61.50, the June 65 put is worth $3.94.

TABLE 5.7   Short Call versus Synthetic Short Call Profit

Real Short Call	Synthetic Short Call
Sell 1 Jun 65 call @ $2.04	Sell 100 shares @ 65.50
	Sell 1 Jun 65 puts @ $1.48
Stock trades down to $61.50	**Stock trades down to $61.50 . . . a**
	$4.00 profit ($400)
Call goes from $2.04 down to	Put goes from $1.48 up to $3.94 . . . a
$0.49 . . . a $1.55 profit ($155)	$2.46 profit ($246)
Total P&L = +$155.00	**Total P&L = +$154.00**

This creates a loss of $2.46 in the put component of our synthetic short call position.

It is time to recap. We made a $4.00 profit in the stock. We lost $2.46 in the put, which gives us a net profit of $1.54. That is almost identical to the $1.55 profit we would have had if we had sold the call outright. Not so fast, though. Remember, you have to add in your cost of carry in the amount of $0.01. Now it matches exactly (Table 5.7).

Finally, let's take a look at our synthetic short June 65 call versus the actual short June 65 call when the stock trades up and we're forced into a loss. Again we will use our June 65 call example with the stock trading at $65.50. The call is worth $2.04. Now let's run the stock up to $71.50. At $71.50, the actual June 65 call is now worth $6.71.

Since we originally sold that June 65 call for $2.04 and it's now worth $6.71, we've incurred a $4.67 loss. Now let us take a look at how that compares to our synthetic short June 65 call position. We create a synthetic short call by selling the stock and selling the corresponding put in a one-to-one ratio. Following that formula's requirements, we first sell the stock at $65.50. Next, we also have to sell the June 65 put. With the stock at $65.50, the theoretical value of the June 65 put is $1.48. For our comparison, we will sell the June 65 put at that $1.48 price. When the stock trades up to $71.50, we incur a loss of $6.00 from the stock component of our short synthetic call. The put component, however, makes money.

Remember, besides selling the stock, we sold the June 65 put at $1.48, when the stock was $65.50. Now, with the stock at $71.50, the July 65 put is only worth 15 cents. This creates a $1.33 profit from the put component of the synthetic short call. To calculate our total profit or loss in the position, we combine the loss in the stock (−$6.00) with the gain in the put (+$1.33) and find that we lost $4.67 in our synthetic short call position. Meanwhile, if we had sold the call outright, we also would have lost $4.67. Again, from a profit and loss scenario, the two positions, the actual short June 65 call and the synthetic short June 65 call, are identical (Table 5.8).

TABLE 5.8 Short Call versus Synthetic Short Call Loss

Real Short Call	Synthetic Call
Sell 1 Jun 65 call @ $2.04	Sell 100 shares @ 65.50
	Sell 1 Jun 65 puts @ $1.48
Stock trades up to $71.50	**Stock trades up to $71.50 . . . a $6.00 loss ($600)**
Call trades up to $6.71 . . . a loss of $4.67 (−$467)	Put goes from $1.48 down to $0.15 . . . a $1.33 profit (+$133)
Total P&L = −$467.00	**Total P&L = −$467.00**

We are again left with the final comparison, the comparison of risk. Even though the profit and loss scenarios match, the positions cannot be labeled identical without a similar risk scenario. To do this, we must survey the Greek sensitivities and evaluate what the similarities of the risks are.

To start, let us compare the deltas of the two positions. First, when we look at the delta of our actual July 65 call, with the stock at $65.50, we see that the delta is 56. Now remember that we are going to sell that call. When we sell that call, we incur a short delta position. This is because calls are a long instrument. When you sell a long instrument, you become short. In this case, we are short exactly 56. In our synthetic short call position, we are going to sell the stock. This is going to give us a short 100 delta position, but we are also going to sell the put. In this case, the June 65 put, and with the stock at $65.50, the June 65 put has −44 deltas.

When we sell a put, we incur long deltas. Since the put is a short instrument, selling it will create a long delta position. In this particular case, we have a long 44 delta position.

When we combine the two to calculate the total delta position of our short synthetic call, we find the stock position is short 100 deltas and the put position is long 44 deltas, which gives us a total delta of short 56 for our synthetic short call position. The synthetic call had the exact same amount of short deltas that the actual call had. Obviously, the deltas, short 56 deltas, match exactly.

Now look at our gammas. If we pan all the way across our trading sheets to the far right, we see under the "G" column that the gamma of the June 65 strike is 7.2 gammas. Do not forget that gamma, vega, and theta are calculated per strike and not by put and call. This means a call and its corresponding put have the exact same gamma, vega, and theta. Remembering that we know that the call's gamma is 7.2 and since we sold the call, we will be short gamma. How many short gammas? We are going to be short 7.2 gammas in the actual call.

Let's take a look at our synthetic short call position. Our first component is the short stock position. In terms of gamma, vega, and theta, stock does not matter because stock has no gamma, vega, or theta. We have already discussed and matched the delta, and that is all stock has. What we will look at is the short put component of the position. In the short put component, we are short the June 65 puts. When we pan all the way across our trading sheet and notice the June 65 gamma, we see that the June 65 gamma is 7.2 for both the calls and the puts. So, our June 65 short put will give us 7.2 short gammas. This is the exact same amount of short gammas as the actual short June 65 call. When we compare the short 7.2 gamma position from our synthetic position with our gamma position from the actual short call, we again have a match.

We see that the deltas and the gammas match. Now let us check vega. We know what the outcome will be by now, but let's review it anyway. The stock has no vega. So, let's just skip the short stock component of the synthetic position. It has no vega. The put component, however, does have vega. According to our trading sheet, the June 65 put will have a 0.05 or a 5-cent vega. Since we are short the put, we will have a short 0.05 vega in our short synthetic call position. Remember, when we sell the call or any option, we acquire short vegas. In this case in particular, it is going to be short 7.2 vegas. So our actual short call position has a short 7.2 vega, just like its synthetic short call counterpart.

Obviously, the exact same thing is true about theta because, as stated earlier, gamma, vega, and theta are all calculated by strike price, not by call and put. Stock does not have theta so we can take that component out of the equation, as we did for both gamma and vega.

Our actual short June 65 call will have a theta, which is obviously going to match its corresponding put's (June 65 put) theta, as per definition. Since the corresponding put is the only component of the synthetic position with theta, and its theta has to match its corresponding call's theta exactly, the two positions must have a matching theta. Because those thetas are going to be identical, our actual short call and our synthetic short call will have the same thetas.

We have compared the two positions: short call and synthetic short call. Both have the same profit and loss scenario as demonstrated earlier. Both have identical deltas, gammas, vegas, and thetas, and thus have similar risks. However, you must remember that with synthetic positions, any time you trade the actual stock from the short side, you are going to incur short stock risks.

There are risks with both short stock and long stock. For example, both are at risk with dividend changes. Long stock is at risk if the dividend is cut. Short stock is at risk if the dividend is increased. However, when you trade a synthetic position, special caution is necessary.

There are risks inherent to short stock positions that are not present in long stock positions. The main risk is a stock being hard to borrow (term applied when the amount of stock available for shorting becomes tight). Suppose a stock is hard to borrow and you sell it short. Your risk comes when whoever loaned it to you wants it back.

Normally, your brokerage can find someone else to lend the stock to you. Then they return the stock to the original lender. But in the case of a hard-to-borrow stock, finding a willing lender can be a problem. And if the brokerage can't find someone new for you to borrow it from, it will have to open a market to purchase it for you.

In that case, the brokerage will buy that stock back for you at whatever the market price is at the time. That is the risk—a costly one: the price you may have to pay to replace the borrowed stock.

How will you know if a stock is going to be hard to borrow? Normally a stock doesn't go from easy to borrow to unbelievably hard to borrow. In general, there is a progression. The tip-off is that in some instances your short stock position is not going to pay you as much interest (short stock rebate) as it normally would.

Why? As the stock gets harder and harder to borrow, your brokerage firm will cease to pay the same amount of interest to you for being short. The stock you are short will pay you less.

For example, say the rate you are receiving on your short stock is 4 percent. The rate then drops from 4 percent in short interest to 2 percent in short interest.

When that happens, beware. Such a move may well be the signal that your stock is hard to borrow. Further, most brokerages have a published hard-to-borrow list, which tells what stocks are hard for the broker to borrow and what ones are currently paying a discounted short rate.

If you are planning on any type of strategy that involves selling the stock short, you have to realize that you have a short stock risk: You must replace any stock you borrowed if the lender wants it back. It could be a very expensive buy-back for you.

Say your brokerage firm is unable to locate someone else to lend the stock to you. So the firm goes out on the open market and buys the stock wherever it is offered at whatever price necessary. You, being short that stock, could incur substantial losses.

You have to be especially aware of your short stock risks if you are using short stock with an option to create a synthetic position. The short-stock risk is the only real risk, but you must be aware of it. It is a risk that can hurt. There are always small risks, but we can deal with small risks. Its the ones that kill you that we have to address. And the hard-to-borrow short stock is a risk that can kill you.

The appendix presents five trading sheets. My suggestion is to construct some synthetic calls, both long and short, and then compare them to their real call counterparts with stock movement.

Synthetic stock is not susceptible to volatility movements, so you can ignore volatility there. But with synthetic calls, you should check how the synthetic position compares with the actual position in terms of stock movement and volatility movements. You have five trading sheets, all having different volatilities, to help you do that.

SYNTHETIC PUT

The final type of synthetic position is the synthetic put. The *synthetic put* will behave like its real counterpart. There are two types of synthetic put positions: the long synthetic put and the short synthetic put.

In the same manner as we observed the relationship and likeness between the synthetic stock and its real counterpart and the synthetic call and its counterpart, we will examine the synthetic put and its real counterpart (Figure 5.5).

First, let's look at the synthetic long put. To establish the synthetic long put, we must sell the stock and purchase the put's corresponding call in a one-to-one ratio. That ratio means that for every 100 shares of short stock we sell, we must buy one call. That will create a synthetic long put that will be equivalent to an actual long put position in virtually every way.

Let's put together an example for testing purposes. Let's set up a synthetic long put position and then compare it to its corresponding actual long put. Then we will take a look at how each position reacts to stock movements.

First, we set up our actual put. For this example, we will use the June 65 puts with the stock at $65.50. With the stock trading at $65.50, the put is worth $1.48. We will buy it at that price. Next, we create the synthetic long June 65 put.

Following the previously stated guidelines, we buy the June 65 put's corresponding call, the June 65 call, for $2.04. We then sell the stock short at $65.50. We now have our two positions: an actual long put and its equivalent, the synthetic long put.

In order to compare the risk/reward scenarios of the two positions, let's first take a look at the profit side of the equation. What happens to our positions if the stock trades down from $65.50 to $61.50? In that case, the actual June 65 put will be worth $3.94. Remember, we bought this put for $1.48; so our profit from the actual June 65 put with a $4.00 downward

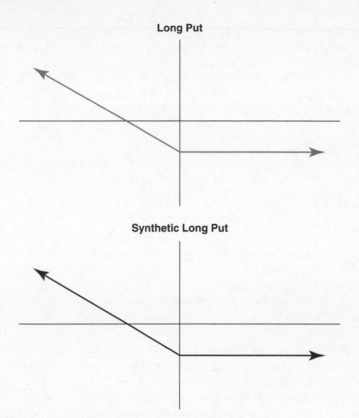

FIGURE 5.5 Long Put versus Synthetic Long Put

movement in the stock is $2.46. Now turn your attention to the synthetic long put.

We constructed it by selling the stock short at $65.50 and purchasing the June 65 call for $2.04. When the stock trades down to $61.50, we have made $4.00 in the stock component. Remember, we are short the stock in the construction of the long synthetic put position. Our other component, the June 65 call, purchased for $2.04 with the stock at $65.50, is now only worth $0.49 with the stock at $61.50.

Where we made money in the stock, we lost money in the put. We lost $1.55 in our June 65 call. A profit of $4.00 from the stock minus a loss of $1.55 from our put gives a net profit of $2.45. Add back in your cost of carry ($0.01), and that is the exact same profit you would have made if you bought the put itself and the stock moved from $65.50 down to $61.50. So, both positions produce an identical profit (Table 5.9).

TABLE 5.9 Long Put versus Synthetic Long Put Profit

Real Long Put	Synthetic Long Put
Sell 1 Jun 65 put @ $1.48	Sell 100 shares @ 65.50
	Buy 1 Jun 65 call @ $2.04
Stock trades down to $61.50	**Stock trades down to $61.50 . . . a $4.00 profit ($400)**
Put goes from $1.48 up to $3.49 . . . a $2.46 profit ($246)	Call goes from $2.04 down to $0.49 . . . a $1.55 loss (−$155)
Total P&L = +$246.00	**Total P&L = +$245.00**

Let's move on to the loss scenario. What will happen to our positions if the stock trades up? We will now compare what happens to the actual long put versus what happens to our synthetic long put if the stock trades in the inverse direction.

First, let's take a look at the actual long put. Remember, we purchased the June 65 put with the stock trading at $65.50 for $1.48. If the stock were to trade from $65.50 up to $71.50, you could see on the trading sheets that the actual June 65 put is now worth $0.15. We bought it for $1.48, and it's now worth $0.15. Our real put will have lost $1.33 with the stock up $6.00 from $65.50 to $71.50.

The question now is how did our synthetic long June 65 put do? Our synthetic long put consists of being short the stock and long the June 65 call. First, let's see how our short stock position did. We sold the stock at $65.50, and now with the stock trading at $71.50, we incur a $6.00 loss in the stock.

The stock portion of our synthetic long put is down $6.00. However, along with selling the stock, we also purchased the June 65 call that was worth $2.04. With the stock up $6.00 to $71.50, our June 65 call will now be worth $6.71. That will give us a profit in the June 65 call. The profit is $4.67.

Now we determine our bottom line. We lost $6.00 in the stock; but we made $4.67 in the call, giving us a total loss of $1.33. The loss in both strategies is a match. From a profit and loss standpoint, these two positions are similar (Table 5.10).

But, there is one more question that needs answering. What about the risk of the two positions?

In order to really be identical, the two positions need not only have the same profit and loss scenario, but they also need to have the same risk scenario. We compare this by looking at our Greek positions. As we know, the Greeks measure a position's sensitivity to outside variables such a stock movement, volatility movement, and time movement. Our Greek

TABLE 5.10 Long Put versus Synthetic Long Put Loss

Real Long Put	Synthetic Long Put
Buy 1 Jun 65 put @ $1.48	Sell 100 shares @ 65.50
	Buy 1 Jun 65 call @ $2.04
Stock trades up to $71.50	**Stock trades up to $71.50 a $6.00 loss ($600)**
Put trades down to $0.15 . . . a loss of $1.33 (−$133)	Call goes from $2.04 up to $6.7 a $4.67 profit (+$467)
Total P&L = −$133.00	**Total P&L = −$133.00**

positions will tell the tale. They will tell us if these two positions are truly similar.

Let's begin by taking a look at the delta of these two positions. First, find the delta of the actual June 65 put. If we go to the June 65 puts on our trading sheet and pan across to a stock price of $65.50, we see the delta we are looking for.

Just below the theoretical value of the June 65 put ($1.48) we see the delta. The delta is 44 and, because the put is a short instrument and we own it, it is a short 44 delta.

Next, we compare this to the delta of our synthetic long June 65 put. Our synthetic long put consists of being short the stock and long the June 65 call in a one-to-one ratio. Using our trading sheet again, we find that the delta of the June 65 calls is 56 deltas.

The call, being a long instrument, will give us positive deltas because we are long it. So we are long 56 deltas from our long June 65 call position and short 100 deltas from our short stock position. This gives us a total position delta of short 44 deltas (−100 + 56), just like the actual long June 65 put. So, the actual long June 65 put delta and the synthetic long June 65 put delta are identical.

What about our gamma? Take a look at the trading sheets again. When we look at the June 65 puts with the stock price at $65.50, we see an option price and we see the deltas. But if you pan all the way over to the far right of your trading sheet, you'll see some additional columns: a "G" column and a "V" column. That "G" column is the gamma value of that strike. Remember we stated earlier that a call and its corresponding put have the same gamma. So let's take a look at this situation.

We are long the June 65 put. Because we are long the put, long an option, we know we will acquire long gamma. What is the gamma of the June 65 put? If you pan over and look under the "G" column next to June 65, you'll see it is 7.2 gammas. So our actual June 65 put position has a long gamma of 7.2.

Does this match our synthetic long June 65 put position? Our synthetic long put position consists of short stock, which has no gamma, and a long June 65 call, which has gamma.

Remember that we stated that the call and its corresponding put have the same gamma. Our long June 65 call will have the same gamma, 7.2, as the actual long June 65 put. The long June 65 put will give you 7.2 gammas. The long June 65 call, used in the construction of the long synthetic June 65 put, also gives you 7.2 gammas. These two positions, the actual put and its synthetic counterpart, both give you 7.2 gammas. They are identical.

What about vega? Vega works much in the same way as gamma worked. Remember we said gamma, theta, and vega do not differentiate between call and put. They are calculated by strike price, and we are dealing with the same strike here. The real put and its synthetic counterpart are both the June 65 strike.

Again, pan over to the far right on your trading sheet along the June 65 strike line, and you'll see the "V" column. That is your vega value. You will see that the vega for the June 65 strike is 0.05, or 5 cents. So the real put has a 5-cent vega. Our synthetic long put position is constructed of short stock (which has no vega) and a long call. As stated by formula, that long call happens to be the June 65 call.

The June 65 call, being the corresponding call to the July 65 put, also has a vega of 5 cents. So the combination of the short stock and the June 65 call gives you a 5-cent vega, the same as the actual put.

The delta, gamma, and vega for both our real position and our synthetically constructed counterpart are identical. Theta, also being calculated by strike price, obviously will work the same way. As you can see, all of the Greeks, which are your measurement of risk, are identical between the real put and its synthetic counterpart; and the profit and loss is the same. The only difference we see is a little bit of money in interest, which is part of your cost to carry and thus part of your calculation.

Now we are going to move on to synthetic short put. How do we construct it? Obviously it will be constructed differently from the synthetic long put. The construction of the synthetic short put is to sell the put's corresponding call and buy the stock in a one-to-one ratio (Figure 5.6).

Since we now know the proper construction of a short synthetic put, let's put one together and see how it compares to the actual short put.

Our first test is the profit and loss test. For our comparison, let us again use the June 65 put. The actual June 65 put, with stock at $65.50, is worth $1.48. In order to create the actual short June 65 put, we must sell the put.

Since its theoretical value is $1.48 with the stock at $65.50, we are going to sell it at that price. We make the sale at $1.48. Let's take a look and see what happens to our actual short put when the stock trades up $4.00 to $69.50. Look at your trading sheet. With the stock price at $69.50, the June

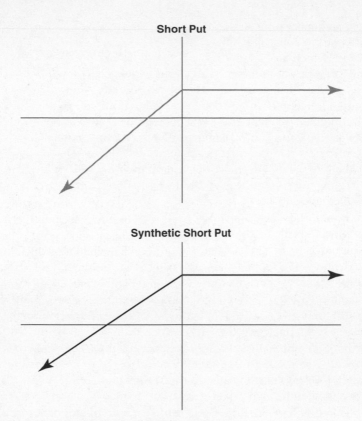

FIGURE 5.6 Short Put versus Synthetic Short Put

65 put is now worth $0.36. Since we sold the put at $1.48 and it is now worth $0.36, we realize a profit of $1.12. With the $4.00 rise in the stock price, we have a profit of $1.12 from selling the actual June 65 put.

Remember, we build the synthetic short put by purchasing the stock and selling the corresponding call in a one-to-one ratio. To construct this for our example, we first buy the stock for $65.50. By the requirements of the formula, we must also sell the corresponding call in a one-to-one ratio with the stock. With the stock at $65.50, the June 65 call has a theoretical value of $2.04. We therefore sell the call at $2.04.

After raising the stock price from $65.50 to $69.50, our long stock position nets us a profit of $4.00. The second component of the synthetic short June 65 put is the short June 65 call. When the stock was trading at $65.50, we sold the June 65 call at $2.04. Now, with the stock trading up at $69.50, the June 65 call is worth $4.92. This creates a loss of $2.88 in the call component of our synthetic short put position.

TABLE 5.11 Short Put versus Synthetic Short Put Profit

Real Short Put	Synthetic Short Put
Sell 1 Jun 65 put @ $1.48	Sell 100 shares @ 65.50
	Buy 1 Jun 65 call @ $2.04
Stock trades up to $69.50	**Stock trades up to $69.50, a $4.00 profit ($400)**
Put trades down to $0.36 . . . a profit of $1.12 (+$122)	Call goes from $2.04 up to $4.92 . . . a $2.88 loss (−$288)
Total P&L = +$122.00	**Total P&L = +$122.00**

It is time to recap. We made a $4.00 profit in the stock. We lost $2.88 in the call, which gives us a net profit of $1.12. That is identical to the $1.12 profit we would have had if we had sold the put outright (Table 5.11).

Finally, let's take a look at our synthetic short June 65 put versus the actual short June 65 put when the stock trades down and we are forced into a loss. Again we will use our June 65 put example with the stock trading at $65.50. The put is worth $1.48. Now let's drop the stock price down to $61.50. At $61.50, the actual June 65 put is worth $3.94. Since we originally sold that June 65 put for $1.48 and it's now worth $3.94, we have incurred a $2.46 loss.

Now let us take a look at how that compares to our synthetic short June 65 put position. We create a synthetic short put by purchasing the stock and selling the corresponding call in a one-to-one ratio. Following that formula's requirements, we first buy the stock at $65.50.

Next, we also have to sell the June 65 call. With the stock at $65.50, the theoretical value of the June 65 call is $2.04. For our comparison, we will sell the June 65 call at that $2.04 price.

When the stock trades down to $61.50, we incur a loss of $4.00 from the stock component of our short synthetic put. The call component, however, makes money.

Remember, besides buying the stock, we sold the June 65 call at $2.04 when the stock was $65.50. Now, with the stock at $61.50, the July 65 call is only worth $0.49. This creates a $1.55 profit from the call component of the synthetic short put.

To calculate our total profit or loss in the position, we combine the loss in the stock (−$4.00) with the gain in the call (+$1.55) and find that we lost $2.45 in our synthetic short put position. Add in our cost of carry of −$0.01, and we have a total of a loss of $2.46. Meanwhile, if we had sold the put outright, we also would have lost $2.46. Again, from a profit and loss scenario, the two positions—the actual short June 65 put and the synthetic short June 65 put—are identical (Table 5.12).

TABLE 5.12   Short Put versus Synthetic Short Put Loss

Real Short Put	Synthetic Short Put
Sell 1 Jun 65 put @ $1.48	Buy 100 shares @ $65.50
	Sell 1 Jun 65 call @ $2.04
Stock trades down to $61.50	**Stock trades down to $61.50... a**
	$4.00 loss (−$400)
Put goes from $1.48 up to $3.94 . . . a	Call goes from $2.04 down to $0.49 . . . a
$2.46 loss (−$246)	$1.55 profit (+$155)
Total P&L = −$246.00	**Total P&L = −$245.00**

We are again left with the final comparison, the comparison of risk. Even though the profit and loss scenarios match, the positions cannot be labeled identical without a similar risk scenario. To do this, we must now survey the Greek sensitivities and evaluate what the similarities of the risks are.

To start, let us compare the deltas of the two positions. First, when we look at the delta of our actual July 65 put, with the stock at $65.50, we see that the delta is −44. Remember, we are going to sell that put. When we do, we incur a long delta position. This is because puts are a short instrument. When you sell a short instrument, you become long. In this case, we are long 44 deltas.

In our synthetic short put position, we are going to buy the stock. This is going to give us a long 100-delta position, but we are also going to sell the call. In this case, with the stock at $65.50, the June 65 call has 56 deltas. When we sell a call, we incur short deltas. Since the call is a long instrument, selling it will create a short delta position. In this case, we have a short 56 delta position.

When we combine the two to calculate the total delta position of our short synthetic put, we find the stock position is long 100 deltas and the call position is a short 56 deltas, which gives us a total delta of long 44 for our synthetic short put position.

The synthetic put has the exact same amount of long deltas that the actual short put had. Obviously, the deltas, long 44 deltas, match exactly.

Now look at our gammas. If we pan all the way across our trading sheets to the far right, we see under the "G" column that the gamma of the June 65 strike is 7.2 gammas.

Do not forget that gamma, vega, and theta are calculated per strike, and not by put and call. This means a call and its corresponding put have the exact same gamma, vega, and theta. Remembering that, we know that the put's gamma is 7.2. Since we sold the put, we will be short gamma. How many short gammas? We are going to be short 7.2 gammas in the actual put.

Let's take a look at our synthetic short put position. Our first component is the long stock position. In terms of gamma, vega, and theta, stock does not matter because stock has no gamma, vega, or theta. We've already discussed and matched the delta, and that is all stock has.

What we will look at is the short call component of the position. In the short call component, we are short the June 65 calls. When we pan all the way across our trading sheet and notice the June 65 gamma, we see that it is 7.2 for both the calls and the puts. So, our June 65 short call will give us 7.2 short gammas. This is the exact same amount of short gammas as the actual short June 65 put.

We see that the deltas and the gammas match. Now let us check vega. We all know what the outcome will be by now, but let's review it anyway. The stock has no vega. So, let's just skip the long stock component of the synthetic position. It has no vega. The call component, however, does have vega. According to our trading sheet, the June 65 calls will have a 0.05 or 5.0-cent vega. Since we are short the call, we will have a short 0.05 vega in our synthetic short put position. When we compare the short 7.2 gamma position from our synthetic position with our gamma position from the actual short put, we again have a match.

Remember, when we sell the put or any option, for that matter, we acquire short vegas. In this case in particular, it is going to be short 7.2 vegas. So our actual short put position has a short 7.2 vega, just like its synthetic short put counterpart. Obviously, I am going to say the exact same thing about theta because, as stated earlier, gamma, vega, and theta are all calculated by strike price, and not by call and put. Stock does not have theta so we can take that component out of the equation, as we did for both gamma and vega. Our actual short June 65 put will have a theta, which is obviously going to match its corresponding call's (June 65 call) theta, as per definition.

Since the corresponding call is the only component of the synthetic position with theta, and its theta has to match its corresponding put theta exactly, then the two positions must have a matching theta.

Because those thetas are going to be identical, our actual short put and our synthetic short put will have the same thetas.

We have compared the two positions: short put and synthetic short put. Both have the same profit and loss scenario as demonstrated earlier. Both have identical deltas, gammas, vegas, and thetas, and thus they have similar risks. However, you must remember that with synthetic positions, any time you trade the actual stock from the short side, you are going to incur short stock risks. Short stock risk is especially dangerous to the investor's bottom line and needs special consideration and attention.

As a reminder, it can be hazardous shorting a stock that is hard to borrow or is being taken over. In both cases, individual investors can be at risk when called to replace the stock borrowed from the loaner on an instant's notice. If the market is not open or that stock is not trading, the broker will be required to buy the stock back for you at any price necessary in order to return it to its rightful owner. The price paid can be much higher than the current stock price. As mentioned, brokers, such as the one I recommend, Think or Swim (www.thinkorswim.com), provide hard-to-borrow information directly on their trading platform.

PART II

Basic Strategies

W*ebster's Dictionary* defines the term *strategy* as "the science of planning and directing larger scale military operations, specifically of maneuvering forces into the most advantageous position prior to actual engagement with the enemy" and "skill in managing or planning, especially by using stratagems or artful means to some end."

When considering the strategy of investing in the market, both definitions should be considered. The investor should pay particular attention to maneuvering into the most advantageous position prior to actual engagement and in managing or planning, especially by using stratagems.

Picking a stock or group of stocks is only half the battle. Making the most from the chosen investment opportunity is the other half. This is where your strategy comes in.

In Part II, we discuss trading strategies involving stock and options: the covered call/buy-write strategy, the covered put/sell-write strategy, the protective put strategy, the synthetic put/protective call strategy, and the collar strategy.

These strategies focus on premium collection and/or limiting risk. In addition, you will also discover the role of "lean" and how to "roll" your position to establish a stream of income.

CHAPTER 6

Introduction to Trading Strategies

The wrong strategy applied to the right opportunity can produce increased risk, decreased profits, and even potential loss. Therefore, understanding and applying the proper strategy is critical. The actual selection of an investment opportunity from those offered normally depends on the type and style of research the investor favors and deems necessary.

This selection process, or investment selection protocol, is a checklist of different types and pieces of data that are favored by the individual investor. These pieces of data can consist of charts, indicators, oscillators, fundamental analysis, news, or even tips.

Each investor has his or her own investment selection protocol. As an investor, once you complete this process and choose your investment opportunity, your strategy takes over. As you will discover, option traders can capitalize on directional as well as neutral outlooks.

However, people invest in stocks based on a directional outlook. That is, investors buy stocks they think will rise in price; conversely, speculators will short stocks they think will fall in price. Therefore, the directional play is where we will start our discussion of option strategies.

DIRECTIONAL TRADING STRATEGIES

As I have said, options were designed to hedge other investments; that is, to be used as insurance against portfolios of stock. Although options are a powerful risk management tool, they can also be used effectively as a

119

stand-alone trading vehicle. In other words, we can trade options all by themselves without the need to ever buy or sell shares of stock.

When an option is not paired or hedged with another asset, it is said to be *naked*. To an option trader, if you buy shares of Microsoft, you are naked long stock. That just means you own an unhedged stock position.

Just as we can trade stock, we can trade naked options. We can buy a call all by itself to capitalize on a bullish outlook on the stock price. If the stock price does rise sufficiently, we can sell the call and collect a profit. We don't ever need to exercise the call and take delivery of the stock. That is trading a *naked long call*.

We can also buy *naked puts* to take advantage of a bearish outlook on the underlying stock price. If the stock price falls sufficiently, we can sell the put and collect a profit. There is no reason to exercise the put in order to sell the shares. Instead, investors and traders can first buy and then sell the puts themselves.

Most investors who are introduced to options believe that they are just cheaper forms of stock and that they should buy calls (or puts) if they feel the stock is going to rise (or fall). There is a fundamental flaw in this thinking. Options are not a form of stock. Not all call options are direct substitutes for long stock; not all puts are direct substitutes for short stock.

As shown in Chapter 4, there is a speed or pace component to an option's price that is not present for stock. That component must be overcome to make a profit with options. In addition, the break-even point of options is different from that of stocks.

For example, let's look at a Microsoft $65.00 call purchased for $2.00. If one investor buys shares of Microsoft for $65.00, she will profit from *any* stock price above $65.00 (ignoring commissions). She only needs the stock price to rise. Another investor buying the $65.00 call for $2.00, however, needs the stock price to rise *above* $67.00 by expiration in order to make money. The call buyer does not profit from all stock prices above $65.00, and he has a time limit. The call is obviously not just a cheaper form of stock. Some calls behave similarly to stock *but not identically*.

It is this speed component that creates one of the biggest paradoxes for new option traders. That is, if you buy an option and the stock moves in your favor, you can still lose money. In the previous example, if Microsoft rises to $66.00, you will lose money even though the stock price rose. For option traders, it is not enough to have proper direction; they must have *sufficient movement* in direction in a specific time frame.

So, on one hand, options provide tremendous benefits due to their low cost and limited risk. However, there is a trade-off: Long options require the underlying stock to move sufficiently and within a specific time frame before a profit can be realized.

Is there a way we can strike a balance between these two extremes? Can we find an option that costs far less than the stock but doesn't expose us to a need for considerable stock price movement?

The answer is yes. And in order to understand why, we need to turn to some option theory. As we've shown, options are not direct substitutes for long or short stock positions. Because of this, option prices do not respond to stock price changes in the same way as stocks. For example, assume Microsoft is $65.00 and you buy the $65.00 call for $2.00. A short time later, the stock raises one full dollar to $66.00. A new option trader might suspect that the $65.00 call's price will also raise a full dollar as well and trade for $3.00. In actuality, the option's price will rise only about half that amount, or 50 cents, and trade for $2.50.

The reason has to do with the fact that the stock price is not guaranteed to retain that full dollar through expiration. With the stock at $66.00, the $65.00 call has $1.00 worth of intrinsic value and $1.50 worth of time value (assuming the call is priced at $2.50). However, the stock's price is not guaranteed to remain at $66.00 through expiration. The price could certainly drop. Because it is not guaranteed, the market will not fully price in that $1.00 increase until expiration.

In our example, the $65.00 call is the at-the-money strike. At this point, the underlying stock has a 50–50 chance of ending up above or below this strike at expiration. Because of this, the market will only price in 50 percent of that $1.00 increase in the stock's price.

The rate at which an option's price changes in relation to the underlying stock is called the delta of the option. We discussed delta earlier. Most option software will provide you with delta values, which range between zero and 1. In most cases, delta is reported as a decimal so an at-the-money option will have a delta of 0.50.

However, some brokers multiply by 100 since each option controls 100 shares and may show it as 50. In either case, 50 delta indicates that the option's price will move about 50 cents with a $1.00 movement of the underlying stock. Put options have negative deltas, which simply shows that put options rise in value as the underlying stock falls.

It is crucial to understand that an option's delta does not stay constant throughout the option's life. Just because an option has a delta of 0.50 today does not mean that it will remain there through expiration. As the stock price changes or as expiration nears, the delta will change.

At expiration, out-of-the-money options have a delta of zero; all in-the-money options have a delta of 1. The market is basically trying to resolve whether the option will be in the money or out of the money at expiration. The more "certain" the market is that an option will be in the money at expiration, the more the crowd will bid for each dollar increase in the stock's price. In other words, the higher the delta becomes, the greater the option value increases with each dollar movement of the stock. At some point, the market will feel that the option is certain to expire with intrinsic value, at which point the delta will be 1.0 and cannot rise beyond that point.

For example, if Microsoft is $70.00 with only a few days until expiration, the market may feel that the $65.00 call option has a 90 percent chance of expiring with intrinsic value. At this point, the option's delta is 0.90. The $65.00 call may be worth $5.10 ($5.00 intrinsic value, 10 cents time value). If the stock suddenly rises $1.00 to $71.00, the option will rise about 90 cents to $6.00. In this case, the crowd bid up the option 90 cents because it is 90 percent certain it will be in the money at expiration.

Of course, just because the crowd feels the option has a 90 percent chance of expiring with intrinsic value does not in any way mean that it is an accurate assessment. But it is the *perception* that counts.

Let's assume the $65.00 call is $5.10, but the crowd feels that the stock is going to make a big upward move soon. Perhaps there is an earnings report coming out or news on a related company. Whatever the reason, the market's perception is that the stock price is going to increase. If so, competition will increase for call options as buyers flock to the market to buy calls. Let's say the $65.00 call price rises from $5.10 to $6.00, but the underlying stock price hasn't budged and remains at $70.00. Now the $65.00 call still has $5.00 intrinsic value but has increased from 10 cents of time value to $1.00 of time value.

How do we explain this? We would say the implied volatility of the option has increased. In other words, the market's perception is that the stock price is going to exhibit more price movement than previously believed. The option's delta must now be reduced from 0.90 to a lower delta. Why? Because with a wider potential range in the stock over the life of the option, there is an increased chance of the stock finishing at a price at expiration where the in-the-money strike in question may no longer be in the money. Since delta tells us the percentage chance that the option will be in the money, the delta will decrease if there is an added chance that the option will not be in the money. The decrease in delta means an increased doubt, thus more extrinsic value.

If volatility has increased, there is, by definition, less chance for the option to expire in the money due to the increased potential range of the stock for the given time period, as indicated by the higher estimated volatility. Recall that volatility is nondirectional. A higher volatility stock has as likely a chance to rise as it does fall. The current stock price, volatility of the underlying stock, and time to expiration all play important roles in determining the delta of an option.

Prior to taking this little theoretical detour on deltas, we asked if we could find an option that costs far less than the stock but doesn't expose us to a need for considerable stock price movement. Now that you have a little option theory behind you, the answer is to buy options with relatively high deltas. **Specifically, I recommend buying naked options in the 80- to 85- (–80 to –85 for puts) delta range if you are using them as a substitute for long or short stock positions.**

Call options with deltas in this range behave in a similar manner to the underlying stock, cost far less, and still provide limited downside protection. Puts with –80 to –85 deltas will behave similarly to short stock positions but have far less upside risk.

IN-THE-MONEY, OUT-OF-THE-MONEY, AND AT-THE-MONEY OPTIONS

In order to find calls or puts with deltas in this range, you must buy in-the-money options. This is the biggest psychological challenge for new option traders to tackle. They reason that it doesn't make sense to pay for intrinsic value. If Microsoft is $65.00 and you think it's going higher, why not buy the $65.00 or $70.00 call option? After all, call options rise with increases in the stock, so you might as well buy the cheapest option you can find to limit your risk. It's exactly this line of reasoning that creates the majority of option losses.

As has been shown, if you buy the Microsoft $65.00 call for $2.00, the stock price must rise to $67.00 at expiration in order to break even. However, you may find that the $55.00 call has an 85 delta and is trading for $10.30, thus creating a break-even point of $65.30 on the option, which is only 30 cents higher than the current stock price. So while all call options theoretically rise in value as the underlying stock rises, they do not rise to the same degree (as shown by delta), and that is what most new option traders fail to recognize. All call options are not created equal.

In-the-money options act like stock. The deeper in the money the calls are, the more they act like the stock. As the call moves deeper and deeper in the money, the call's delta approaches 1.0 (100), which means its price movement will reflect 100 percent of the stock's movement. An option with a delta of 1.0 is no longer an option; it is now a perfect stock substitute. (This is discussed in more detail later in "The Stock Replacement Covered Call Strategy" in Chapter 14.)

Figure 6.1 shows the $55.00 call trading for $10.30 compared to the underlying stock trading for $65.00. You can see how closely this high-delta call mimics the upward movement of the stock. In fact, it's rather hard to distinguish between the stock and the call, since the dotted and solid

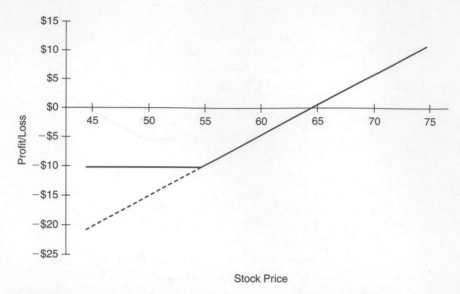

FIGURE 6.1   Long Stock (Dotted) versus Deep ITM Call (Solid) (85 Delta)

lines nearly overlap each other for all stock prices above $55.00. That is the benefit of buying calls with deltas in the 80 to 85 range. They are very good substitutes for stock yet cost a fraction of the stock's price.

Now take a look at Figure 6.2, which shows the $65.00 call compared the stock over the same price ranges as Figure 6.1.

You can see that there is no longer such a strong overlap between the two profit and loss curves. The profit and loss diagram for the $65.00 call is shifted significantly to the right when compared to the $55.00 call in Figure 6.1. Granted, the $55.00 call costs $10.30, which is a lot more than the $65.00 call trading for $2.00. **However, the $55.00 call at $10.30 costs far less than the $65.00 stock yet is a much better approximation for the underlying stock.** Further, the $55.00 call still provides a lot of downside protection should the stock price plummet below $55.00. If it does, the most the option trader can lose is the $10.30 spent on the call. The stock investor can make no such claim to limited losses, even if he or she uses stop or stop limit orders.

Most new option investors, however, tend to buy out-of-the-money options because of the cheap price. The stock trades in their favor, but the option still loses money and the investors wonder why. By now you should understand the reason. Out-of-the-money calls have a much greater speed component to their price. They require a significant, aggressive price move in the underlying stock before a profit can be earned. And this puts the

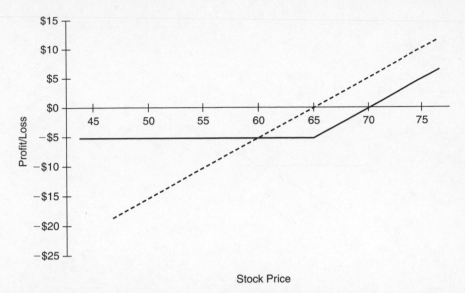

FIGURE 6.2 Long Stock (Dotted) versus ATM Call (Solid) (50 Delta)

option buyer at a disadvantage. It is the very reason for many of the losses incurred by new option traders.

As we move to the out-of-the-money options, we see that there is even less of a close match to the stock. The out-of-the-money option has very little in common with the stock and therefore is not a good replacement vehicle for the stock in most cases. The large amount of extrinsic value, the low delta, and the distant break-even creates too large of a difference in the out-of-the-money option for stock replacement (see Figures 6.3 and 6.4).

High delta options (in the 80 to 85 range) have a very small speed component and acquire the vast majority of their value from changes in the stock's price. In-the-money options will therefore perform much like the stocks you are already used to trading.

Buyers of in-the-money options not only get an advantageous break-even point, they also lose less money from the passage of time. As shown, in-the-money options have a relatively small amount of time value, which is why they provide us with favorable break-even prices; less time value means there is less to decay from the passage of time.

Table 6.1 shows a hypothetical stock trading for $35.00 along with the $30.00, $35.00, and $40.00 strikes and their theoretical prices.

The last column shows the extrinsic value for each of these strikes. Notice that the $35.00 strike (at the money) has the highest time value

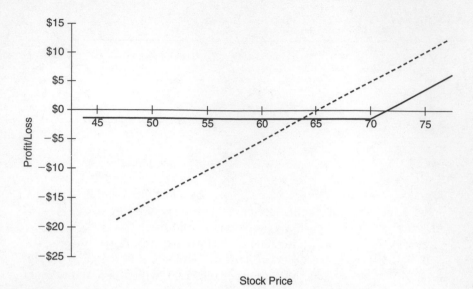

FIGURE 6.3 Long Stock (Dotted) versus OTM Call (Solid) (25 Delta)

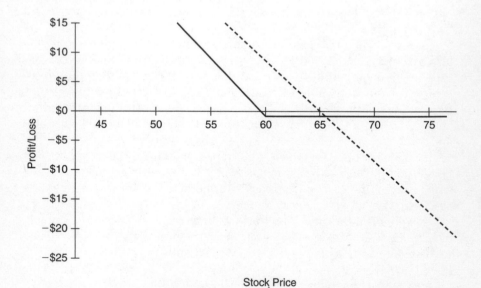

FIGURE 6.4 Short Stock (Dotted) versus OTM Put (Solid) (−25 Delta)

TABLE 6.1	ITM and OTM Calls Less Extrinsic Value than ATM Calls (Stock $35.00)			
Strike Price	**Option Price**	**Delta**	**Break-Even**	**Extrinsic Value**
30	5.20	85	35.20	.20
35	1.00	52	36.00	1.00
40	.30	20	40.30	.30

at $1.00. The $30.00 strike (in the money) has a time value of only 20 cents. The $40.00 strike (out of the money) also has a relatively small time value (30 cents); however, that strike also has a very low delta and is in no way behaving like shares of stock. It requires that the underlying stock rise past $40.30 at expiration before any profit can be realized.

If the underlying stock remains at $35.00 at expiration, the buyer of the $30.00 call will only lose 20 cents on the investment, or less than 4 percent. The buyer of the $35.00 call loses the full $1.00, which is a 100 percent loss. The $40.00 call buyer loses less money (30 cents) but still takes a 100 percent loss.

It is the connection between delta and time decay that is so important for new options traders to understand. If you want to buy naked calls and puts as a *substitute* for long or short stock positions, you need to buy relatively high delta strikes in the 0.80 to 0.85 range.

Many new traders make the mistake of thinking the at-the-money call option is the best choice as a long stock substitute. After all, why pay for any intrinsic value? Isn't the purpose of buying calls to *avoid* controlling all of the stock prices below the current stock price? They continue to rationalize that the at-the-money strike "immediately" begins to make money since it becomes in the money with the next 1-cent tick in the stock's price. While this may sound sensible, it is flawed reasoning because **the at-the-money strike carries the *highest* extrinsic value (time value) and therefore has the highest rate of decay.** The at-the-money strike requires that the stock price make a sizable change by expiration in order to show a profit.

In order to profit from buying an at-the-money option, you need the stock to make a fast, aggressive move because of the large extrinsic value. If the stock price doesn't move quickly, you will be battling the option's daily rate of decay.

Table 6.2 lists stats from the $30.00 and $35.00 strikes. Notice the break-even points for each (remember, that is where the profit and loss curve crosses the horizontal axis). You can clearly see that the curve is shifted farther to the right for the at-the-money $35.00 call, which means the stock must rise further before you can earn a profit.

TABLE 6.2	ITM Have Lower Break-Even Points than ATM Calls (Stock $35.00)		
Strike Price	**Option Price**	**Extrinsic Value**	**Break-Even**
30	5.20	.20	35.20
35	1.00	1.00	36.00
40	.30	.30	40.30

You can see in Table 6.2 that, while the $30.00 strike costs more, it has the distinct advantage that it carries a much lower break-even point. **In-the-money calls therefore have a much higher chance for profit.**

While the break-even points for the $30.00 and $35.00 strikes may not appear to be too different graphically, that small space between them makes all the difference in the world as to whether the option will behave like the underlying stock. Remember, if you are learning to use options after years of stock investing, you don't want to choose an asset (such as an at-the-money option) that behaves nothing like stock. Start out by using assets that behave similarly to the stocks you are already used to.

If a small time value reduces the effect of time decay, why not buy out-of-the-money options, since they also have small amounts of time value? Remember, reduced time decay is not the total story. We want reduced time decay *and* low break-even points.

As shown in Table 6.2, out-of-the-money call options have even higher break-even points than their in-the-money and at-the-money counterparts. While it might appear to be an advantage to spend only a small amount of total dollars for an out-of-the-money strike, you must remember that it comes at a very big cost: a high break-even point.

Figure 6.5 compares the break-even points for the at-the-money $35 strike and the out-of-the-money $40 strike:

While out-of-the-money options are cheaper, they require bigger price moves from the underlying stock to become profitable and are therefore riskier. Riskier? How can that be? If there is less money to lose, isn't there *less* risk? To understand why it is not less risky, you must understand the risk and reward relationship.

LEVERAGE AND RISK

People don't like risk. With all else being equal, people prefer less risk to more. Therefore, if two assets offer the same reward but have different risks, people will bid *down* the price of the riskier asset. For example, imagine that you are in room with hundreds of people all bidding on a

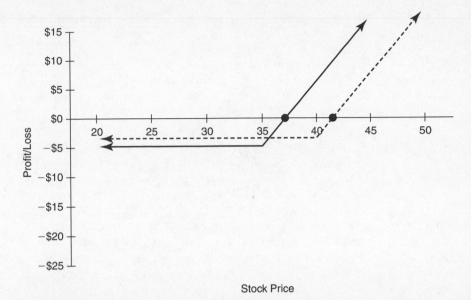

FIGURE 6.5 OTM Calls Have Much Higher Break-Even Points than ATM Calls

$100 bill. The highest bidder gets the $100 bill. No gimmicks, no strings attached.

Now imagine the same opportunity, but this time the highest bidder must correctly guess the outcome of a coin flip. With this condition, the $100 bill is no longer guaranteed; we have introduced some risk.

While we can never be sure of the highest price that will be bid for either scenario, we do know one thing: The highest price paid will be for the guaranteed outcome. The certainty of the reward will command a higher bid because the percentage of the return can be calculated with each bid and the possibility of losing the amount bid has been eliminated. The uncertainty of the second scenario will affect the amount the bidder is willing to risk since there is a chance of losing 100 percent of the amount if the toss goes against the bidder.

When it comes to the financial markets, the same concept applies. A government bond may cost $9,500 and mature to a $10,000 face value, which doesn't sound like much of a reward. The reason for the relatively high price (and relatively low reward) is that there is no risk. The markets will bid up the price very close to the $10,000 value just like our hypothetical crowd bidding on the guaranteed $100 bill.

However, if you look up a quote on a corporate bond with the same face value and maturity in "junk bond," status and you will see that it costs far less than the government bond. The crowd will never bid the price of the junk bond to the same level of the government bond due to the risk.

Understanding the risk-reward relationship makes it easier to see that deep-in-the-money options are *less risky* when compared to at-the-money or out-of-the-money strikes. There is a better chance for deep-in-the-money options to expire with intrinsic value; market participants therefore will bid their prices higher relative to other strikes.

For call options deep in the money, the lower the strike, the higher the price for any given expiration month. For put options the reverse is true; higher strikes will always cost more than lower strikes for a given expiration month.

Despite the number of ways we have shown that in-the-money options are relatively less risky than at-the-money or out-of-the-money strikes, new option investors tend to gravitate toward purchasing the riskier strikes.

They do so because they are convinced that spending a small amount of money in exchange for a potentially large reward means they are taking less risk. They consider only price without any regard to the *probability* of reaping the reward.

For similar reasons, **new option investors must understand that the odds of profiting from the purchase of a naked out-of-the-money option are very slim.** While those strikes may be tempting to buy due to their low price, you must realize those prices are low for a reason; that reason is risk. When purchasing a naked out-of-the-money option, be prepared to lose your entire investment.

When starting out in options, buy in-the-money calls and puts as directional substitutes for your long and short stock positions. It will take some faith to accept the fact that you must spend more money than "necessary," but the added safety provided through the low time value and break-even point will be your reward. The 80 to 85 delta option will still cost far less than the stock and provide all the leverage and protection you need.

Although options can be traded by themselves for directional plays, they can also be used in coordination with stock or other options. Chapter 7 looks at one of the most popular combination strategies for new option investors: the covered call/buy-write strategy.

Covered Call/Buy-Write Strategy

F or better or worse, the majority of main stream investors purchase stock with the expectation of holding their shares for an extended period of time. Investors do this mainly because the media and industry professionals have drilled, year after year that it is best to buy and hold; and there is a certain comfort level for many investors in that strategy. The recent bull market phenomenon also fueled this mind-set because the buy-and-hold strategy worked extremely well—for a while. Whether the buy-and-hold strategy is still the most efficient way of investing remains a topic for discussion especially after the 2008–2009 market meltdown. However, it has been and remains the strategy that most investors are comfortable with and tend to follow.

FOUNDATIONS OF THE STRATEGY

The first strategy we will be discussing is a hybrid of the buy-and-hold strategy. This strategy provides for better and more consistent returns on your initial investment when compared to naked stock ownership alone.

When we buy a stock, there are three possible outcomes. Two of these scenarios are generally negative, and only one outcome is generally positive. If the stock goes up, that is good. If the stock goes down, that is bad. And if the stock stays still, that is also a bad outcome. Not only do you have a loss in opportunity cost (the money invested in your stagnant stock could be making you money if it was somewhere else), but also you have incurred commission costs on both the way in and the way out.

131

Thus, in the case of buying stock, only one of the three scenarios provides a positive return.

For the sake of description, the three potential scenarios as the *up scenario*, the *down scenario*, and the *stagnant scenario*. By employing the covered call or buy-write strategy, you can change the potential outcome of the scenario profile so you have two positive potential results instead of only one.

If you employ the covered call or buy-write, you still have the up scenario as a positive result, but now the stagnant scenario also produces a positive result since you collect a premium, and the third scenario, the down scenario, will not be as negative. Thanks to the covered call strategy, now two of three scenarios end in a positive result and the third has a result that is less negative.

There are two components of the covered call strategy: the stock component and the option component.

The *stock component* consists of a long stock position (you own the stock). The *option component* consists of selling 1 call per every 100 shares of stock owned.

Remember, 1 option contract is worth 100 shares of stock. For example, 1,000 shares of stock equals 10 call contracts; 200 shares of stock equals 2 call contracts. Note that the ratio of stock to calls always must be exactly 100 shares to 1 option contract.

The philosophy behind the covered call strategy is not complicated. It entails acquiring a long stock position along with a short call option to create a positive stream of additional income, much in the same way a person would purchase a house and then lease it out to collect rent in order to pay the mortgage.

Another analogy is that of the insurance company. An insurance company receives premiums month in and month out. Over a period of time, this constant stream of income easily builds to a point where it outweighs any payout the insurance company may face, even for catastrophic events.

The constant and recurring collection of option premiums works better if done over longer periods of time (e.g., twelve months).

While the premium received from the sale of any given call may not be too significant, the constant and recurring collection of option premiums is what makes the strategy so successful. For this reason, the covered call usually works better if done over longer periods of time (e.g., one year). This time frame increases probability for a successful outcome.

By selling the call, the investor reduces the cost basis of the stock, which lowers the break-even point. The lowering of the break-even point allows the investor to profit even when the stock price is stagnant. In fact, as long as the stock price doesn't fall below the break-even point, the investor is still able to realize potential gains.

For example, assume you purchase 100 shares of stock for $50.00 and sell a one-month $50.00 call for $2.00. You will spend $5,000.00 for the stock but receive $200.00 for the sale of the call thus spending a total of $4,800.00, or $48.00 per share.

However, in exchange for that benefit, you are now giving up all price appreciation above $50.00. If the stock price is above $50.00 at expiration, you will be assigned on the short call and be required to deliver your 100 shares for the $50.00 strike. No matter how high the price of the stock may be, the most you will receive is $50.00.

From a profit and loss standpoint, this covered call example looks like Figure 7.1.

Figure 7.1 shows that the profit and loss curve flattens out for all stock prices above the $50.00 strike. Again, that is because the most you will ever receive is $50.00 for the sale of those shares. You have effectively sold off the rights to that portion of the profit and loss chart. Notice that the break-even point is, in fact, shifted lower, to $48.00. That's due to the $2.00 premium received from the sale of the call.

Probably the most notable observation of the profit and loss diagram is that the covered call writer retains 100 percent of the downside risk in the stock. That's important to understand. The reason is that many new investors learn about the covered call and buy the stocks that provide the

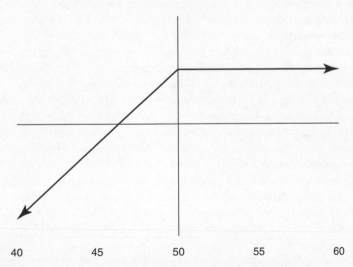

| 40 | 45 | 50 | 55 | 60 |

FIGURE 7.1 Covered Call P&L (Buy Stock for $50.00, Sell $50 Call for $2.00)

greatest option premiums. That's a roundabout way of searching for the stocks with the highest volatility and therefore the highest risk.

Figure 7.1 clearly shows that the covered call strategy is neutral to slightly bullish in nature. You would not sell a call against shares you thought were going to take off to the moon, and, more important, you should not buy stock to write calls against if you feel the stock price is going to fall.

Now let's talk about the odds. Several studies have been done on the topic of premium buying versus premium selling. The primary goal of the studies was to determine whether it is better to buy or sell options. Several option trading units tracked premium buying versus premium selling. The goal was to determine whether it was better to buy or sell options. The year-long tracking found that selling the premium was the correct trade 75 to 83 percent of the time. That is a very high percentage and is worth taking advantage of when a good opportunity presents itself.

Let's recall some of the terms we have studied before and see how they apply to this strategy.

The *covered call strategy* takes advantage of the fact that an option is a depreciating asset because its extrinsic value goes to zero at expiration. The process by which an option's extrinsic value dissipates is called time decay.

Time decay, also known as theta, is defined as the rate by which an option's value erodes into expiration. The value of the option over parity to the stock is called extrinsic value.

Since an option is a depreciating asset, meaning it has a limited life, the extrinsic value in the option will wither away daily until expiration. This "decay" is not a linear function. (It is not equally distributed between all of the days to expiration.) As the option gets closer to expiration, the daily rate of decay increases and continues to increase daily until expiration of the option. As more time goes by, the option's *extrinsic value* decreases. At expiration, all options in the expiration month, calls and puts, in the money and out of the money, will be completely devoid of extrinsic value. Again, it is important to note that the rate of this decrease is not linear; it is not smooth and even throughout the life of the option contract.

An option contract learns to experience the decay curve increasing when the option has about 45 days to expiration. It increases rapidly again at about 30 days out and really starts losing its value in the last two weeks before expiration. This is like a boulder rolling down a hill. The farther it goes down the hill, the more steam it picks up until the hill ends. By selling the option and owning the stock, the covered call seller captures the extrinsic value in the option by holding the short call until expiration. As mentioned earlier, an option's loss of extrinsic value over its life is called time decay. In the covered call strategy, the option's time decay works to the seller's advantage in that the more that time goes by, the more the extrinsic value decreases. As the extrinsic value decreases, the price of the option decreases. As the price of the option decreases, the option seller benefits from having sold the option at a higher price.

 KEY POINT

The covered call strategy provides the investor with an additional opportunity to gain income from a long stock position. The strategy not only produces gains when the stock trades up but also provides above average returns in a stagnant period while offsetting losses when the stock declines in price.

We have now seen how a covered call strategy is constructed and how it is intended to work. Keep in mind that the trade can be entered into in two ways: You can either sell calls against stock you already own (covered call), or you can buy stock and sell calls against them simultaneously (buy-write).

PERFORMANCE IN DIFFERENT SCENARIOS

Take this example: you own 1,000 shares of Oracle at $9.50.

The stock has been stuck around this level for a long time now, and you have grown impatient. You finally give in and sell the front month (e.g., November) at-the-money calls. The at-the-money calls would have a strike price of $10.00 if the stock was trading at $9.50.

You sell the calls at a $0.50 premium per contract, which creates a $10.50 break-even point. Remember, in a buy-write or covered call, the break-even point is the strike price plus the option premium. Let's look at what our returns will be in each of the three scenarios.

Up Scenario

In the up scenario, the maximum gain that can be attained is the stock finishing at $10.00. At $10.00, you would profit from the full value of the extrinsic value of the option, which is $0.50, and you would also have $0.50 of capital appreciation from the stock, for a total of $1.00. This represents a 10.52 percent one-month return, or an annualized return of 126.32 percent.

It is not realistic to expect this type of return every month, but remember, recent studies show that premium selling works approximately 80 percent of the time, which is still very good. We stated earlier that the maximum return of this buy-write will be actualized when the stock reaches $10.00 and the maximum return will be $1.00, and no more than $1.00. As the stock goes higher, the option will earn less in direct proportion to the increase in capital appreciation.

For example, if the stock closes at $10.30, you would receive only $0.20 from the option. The option would now be worth $0.30 because with the stock at $10.30, the 10 strike call would have $0.30 of intrinsic value. Since you sold the option at $0.50, you would see a $0.20 profit now that the value of the option you are short has declined in value ($0.50 − $0.30 = $0.20). Since you bought the stock at $9.50 and it is now $10.30, you have $0.80 of capital appreciation. Combine the two and you have a $1.00 profit.

In a third example, if the stock trades up as little at $0.10, you still have a $0.60 gain. You will receive $0.50 from the sale of the call that would expire out of the money (i.e., worthless) plus $0.10 of capital appreciation. That $0.60 represents a 6.3% one-month return.

Take note that if the stock closes over $10.00, your stock will be called away because your short calls will be exercised. We will talk about position management later. For now, let's get back to our three scenarios.

In the up scenario, you would profit with the buy-write when the stock is up as little as $0.01, but you are also limited on your maximum profit, as defined by this formula:

Maximum Profit = Strike Price + Option Price − Stock Price.

This method of calculation will work every time. As you see, the buy-write has a positive but limited upside potential.

Stagnant Scenario

When the covered call strategy is applied to the stagnant stock scenario, a negative return scenario is turned it into a positive one. Remember, when we sell an option, we receive a premium for doing so. When the stock does not move during the option's life, the extrinsic value of the option goes to zero. The amount of money paid for the option goes to the seller. Take a look at how this sets up. Let's go back to our previous example with the stock trading at exactly $9.50. We sell the front-month, at-the-money call, which would be the 10 strike call. We sell the front-month 10 strike calls at $0.50.

As time goes by, there is less chance for the option to become in the money. As this happens, the extrinsic value lessens and finally, after Friday expiration, the option is worthless. The stock finishes at $10.00 and you have received no capital appreciation, but you have received the full $0.50 of extrinsic value from the option sale. If the studies are correct and selling the premium works 78 to 80 percent of the time, then you will collect approximately $4.00 per contract sold over the course of the year.

As the examples demonstrate, writing covered calls against a stagnant stock can provide you with an acceptable return instead of frustration and wasted time and capital.

Down Scenario

In the final scenario, where your stock purchase is headed down into negative territory, the covered call strategy can help minimize your losses. Although you can't avoid picking losers and incurring losses, you can minimize and control these problems. Let's take a look at how the buy-write can help us do that.

For example, let's say you bought a stock for $9.50 and at the end of the month it had traded down to $8.50. You would have a $1.00 loss on our investment. However, if you had sold the 10 strike calls for $0.50, you would have only a $0.50 loss. You would have a $1.00 capital loss in the stock but a $0.50 option gain from selling the option, which would expire worthless. If you were going to buy the stock anyway and incur a possible loss, it is better to take a $0.50 loss than a $1.00 loss. In this down scenario, the option premium received helped to offset the capital loss. If the stock is down more than the amount you received for selling the call, then the option premium serves as an offset to the loss of the stock.

However, you can still make money in the down scenario using the covered strategy if the stock is down only a small amount. There is a scenario in the buy-write strategy where you can profit from owning a stock that is lower than where you bought it. Going back to the previous example, you bought a stock for $9.50 and you sold the front-month 10 strike calls for $0.50. At expiration, the stock finishes down $0.20 at $9.30. You would have incurred a $0.20 loss on your stock. However, with the stock at $9.30, the 10 strike call that you sold for $0.50 is now worthless. So, you have a $0.20 loss on the stock and a $0.50 gain from the option premium sold. This leaves you with a gain of $0.30 on a stock that is down $0.20 since the time you purchased it.

To recap: In the down scenario, your loss will be offset by the option premium you received, so your loss will not be as severe. You still may incur a loss, but it will be minimized, and minimizing losses is a key to successful investing.

Summary

For a complete breakdown of these three scenarios and the profit and loss occurring, refer to Table 7.1.

TABLE 7.1 Covered Call Profit and Loss (Stock Price $9.50)

Strike Price	Stock P&L	Option P&L	Total P&L
12.00	+2.50	−1.50	+1.00
11.50	+2.00	−1.00	+1.00
11.00	+1.50	−.50	+1.00
10.50	+1.00	0	+1.00
*10.00	+.50	+.50	+1.00
9.75	+.25	+.50	+.75
9.50	0	+.50	+.50
9.25	−.25	+.50	+.25
9.00	−.50	+.50	0
8.50	−1.00	+.50	−.50

*ATM option $0.50.

Now that we have discussed how to construct a buy-write strategy and how it will provide returns in the three different scenarios, I feel it is sensible to talk about the concept of lean.

LEAN

As mentioned, professional traders use the term *lean* to refer to one's perception about the directional strength of a stock. When you own a stock and intend to hold it for a period of time, you are aware that you will probably be holding it while it goes up and while it goes down. This means that at any given time, you might have a different opinion of the potential movement of that stock. Knowing this, there is a way to address your current level of confidence, or lean. You do this by your choice of which option you sell.

While it is true that the at-the-money option has the most extrinsic value, it might not always be the ideal option to sell in every situation. For instance, if you feel that the stock itself has a very high chance of producing capital appreciation above the potential amount of premium you could receive from selling an at-the-money call, sell an out-of-the-money-call so you can allow yourself a little more room to the upside on the stock.

For example, let's say the stock is trading at $27.00. Normally, you would sell the 27.5 calls at, say, $1.00. If the stock were to rise quickly and eclipse the $28.50 mark, then with the buy-write strategy, your position would have maxed out at $28.50, and you would have a $1.50 one-month gain. Not bad, but if the stock went to $29.50, then you would have missed out on another $1.00 profit. However, if you had sold the 30 calls for $0.30, you would have another outcome. You bought the stock at $27.00 and sold the 30 calls for $0.30 and the stock goes to $29.50. You would have made $2.50 in capital appreciation and $0.30 in option premium for a total of a $2.80 return.

Therefore, if you feel the stock has a real good shot at taking a run up, you can lean your position long by selling an out-of-the-money call. If you have a more neutral view on your stock, you would sell an at-the-money-call in order to receive a bigger premium, which allows for greater downside protection if the stock trades down and higher potential profit if the stock becomes stagnant.

This strategy also works on the downside. If, by chance, you feel that the stock may trade down a bit during the life of the option, then you can sell an in-the-money call. The effect of doing this would be to provide you with a little extra premium to cover more downside risk.

Remember, when you sell an option, you seek to capture extrinsic value. An in-the-money option not only has extrinsic value but also some intrinsic value. When you feel that you want to lean your covered call strategy (buy-write) a little short, choose to sell an in-the-money call so you can also have some intrinsic value to cover your downside.

As an example, say your stock is trading at $29.00. You feel that your stock may trade down a little but still remain in an uptrend cycle. You don't want to get rid of the stock but you also don't want to lose any money so you sell the 27.5 call at $2.00. The stock starts to trade down and finishes at $26.00. If you had owned the stock naked, you would have lost $3.00, since you owned the stock at $29.00 and it closed at $26.00 on expiration. However, because you sold the 27.5 calls at $2.00, you would realize only a $1.00 loss in the stock. The premium received will offset the loss due to the fact that you identified and adjusted for a likely move. As you can see, the buy-write strategy can be altered to fit any directional view you have on your selected stock.

Finally, if you intend to use the buy-write strategy successfully, you generally need to sell the calls against your stock on a consistent, recurring interval over a period of time. This means that you will have to be prepared to roll your calls out to the next month come expiration. Sometimes all you will need to do is to sell the next month out call.

ROLLING THE POSITION

In options, *rolling* is defined as moving a position from one strike to another vertically in the same month, horizontally to another month, or some combination thereof. Other times you may have to buy your short call back so that you will not lose your stock. Sometimes you may even want to allow the stock to be called away if you have decided that it has reached a level where you want to take your profits and begin to look for another opportunity.

The term *roll* means to move your position either out to the next strike or to move your position up or down a strike in the same month. It means *to move*.

Rolling is normally done via time spread and vertical spreads. Without getting into the trading of spreads, which is a unique strategy in itself, I will talk a little about the roll.

As stated, the covered call strategy is most effective when executed month in and month out over an extended period of time. In order to do this, investors must reinitiate the position every month at the option expiration. The reinitiation of the position every month is where the term *rolling* comes from. However, there may be times when you want to give yourself a little more upside room for capital appreciation. In those rare cases, you will not want to roll the position, because it might be called away if the call you sold is exercised when it becomes in the money.

When option expiration approaches, your short option can be either in the money or out of the money. As we discuss the two potential outcomes, let's first assume that we want to hold onto our stock.

If the option is going to finish out of the money, you would let it expire worthless and then sell the next month's call. If the option is going to expire in the money and you want to keep the stock, you will need to buy the short option back and sell the next month's call.

This trade will consist of two option trades. You will be buying one option and selling another, which is commonly known as a *spread* and is referred to as a *single trade*.

So, when you roll out your covered call or buy-write, you do it by doing a spread. The front-month option, the one that you happen to be short, will be bought back, thus ensuring you keep your stock.

The second-month option will be sold short, thus reinitiating your covered call strategy. The position that remains is long stock and short calls. There are some choices regarding the selection process for the spread used to roll the position.

Of course, there is no choice for the front-month option; you must buy back the option you are short. However, you do have a choice regarding the next month's option you are going to sell; will it be near term or farther out in expiration?

This goes back to our earlier discussion about lean. If you are no longer bullish, you would not have bought back your short call. You would have allowed it to be exercised and have the stock called away from you. If you choose to roll the position, you must be somewhat bullish on the stock. Your lean will dictate which new option you should sell.

EXAMPLES

For now, let's look at four good candidates for the covered call/buy-write strategy.

Example 1: McDonald's

Figure 7.2 shows a chart for McDonald's (MCD) covering a period of a little more than one year.

Notes

Covered Call

1. Around June 2, 2003, McDonald's breaks out through a resistance level established back in late November–early December 2002 after failing to break that resistance level in mid-May 2003.

FIGURE 7.2 MCD Daily Chart
Source: Courtesy of Think or Swim (www.thinkorswim.com)

2. McDonald's climbs up from $20.00 to the $25.00 range in a slow gradual uptrend steplike pattern. This type of pattern is an opportunity for buy-writers because this type of gradual rise normally brings about a decreasing implied volatility period, which is great for premium selling.

3. Notice the size of the daily vertical lines during the period from mid-August 2003 to December 2003. The size of the lines represents the daily trading range of the stock. As you can see, the lines are very short, which indicates that the stock does not move much intraday. Again, this is an indication of decreasing volatility, which is a positive sign for buy writers.

Conclusion　The two most prominent and noticeable patterns both bode well for buy writers. The covered call strategy does not need a lack of movement as much as slow, consistent nonvolatile movement.

So, in the case of McDonald's, the slow trending movement of the stock brings about a decreasing volatility. Added to this is the contraction of intraday movement, shown by the decreasing range of daily trading.

These two factors each contribute to decreasing volatility and provide an opportune time to write a covered call. This type of pattern offers both capital appreciation and premium returns.

Example 2: J. P. Morgan

Figure 7.3 shows J. P. Morgan (JPM) over a nine-month period from April 2003 to mid-January 2004

Notes

Covered Call

1. By June of 2003, J. P. Morgan had traded up from a lower trading range in the $25.00 area to a new range around $35.00.

2. Since entering the new trading range in June, the stock has consolidated into a relatively flat, horizontal trading channel. For the most part, this channel is only around $3.00 to $4.00 wide.

3. This trading channel is not only tight, but it seems to be equally dispersed around the $35.00 mark. The stock does not seem to venture very far on either side of $35.00.

4. From the time that the stock enters the trading channel, the range of the channel has been decreasing, or tightening, which indicates decreasing volatility.

JPM	⬇️🔖JPMorgan Chase & Co.	✂️🖊 D 📈 Style ✏️Drawings 📊Studies

JPM 10 y D │ D: 12/19/08 │O: 30.11│H: 31.25│L: 29.78│C: 30.32│ R: 1.47

FIGURE 7.3 JPM Daily Chart
Source: Courtesy of Think or Swim (www.thinkorswim.com)

Conclusion J. P. Morgan sets up a classic textbook buy-write opportunity. After finding a new trading range, the stock consolidates into a tight trading channel that is almost horizontal. Further, this channel tightens and does not deviate from $35.00 to the point where it even comes close to a channel line violation.

Here an investor would most likely be interested in writing the 35 strike price calls to collect premium as the stock trades sideways. Obviously, there is no way to predict how long a stock will consolidate like this, but the risks are low, and in this case, the covered call strategy would have returned some very nice, low-risk returns over this period.

Example 3: Dell Computer

Figure 7.4 is a chart of Dell Computer (DELL) from November 2002 through December 2003. It shows another great technical setup for the covered call.

Notes

Covered Call

1. After dropping out of a higher trading range, Dell trades down throughout the months of December 2002, January 2003, and into

FIGURE 7.4 DELL Daily Chart
Source: Courtesy of Think or Swim (www.thinkorswim.com)

mid-February 2003 before bottoming out. During this period, the drop was a low-volatility, gradual one in which the stock loss could have been well offset by premium collection.

2. After rebounding off a low around $22.50 in mid-February, Dell rebounded quickly to the $26.00–$27.00 level, where it consolidated until mid-March. The stock traded in a tight band until starting to trade up.

3. After the consolidating period, Dell began a slow, deliberate rise over the course of the next nine or so months, with most months showing an overall trading range of $2.00 or less. The long, slow, steplike growth pattern can be seen both in the daily trading ranges and in the monthly trading ranges. This is very favorable to writing covered calls.

Conclusion   Dell spent the better portion of nine months trading up in a manner that is suggestive of decreasing volatility. Because the stock was in a gradual up trend, a buy writer would have been able to profit from capital appreciation and have a good chance at seeing a positive return in terms of the collection of premiums.

Furthermore, during Dell's down cycle, the stock traded down slowly enough to be able to receive several months of premium. This should have at least partially offset enough of the loss to allow the trader time to profit from the subsequent recovery.

FIGURE 7.5 FON Daily Chart
Source: Courtesy of Think or Swim (www.thinkorswim.com)

Example 4: Sprint Corporation

Let's take a look at one last chart. Figure 7.5 shows Sprint Corporation (FON) from November 2002 through December 2003.

Notes

Covered Call

1. After a large drop at the end of January 2003, Sprint consolidates around $12.00 and trades in a relatively tight range, around $12.00, for approximately five months, until mid-May 2003. This period is the first opportunity for premium collection.

2. At the end of May 2003, Sprint trades up to the top of its trading range in a slow, methodical way, indicating a period of decreasing volatility.

3. Sprint breaks out of its old trading range by trading through resistance set by the two highs in February, around $13.25. It develops a new trading range at the $15.00 level by trading up in a slow, steplike pattern which also indicates a period of decreasing volatility.

4. Sprint trades around the $15.50 range and really tightens up from October 2003 through January 2004. This again is a long period of decreasing volatility.

Conclusion   Sprint shows two favorable patterns here that are friendly to covered call writing. The first is that Sprint shows the tendency to trade in a tight range for extended periods of time, as seen in February–May 2003 and July–December 2003. This is advantageous for premium collection.

The second is that when Sprint does move, it mostly trades up in a slow, directional way, as opposed to gapping (with the exception of January 2003). These slow upward directional moves work well for covered call writers in two ways: capital appreciation and premium capturing.

COVERED CALL/BUY-WRITE SYNOPSIS

Construction. Long stock, short one call for every 100 shares of stock owned.

Function. To enhance profitability of stock ownership and to provide limited downside protection against adverse stock movement.

Bias. Neutral to slightly bullish.

When to Use. When you feel stock will trade up slightly or in a tight range for a period of time and you plan on holding the stock for longer term.

Profit Scenario. If stock rises, your profit will be enhanced by the premium received. If stock stagnates, you will profit from the premium received from the call sale.

Loss Scenario. If stock trades lower than the point defined by your purchase price minus the premium received from call sale, you will lose dollar for dollar. The call premium received will act as an offset to the loss in the stock.

Key Concepts. If stock trades up aggressively, you will profit only up to a stock price defined by the strike price plus the option price. If stock continues higher above that point (break-even), you will incur lost opportunity. Further, if stock closes above strike price, stock will be called away unless you make the necessary adjustment. This is philosophically identical to the sell-write position except it is in opposite direction. Time decay helps the position.

CHAPTER 8

The Covered Put/Sell-Write Strategy

Many investors and traders would assume that the covered put or sell-write strategy is the opposite strategy of the covered call or buy-write strategy. From the sounds of their names, that would be a logical conclusion. However, in actuality, the covered put (sell-write) and the covered call (buy-write) are philosophically identical strategies. If you understand the covered call, then you understand the covered put.

The philosophy behind these strategies is not complicated. They are both premium collection strategies. Both of these provide profit opportunity when stocks are stagnant (i.e., the stock moves in a very tight trading range). Two different strategies are needed because the covered call, is used when the stock is stagnant but has the possibility of upward movement. The covered put is used when stock is stagnant but a possible downward movement is anticipated.

As an investor, if you feel that a stock is going to trade in a tight range for a period of time but may possibly trade up slightly, the covered call strategy would be a good selection. Likewise, if you feel that a stock is going to trade in a tight range for a period of time but may possibly trade down slightly, the covered put is the strategy you want to use.

We previously discussed the covered call/buy-write; now let's look at the covered put/sell-write strategy.

REVIEWING SELLING SHORT

Before we start, it is important that we first define and explain (or review for some of you) what is meant by selling a stock short. *Selling stock short* is the process by which investors/traders sell a stock that they do not own. To do that, they investor/trader "borrow" the stock from their broker or clearing firm for a fee, which is usually an interest rate charge. The idea is for investors to borrow the stock from their broker, sell it to someone else, then replace (at a lower cost) the borrowed stock.

Let's use an example to see how this works.

You feel that Google (NASDAQ symbol GOOG) is extremely over-priced at $200.00 per share. You call your broker and say, "Sell 100 shares of Google short at $200.00."

Your broker sells the shares for you, and your position reflects the sale of short stock as a −100 shares. Your brokerage firm, meanwhile, has lent you the shares itself or has borrowed the shares from another brokerage.

Three weeks later, Google has traded down to $170.00. You instruct your broker to buy back the 100 shares of Google, or *cover* your short position. Those 100 shares are sold and then returned to your brokerage firm.

You now have no position in Google and whoever lent you the stock now has their shares back. But remember, you originally sold the 100 shares at $20,000.00. Now you have now bought back the borrowed 100 shares for $17,000.00—a $3,000.00 profit.

From that $3,000.00 profit, you have to deduct a fee for borrowing the stock. This fee is generally the normal margin rate your broker charges you on your margin account.

Needless to say, you will still be sitting on a profit.

Of course, there also exists the possibility of loss. So, as always, first discuss with your broker your intentions or interest in short selling and ask what criteria and collateral are necessary to set up such an account. Every brokerage firm has different rules and guidelines on margin accounts. Make sure they explain all of the rules, procedures, risks, and rewards of short selling and margin accounts.

FOUNDATIONS OF THE STRATEGY

We reviewed selling short because using the covered put entails using a short stock position along with a short put option to create a positive stream of additional income.

The process is similar to a person purchasing a house and then leasing it out to collect rent in order to pay for the mortgage.

The sell-write provides the option seller with a premium. While the stock may remain stagnant, offering no capital gain, the premium from the option sale provides a stream of profit. The constant and recurring collection of option premiums works better if done over longer periods of time (e.g., twelve months). That time frame increases your probabilities for a successful outcome.

Seller or Buyer

Remember from past discussions what we've learned about the odds. Studies have been done on the topic of premium buying versus premium selling to determine whether it is better to buy options or sell options. The studies have found that selling the premium was the correct trade 75 to 83 percent of the time, though that finding has been disputed. However, the stream of premiums is worth taking advantage of when a good opportunity presents itself.

When a stock is purchased, there are three possible outcomes. As we discussed previously, two of those outcomes are generally negative while only one outcome is positive.

The same ratio applies to selling a stock short. Of the three potential outcomes, two are bad and only one is good. If the stock goes down, that is good. If the stock goes up, that is bad. If the stock stays still, that is also bad because you have incurred commission costs on both the way in and on way out.

Effect of the Covered Put

Let's see what happens to our three potential outcomes (up, down, and stagnant) using the covered put strategy. By employing the covered put or sell-write strategy, you can change the outcome of the scenario profile so you have two positive potential results instead of only one. You change the good to bad ratio and limit your risk while providing an opportunity for profit.

Using the covered put or sell-write, we still have the down scenario as a positive result, but now the stagnant scenario will also produce a positive result, since we collect a premium. The third scenario, the down scenario, will not be as negative. Thanks to the covered put strategy, now two of three scenarios end in a positive result and the third has a result that is less negative.

Construction

There are two components of the covered put strategy, the stock component and the option component. The stock component consists of a short stock position (you sell the stock short). The option component consists of selling 1 put per every 100 shares of stock sold short. Please take special note that the ratio of short stock to short puts must be exactly 1 short put option contract per every 100 shares sold short.

How It Works

The *covered put strategy* takes advantage of the fact that an option is a depreciating asset, because its extrinsic value or time value goes to zero at expiration. The process by which an option's extrinsic value dissipates is called *time decay*.

Since an option is a depreciating asset, meaning it has a limited life, the extrinsic value in the option will wither away daily until expiration. This "decay" is not a linear function, which means it is not equally distributed among all of the days to expiration.

As the option gets closer to expiration, the daily rate of decay increases and continues to increase day after day until expiration of the option. At expiration, all options in the expiration month, both calls and puts, in the money, at the money, and out of the money, are completely devoid of extrinsic value, as noted in the time value decay charts (Figure 4.12).

Remember, as more time continues to pass, the option's extrinsic value progressively decreases. Again, it is important to note that the rate of this decrease is not linear; it is not smooth and even throughout the life of the option contract.

As mentioned, the option contract begins to experience the decay curve increasing when the option has about 45 days to expiration. It increases rapidly again at about 30 days out and really starts losing its value in the last two weeks before expiration.

By selling the put option and shorting the stock, the covered put seller captures the extrinsic value in the option by holding the short put until expiration. It is hoped that the option expires worthless and you have the premium paid for its sale.

In the covered put strategy, the option's time decay works to the seller's advantage in that the more time that goes by, the more the extrinsic value decreases.

While the stock may remain stagnant, offering no capital gain, the premium from the option sale provides a stream of profit. Just as with the covered call, the constant and recurring collection of option premiums works better if done over longer periods of time to allow the odds to play into your favor. By selling the put against short shares of stock, you shift the odds in your favor for a profit since two of the three possible stock price sequences become profitable.

Because a stock price can go up, down, or sideways, a short stock position by itself makes money only if the stock price falls. If the stock price rises, losses result. If the stock price moves sideways, nominal losses result due to commissions and possible interest charges from the broker.

While interest charges may seem insignificant, they are the primary reason that most short sellers do not make a profit.

The daily accrual of interest effectively reduces the credit balance you received from shorting the shares. Unless the stock makes a quick, aggressive downward move, most short sellers lose money for no other reason than interest charges. However, after selling the put, short sellers increase their chance for profit since they can now profit from a sideways stock price as well as a downward move.

KEY POINT

The covered put strategy provides investors with another opportunity to gain income from a short stock position. The strategy not only produces gains when the stock trades down but also provides above-average returns in a stagnant period, while offsetting losses when the stock increases in price.

Remember that one component of the covered put is the short stock. Keep in mind that you can enter this position in two ways: You can either sell puts against stock you are already short (covered put) or you can short stock and sell puts against those shares at the expiration.

PERFORMANCE IN DIFFERENT SCENARIOS

Take this example: You sell short 1,000 shares of IBM at $101.00.

The stock has been running up aggressively and has finally settled down around this level for a while. Volume has declined steadily over the last several days. Now you feel that the stock has exhausted itself and is likely to stagnate or even pull back a bit. Seeking to take advantage of this perceived opportunity, you sell the stock short and sell the front month (e.g., December) at-the-money puts. The at-the-money puts would have a strike price of $100.00 if the stock was trading at $101.00.

You sell the puts at a $3.50 premium per contract, which creates a $104.50 break-even point. In a sell-write, the break-even point is calculated by adding the stock sale price plus the option premium. Let's look at what our returns will be in each of the three scenarios.

Down Scenario

In the down scenario, the maximum gain that can be realized is at expiration, when the stock closes at $100.00 or lower.

At $100.00, you would profit from the full value of the extrinsic value of the option, which is $3.50, and you would also have $1.00 of capital appreciation from the stock for a total of $4.50. This represents a 4.5 percent one-month return or an annualized return of 53.5 percent. Remember, it is not realistic to expect this type of return every month.

We stated earlier that the maximum return of this sell-write will be actualized when the stock reaches $100.00 or below and the maximum return will be $4.50, and no more than $4.50. As the stock goes lower than $96.50, the put option will actually start to lose but in direct proportion to the increase in capital appreciation, thus fixing your maximum gain at $4.50.

Let's look at what happens when the stock trades down to $90.00 and see if you again have a $4.50 return on the position. At $90.00, the option will have $10.00 of intrinsic value (stock price – strike price) because it is in the money.

You sold the put option at $3.50 so you have a $6.50 loss. However, you sold the stock for $101.00; therefore, you have an $11.00 capital gain. Combined, you again have a $4.50 profit.

In a third example, if the stock trades down as little at $0.50, you still have a $4.00 gain.

You will receive $0.50 from the sale of the stock via capital appreciation, but you will also receive the full amount of premium ($3.50) from the sale of the put that would expire out of the money, thus worthless.

Refer to Table 8.1 for examples of total dollar profits per number of contracts, remembering that each contract controls 100 shares of stock.

Understand that in the down scenario, with the stock closing below $100.00, stock will be put to you (assigned) because your short puts will be exercised. The effect will be that you will have to have your short stock position bought back for you. This will close out your position but will not affect the previously discussed profit.

Depending on your opinion of the future movements of the stock, there are several different ways to proceed. You can continue the position,

TABLE 8.1 Total Dollar Profits

Contracts	Stock Profit	Option Profit	Total Profit
1	$0.50	$3.50	$400.00
5	$0.50	$3.50	$2,000.00
10	$0.50	$3.50	$4,000.00
20	$0.50	$3.50	$8,000.00
50	$0.50	$3.50	$20,000.00
100	$0.50	$3.50	$40,000.00

change the position, or just allow the position to close out. We will talk about position management later.

For now, let's get back to our three scenarios. In the down scenario, you would profit with the sell-write when the stock is down as little as $0.01, but you are also limited on your maximum profit, as defined by this formula:

Maximum Profit = Stock Price – the sum of (Strike Price – Option Price)

This method of calculation will work every time. As you see, the sell-write has a positive but limited profit potential to the downside.

Stagnant Scenario

When we apply the covered put strategy to the stagnant stock scenario, we take a negative return scenario and turn it into a positive return scenario. Remember, when we sell an option, we receive a premium for doing so.

When the stock does not move during the option's life, the extrinsic value of the option goes to zero. The amount of money paid for the option goes to the seller. Let's look at how this sets up.

Let's go back to our previous example with the stock trading at exactly $101.00. We sold the front-month, at-the-money put (the December 100 put) at $3.50.

As time goes by, there is less chance for the option to move to becoming in the money. As this happens, the extrinsic value lessens and finally, after Friday expiration, the option is worthless.

The stock finishes at $101.00, and you have received no capital appreciation, but you have received the full $3.50 of extrinsic value from the option sale due to time decay. If the studies are correct and selling the premium works 80 percent of the time, then you will collect your premium as a profit approximately 9.6 months over the course of the year.

This total should be more than sufficient to offset the losses when the strategy does not work the remaining 2.5 months, leaving you with a respectable profit.

As the example demonstrates, selling covered puts against a stagnant short stock position can provide you with an acceptable return instead of frustration and wasted time and capital.

Up Scenario

In the final scenario, where the stock you shorted has traded up into an area that has created a capital loss, the covered put strategy can help minimize your losses.

Although picking losers and incurring losses is inescapable, it can be minimized and controlled.

Let's take a look at how the sell-write can help us do that.

Looking back at our example, let's say you sold IBM stock short at $101.00. If at the end of the month the stock had traded up to $105.00, you would have a $4.00 loss on your investment.

However, if you had sold the 100 strike puts for $3.50, you would have only a $0.50 loss.

You would have a $4.00 capital loss in the stock but a $3.50 option gain from selling the put, which would expire out of the money and worthless. In this up scenario, the option premium received from the put sale helped to offset the capital loss in the stock.

So, if the stock is up more than the amount you received for selling the put, the option premium serves as an offset to the loss of the stock position.

However, you can still make money in the up scenario using the covered put strategy if the stock is up only a small amount (the stock price is up less than the amount of premium received from the put sale). There is a scenario in the sell-write strategy where you can profit from shorting a stock that is higher than where you shorted it.

Again, going back to the previous example, you shorted IBM at $101.00 and you sold the front-month (December) 100 strike put for $3.50. At expiration, the stock finishes up $2.00 at $103.00. You would have incurred a $2.00 loss on your stock.

However, with the stock closing at $103.00 on expiration Friday of December, the 100 strike put that you sold for $3.50 is now out of the money and worthless. So, you have a $2.00 loss on the stock but a $3.50 gain from the option premium sold. This leaves you with a net gain of $1.50 on a stock that is up $2.00 since the time you shorted it.

To recap: In our third scenario, the up scenario, your loss will be offset by the option premium you received so it will not be as severe as if you were naked short the stock. You still may incur a loss, but it will be minimized, and minimizing losses is a key to successful investing.

For a complete breakdown of these three scenarios, refer to Table 8.2.

LEAN

Now that we have discussed how to construct a sell-write strategy and how it will provide returns in the three different scenarios, it is time to revisit lean.

TABLE 8.2 Profit and Loss: Sell-Write Scenarios

Stock Price	Stock P&L	Option P&L	Total P&L
93.00	+8.00	−3.50	+4.50
94.00	+7.00	−2.50	+4.50
95.00	+6.00	−1.50	+4.50
96.00	+5.00	−.50	+4.50
97.00	+4.00	+.50	+4.50
98.00	+3.00	+1.50	+4.50
99.00	+2.00	+2.50	+4.50
100.00	+1.00	+3.50	+4.50
101.00	0	+3.50	+3.50
102.00	−1.00	+3.50	+2.50
103.00	−2.00	+3.50	+1.50
104.00	−3.00	+3.50	+.50
105.00	−4.00	+3.50	−.50
106.00	−5.00	+3.50	−1.50

Professional traders use the term *lean* to refer to one's perception about the directional strength of a stock. As a trader/investor, you may follow a stock until you feel you know how it will behave.

At some point, you may short the stock. When you short a stock and intend to hold that position for a period of time (to earn capital appreciation), you are aware that you probably will be holding the position while the stock goes against you from time to time. The stock may take a little time to start its movement in the direction you have anticipated. During that period, the stock's normal gyrations may take it to a point where your confidence level may change.

For example, you may be very confident that a stock that ran up from $70.00 to $110.00 is going to sell off a bit. As it sells off and trades down to $100.00, it is possible—even quite probable—that your level of confidence for a continued sell-off to lower prices is not as high as it was when the stock was trading at $110.00.

With the stock at $100.00, already down $10.00, you may be pretty confident, but not very much so, that the sell off will continue. Obviously, you're not as confident as before but probably more confident than if the stock was trading down around $90.00. As the stock moves, so may your level of confidence, your lean. Does it make sense to make the same bet at different levels of confidence? Of course not!

Your lean must acknowledge the fact that at any given moment, you might have a different opinion of the potential movement of a stock. The way to address your changing levels of confidence is by leaning your position. You do this by choosing to sell options that give a certain level of protection and/or additional premium to your position, depending on your outlook on the stock.

While it is true that the at-the-money option has the greatest amount of extrinsic value, it is not always the ideal option to sell in every situation.

For instance, if you feel that a stock itself has a very high chance of trading down, producing capital appreciation above the potential amount of premium you could receive from selling an at-the-money put, then sell an out-of-the-money put. That will allow a little more room for capital appreciation to the downside on the stock.

Let's say a stock is trading at $30.00 at the beginning of May and you sell it short. Normally, in most cases with premium collection strategies, you would sell the at-the-money option, which is where the greatest amount of extrinsic value is located. In this example, you would select the front-month at-the-money puts (May 30 puts at $2.00). If the stock were to sell off quickly and break below the $28.00 mark, then with the sell-write strategy, your position would have maxed out at $28.00, and you would have a $2.00 one-month gain.

Not bad, but if the stock went to $27.00, you would have missed out on another $1.00 profit. However, if we had sold the $27.50 puts for $1.00, we would have another outcome. You sold the stock at $30.00 and sold the $27.50 put for $1.00 and the stock goes to $27.00.

You would have made $3.00 in capital appreciation and $0.50 in option premium for a total return of a $3.50. So, if you feel the stock has a good shot at really trading down, you can lean your position short by selling an out-of-the-money put.

If you have a more neutral view on your stock, you could sell an at-the-money put in order to receive a bigger premium that allows for greater protection if the stock trades up and higher potential profit if the stock becomes stagnant.

If, by chance, you feel that the stock may trade up a bit during the life of the option, you can sell an in-the-money put. The effect of this would be to provide you with a little extra premium to cover more upside risk.

Remember, when you sell an option, you seek to capture extrinsic value. An in-the-money option not only has some extrinsic value but also some intrinsic value.

When you feel that you want to lean your covered put strategy (sell-write) a little long, sell an in-the-money put so you can also have some intrinsic value to cover your upside risk.

As an example, say a stock you had sold short is trading at $47.50 and you feel that the stock may trade up a little but still remain in a down-trend cycle. You don't want to buy back the stock, but you also don't want to lose any money, so you sell the $50.00 puts at $3.50. The stock starts to trade up and finishes at $52.00. If you had shorted the stock naked, then you would have lost $4.50 since you shorted the stock at $47.50 and it closed at $52.00 on expiration.

However, because you sold the $50.00 puts at $3.50, you would have only a $1.00 loss in the position. The premium received will offset the loss since you identified and adjusted for a likely move.

As you can see, the sell-write strategy can be altered to fit any directional view (lean) you have on your selected stock.

ROLLING THE POSITION

Finally, if you intend to use the sell-write strategy successfully, you should sell the puts against your short stock on a consistent, recurring interval over a period of time.

This means that you will have to be prepared to "roll" your puts out to the next month come expiration. Sometimes all you'll need to do is to sell the next month-out put when your current short put expires worthless. Other times it may be necessary to do a little more.

For example, you may have to buy your short put back so that you will not lose your short stock position. Sometimes you may even want to allow the stock to be assigned to you if you have decided that it has reached a level where you want to take your profits and begin to look for another opportunity.

Remember, the covered put/sell-write strategy is a premium collection strategy that is philosophically identical to the covered call/buy-write except for anticipated stock direction. The covered put is used when you feel the stock will be stagnant or trade down a little. Like most premium collection strategies, it is most effective when executed month in and month out over an extended period of time.

Unless there has been a definite change in your confidence level about the future movements of your stock, stick with the covered put/sell write strategy for optimum results.

EXAMPLES

Let's take a look at several examples of when you might use the covered put/sell-write strategy in your trading.

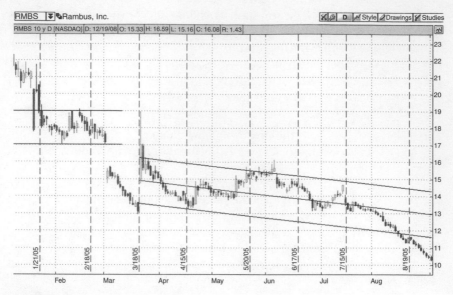

FIGURE 8.1   RMBS Daily Chart
Source: Courtesy of Think or Swim (www.thinkorswim.com)

Example 1: Rambus

Figure 8.1 shows a chart of Rambus (RMBS) from mid-January through August 2003 and a good technical setup for the covered put strategy.

Notes

Covered Put/Sell-Write

1. After breaking down out of a higher trading range in late February/early March, Rambus begins a new slow, steady downward trading channel.

2. The channel begins in a relatively volatile way, as shown in Figure 8.1 by the large gap breakdown, which puts in a new low and establishes the lower end of the new trading range. This is followed by a large gap opening several weeks later, which puts in the upper range of the new trading range.

3. Following this, volatility decreases, as can be seen by smaller-percentage moves and smaller candles within the trading range. This is a perfect time for the sell-write strategy, which takes advantage of slow, gradual downward stock moves.

4. The sell-write strategy will take advantage of the stock trading down via its short component, and also the passage of time and decreasing volatility via the short put.

5. When using the sell-write strategy, the premium received from the sale of the put will provide some protection toward the sale of the stock in case of a small upward movement of the stock.

Conclusion   Although the down-trending channel in Rambus starts out in a volatile fashion, the stock never really breaks out of its trading channel, which is good for sell writers.

The volatile start, however, actually benefits the position because the increased volatility will increase the price of the put the sell writer will be selling, which allows for even greater premium capture. Again, it is fortunate that the stock stays in the trend, even though it started out in such a volatile manner, but this turns out to benefit the sell writer.

Example 2: Bristol Myers

Figure 8.2 is a chart of Bristol Myers (BMY) from February through August 2003 and another good technical setup for the covered put strategy.

FIGURE 8.2   BMY Daily Chart
Source: Courtesy of Think or Swim (www.thinkorswim.com)

Notes

Covered Put/Sell-Write

1. After running up from late January to mid-April, Bristol Myers starts a new downward trading channel after failing to maintain new highs.

2. This downward trading channel is marked by a slow, gradual movement from a price of $26.50 in mid-April to a low of $24.50 in late August.

3. During this four-month gradual decline, we see a continuing pattern of lower highs and lower lows.

4. A sell-write position not only takes advantage of the downward movement of the stock by being short stock but also takes advantage of time decay and the decrease in volatility of the short put.

5. The short put also provides a minimal amount of protection to the upside for your short stock position, by the amount of premium brought in by your put sale.

Conclusion   Bristol Myers' well-defined down-trending trading channel is characteristic of a low- or decreasing-volatility event, due to the slow and consistent pace of the downward movement of the stock. The short delta of the position will benefit from the decreasing stock price, while the short put will benefit from decreasing volatility and the erosion of time.

Example 3: Merck Co.

Figure 8.3 is a chart of Merck Co. (MRK) from February through August 2003. It is a good chart pattern for the covered put strategy.

Notes

Covered Put/Sell-Write

1. Drug giant Merck begins trading into a long slow downside trading channel starting in April, which extends through late August.

2. This trend shows several lower highs and lower lows, indicating a continued, prolonged movement. This is an ideal pattern for the sell-write.

3. The downside movement of the stock is exactly what our sell-write short stock component needs, while the slow, gradual pace of the movement allows for a decreasing level of volatility. This combines to speed the rate of decay of the short put component of the sell-write.

FIGURE 8.3 MRK Daily Chart
Source: Courtesy of Think or Swim (www.thinkorswim.com)

4. Risk of the position lies within the construction of the sell-write itself. If the stock were to trade up, our short stock position could lead to sharp losses. The sell-write short put position allows for some protection, but only up to the amount of premium received from the sale of the put.

Conclusion   Merck begins a multi-month gradual decline in late March, which is a very good opportunity for sell writing. The pattern is tight, with many small candlesticks, which indicates small intraday movements. These types of movements indicate a lower of declining volatility, which is an excellent opportunity for premium collection.

The short put component of our sell-write will allow us to collect premium as the stock trades lower over time.

Example 4: Johnson & Johnson

Figure 8.4 shows a chart of Johnson & Johnson (JNJ) from November 2004 through September 2005. It is a good covered put opportunity, coming off the April highs.

FIGURE 8.4 JNJ Daily Chart
Source: Courtesy of Think or Swim (www.thinkorswim.com)

Notes

Covered Put/Sell-Write

1. Starting in early April, Johnson & Johnson breaks down below its lower support trend line, after putting in a bearish engulfing candle at support. It continues to trade lower in a slow, gradual, nonvolatile manner, which is idea for sell writers.

2. This gradual down-trending channel continues through August, which allows sell writers to roll their positions several times, allowing for the repeated capture of premium during the course of this movement.

3. The premiums received from the sale(s) of these put(s) will provide limited upside protection against an upward movement in the short stock.

Conclusion After running up and peaking at a high of around $70, Johnson & Johnson proceeds to give back almost the entire run in a slow, gradual, and steady downward trading channel. This channel lasts for at least four months, providing sell writers the opportunity to get a nice ride down in their short stock position, and also capture of premium from the sale of the put as it trades down in a slow, decreasing volatility fashion.

COVERED PUT/SELL-WRITE SYNOPSIS

Construction. Short stock, short 1 put for every 100 shares of stock shorted.

Function. To enhance profitability of short stock position and to provide limited protection against adverse stock movement.

Bias (Lean). Neutral to slightly bearish.

When to Use. When you feel the stock will trade slightly down or in a tight range for a period of time.

Profit Scenario. If the stock falls, the profit will be enhanced by the premium received. If the stock stagnates, you will profit from the premium received from put sale.

Loss Scenario. If the stock trades higher than the point defined by your stock sales price plus the premium received from put sale, you will lose dollar for dollar. The put premium received will act as a stock loss offset.

Key Concepts. If the stock trades down aggressively, you will profit only down to a stock price defined by the strike price minus the option premium. If the stock continues down below that point (break-even), you will incur lost opportunity. Further, if stock closes below the strike price, the stock will be assigned to you unless necessary adjustment is made. Time decay helps the position. The covered put/sell-write strategy is philosophically identical to the buy-write strategy, except it is in the opposite stock direction.

CHAPTER 9

The Protective Put Strategy

A s a reminder, a put gives an owner the right but not the obligation to sell a certain stock, at a specific price, by a specified date. For this opportunity, the buyer pays a premium. The seller, who receives the premium, is obligated to take delivery of the stock should the buyer wish to sell the stock at the strike price by the specified date. A strategically used put offers maximum protection against substantial loss.

FOUNDATIONS OF THE STRATEGY

The *protective put*, also referred to as a married put, puts and stock, or bullets, is an ideal strategy for an investor who wants full hedging coverage for a position.

Whereas the *covered call strategy* covers an investor down only as far as the premium received, the protective put strategy protects the investor from the break-even point down to zero.

This strategy's philosophy is different from the covered call (buy-write) strategy in two major ways. The covered call is a premium selling strategy, while the protective put is a premium purchasing strategy; and the covered call is most effective in a less volatile situation while the protective put is more effective in high-volatility situations.

When you purchase a stock, you can either sell the call (buy-write) or buy the put (protective put) to provide a proper hedge. The construction of the protective put position is actually quite simple. You buy the stock and you buy the put on a one-to-one ratio, meaning 1 put for every 100 shares.

Remember, 1 option contract is worth 100 shares. So, if you have 400 shares of IBM, then you would need to purchase exactly 4 puts.

From a premium standpoint, you must keep in mind that by purchasing an option, you are paying out money as opposed to collecting money. For this reason, your position must outperform the amount of money you put out, which is the opposite of what you did in the covered call strategy.

If you were to pay $1.00 for a put and you owned stock against it, you would need to have the stock increase in price $1.00 just to break even. Unlike the covered call, the protective put strategy has the premiums working against it; thus the stock needs to move more to offset the cost of the put.

This is why long option strategies need more volatility than short option strategies. Earlier I discussed how the covered call strategy needs to be done over a decent period of time (a year or so) in order to take advantage of the odds.

I previously said that selling options and collecting the premium was the right thing to do 75 to 82 percent of the time. If this is true, then buying an option and paying out premiums is going to be right only 18 to 25 percent of the time.

Those are not good odds. So, you should try to stay away from employing this strategy over a long period to avoid having the odds fall against you. However, a protective put can be used extremely effectively in the proper situation.

Let's take a look at the risks and rewards of the protective put strategy over three different scenarios.

PERFORMANCE IN DIFFERENT SCENARIOS

As previously stated, when we buy a stock, three potential outcomes exist. The stock can go up, go down, or remain stagnant. Let's hypothesize results across these three scenarios. In the first scenario, you buy the stock for $31.00 and buy the front-month 30 put for $1.00.

Up Scenario

In the *up scenario*, let's assume the stock price is $31.50 at expiration. The results are that you have a $0.50 gain from capital appreciation and a $1.00 loss from the purchase of the put, which combined gives us a $0.50 overall loss.

It is important to realize that the up scenario will produce a positive return only if the stock gain is greater than the amount paid for the put. That being the case, you calculate the break-even point for the protective put strategy by adding the purchase price of the stock to the price of the put.

In the up scenario, add the stock price, $31.00, plus the option price, $1.00. The break-even point is $32.00. So, until the stock reaches $32.00, the position will not produce a positive return. Above $32.00, the position will gain the amount equal to the stock price minus the premium paid for the option.

Stagnant Scenario

In the *stagnant scenario*, the position will produce a loss. Since the stock hasn't moved, there will be no capital gain or loss, and with the stock at $31.00 at expiration, the puts are worthless. The position lost $1.00, the amount you paid for the puts.

Down Scenario

In the *down scenario*, the position will again produce a loss. If the stock price were to trade down $1.00 to $30.00, then you would have a $1.00 capital loss. With the stock at $30.00, the 30 puts will be worthless; thus you incur a $1.00 loss because that is what you paid for them. Your total loss will be $2.00.

Table 9.1 shows the profit and loss of the protective put strategy in the three scenarios just discussed.

However, in the down scenario, the protective put will set a cap on your losses. Let's see how that works. We'll set the stock price down to $28.00. Since you purchased the stock at $31.00, there will be a capital loss of $3.00. The puts, however, are now in the money with the stock below

TABLE 9.1 Profit and Loss: Protective Put Scenarios

Stock Price	Stock P&L	Option P&L	Total P&L
25.00	−6.00	+4.00	−2.00
26.00	−5.00	+3.00	−2.00
27.00	−4.00	+2.00	−2.00
28.00	−3.00	+1.00	−2.00
29.00	−2.00	0	−2.00
30.00	−1.00	−1.00	−2.00
31.00	0	−1.00	−1.00
32.00	+1.00	−1.00	0
33.00	+2.00	−1.00	+1.00
34.00	+3.00	−1.00	+2.00
35.00	+4.00	−1.00	+3.00
36.00	+5.00	−1.00	+4.00
37.00	+6.00	−1.00	+5.00

$30.00. With the stock at $28.00, the 30 puts are worth $2.00. You paid $1.00 for them so you have a $1.00 profit in the puts.

Combine the put profit ($1.00) with the capital loss (–$3.00), and you have an overall loss of $2.00. The $2.00 loss is the maximum amount you can lose regardless of how low the stock declines, even if it goes as low as zero. This is what is meant by *maximum protection*.

In every protective put position, it is possible to calculate your anticipated maximum loss. Use the formula:

Maximum Loss = (Stock Price – Strike Price) – Option Price

For example, suppose you paid $31.00 for your stock. You bought the front-month 30 put for $1.00. Next, assume the stock closes at $30 on expiration day.

Your maximum loss calculation would be:

$$($31.00 – $30.00) – $1.00 = –$2.00$$

$$$31.00 \,(\text{stock price}) – 30 \,(\text{strike price}) = $1.00 \text{ capital loss}$$

Do not forget that with the stock at $30.00, the 30 puts will be worthless at expiration.

Add the capital loss ($1.00) plus the option loss ($1.00). The total is –$2.00, which is your maximum possible loss in that position. This formula will work every time.

Summary

Looking at the three scenarios, we find that only one scenario, the up scenario, can produce a positive return, and that is only when the stock increases more than the amount you paid for the puts.

The other two scenarios produced losses. If the stock is stagnant, you lose the amount you paid for the put. If the stock goes down, you lose again, but the loss is limited. **The limiting of loss is what makes the protective put an attractive and useful strategy.**

LEAN

The protective put strategy can be adjusted to address the particular lean that the stock owner has at a particular time. (The term *lean* describes the stock owner's perception of the directional strength of the stock.)

At any given time, an investor could feel that a stock may go up or down, a little or a lot, or just stay where it is. The protective put is not a position you would take if you feel that the stock you own was going to consolidate for a while. You would have a loss in the stagnant lean scenario since the stock made no gain but you would be out the cost for the purchase of the put.

However, the situation is different in a bullish lean scenario. A stock that has the potential to rise quickly has the potential to fall just as quickly. A stock that has substantial potential gain has an equal potential loss.

An investor choosing to buy a stock like this should have more protection to the downside than a covered call can provide and at the same time more allowance for a larger upside potential than the covered call allows.

This is a perfect time to use the protective put strategy. The purchase of an out-of-the-money put will be a relatively inexpensive investment but will provide the kind of results that will best fit a bullish lean.

You will have maximum downside protection with all the room you need for your stock's potential run up. Of course, this protection comes at a price. You must pay for the protection and freedom this position can provide.

The protective put also can be used when you have a little bearish lean on your stock.

Let's say that you own a stock that has taken a very nice run up. The stock has gotten to a point where you think about possibly selling and taking your profits, but you are afraid to because you feel it may still run up more and you do not want to get out too early.

Instead of selling the stock and missing out on the continued run, look into buying a put for protection. It will allow you to continue your capital appreciation as the stock trades up while limiting your loss to a fixed, known amount.

In cases such as this one, the purchase of an at-the-money or slightly in-the-money put will ensure you get a good sale price if the stock heads down and allows you ongoing profit if the stock continues up.

Of course, if the stock stays still, you would lose the amount of premium you spent on the put. If the stock goes up, it would have to trade higher than the amount you spent on the put before your long stock's upward movement starts to make you money again.

 KEY POINT

The protective put strategy, when used correctly, allows investors to take advantage of some opportunities that can provide large potential gains without being exposed to the severe risks that normally accompany such opportunities. With the proper protection in place, investors can profit from aggressive upside moves in the stock while having a fixed, limited loss.

WHEN TO USE THE PROTECTIVE PUT STRATEGY

As stated, the protective put strategy is not going to work all the time. However, there are some especially favorable opportunities for implementing it.

One is the case of a stock in the process of a steep decline. Quite often, stocks experience bad news or break down through a technical support level and trade down to seek a new, lower trading range.

Everyone wants to find the bottom to buy and go long, catching the technical rebound, or start accumulating the stock at lower levels for the longer term.

Although this scenario sounds good, these types of trades are risky. The risk is in identifying the true bottom. A stock that is in a free fall or rapid decline might give a false indication of a bottom, which could lead to substantial losses. The protective put will provide protection against this kind of substantial loss.

A stock that goes through a free fall finally "exhausts," or works through, the sellers. The stock proceeds down to lower levels where sellers are no longer interested in selling the stock.

At this level, the stock consolidates and buyers move in. Because the sellers are now done (exhausted), the pressure is lifted from the stock, and it proceeds up as buyers outnumber sellers.

Models are used to calculate where this bottom may lie, commonly referred to as exhaustion models. The problem is that the stock, on the way down, may stop and give the appearance of exhaustion but then continue farther down. If you had bought at the false appearance of exhaustion, you could be looking at a big loss.

There is a potential for a very big reward if you pick the right bottom. However, with the big potential gain comes the big potential loss that is common in these types of risk/reward scenarios. Here is a perfect opportunity to employ the protective put strategy!

Remember, the protective put allows for a large potential upside with a limited, fixed downside risk. If you feel that the stock has bottomed out and is starting to consolidate, you purchase the stock and purchase the put.

If you are right, and the stock runs back up, the stock profit will well exceed the price paid for the put. Once the stock trades back up, consolidates, and develops its new trading range, the need for the protective put is over. At this time, if you still like the stock and want to hold on to the long position, you could always start selling calls against it.

Use the formula for maximum loss discussed earlier. Calculate the loss in the stock and the amount you paid for the put, and add them together for your maximum loss in this position. The protective put has limited your loss.

$$\text{Maximum Loss} = (\text{Stock Price} - \text{Strike Price}) - \text{Option Price}$$

This protection will save you enough money when you pick a false (wrong) bottom that you may, if you like, try to pick the bottom again at a lower point. The exhaustion scenario, as described here, is a perfect opportunity to apply the protective put strategy.

As seen with the exhaustion example, the protective put strategy is best used in situations where the stock has a potential for an aggressive upside move and the chance of a big downside move.

Another potential opportunity for using the protective put is in combination with technical analysis. *Technical analysis* is the study of charts, indicators, oscillators, and the like. Charting has proven to be more than reasonably accurate in forecasting future stock movements.

Stocks travel in cycles that can and do form repetitious patterns. These patterns are predictable and detectable through charts, indicators, and oscillators.

Although there are many, many forms and styles of technical analysis, they all have several similarities. The one we want to focus on is the technical breakout. A *breakout* is a movement of the stock where its price trades quickly through and beyond an obvious technical resistance, or resistance point.

For a bullish breakout, this level is at the very top of its current trading range. Once through that level, the stock is considered to have broken out of its trading range and now often trades higher and establishes a new higher trading range.

The breakout is normally a rapid, large upward movement that usually offers an outstanding potential return if identified properly and acted on in a timely fashion.

However, if the breakout fails, the stock could trade back down to the bottom of the previous trading range.

If this were to happen, you would have incurred a large loss because you would have bought at the upper end of the previous trading range. Therefore, the breakout scenario is an opportunity that has large potential rewards but can, on occasion, have a large downside risk.

An excellent scenario for application of the protective put strategy is described next.

Stock XYZ is currently at the top of a trading range. The upper end of the range is $66.00 and the bottom end of the range is $58.00. When the chart, indicator, or oscillator you are using identifies the breakout of the stock (when it trades through $66.00), you should buy the stock immediately.

The risk of the stock not following through with its breakout is not large, but it does happen. The stock could trade back down to $58.00, the bottom of the trading range. If you had bought the stock naked above $66.00, you would experience a minimum $8.00 loss.

However, if you were to apply a protective put strategy with the stock purchase, you can drastically limit your downside exposure. For instance, when you buy the stock, you also buy the 65 strike put for $2.00. If the stock trades up to $75.00, you would make $9.00 if done naked but only $7.00 if done with the protective put.

This difference is the cost of the put. This $2.00 investment is more than worth it should the stock go down. If the breakout turns out to be a false breakout and the stock reverses and trades down, your 65 put will allow you to sell your stock out at $65.00 minus the $2.00 you paid for the put. This limits your loss to $3.00 instead of a potential $8.00 loss. This is a much better risk/reward scenario.

EXAMPLES

Let's look at three examples where the protective put could have been used effectively.

Example 1: Amgen

Figure 9.1 shows a chart Amgen (AMGN) from January 2002 through January 2004. It is a good example of when you would use the protective put strategy.

Notes

Protective Put

1. With the use of technical analysis, Amgen is identified to be poised to break down through a technical support as determined by a line drawn through three bottoms points, occurring in January 2002.

2. Then, in May 2002, the stock breaks down below the support line, indicating an upcoming drop to a new, lower trading range.

3. The stock begins to consolidate at around $46.00 and attempts to rebound. A protective put can be used here with the purchase of the stock in case the stock has a false bottom.

FIGURE 9.1 AMGN Daily Chart
Source: Courtesy of Think or Swim (www.thinkorswim.com)

4. Indeed, this level is a false bottom, as the rally fails, and the stock heads lower before the next consolidation level at point around $41.00. Again, stock may be purchased here with a protective put.

5. The rally fails again, and the stock falls to around $32.00 before putting a final bottom and reversing. Again, a protective put can be purchased here to guard against further downside. At this level, the stock begins its real rally and rises quickly from this point to provide an outstanding return from $32.00 to a high of $72.00 in one year.

6. In September 2002, at a stock price around $41.00, you could also buy a protective put as the stock pauses in its uptrend before continuing higher. At this level, the stock could be gathering up strength for the next leg of the rally (which it does), or it can become tired and begin to trade down again.

Conclusion The protective put allows the investor the room to be wrong by limiting the total loss. Because the loss is limited, protective put investors have staying power not afforded to naked stock buyers who would feel the full brunt of the loss.

This ability to play again increases the protective put buyer's chance of being right and therefore more profitable than the naked stock buyer would be. The Amgen chart is a textbook example of a stock in position for the use of the protective put strategy.

Obviously, this was a risky trade, but one that could—and in this case did—provide an outstanding return. This is the perfect time to use the protective put. The protective put provides maximum protection in risky situations while allowing you to have almost the maximum available upside.

If you did buy the wrong bottom, the put would have bailed you out by limiting your downside and saving you enough money to try again. As you see from the chart, within 12 months of the July 2002 low of around $32.00, the stock traded to a high of over $72.00. This profit is more than enough to have covered the purchase of a few puts.

As stated earlier, this is a textbook case and one that should be studied to see why and when to use the protective put.

Example 2: Wal-Mart

Figure 9.2 shows a chart of Wal-Mart (WMT) from April 2003 through January 2004. It is and a good technical setup where you would use the protective put strategy.

FIGURE 9.2 WMT Chart
Source: Courtesy of Think or Swim (www.thinkorswim.com)

Notes

Protective Put

1. In mid-November 2003, Wal-Mart opens down $1.50 to $56.25 and proceeds to trade down from there, breaking the lower end of an uptrend channel.

2. Wal-Mart then has a quick consolidation in mid-November around the $54.50–$55.00 level followed by a small technical rebound back to about $56.25. This may have been due to some investors thinking that the consolidation was a bottoming and thus a buying opportunity. As it turned out, it was a false bottom, and the stock traded back down rapidly to lower lows. A purchase at that level probably led to losses.

3. In early December, Wal-Mart starts another consolidation around the $52.50 level. It seems to be another buying opportunity for bottom fishers. There has already been one false bottom that has cost someone a lot of money. If that investor employed a protective put, the loss would have been limited, and he or she may have been able to purchase again at this level if desired.

4. The $52.50 level turns out to be another false bottom, and the stock trades down another $2.00 to $50.50. Here again, the same opportunity exists. Is this the bottom? If it is, a nice profit can be made quickly. If not, losses can mount quickly as another false bottom occurs and the stock trades down rapidly. This level, so far, turns out to be a good buying opportunity, as the stock rebounds back up to $52.50 quickly.

Conclusion Bottom fishing can be a very risky endeavor; however, investors cannot ignore the potential reward that comes with the risk. If the risk can be minimized without affecting the potential reward to a significant degree, the risk/reward scenario will be an advantageous one for a potential investment.

The protective put will accomplish this perfectly. In a case like this, you should employ the protective put strategy at any level where you deem it worthy of a capital commitment.

Example 3: General Motors

Figure 9.3 shows a chart of General Motors (GM) from July 2003 through January 2004, and a slightly different example of when you could use the protective put strategy.

FIGURE 9.3 GM Chart

Source: Courtesy of Think or Swim (www.thinkorswim.com)

Notes

Protective Put

1. After trading in a tight range for a considerable period of time with low volatility, General Motors' volatility spiked in early December 2003, and the stock gapped open considerably higher, followed by another breakout gap opening several days later.

2. This second gap opening forced the stock up through a previous resistance level, as the stock broke out and began a new, higher trading range.

3. The stock then advanced five of the next seven trading days with bigger intraday ranges than average during the previous 12 months, indicating increasing volatility.

4. The initial General Motors' breakout, when it traded through $44.00 and quickly proceeded to trade up to the $54.00 range in less than one month, represented a 2 percent return in a very short period of time.

Conclusion   General Motors is a perfect example of an opportunity to use the protective put strategy to provide protection against a false breakout when buying a stock on a technical breakout.

In this case, General Motors had been trading in a lower volatility pattern for several months, which would have kept option premiums down. This would have allowed the investor to purchase the put at an advantageous price.

With the protective put in place, and at a relatively inexpensive price, the investor could ride the breakout with patience and confidence, with limited loss and controlled risk.

Even though this stock was in a rapid uptrend after breaking out of its previous trading range and the protective puts purchased would have expired worthless, it still would have been a good idea to put on this protection in case the stock pulled in.

Gap openings tend to get filled at some point before proceeding higher. In the case of a rapid sustained rally, there is usually some type of pullback when the stock is overbought.

In this case, the puts would not have been profitable but would have provided the necessary protection in case the rally failed or temporarily retraced.

I wanted to show this example where the puts would not have been profitable, because you never know where the stock is going to go. But even though the puts would have expired worthless, the rise in stock price would have clearly offset the cost of these puts.

So again, the protective put strategy here would have provided a cost-effective insurance policy against the stock's pulling back or a failed rally.

PROTECTIVE PUT SYNOPSIS

Construction. Long stock, long 1 put per every 100 shares of stock.

Function. To provide maximum downside protection for long stock position; long stock insurance policy.

Bias (Lean). Bullish but cautious.

When to Use. When you wish to protect profits of long stock position while retaining position; also, to protect speculative stock purchases (i.e., purchasing stock on potential chart breakout from the current trading range according to technical analysis).

Profit Scenario. If the stock continues to trade up by more than the amount paid for the puts. Once above that level, the position makes dollar for dollar with stock.

Loss Scenario. If the stock trades down, the loss will be felt until the stock reaches the point defined by the put's strike price minus the put price. At that level, the position will cease losing. If the stock stagnates, the loss will equal the put price due to decay.

Key Concepts. Due to the acquisition of time decay from the long put, the position is best used to protect already existing profits or when a potentially aggressive or explosive upside move in the near future is a good possibility. It is the other side of the sell-write position. It is philosophically identical to the synthetic put strategy except for the anticipation of the stock going up.

CHAPTER 10

The Synthetic Put/Protective Call Strategy

W hile, as previously explained, the protective put provides the investor maximum downside coverage for a long stock position, the *protective call* (*synthetic put*) provides the investor maximum upside coverage for a short stock position.

FOUNDATIONS OF THE STRATEGY

Many might think that the protective call is the opposite strategy from the protective put; it is, in fact, philosophically identical. Both positions work in the same way. That is, they both provide maximum protection for a directional stock play. The only difference is that the protective put is used to protect a long stock position while the protective call is used to protect a short stock position. The protective call position received its more commonly used nickname, synthetic put, not from how it is constructed but from how it acts. This position simulates the behavior patterns of a long put in both risk/reward and profit/loss. The position, from the buyer's standpoint, allows for a fully hedged downside play.

Please take special note that this strategy, in the investment world, is called the synthetic put. I refer to it as the protective call for educational purposes because of its philosophical and fundamental relationship to the protective put. If you understand the function of the protective put, you will understand the protective call.

For the opportunity of protection, the buyer pays a premium in the form of purchasing a call. The seller, who receives the premium for the sale of the call, is obligated to deliver the stock to the buyer (should the buyer wish to buy the stock) at the strike price by the specified expiration date. A strategically used long call offers maximum protection against substantial loss in the event the stock that you are short trades up.

The covered put strategy (sell-write), discussed in Chapter 9, covers investors up only as far as the premium they receive from the put sale, whereas the protective call strategy protects investors from the break-even point up to infinity (theoretically) via the purchase of the call.

This strategy's philosophy is different from the covered put strategy in two major ways. While the covered put is a premium selling strategy, the protective call (synthetic put) is a premium purchasing strategy; also, the covered put is most effective in a stagnant or decreasing volatility situation while the protective call is more effective in increasing volatility situations.

When investors sell a stock short, they can either sell the put (sell-write) or buy the call (protective call or synthetic put) to provide a proper hedge. The construction of the protective call position is actually quite simple. You sell the stock short and you buy the call on a one-to-one ratio, meaning 1 put for every 100 shares.

Remember, 1 option contract is worth 100 shares. So, if you have shorted 400 shares of IBM, then you would need to purchase exactly 4 calls.

From a premium standpoint, keep in mind that by purchasing an option, you are paying out money as opposed to collecting money. This means that your position must outperform the amount of money that you put out, which is the opposite side of what you did in the covered put strategy.

Consider: If you were to pay $1.00 for a call and you shorted the stock against it, you would need to have the stock decrease in price $1.00 just to break even. Unlike the covered put, the protective call strategy has the premiums working against it; thus the stock needs to move more to offset the cost of the call.

This is why long option strategies need more volatility than short option strategies. I discussed that short option strategies need to be done over a decent period of time (a year or so) in order to take advantage of the odds. Meanwhile, long option strategies like the protective call need relatively quick, aggressive movements in order to maximize profit potential.

As mentioned, selling options and collecting the premium is the right thing to do 75 to 83 percent of the time. If this is true, then buying an option and paying out premiums is going to be right only 17 to 25 percent of the time. Those are not good odds. You should avoid using this strategy over a long period so the odds do not fall against you. However, like the protective put, a protective call can be extremely effective in the right situation.

PERFORMANCE IN DIFFERENT SCENARIOS

Let's take a look at the risks and rewards of the protective call strategy over three different scenarios.

As previously stated, when we short a stock, three potential outcomes exist: The stock can go up, go down, or remain stagnant. Let's hypothesize results across these three scenarios. Our basis is that you short the stock for $29.00 and buy the front-month 30 call for $1.00.

Down Scenario

Consider the down scenario. Assume the stock price is $28.50 at expiration. The results are that you have a $0.50 gain from capital appreciation and a $1.00 loss from the purchase of the call, which, combined, gives a $0.50 overall loss.

It is important to realize that the down scenario will produce a positive return only if the gain on the short stock is greater than the amount paid for the call. You calculate the break-even point for the protective call strategy by subtracting the price of the call from the sales price of the stock.

In the down scenario, subtract the option price of $1.00 from the stock price of $29.00 and you get a break-even of $28.00. Until the stock reaches $28.00, the position will not produce a positive return. Below $28.00, the position will gain the amount equal to the stock price minus the premium paid for the option.

However, if the stock were to trade down aggressively, say down to $22.00, you would see a healthy gain of $6.00. You would have a $7.00 gain from capital appreciation and a $1.00 loss from the purchase of the call you used as insurance.

Stagnant Scenario

In the stagnant scenario, the position will again produce a loss. Since the stock hasn't moved, there will be no capital gain or loss, and with the stock at $29.00 at expiration, the calls are worthless. The position lost $1.00, the amount you paid for the calls.

Up Scenario

In the up scenario, the position will again produce a loss. If the stock price were to trade up $1.00 to $30.00, then you would have a $1.00 capital loss.

Further, with the stock at $30.00, the 30 calls will be worthless; thus you incur a $1.00 loss because that is what you paid for them. Add that to your capital appreciation loss and your total loss will be $2.00 with the stock expiring at $30.00.

Summary

Table 10.1 recaps the profit and loss of the protective call.

With a loss possible in all scenarios, why use this strategy? The reason is because, in the up scenario, the protective call will set a cap on your losses. Let's see how that works. We will set the stock price up to $32.00. Since you shorted the stock at $29.00, there will be a capital loss of $3.00. The calls, however, are now in the money with the stock above $30.00. With the stock at $32.00, the 30 calls are worth $2.00. You paid $1.00 for them, so you have a $1.00 profit in the calls.

Combine the call profit ($1.00) with the capital loss (−$3.00), and you have an overall loss of $2.00. The $2.00 loss is the maximum amount you can lose regardless of how high the stock increases. This is what is meant by maximum protection.

In every protective call position, it is possible to calculate your anticipated maximum loss. Use the formula:

$$(\text{Option Strike Price} + \text{Option Price}) - \text{Stock Price}$$
$$\text{Maximum Loss} = (\text{Strike Price} + \text{Option Price}) - \text{Stock Price}$$

For example, suppose you sold a stock short at $29.00. You bought the front-month 30 call for $1.00. Next, assume the stock closes at $30 on expiration day.

TABLE 10.1 Profit and Loss of Protective Call Scenarios

Stock Price	Stock P&L	Option P&L	Total P&L
24.00	+5.00	−1.00	+4.00
25.00	+4.00	−1.00	+3.00
26.00	+3.00	−1.00	+2.00
27.00	+2.00	−1.00	+1.00
28.00	+1.00	−1.00	0
29.00	0	−1.00	−1.00
30.00	−1.00	−1.00	−2.00
31.00	−2.00	0	−2.00
32.00	−3.00	+1.00	−2.00
33.00	−4.00	+2.00	−2.00
34.00	−5.00	+3.00	−2.00
35.00	−6.00	+4.00	−2.00
36.00	−7.00	+5.00	−2.00

Your maximum loss calculation would be:

$$(\$30.00 + \$1.00) - \$29.00 = -\$2.00$$
$$\$30.00 \, (\text{closing price}) - \$29.00 \, (\text{stock price}) = \$1.00 \, \text{capital loss}$$

However, do not forget that with the stock at \$30.00, the 30 calls will be worthless.

Add the capital loss (\$1.00) plus the option loss (\$1.00) together. The total is \$2.00, which is your maximum possible loss in that position. This formula will work every time.

Looking at the three hypothetical scenarios, we find that only one, the down scenario, can produce a positive return, and that's only when the stock decreases more than the amount you paid for the calls.

The other two scenarios produced losses. If the stock is stagnant, you lose the amount you paid for the put. If the stock goes up, you lose again, but the loss is limited. It is the limiting of loss that makes the protective call an attractive and useful strategy.

LEAN

The protective call strategy can be adjusted to address the particular lean that investor or trader has at any particular time. (The term *lean* describes the investor's perception of the directional strength of the stock.)

At any given time, an investor can feel that a stock may go up or down, a little or a lot, or just stay where it is. The synthetic put is not a position you would be in if you feel that the stock you own was going to consolidate for a while. You would have a loss in the stagnant lean scenario since the short stock position made no gain or loss, but you were out \$1.00 for the purchase of the call.

However, the situation is different in a bearish lean scenario.

A stock that has substantial potential gain has an equal potential loss. If a stock has broken down through a support level, that stock could see a rapid, sharp, downward move. There may be an opportunity to capitalize on this event by shorting the stock.

An investor choosing to short a stock like this should have more protection to the upside than a covered put can provide and at the same time more allowance for a larger downside potential than the covered put allows.

This is a perfect time to use the protective call (synthetic put) strategy. The purchase of an out-of-the-money call will be a relatively inexpensive investment but will provide the kind of results that will best fit a bearish lean.

You will have maximum upside protection with all the room you need for your stock's potential decline. Of course, this comes at a price. You must pay for the protection and freedom this position can provide.

The protective call also can be used when you have a little bullish lean on your short stock position. Let's say that you shorted a stock that has traded down very nicely. The stock has gotten to a point where you think about possibly buying it back and taking your profits, but you are afraid to do so because you feel it may still trade down more.

Instead of buying the stock back and missing out on the continued decline, look into buying a call for protection. It will allow you to continue your capital gains as the stock trades down while limiting your loss to a fixed, known amount.

In cases such as this one, the purchase of an at-the-money or slightly in-the-money call will ensure you get a good purchase price if the stock heads up and allows you ongoing profit if the stock continues down.

Of course, if the stock stays still, you would lose the amount of premium you spent on the call. If the stock continues down, however, it would have to trade lower than the amount you spent on the call before your short stock's downward movement starts to make you money again.

 KEY POINT

The protective call strategy, when used correctly, allows investors to take advantage of some opportunities that could provide large potential gains without being exposed to the severe risks that normally accompany such risky opportunities.

With the proper protection in place, you can profit from aggressive downside moves in the stock while having a fixed, limited loss. As stated before, this strategy is not going to work all the time. However, there are some especially favorable opportunities for implementing the protective call strategy.

WHEN TO USE THE PROTECTIVE CALL STRATEGY

One is the case of a stock in the process of a steep incline. Quite often, IPO (initial public offering) stocks trade up wildly on inadequate supply, as many Internet stocks did during the late 1990s and even some IPOs today.

We have all seen these stocks trade to ridiculously high levels that we all knew could not be maintained.

Everyone knew these stocks were way overvalued and knew that they would sell off as radically as they traded up. It seemed like an easy trade to just short stocks of this nature, wait for them to come back down to reality, and cash in on big profits.

Although this scenario sounds good, these types of trades are risky. The risk is in identifying the true top. A stock that is in a rapid incline might give a false indication of a top (or exhaustion level), which could lead to substantial losses. The protective call will provide protection against this kind of substantial loss.

A stock that explodes to the upside will finally exhaust, or work through, the buyers. The stock then proceeds up to higher levels, where buyers are no longer interested in buying the stock. At this level, the stock consolidates and sellers move in. Because the buyers are now done (exhausted), the demand is lifted from the stock and moves down as sellers now outnumber buyers.

Models are used to calculate where this top may lie. They are commonly referred to as exhaustion models and are based largely on volume analysis. The problem is that the stock, on the way up, may stop, consolidate, and give the appearance of exhaustion but then continue farther up. If you had shorted the stock at the false appearance of exhaustion, you could be looking at a big loss.

There is a potential for a very big reward if you pick the "right" top. However, with the big potential gain comes the big potential loss that is common in these types of risk/reward scenarios. Here is a perfect opportunity to employ the protective call strategy.

Remember, the protective call allows for a large potential profit with a limited, fixed potential loss. If you feel that the stock has topped out and is starting to trade down, you short the stock and purchase the call.

If you are right and the stock gaps down, the profit from the short stock position will well exceed the price paid for the call. Once the stock trades back down, consolidates, and develops its new, lower trading range, the need for the protective call is over. At this time, if you still like the short side of the stock and want to hold on to the short position, you could always start selling puts against it and begin a covered put position.

The protection provided by the protective call strategy will save you enough money when you pick a false (wrong) top that you may try to pick the top again at a higher point. The buyer exhaustion scenario, as described here, is a perfect opportunity to apply the protective call (synthetic put) strategy.

As seen with the exhaustion example, the protective call strategy is best used in situations where the stock has a potential for an aggressive downside move.

Another potential opportunity for using the protective call is in combination with technical analysis—the study of charts, indicators, oscillators, and so on. Charting has proven to be more than reasonably accurate in forecasting future stock movements.

Stocks travel in cycles that can and do form repetitious patterns. These patterns are predictable and detectable by the use of any number of charts, indicators, and oscillators.

Although there are many, many forms and styles of technical analysis, they all have several similarities. The one we want to focus on is the technical break down. A *break out* is described as a movement of the stock where its price trades quickly through and beyond an obvious "technical support."

For a *bearish break down*, we are speaking of a level at the very bottom of a stock's present trading range. Once through that level, the stock is considered to have "broken down" of its trading range and now will often trade lower, seeking to establish a new lower trading range.

The break down is normally a rapid, large downward movement that features an expansion in implied volatility and usually offers an outstanding potential return if properly and acted on in a timely fashion. However, if the break down fails, the stock could trade back up to the top of the previous trading range and implied volatility could contract.

If the break down should fail, you would incur a large loss because you would have shorted the stock at the lower end of the previous trading range. Now, with the stock more likely than not on its way back to the upper end of the trading range, you will be facing a loss. As you can see, the break-down scenario is an opportunity that has large potential rewards but can, on occasion, have a large potential risk.

Therefore, this is an excellent scenario in which to apply the protective call strategy.

For example, XYZ is currently at the bottom of a trading range; the upper end of the range is $68.00 and the bottom end of the range is $58.00. When the chart, indicator, or oscillator you are using identifies the break-down of the stock (when it trades below $58.00), you would short the stock immediately.

The risk of the stock not following through with its break down is not large, but it does happen. The stock could trade back up to $68.00, which is the top of the trading range.

If you had shorted the stock naked below $58.00, you would realize a minimum $10.00 loss if the stock did indeed trade back up to $68.00.

However, if you were to apply a protective call strategy with the stock purchase, you can limit your negative exposure greatly. For instance, say you were to buy the 60 strike call for $2.00. If the stock trades down to $49.00, you would make $9.00 if you shorted the stock naked but make only $7.00 if traded with the protective call.

This difference is the cost of the call. This $2.00 investment is more than worth it should the stock go back up. If the break down turns out to be a false one, and the stock reverses and trades up, your 60 call will allow you to buy your stock back at $60.00 plus the $2.00 you paid for the call. This limits your loss to $4.00 instead of a potential $10.00 loss. Shrewd investors would agree that this is a much better risk/reward scenario.

The protective call (synthetic put) gives investors the room to be wrong by limiting their total loss; it thereby increases the amount of opportunities investors can capitalize on. Because the loss is limited, protective call investors have a staying power not afforded to naked short stock players who would feel the full brunt of the loss if wrong.

This ability to play again increases the chances of protective call buyers being right and therefore more profitable than naked stock buyers would be. So, if you feel a stock has a good chance of trading down aggressively because it has become overextended or is about to break down, you may want to explore the use of the protective call (synthetic put) strategy.

EXAMPLES

Let's take a look at some chart examples.

Example 1: Qlogic Corp.

Figure 10.1 shows a chart of Qlogic Corp. (QLGC) from November 2004 through August 2005 and a good technical setup for the synthetic put strategy.

Notes

Synthetic Put

1. Qlogic trades in a strong uptrending trading channel, which started in late 2004 and continues into early April 2005.

2. Qlogic then breaks down through the lower support channel line in mid-April 2005 and begins a precipitous drop, losing much of its value quickly.

3. Selling the stock short after the trend-line violation would put the investor in an excellent position to take advantage of the upcoming downside movement.

4. The simultaneous purchase of a call (in this case the 40 strike) would protect the short stock position in the event it makes an unexpected upward movement. If it does, the long call will act as a guaranteed

FIGURE 10.1 QLGC Daily Chart
Source: Courtesy of Think or Swim (www.thinkorswim.com)

> stop, limiting our loss in the short stock position and capping it to a fixed amount.

5. When the stock finally collapses, the investor will profit dollar for dollar on the way down with the stock minus the amount paid for the call. The long call acts as an insurance policy for the short stock position.

Conclusion   Qlogic shows a classic example of a stock breaking down out of an uptrending trading channel. This type of downside violation or breakdown formation often leads to a precipitous drop in the price of the stock. A short stock position can profit generously in this situation. However, some stocks demonstrate false breakdowns but then bounce back up quickly.

This could be disastrous for a short stock position. A long call attached to the short position will create a synthetic put position and offer upside protection by limiting your risk to a fixed manageable amount.

Example 2: Martek Biosciences

Figure 10.2 shows a chart of Martek Biosciences (MATK) from November 2004 through August 2005; it is another good technical setup for the synthetic put strategy.

FIGURE 10.2 MATK Daily Chart
Source: Courtesy of Think or Swim (www.thinkorswim.com)

Notes

Synthetic Put

1. Martek forms a classic bearish pennant formation, which comes to a head in late April. As the formation tightens, an investor could short the stock in preparation for a potential breakdown and downside move. However, being naked the short stock position puts the investor at risk in the event of an upside stock movement.

2. To protect against this risk, an investor could buy an at-the-money or slightly out of-the-money call, which would minimize the risk and actually cap the total dollar loss potential to a fixed amount.

3. When the stock drops from around $60.00 down to around $32.00, the synthetic put investor will see the full dollar gain of the drop of the stock minus the cost of the call. Here the call will act as an insurance policy, protecting the short stock position while waiting on the expected downward movement.

Conclusion When Martek begins to form a downside pennant formation (a charting formation that indicates a coming downward movement), it appears as if it is ripe for a breakdown, but in order to best take advantage of this potential opportunity, the short stock position needs to be established early.

A large-gap down movement offers very large potential profits, but you must be in on the position, in the correct direction, before the gap, or you will miss the opportunity.

However, holding a naked short stock position for any length of time is potentially very risky. If an investor has to hold the short stock position while waiting on the final leg of the charting formation, a call purchase would ensure a maximum fixed loss potential.

The long call would provide protection for the short stock position if the stock rallied, limiting the loss to a more manageable level, as opposed to a potentially catastrophic situation by simply being naked in the short stock position and having the stock bounce.

Example 3: Wynn Resorts

Figure 10.3 shows a chart of Wynn Resorts (WYNN).

FIGURE 10.3 WYNN Daily Chart
Source: Courtesy of Think or Swim (www.thinkorswim.com)

Notes

Synthetic Put/Protective Call

1. Wynn Resorts trades in a strong upward trading channel before breaking down sharply through its support in early April.
2. The early clue was the bearish engulfing candle formation, which was followed by a dramatic drop in the stock price. The short sale of the stock would allow an investor to take advantage of the downside movement but would expose him or her to upside risk if the stock rallied. The purchase of an at-the-money or in-the-money call would protect against the upside risk of a naked short stock position.
3. Here the synthetic put position allows the investor to profit from selling the stock short, while the long call provides upside protection, to the degree of maximizing losses to a predefined (and more acceptable) level.

Conclusion   Wynn Resorts breaks down to a technical support level, at its lower trading range around the $68 level in late March. The bearish engulfing candle precedes a major precipitous drop in the stock price. By mid-May, the stock has dropped below $45.

Stocks like these that break technical support levels with explosive downward movements offer users of the synthetic put strategy the opportunity to benefit from their short stock position while maintaining very acceptable risk parameters that are maximized and controlled by the ownership of the call option. This provides an insurance policy to protect the naked risk of the short stock position.

SYNTHETIC PUT SYNOPSIS

Construction. Short stock, long 1 call per every 100 shares of stock.

Function. To provide maximum upside protection for a short stock position. Short stock insurance policy.

Bias (Lean). Bearish but cautious.

When to Use. When seeking to protect profits of short stock position or while continuing to retain short position. Also can be used to protect a speculative stock sale (i.e., selling stock on a potential chart breakdown through support from the current trading range according to technical analysis).

Profit Scenario. If the stock continues to trade down by more than the amount paid for the calls. Once below that level, the position makes dollar for dollar with stock.

Loss Scenario. If the stock trades up, the loss will be felt until the stock reaches the point defined by the call's strike price plus the call's price. At that level, the position will cease losing. If the stock stagnates, the loss will equal the call price due to decay.

Key Concepts. Due to the acquisition of time decay from the long call, the position is best used for protection of already existing profits or when a potentially aggressive or explosive downside move in the near future is a good possibility. It is the other side of the buy-write trade. It is philosophically identical to the protective put except for the anticipation of the stock going down.

CHAPTER 11

The Collar Strategy

Another protective strategy that allows for some upside capital gain while providing maximum down side protection is the *collar strategy*.

FOUNDATIONS OF THE STRATEGY

The collar is a combination of the covered call and protective put strategies. The collar uses a long put position in coordination with a short call position along with a long stock position. The ratio is 1 short call, 1 long put (not of the same strike), and 100 shares of stock. As you remember, 1 contract is equal to 100 shares. The options that we will use to construct this strategy will be out-of-the-money puts and calls.

The object here is to construct a protective put strategy without having to pay for the purchase of the put. I discussed premium in the covered call strategy and how you are better off collecting premiums over a period of time, not paying them out. By selling the call, you collect premiums that can be used to offset the capital outlay you incurred for the put purchase.

I said that two of three scenarios in the covered call strategy were positive while the protective put scenario had only one scenario that produced a positive outcome.

However, the protective put was the strategy that provided the most downside protection. The challenge was to construct a protective put strategy without paying out money. The solution is the collar strategy.

The collar takes on the characteristics of both the protective put and covered call strategies. Like the covered call, there is an upside cap on profits; like the protective put, there is unlimited downside protection.

Ideally, the collar is set up to be an even trade, meaning you neither receive nor pay out any money. Realistically, depending on the options used, you may have to pay out a small premium or even receive a small premium, but the goal of the collar in terms of premium is to be neutral.

As mentioned previously, to construct a collar, buy 1 out-of-the-money put and sell 1 out-of-the-money call per every 100 shares of stock owned.

Obviously, the put and the call must be of differing strikes. (It is impossible for both a put and a call of identical strike price to be out of the money or be in the money.)

For example, with a stock priced at $28.50, a collar may be constructed by the purchase of the December 27.5 puts and the sale of the December 30 calls. It is hoped that the price of the call and put are close enough so that the funds generated by the sale of the call are enough to offset the cost of the put purchase.

Let's take a look at how the strategy works with this position. For the sake of our illustration and to make our calculations easy, let's establish the collar using the December 27.5 put and the December 30 call, with both trading at $1.00. Remember our stock price was $28.50. The cost of the collar will be $0 because you paid $1.00 for the put but you collected $1.00 from the sale of the call.

PERFORMANCE IN DIFFERENT SCENARIOS

How does the collar work in our usual three scenarios: up, down, and stagnant?

Up Scenario

In the up scenario, we find that when the stock rises, the investor gains penny for penny until the stock reaches the call strike. Once the stock reaches that level, the position no longer gains because the stock is at the point where it will be called away.

Capital gains of the position are maximized when the stock reaches the call's strike price. Let's take a closer look at what happens as the stock price goes up. With the stock at $29.00, both the December 30 calls and the December 27.5 puts are out of the money and thus worthless. Since there was no debit or credit incurred in the options, the option profit (loss) is

$0. Only the stock position remains. The stock purchased at $28.50 is now trading at $29.00 for a $0.50 profit.

Let's raise the stock price to $30.00. The puts and calls are again worthless, so your profit (loss) is solely determined by the stock. The stock, which was purchased for $28.50, is now worth $30.00 and represents a gain of $1.50. This $1.50 gain is the maximum gain the position allows.

Once the stock goes over $30.00, the December 30 call, which we are short, would become in the money; therefore, the stock position would be called away at that price.

When the stock price rises to $31.00, the puts would be out of the money, thus worthless, but the calls would be worth $1.00.

You received no money for the establishment of the collar so you would have a $1.00 loss in the options. Meanwhile, the stock that you purchased at $28.50 is now worth $31.00 at expiration, which is a $2.50 gain.

Combine the $2.50 gain in the stock with the $1.00 options loss; you have a $1.50 profit again. You may do this calculation with higher and higher stock prices, but the outcome will always be the same. This example shows how your upside potential is limited.

Obviously, if the option portion of the collar incurred a debit or credit, that inflow or outflow of money must be added to or subtracted from the stock gain to get the overall return of the position.

Normally, there will be a debit or credit incurred in the collar. It is usually difficult to find an appropriate put and a call to use in the collar trading at an equal value.

Let's use our last example with some minor price changes.

If the put had been trading at $1.25 instead of $1.00, then there would be a $0.25 capital outflow that would have to be subtracted from the $1.50 gain to reduce it to an overall gain of only $1.25.

If the call was trading at $1.25, however, you would have collected an extra $0.25, which, added to the $1.50 gain, would produce a $1.75 gain. The cost of the collar always impacts the bottom-line profit or loss of the position.

Stagnant Scenario

Looking at the collar in the stagnant scenario, the stock price would be unchanged, thus neutral in terms of return. Therefore, the potential profit or loss would come strictly from the debit or credit of the two options.

If the stock does not move, as in our example, both the put and call would finish out of the money and be worthless.

Our profit or loss simply would be calculated from whether you paid for the collar or collected from the collar and how much that amount was.

Using the same prices as the previous example (the stock purchase price of $28.50, the December 27.5 put of –$1.00, and the December 30 call of $1.00), we will now take a look at the down scenario.

Down Scenario

Let's set the stock price at $28.00 on expiration. At this price both the December 27.5 put and the December 30 call are out of the money and worthless. Since there is no credit or debit incurred in the option position ($1.00 inflow from the calls, $1.00 outflow from puts), the total return of the position is simply the gain or loss from the stock.

Since there is a $.50 loss with the stock price at $28.00 at expiration ($28.50 purchase price – $28.00 value at expiration) there is a $.50 loss with this position.

With the purchase price of the stock $28.50 and the stock price at expiration $27.50, there will be a $1.00 loss. In this case with the stocks at $27.50 or lower, you have reached the maximum loss. No matter how low the stock goes, you can only incur a maximum loss of $1.00.

Now let's set the stock price at $26.00 and see if this holds true. With the stock at $26.00 on expiration, the December 30 calls are out of the money and worthless. The December 27.5 puts, however, are in the money and now worth $1.50. The stock you purchased for $28.50 is now worth $26.00 on expiration, which is a $2.50 loss. Combine the $2.50 stock loss with the $1.50 gain in the puts, and you have a $1.00 loss in the overall position.

This demonstrates that $1.00 is the maximum loss of the position. Keep in mind that if the option position creates a debit or a credit, it must be added to or subtracted from the stock loss or gain to get the profit or loss of the total position.

Most of the time, there will be a small debit or credit incurred in the option position. It is relatively infrequent that the put and call used in the collar are trading at the exact same price.

Summary

Check Table 11.1 for a summary of the profit and loss scenarios with the collar. Purchases: Stock $28.50, December 27.5 put (–1.00), December 30 call (+1.00).

Like other strategies, the collar can be leaned toward the investor's perception of the stock's direction and strength.

TABLE 11.1 Profit and Loss Scenarios: Collar

Stock Price	Stock P&L	Option P&L	Total P&L
24.00	−4.50	+3.50	−1.00
25.00	−3.50	+2.50	−1.00
26.00	−2.50	+1.50	−1.00
27.00	−1.50	+.50	−1.00
28.00	−.50	0	−.50
28.50	0	0	0
29.00	+.50	0	+.50
30.00	+1.50	0	+1.50
31.00	+2.50	+1.00	+1.50
32.00	+3.50	+2.00	+1.50
33.00	+4.50	+3.00	+1.50
34.00	+5.50	+4.00	+1.50

LEAN

Let's look at the potential leans that can be taken. Say that you have a very strong feeling that XYZ is going to go up. Instead of buying a put and selling a call with strikes that are roughly equidistant from the stock price, you would sell a call that is farther out of the money. This would allow more room for a larger increase in stock price because the stock would not be called away as early. You retain ownership for a longer period of time during the increasing price period.

Of course, by increasing the distance of the option's strike away from the stock, the amount of the call's premium will decrease. The overall effect is that you will have to pay more to own the position. (You will pay out more money for the put than you will receive from the call.)

Again, we will start with the same prices as in our original case (stock $28.50, December 27.5 put at −$1.00, and December 30 call at $1.00), only now we will change the December 30 call at $1.00 to the December 32.5 call at $0.35.

In our other examples, we incurred no debit or credit from our option position. This time, with the bullish lean, a debit is incurred. The purchase of the December 27.5 put for −$1.00 combined with the receipt of $.35 from the sale of the December 32.5 call produces a $0.65 debit.

Remember, this debit must be subtracted from the bottom-line profit or added to the bottom-line loss of the stock's capital result. This means that before you make any money from the position, the stock must trade up $0.65.

If the stock stays stagnant you will lose $0.65, and any capital loss you incur will be $0.65 worse.

Now back to the position in our previous example. With the selling of the December 30 call, we had an upside potential of $1.50. In this next example, things change.

As stated, the maximum upside potential is calculated by setting the stock price at the strike price of the short call, which is $32.50 in this case. With the stock at $32.50 at expiration, you would have a $4.00 stock gain, since the stock was purchased for $28.50.

Remembering your $0.65 debit to enter the position, we subtract that from the $4.00 and we have a total maximum profit of $3.35. This is significantly more potential reward than our original example using the December 30 call.

As in all trading situations that offer a higher potential reward, there comes a higher potential risk. If the stock stays at $28.50 (the stagnant scenario), you have a loss of $0.65 in option costs.

In the down scenario, calculating the maximum risk is done by setting the stock price at $27.50 on expiration. The stock, purchased at $28.50, has lost $1.00. The options, not neutral as in the first example, resulted in a $0.65 loss. The total loss is $1.65.

In both the stagnant and down scenarios, the loss increased over that in our original example. As you can see, **the higher potential gain is accompanied by an increased potential risk**.

 KEY POINT

The collar strategy allows for a limited but continued capital appreciation of a long stock position while providing for a limited, fixed downside exposure. The position is very inexpensive to initiate due to the offsetting premiums of the long (purchased) put and short (sold) call.

The collar is an excellent protective strategy for an investor who has a bullish opinion on a stock.

In looking at the bullish lean example, one of the flaws is the fact that if you move that upside call to the higher strikes, you may overly decrease the amount of premium you receive for the sale of that call, which, as you know, is supposed to compensate for the amount spent on your protective put.

One way to adjust for this is to look farther out across the months in the strike you are interested in. Selling a call out two or three months may generate enough premiums to fully offset the price of the put.

Remember, premiums increase over time for all options. You do not have to be confined by the idea that your long put and short call have to be in the same expiration month.

This adjustment provides more acceptable premium balance, allowing extra room for a strong upward stock move while still giving you maximum downside protection.

EXAMPLES

Now let's look at some examples with the collar strategy.

Example 1: Eli Lilly Co.

Figure 11.1 shows a chart of Eli Lilly Co. (LLY) from mid-November 2002 through December 2003 and a chart of when you might use the collar strategy.

Notes

Collar

1. In a one-month span from November 18, 2002, to December 18, 2002, Lilly traded from just below $60.00 to just below $70.00 and back down to $62.00.

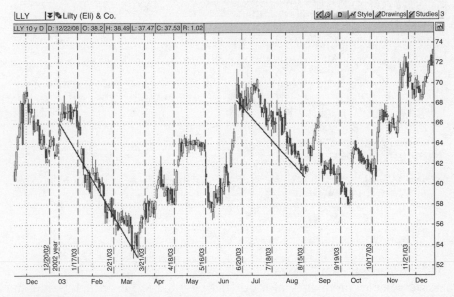

FIGURE 11.1 LLY Chart
Source: Courtesy of Think or Swim (www.thinkorswim.com)

2. In another one-month span from late May 2003 to mid-June 2003, Lilly traded from $56.00 up to $72.00.

3. Several gap openings are also apparent: one in mid-January 2003, one in late August, and one in very late September. These all point to periods of high or increasing volatility.

4. Notice the individual daily trading ranges. The length of the lines shows the number of large range-days. The longer lines indicate larger intraday ranges. In Figure 11.1, Lilly shows a very high number of large intraday movement days, again pointing to high volatility.

5. As much as Lilly had strong run-ups, it had some large down periods also. In a two-month period from mid-January to mid-March 2003, Lilly traded down from $68.50 to $58.00. Then in another two-month period, mid-June to mid-August 2003, Lilly traded down from $71.00 to $61.00.

Conclusion　Lilly appears to be a very volatile stock during the observed period charted in Figure 11.1. The stock began this period at around $60.00 and finished the period at $67.00, which is not necessarily a large move. But when we look at the large intramonth ranges, it's clear that Lilly has been very volatile during this period.

With this type of movement, a maximum protection strategy is necessary, but, with such high volatility, premiums will likely be expensive. The outright buying of a put may cut too deeply into potential profits, making the risk/reward scenario unjustified.

The collar strategy, however, will provide the necessary downside protection while still allowing room for some capital appreciation. The sale of the call will offset the cost of the put purchase to make the trade's risk/reward scenario more viable. The collar can be leaned to provide either more protection or more capital appreciation, depending on the investor's short-term outlook.

Example 2: eBay

Figure 11.2 shows a chart of eBay (EBAY) from June 2003 through January 2004 and a good technical setup for the collar strategy.

Notes

Collar

1. eBay traded in a very wide range during July 2003. It started the month around $25.87 and traded up to $28.76 before trading down to $26.78. Within a week it traded to a high of $29.46. The week after that, at the end of the month, the stock was down to $24.94.

FIGURE 11.2 EBAY Chart
Source: Courtesy of Think or Swim (www.thinkorswim.com)

2. August was another volatile month. The stock had a high of $28.54 and a low of $24.94.

3. The stock started the month of September trading at $28.21. It traded down to $25.22 then back up to $28.62.

4. Volatility continued in October. The stock had quite a range with a high of $30.80 and a low of $26.65. Moreover, the stock had no less than five gap openings. The gap openings were almost evenly divided between ups and downs.

5. The pattern continued in November 2003. The stock started the month by quickly putting in a high around $29.28. It then traded down, reaching a low around $25.32, before rallying and trading back up to $28.10 before the month's end.

6. December began with the stock trading around $28.50. It then moved down quietly to $27.26 by the middle of the month. By the end of the month, eBay was trading at $32.40, up a modest $5.14 in a little more than two weeks.

Conclusion A stock this volatile requires a hedging strategy that provides maximum protection. The collar, more than the covered call, allows you to extract impressive profits while minimizing the risk to your long stock position.

The protective put strategy would work in terms of maximum downside protection, but at what cost? With volatility this high, the puts will be very expensive, maybe too expensive. This situation is perfect for employing the collar.

The sale of a call against the purchase of the put will at least partially offset the expense of the put, making the downside maximum protection affordable, while still leaving room for capital appreciation.

Example 3: Yahoo!

Our third example, shown in Figure 11.3, is Yahoo! (YHOO) from mid-June 2003 through early January 2004.

Notes

Collar

1. Yahoo!, historically a volatile stock, bottoms out and then trades through resistance of a downtrend in mid-August 2003.

2. Yahoo! then trades in an uptrend from a price around $14.00 in late August out through January 2004 with a price high of $25.20. This represents a 35.7 percent increase in four months.

FIGURE 11.3 YHOO Chart
Source: Courtesy of Think or Swim (www.thinkorswim.com)

3. During this uptrend, Yahoo! had several gap openings, which are considered very volatile events. There are three of these gaps in October 2003 and two in November 2003.

4. Further, Yahoo! has many large intraday range days. This also points to a higher level of volatility for this stock.

5. This uptrend that Yahoo! trades in has a wide range. The stock fluctuates widely from the midline of the range. Again, this is indicative of higher volatility.

Conclusion   Yahoo! offers the investor a good upside opportunity. However, in a stock as volatile as Yahoo!, there is also large potential for loss.

Here a maximum protection strategy is advised. Under these higher volatility situations, the collar would be better than the protective put because of overall cost.

When trading a stock with such high volatility, the investor must be aware that option premiums will be expensive if not prohibitive. The collar gives the investor the needed downside protection at a much lower cost (due to premiums received from the sale of the call) while still allowing room for capital appreciation.

Example 4: Merrill Lynch

Figure 11.4 shows a chart of Merrill Lynch (MER) from June 2003 through January 2004 and another possible chart setup for the collar strategy.

Notes

Collar

1. During this viewing period, Merrill (MER) trades in an uptrend from late June 2003 at a price of about $45.00 through January 2004 with a high of around $60.00.

2. This is a wide trend with some intramonth ranges as much as $5.00 and $6.00 wide, indicating a volatile trend.

3. There were a few gap openings early on in the uptrend during July, but we also want to look at the large intraday ranges, displayed by the length of the daily candles.

4. The stock also deviates frequently from the midline of the trend. Although it stays within the trading channel nicely, this still is a volatile trading pattern.

FIGURE 11.4 MER Chart
Source: Courtesy of Think or Swim (www.thinkorswim.com)

Conclusion   With volatility high, option premiums probably will be expensive. In Merrill's case, investors should look to obtain maximum protection, but the protective put would not be the best choice.

Although the stock is very volatile, the uptrend is not a steep one. During the observed period of six months, the trend's midline capital appreciation is only a little more than $6.00, not much compared to many other stocks during this period. With the high volatility, the price of a protective put for any length of time would quickly eat away any profits from the stock's rise.

A collar would allow the investor the protection needed, at a reasonable and warranted cost, to justify the potential reward of the capital appreciation.

COLLAR SYNOPSIS

> **Construction.** Long stock, simultaneously long one out-of-the-money put and short one out-of-the-money call per every 100 shares of stock owned.
>
> **Function.** Provides a low cost to no cost maximum profit protection for a long stock position.

Bias. Cautious or even short-term bearish.

When to Use. When you feel that your long stock position appears to be headed toward volatile market conditions, you want to continue holding the long stock position.

Profit Scenario. Depending on how you set up the collar and the prices of the put and call, you may make a very negligible amount. If the stock trades up, you may make a little.

Loss. Depending on how you set up the collar and the prices of the put and call, you may lose a little money. If the stock trades down, you may also lose a little, but the collar will limit it to a set amount regardless of how low the stock goes.

Key Concepts. Collars are not designed to make money. They are designed to provide maximum downside protection, similar to the protective put, but at a much better price. The premium received from the sale of the call will offset the amount paid for the put.

PART III

Advanced Strategies: Spread Trading, Straddles, and Strangles

I n previous chapters, I demonstrated how well options function in unison with a stock position. They enhance potential gains, provide profit protection, and limit the risk of the entire investment. They enable us to manage risk in a single stock as well as an entire portfolio. But as good as options are in conjunction with stocks, they can be even better when traded against each other.

Spreads are strategies that do not involve the use of any security other than another option. Their positives are that they are inexpensive, they offer protection for both buyer and seller, and they are in effect automatically hedged trades.

Spreads can provide large-percentage returns with low risk and can be entered into with small capital outlay. A spread involves the purchase of one option in conjunction with the sale of another option. This might be the place and time to review the obligations, rights, risks and rewards of buying and selling calls and puts. Those components are what make the spreads possible.

There are many types of spreads. Some take advantage of stock movements while others are set up to take advantage of movements in implied volatility and even the passage of time. There are calendar or time spreads, diagonal spreads, ratio spreads, and also vertical spreads, which we will discuss in depth here.

Spreads are more advanced and sophisticated than the strategies discussed earlier. While certain spreads, such as a one-to-one vertical spread, can be less risky than a buy-write, trading the spread is more complicated because there are more variables to consider and control.

When you trade a spread you are dealing with three elements: the spread as a whole (which you can buy or sell) and its component parts: the option you buy and the option you sell.

Although most spreads are relatively inexpensive to initiate, they can provide a large percentage return and provide protection (limits) to both sides of the trade. Therefore, even experienced investors can profit from learning about spreads and their investment potential.

CHAPTER 12

Vertical Spreads

There are two primary vertical spreads: the vertical call spread and the vertical put spread. Each spread can be bought, making you long the vertical spread, or sold, making you short the vertical spread. Both can be executed to take advantage of directional stock plays. When I use the term *directional stock play*, I mean using vertical spreads to capitalize on anticipated stock movements either up or down.

A *bull spread* is used by the investor in anticipation that the stock will rise. Remember, **bullish means to have a positive outlook on a stock's future movement.** There are two ways to set up a bull spread. The first is with the use of calls. In this case, a bullish investor would buy a vertical call spread (*bull call spread*) by buying a call with a lower strike price and selling a call with a higher strike price. This would create a debit trade.

The second way to construct a bull spread is with the use of puts. A bullish investor could sell a vertical put spread (*bull put spread*) hoping to profit from an increase in the stock's value. The investor would sell a put with a higher strike price and buy a put with a lower strike price. This would create a credit trade. Figure 12.1 shows a bull spread profit and loss chart.

Vertical spreads can be classified in another way besides bull spreads and bear spreads. They can also be categorized as debit spreads and credit spreads as determined by whether you are paying out money (debit) to buy a vertical spread or taking in money (credit) by selling a vertical spread.

To recap, if you feel a stock will be increasing in value, you may put on a bull spread by either buying a vertical call spread (bull call spread: debit) or selling a vertical put spread (bull put spread: credit).

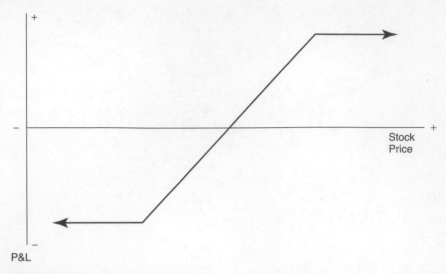

FIGURE 12.1   Bull Spread P&L Chart

A *bear spread*, however, is used when you feel a stock is likely to trade down. Remember, **bearish means having a negative outlook on the future movement of a stock.** To take advantage of this expected downward movement, the investor would put on a bear spread.

This can be done in either of two ways. First, you can do it using a vertical put spread (*bear put spread*) by purchasing a put with a higher-priced strike and selling a put with a lower-priced strike. This would create a debit trade as you would be paying out money by purchasing a more expensive option and selling a less expensive option.

Another way to construct a bear spread is by using calls: specifically sell a vertical call spread (*bear call spread*). You do that by selling a call with a lower strike price and purchasing a call with a higher strike price. This will create a credit trade. Instead of putting out money to purchase a spread, you will be receiving money for selling the spread. It is important to note that just because you are receiving money from the sale of the spread does not mean that the spread is a premium collection spread. If you think that a stock is likely to decrease in value, you can sell a vertical call spread (bear call spread) or purchase a vertical put spread (bear put spread). Figure 12.2 shows a bear spread profit and loss chart.

CONSTRUCTION OF A VERTICAL SPREAD

A vertical spread is constructed by the purchase of a call (or put) and the sale of a call (or put) in the same stock and in the same month. The only

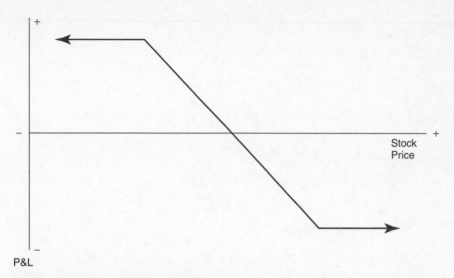

FIGURE 12.2 Bear Spread P&L Chart

difference between the two options is the strike price. For instance, a vertical spread can be constructed by purchasing the IBM June 55 call while selling the June IBM 60 call. This trade would be called the IBM June 55–60 call spread. Similarly, a purchase of the IBM July 45 put and sale of the IBM July 60 put would be called the IBM July 45–60 put spread.

The key to the construction of vertical spreads is that you choose the options that are in the same stock, same month, but different strikes and in a one-to-one ratio. That is, you must purchase one option for every one you sell or sell one option for every one you buy.

VALUE AND THE VERTICAL SPREAD

Two fundamentals are universal to understanding the value of all vertical spreads: You can determine a vertical spread's maximum value by taking note of the difference between the two strikes, its minimum value ($0); and vertical spreads have intrinsic as well as extrinsic value.

Maximum Value

A vertical spread's maximum value is the difference between the two strikes chosen for the spread. The difference between the strikes is the maximum value of all vertical spreads regardless of the distance between the two strikes. For example, the maximum value of the June 55–60 call spread is $5.00: [60 − 55] = $5.00. The maximum value of the July 45–60 put spread is $15.00 [60 − 45 = 15]. It does not matter whether the spread is $5.00 wide, $10.00 wide, $20.00 wide, or even $50.00 wide; the spread's maximum value is the difference between the two strikes. When choosing a spread, you are able to calculate in advance the maximum potential gain in that spread by checking that difference between the two strikes and then subtracting the amount of money you spent buying the spread.

Where does the spread get its value? Basically, from its two components—the call (or put) you buy and the call (or put) you sell. The value of the spread changes during its lifetime as the two options will be influenced by the movement of the stock price, the movement of volatility, and the passage of time. The value of the spread is definitive at expiration, determined by the price of the stock at that point in time.

Let's look at a spread's value with different closing stock prices. Using the June 55–60 call spread example, we will set the date to June expiration on Friday. On that day, all the June options will expire and the options will be worth parity, as all of the extrinsic value will have eroded away.

If the stock closes at $55.00, then both the 55 strike and the 60 strike will be out of the money and thus worthless. The value of the spread will be zero as both options are worth $0.

However, if the stock closes at $57.50, the June 55 calls will be worth $2.50. The June 60 calls will be out of the money and thus worthless; therefore, the spread will be worth $2.50 (June 55 call $ 2.50 − June 60 call $0 = $2.50).

If the stock closes at $60.00, then the June 55 calls will be worth $5.00. Meanwhile, the June 60 calls will be worth $0. This means that the spread will be worth $5.00 (June 55 call $ 5.00 − June 60 call $0). This is the maximum value of the spread. Note that this shows that the maximum value is identical to the difference between the strikes.

As the stock goes higher, the June 60 call becomes in the money and gains intrinsic value. Now, for every penny that the stock increases in value, the June 55 calls and June 60 calls gain value equally, keeping the $5.00 spread between the two strikes constant. The gains both calls experience is due to the deltas of both options increasing to 100 and having both options now increasing in price at the identical rate, holding the price of the spread constant.

Remember, one of delta's definitions is that of percent change. If two options under the same stock have the same delta, then both options will increase (and decrease) in price at the same rate. If both options increase at the same rate, the difference between the two prices will remain the same. Thus the value of the spread will stay the same, as seen in Table 12.1. (The spread value is the difference between the price of the call you bought and the price of the call you sold. You have a gain with the one but a loss with the other.)

TABLE 12.1   Value of Spread: Call

Strike Price	June 55 Call	June 60 Call	Spread Value
50	0	0	0
55	0	0	0
60	5	0	5
65	10	5	5
70	15	10	5
75	20	15	5
80	25	20	5

The maximum value of the vertical spread (the difference between the two strikes) holds true for vertical put spreads as well as vertical call spreads. Let's look at an example, using puts: the July 50–60 put spread (spread difference $10.00).

Again we set time forward to Friday, July expiration. We set the stock closing price at $60.00. At $60.00, both the July 50 puts and the July 60 puts will be out of the money and thus worthless. With both the July 50 puts and July 60 puts worthless, the spread is also worthless (July 60 put $0–July 50 put $0).

But if the stock finishes at $52.50, then the July 60 puts will be worth $7.50 while the July 50 puts will still be worthless. In this scenario the July 50–60 put spread will be worth $7.50 (July 60 puts $7.50–July 50 puts $0).

If the stock finishes at $50.00, then the July 60 puts will be worth $10.00 while the July 50 puts will be worth $0. At this level, the spread will be worth $10.00 (July 60 puts $10.00–July 50 puts $0). This is the maximum value of the spread. As you can see, it is identical to the $10.00 difference between the strikes.

As the stock goes lower, the July 50 puts become in the money and gain intrinsic value (Table 12.2). Now, for every penny that the stock decreases

TABLE 12.2   Value of Put Spread

Strike Price	July 50 Put	July 60 Put	Spread Value
35	15	25	10
40	10	20	10
45	5	15	10
50	0	10	10
55	0	5	5
60	0	0	0
65	0	0	0

in value, the July 60 puts and the July 50 puts will gain value equally, keeping the $10.00 spread between the two strikes constant.

As a vertical spread buyer, your ability to calculate the maximum value of the spread is essential for calculating your maximum potential gain. If you know the maximum value of the spread (difference between two strikes) and you know how much the spread costs us, you can calculate how much you could make by simply taking the maximum potential value of the spread and subtracting what you paid for it. The difference is your maximum potential gain.

As stated, the maximum value of a vertical spread is the difference between the two strikes while the minimum value of the spread is, of course, $0. This means that in this strategy, **both the buyer and the seller have a limited, fixed maximum loss.**

Buyers of a vertical spread can lose only what they spend. So, if buyers spend $2.20 to purchase the August 35–40 call spread, the most they can lose is the $2.20 they spent.

For sellers, the maximum loss is the difference between the maximum value of the spread (difference between the strikes) and the amount of money received for the sale of the spread. For example, if you sold the August 35–40 call spread for $2.20, then your maximum loss will be $2.80. Remember, the maximum value of the spread is the difference between the two strikes or in this case $5.00 (40–35). The difference between the maximum value of the spread ($5.00) and the amount the seller received for the sale ($2.20) leaves a $2.80 maximum loss.

 KEY POINT

It is important to understand and remember that vertical spreads have both a limited profit and a limited loss scenario for both the buyer and the seller.

Intrinsic Value

In looking at vertical spreads, an investor must take note that they have an intrinsic value as well as extrinsic value. Since vertical spreads have intrinsic value, they can be considered to be in the money.

Any spread that has intrinsic value is considered in the money. How can you identify the value of a vertical call spread or a vertical put spread? Compare the stock price to the strike prices.

Look at any vertical call spread. If the stock price is above the lower strike of the spread, then the spread is in the money. For example, in the February 50–55 call spread, if the stock is trading at $52.00, then the spread would be in the money by $2.00. This is because if the spread expired at that moment, the February 50 calls would finish $2.00 in the money. The February 55 calls would finish worthless because they are out of the money. The spread, however, would be in the money with a value of $2.00. Remember, when looking at the value of the spread as a whole, you must look at each of its component parts.

The rule is similar for determining whether a spread is out of the money. If the stock price is lower than the lower strike of the spread, then the spread is out of the money. Again, looking at the February 50–55 call spread, if the spread expired today and the stock price closed at $48.00 (lower than the lower strike), then the spread would be out of the money.

And, of course, if the stock is trading at the same price as the lower strike price, then the spread will be considered at the money.

For vertical put spreads, a spread is determined to be in the money if the stock price is lower than the higher of the two strikes of the spread. For example, let's look at the September 40–45 put spread. If the stock were to close at $42.00 on expiration day, the September 45 put would end up in the money and be worth $3.00. The September 40 puts would be out of the money, creating a $3.00 intrinsic value for the spread. Since the spread has an intrinsic value, it is in the money.

A vertical put spread is considered to be out of the money if the stock price is higher than the higher strike of the spread. So, going back to our September 40–45 put spread example, if the stock were to close at a price of $46.00 (higher than the higher strike), then both the September 40 and 45 put will expire worthless. Thus the spread will be worthless and out of the money.

A vertical put spread is considered at the money when the stock price is equal to the higher strike price.

Cost Relationship between Corresponding Put Spreads and Call Spreads

We have seen that vertical spreads can have intrinsic value and that we can roughly determine their value by comparing stock price to strike prices. There is another relationship that can help investors determine value.

That is the relationship that exists between corresponding vertical spreads. The term *corresponding* here refers to the same month, the same strikes, in the same stock. The only difference is between calls and puts. For example, the XYZ September 30–35 vertical call spread's corresponding spread would be the XYZ September 30–35 vertical put spread. Similarly, the spread of the ABC June 70–80 put would be the ABC June 70–80 call spread.

KEY POINT

The sum of a vertical call spread and its corresponding vertical put spread equals the difference between the two strikes.

If the May 40-45 call spread trades at $2.00, then the May 40-45 put spread will be worth $3.00. Let's review this. The difference of the two strikes is $5.00 and the value of the call spread is $2.00. That means the value of the put spread will be $3.00. Table 12.3 is a floor trader's pricing sheet that shows where individual options would be trading and what they would be worth at expiration based on each trader's individual inputs.

From this table, we can calculate the price of any corresponding spread. Pick any stock price. Now calculate the value of a vertical call spread or a vertical put spread by determining how much your call or put is in the money. Once you've done that, calculate the value of its corresponding vertical spread. Add the two spreads together, and see if that sum is equal to the difference between the two strikes.

Perform the calculations several times at different stock prices on the different vertical spreads. This relationship is just one of the mathematical relationships between the price of a call and its corresponding put and is true with $5, $10, $15 and, in fact, with all corresponding spreads. Remember note the difference in the strikes of the spread, then check the costs of the call and its corresponding put. Adding both should equal the difference in the spread.

It is not necessary to understand why this works. For now, it is important to understand that these spreads are related and the price of one can help you calculate the price of the other.

TABLE 12.3   Relationship between Calls and Corresponding Puts at Expiration

Stock Price	May 40–45 Call Spread Price	May 40–45 Put Spread Price
38	0	5
39	0	5
40	0	5
41	1	4
42	2	3
43	3	2
44	4	1
45	5	0
46	5	0
47	5	0

SPREAD PRICES FLUCTUATE

While the value of the spread at expiration is definitive and consists of only intrinsic value, during the life of a vertical call spread, the spread will trade between its minimum and maximum values (between zero and the difference between the two strikes) and include both intrinsic and extrinsic value. In the case of a vertical call spread, the spread will trade closer to zero when the stock trades closer to or lower than the lower strike price. The spread will trade closer to maximum value when the stock trades closer to or higher than the higher strike price.

For example, let's refer back to the May 40–45 call spread chart in Table 12.3. In the column marked May 40–45 call spread price, you can see that with the stock at $39.00, the spread is worthless. As the stock price climbs toward $45.00, the call spread price increases until finally it reaches its maximum value which is the difference between the two strikes

Remember, this maximum gain occurs *at expiration*. Before that time, the spread will trade with a premium or a discount to its intrinsic value. Depending on where the stock is located in relationship to the two strikes, the spread may be worth more or less than its intrinsic value. This is due to the extrinsic value component of the two options.

Starting from a stock price of $42.50, a price located directly between the two strikes (using our example of the May 40–45 call spread), the approximate value of the spread will be roughly $2.50. This is because the May 40 calls and the May 45 calls are equidistant from the current stock price of $42.50. Being equidistant from the stock, both the May 40 and 45 calls will have almost the same amount of extrinsic value.

Thus, in the spread, the extrinsic values of the two options cancel each other out since you are long one call and short the other. This would leave each option value consisting of intrinsic value only. With the stock at $42.50, the value of the May 40–45 call spread will be $2.50. The May 40 calls will have $2.50 in intrinsic value while the May 45 calls will have $0 in intrinsic value. The difference gives you a spread with a value of $2.50.

A general rule of thumb is: If the stock price is located evenly between the two strike prices, the vertical spread should be worth roughly half of the value of the distance between the two strikes. This is true for vertical put spreads as well as call spreads.

From this rule, we can roughly estimate the vertical spread's price for different stock prices.

For vertical call spreads, if the spread is worth roughly half of the difference between the two strikes with the stock price directly between the two strikes, then as the stock falls to the lower strike and below, the spread's value will decrease and move closer to $0.

Time left until expiration and volatility will dictate how close and how quickly it will approach $0. On the other side, as the stock climbs toward and above the upper strike, the spread's value will increase toward the maximum value described by the difference between the two strikes.

For vertical put spreads, as the stock price decreases toward the lower strike price, the spread will increase in value and approach its maximum value as defined by the difference between the two strikes. As the stock price increases toward the higher strike, the spread will decrease in value and will approach $0. Again, time until expiration and volatility will determine how quickly and how close the spread will approach $0.

FACTORS THAT AFFECT SPREAD PRICING

The determination of pricing as just described works in most cases, assuming that the implied volatility in both the 35 and 40 calls is the same.

Most of the time, these two options will have a slightly different implied volatility. This intramonth difference in implied volatility values through different strikes is known as a *vertical volatility skew*. Markets run volatility skews to make sure that out-of-the-money options have enough premium in them to justify the individual option's risk/reward scenario.

For now, it is enough to know that volatility skew exists. As long as it is a tight skew (little deviation of implied volatility from strike to strike), the values should hold pretty consistent to our previous examples.

Whatever factors affect the vertical spread, they are contingent on where the stock is in relation to the spread. As stated, changes in implied volatility affect the price of a spread, but the position of the stock in relation to the strikes of the spread is the key determinant of price.

ROLLING THE POSITION

The selection of a vertical spread is only the beginning. Once you have the spread, you need to know how to manage (roll or morph) or close the position. Closing out, rolling, or morphing the position has to be analyzed and executed with the same due diligence as was used in the selection process.

Looking to the closing out of a vertical call spread, there are three possible outcomes. The spread can finish out of the money and valueless. For a call spread, this scenario occurs when the stock closes at or below the lower strike of the spread. In this scenario, in order to close out the spread, you would just let it expire. Both options finish out of the money, so no residual position will be left.

If the spread finishes fully in the money (at maximum value)—that is, with both options in the money—then both options will be exercised. You will exercise your long call, and your short call will be assigned. They will cancel each other out, and you will be left with no residual position. This scenario occurs when the stock price closes higher than the higher strike call involved in the spread.

The difficult scenario is when the stock closes in between the two strikes of the spread. This scenario creates a situation where one strike winds up in the money while the other ends up out of the money. When both options expire in the money, they are both exercised—one creating a long stock position, the other creating a short position; thus they cancel each other out. This is not the case here. Here one option, the one that is in the money, will leave a residual stock position. Since the other option is out of the money, it will not be able to be used to offset the residual stock position created by the expiring in-the-money option.

Two actions could be taken: trade out of the spread or go through the expiration process. Choice one involves trading out of the spread on expiration Friday just before the close. Because of the bid/ask spread of the two options, you probably will have to give away some of your profits in order to close out the position in its entirety. Giving up a portion of the profits may be the best thing to do in order to avoid a potential naked short position, which brings with it unlimited risk.

Remembering that the stock is in between the two strikes, you may decide not to trade out of the entire spread. If you decide only to trade out of the in-the-money option, you run the risk (albeit short-lived because you are doing this late on expiration day of the expiring month) that the stock moves adversely and the out-of-the-money option suddenly becomes in the money. If that happens, you will now be naked the residual stock position. Depending on whether you are short or long the strike that was out of the money and has now become in the money and whether you are trading a call spread or a put spread, you will wind up either long stock or short stock on Monday morning with no hedge.

However, if the stock is at a relatively safe distance from out of the money, you may want to just close out the in-the-money option and let it expire worthless.

The two factors that must be considered are:

1. The combination of the distance of the strike from the stock price in relation to the short amount of time for the stock to get there

2. The amount of money saved by not buying back the out-of-the-money option

Remember, you are making this trade at the very end of the day on expiration day. These options only have minutes of life left. So, knowing this, the risk is somewhat mitigated, but it still there.

The catch is the proximity of the stock to the out-of-the-money option. If the stock is close to the out-of-the-money option, you would be best advised to trade out of the spread entirely.

Again, as stated before, if the stock closes either with the spread fully in the money or fully out of the money, the position will adjust itself through the exercise process, leaving no residual position. If the stock price finishes between the two strikes, there will be a residual position. We discussed how to trade out of this position.

Choice two is not to trade out and allow yourself to go through the expiration process. You must remember that if you are going to accept a residual stock position, you must be able to afford it.

For example, if you have 10 July 50 calls and you exercise them, you will be receiving 1,000 shares of stock at $50.00 per share. Thus, you must have $50,000.00 of cash and/or margin in your account to receive the stock. If you do not have enough cash and/or margin to accept delivery, you must trade out of the position before it expires.

TIME DECAY AND VOLATILITY TRADING OPPORTUNITIES

When vertical spreads are mentioned, they quite often come with additional names, such as bull and bear. Because of this, most people think of vertical spreads as directional plays—which is true. However, vertical spreads can be used to take advantage of two other potential trading opportunities: time decay and volatility movement.

If you are looking for a fully hedged way to take advantage of time decay, a vertical spread can be an excellent tool. You will recall that a vertical spread has a limited profit potential but also a limited loss scenario for both the buyer and the seller. So, how do we use this covered trade to take advantage of time decay?

At-the-money options have more extrinsic value than their similar month in-the-money or out-of-the-money options. Since it is an option's extrinsic value that decays away over time, you could set up a vertical spread by selling an at-the-money option and buying either the out-of-the-money option (creating a credit spread) or an in-the-money option (creating a debit spread). If the stock holds tight to the out-of-the-money option, the option's extrinsic value will decay away at a faster rate than either the in-the-money or the out-of-the-money option, due to the fact that the at-the-money option has more total extrinsic value to decay in the same amount of time as the others.

Creating the vertical spread by selling an at-the-money option and buying an out-of-the-money or in-the-money option as a hedge looks like a good idea, but there are other choices. Should you do the put spread or the call spread? Should you buy it or sell it? The decision of what to do from this point should be based primarily on which way you think the stock will move. Although you are playing for time decay and assuming an overall lack of movement, you can't expect the stock not to move at all. So even though you are playing time decay, you still want to form an opinion about in which direction the stock is most likely to move. By doing this, you have now given yourself another way of making the trade profitable. You are playing for a lack of movement, but now you can still win if you pick the right direction. This scenario presents you with two ways to win and only one way to lose.

Now that you have picked which at-the-money strike you are going to sell and you have picked your anticipated stock position, you have yet another decision to make. Do you do the call vertical spread or the put vertical spread? Remember, both the vertical call spread and the vertical put spread allow you to participate in either stock direction. For the bulls, you can buy a vertical call spread or sell a vertical put spread if you think that the stock will go up.

For the bears, you can buy a vertical put spread or sell a vertical call spread.

For each direction, there are two choices: a purchase or a sale. The best way to decide which to do, other than deciding based on your own style or comfort ability, is a simple risk/reward analysis.

By selecting an at-the-money option to sell as part of a vertical spread, you can execute a time-decay play with a hedged position.

A vertical spread can be used as a volatility play in much the same way as a time decay play can be used. As stated, an at-the-money option has more extrinsic value than any other option in its expiration month.

This is due to a number of contributing factors including time, but it is in no small way due to volatility. Volatility is a huge component of an option's extrinsic value. An option's dollar sensitivity to movements in implied volatility is known as *vega*. Obviously, an at-the-money option will have a higher vega (volatility sensitivity) then will an in-the-money or out-of-the-money option in the same month.

As volatility increases, the at-the-money option will increase in price to a greater degree than will an in-the-money or out-of-the-money option in the same month. As volatility increases, the at-the-money option will increase in price to a greater degree than will an in-the-money or out-of-the-money option whose vega will be less.

Conversely, the at-the-money option will lose value at a greater rate than an in-the-money or out-of-the-money option should implied volatility decrease. The question now is how to use the vertical spread to take advantage of anticipated movements in implied volatility. Remember, the vertical spread affords you the luxury of being hedged on either side of the trade, as both a buyer and a seller of the spread.

If you think that implied volatility is likely to increase, you can set up a vertical spread by buying an at-the-money option and selling either the in-the-money or out-of-the-money option against it. Conversely, if you feel implied volatility will decrease, you can set up a vertical spread by selling an at-the-money option and buying either an out-of-the-money or an in-the-money option against it.

To set it up, you would follow the same guidelines as you would for setting up a vertical spread to take advantage of time decay. Decide in which direction you feel the stock would most likely move. If you feel the stock would most likely rise, you will have to decide between buying a vertical call spread and selling a vertical put spread.

Either way, you will have to construct the spread with the at-the-money option being long if you feel volatility will increase or short if you feel volatility will decrease. If you feel the stock would most likely fall, you will have to decide between buying a vertical put spread and selling a vertical call spread. Again, either way, you will have to construct the spread with the short option being at the money.

As you can see, the vertical spread does not have to be used only in directional scenarios. It is very versatile, allowing the investor several choices among a diverse group of potential uses. It also affords limited risk, albeit limited profit potential, to both the buyer and the seller.

AN IMAGINARY SPREAD SCENARIO

Let's develop an imaginary spread scenario and set it in real life events.

In October, you begin to hear about IJK stock. It looks interesting, so you then use a variety of sources to learn about it: news, charts, outside analysts, Internet research, and so on. From your investigations, you decide that this stock is poised for a strong upward move and you would like to take advantage of it. However, each share is $50.00, and you question whether you want to put out the capital for enough shares to make the trade worthwhile.

That is the time to investigate IJK spreads. Since you are bullish on the stock, you investigate the bullish plays of the call spreads and the put spreads. You check the pricing of both since you are aware that implied volatility and time decay will affect both your purchase price and your selling price if you decide to sell out the spread before expiration.

Let's say that you set the spread's maximum potential gain at $5.00 using our formula.

Then you decide you want to buy a call spread, so you buy 10 IJK November 50 calls and sell 10 IJK November 55 calls. The spread is called November 50–55. The spread's cost is $2.50, which means you pay $2,500 for the trade—inexpensive when you consider that purchasing 1,000 shares of IJK stock would have cost you $50,000.

Now you wait and follow the stock price of IJK. If you hold the position to expiration, you face these losses or gains.

1. If the stock does not move up as you expected and stays at $50.00 or decreases in value, your spread is worthless, and you lose the $2,500 that you paid for it.
2. If the stock begins to move up, you first recoup your investment and then move into profits. After the stock has moved up to $52.50, you are at the break-even point. Every money advance after that represents profit.

Table 12.4 represents the spread's losses and gains and your total profit.

Table 12.4 is based on stock prices at expiration Friday in November. Until then the spread's value fluctuates between $0 and its maximum (the difference between strike prices) of $5.00.

At any time until expiration, you can sell out of the spread, but what you receive for the price may be influenced by implied volatility and time

TABLE 12.4 Vertical Spread's Profit and Loss

Stock Price	50 Calls	55 Calls	Spread	Your Cost	P&L
48	0	0	0	2500	−2500
49	0	0	0	2500	−2500
50	0	0	0	2500	−2500
51	1	0	1	2500	−1500
52	2	0	2	2500	−500
53	3	0	3	2500	+500
54	4	0	4	2500	+1500
55	5	0	5	2500	+2500
56	6	1	5	2500	+2500
57	7	2	5	2500	+2500

decay, and that will change your profit or loss. If you hold the spread until expiration and your bullish lean proves true, your maximum profit on your $2,500 investment is $2,500.

You paid $2,500 for the spread and received $5,000 at expiration with the stock at $55.00 or higher. That represents a $2,500 profit, which is a 100 percent return.

If you had invested $50,000 for 1,000 shares of IJK and at expiration sold the stock for $55,000, your profit is $5,000 for a 10 percent return.

For many investors, the reward/risk scenario of the spread is attractive. They can limit the capital at risk and the time of risk/reward exposure. The spread also offers protection whether your lean is bullish or bearish. Finally, the spread has the potential of a large-percentage return on investment.

RECAP WITH SPECIAL INSIGHTS

Vertical spreads can have various names. Different people may call the same vertical spread several different things. We have used two terms only: vertical call spread and vertical put spread. Each of these two spreads allows for two positions, long and short.

The long vertical call spread is constructed by buying one call option with a lower strike price while simultaneously selling another call option in the same month with a higher strike price. In a one-to-one ratio, this trade, the long vertical call spread, is labeled a bullish trade. This means that when engaging into a long vertical call spread, the investor expects the stock to increase in value. An investor who engages in a trade with the expectation of the stock going up is said to be bullish. Thus, a long vertical call spread is a bullish trade.

A short vertical call spread is constructed by selling a call with a lower strike price while simultaneously buying a call in the same month with a higher strike price. Since owning a vertical call spread created a long position for the owner, then the seller of the vertical call spread must be short.

An investor who takes a short position anticipates a decrease in the price of a stock and is considered to be bearish on the stock. Thus, a short vertical call spread is considered a bearish position.

The maximum profit for the seller of a vertical call spread is attained when the price of the stock closes at or below the lower priced strike. The maximum loss is attained when the stock closes at the higher strike.

The vertical put spread functions in much the same way as the vertical call spread, just in the opposite direction. Like the vertical call spread, the construction of the vertical put is done in a one-to-one ratio. The vertical put spread is constructed by purchasing one put and simultaneously selling another put in the same month but in a different strike.

A long vertical put spread is considered to be a bearish trade. This means that the purchaser of a vertical put spread is expecting the stock to go down. Further, a long vertical put spread is considered a debit spread, which simply means that the purchaser had to put out money to buy the spread.

Now, if the stock proceeds down, the spread's value will expand. As stated before, a spread's maximum value is equivalent to the difference between the strikes. A spread's minimum value is $0.

In the case of a put spread, maximum value is attained when the stock trades at or below the lower strike. Conversely, a put spread's minimum value is attained when the stock trades to the higher strike.

A short vertical put spread is constructed by purchasing a put with a lower strike price while simultaneously selling a put with a higher strike in the same stock in the same month and in a one-to-one ratio: for example, buying 1 February 65 put while selling 1 February 70 put or buying 10 May 20 puts while selling 10 May 30 puts. It is considered to be a bullish trade because the seller expects the stock to go up or increase in value.

Further, it is considered a credit spread, meaning that the seller receives cash into his or her account upon execution of the trade.

Suppose you were to sell the June 50–60 put spread for $5.50. As the seller, your maximum profit will be the $5.50 you received for the sale of the spread. The maximum profit will be attained if the stock closes at $60.00 or above. At that level, both the June 50 and 60 puts will be worthless because both will be out of the money. Thus, the spread will have no value.

The maximum loss of the trade will be defined by the difference between the two strikes minus the amount you received from the sale of the spread. In this case, the difference between the strikes is $10.00 (60 strike–50 strike). The spread was sold for $5.50, so $4.50 is the maximum loss of the position to the seller.

In conclusion, **vertical spreads provide the buyer and the seller an excellent percentage return. At the same time, they provide limited loss scenarios.** Vertical spreads allow for two types of bullish trades, the purchase of a vertical call spread and the sale of a vertical put spread. Vertical spreads also offer two bearish trades: the purchase of a vertical put spread and the sale of a vertical call spread.

EXAMPLES

The next four examples show vertical spreads.

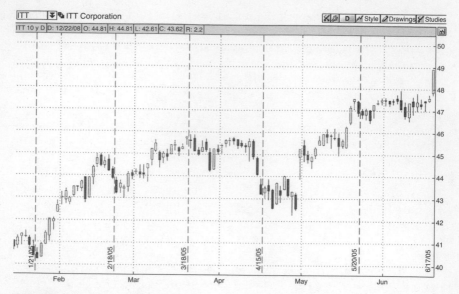

FIGURE 12.3 ITT Daily Chart
Source: Courtesy of Think or Swim (www.thinkorswim.com)

Example 1: ITT Industries

Figure 12.3 shows the daily chart of ITT Industries (ITT).

Notes

Vertical Bull Spread

1. Dating back to January 2005, ITT was in a steady consistent upward trading pattern that actually turns into a bit of a tear starting in early May. Although the pattern is aggressive, it is consistent over the course of several months.

2. Some investors would choose this opportunity to do a buy-write. Purchasing the stock and selling a call for premium collection is not a bad idea. However, a stock having this kind of run has to get you a little nervous about the depth and rapidness of a reversal. Downside risk becomes a legitimate source of concern.

3. A long vertical call spread consisting of a long in-the-money call and short at-the-money or slightly out-of-the money call will assure a profit from the upward movement of the stock as well as a capture of some premium.

4. The spread can be rolled out a month and up strikes in order to lock in some profit from month to month and to better continue the

position for future profitability. This is all accomplished in a limited loss scenario using much less cash in a more efficient way. The buy-write does not match this risk/reward scenario, so the vertical bull spread is a better option.

Example 2: General Electric

Figure 12.4 shows the daily chart for General Electric (GE).

Notes

Vertical Bear Spread

1. General Electric spends a large chunk of time in a sideways trading pattern into early May. At this point, General Electric breaks out in search of a higher trading range but fails to hold that range and trades down to find a lower range.

2. During this time, General Electric begins trading down in a slow, gradual motion that starts in mid-June. As the stock continues down, there are two noticeable bounce-backs. The first bounce was in July. This bounce could have fooled you into taking off your position, because it may have look as if the stock was ready for a real recovery. If you had been in a sell-write position (which has unlimited risk), the thought of

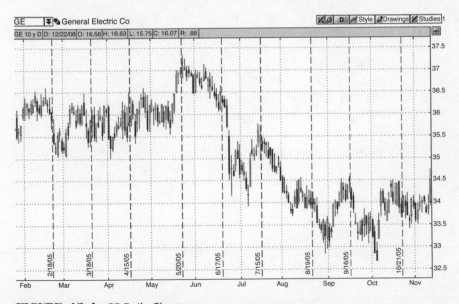

FIGURE 12.4 GE Daily Chart
Source: Courtesy of Think or Swim (www.thinkorswim.com)

unlimited loss or of losing already earned profits may have made you want to take the money off the table and run.

3. If you had given up on the position in July, you would have missed out on at least another 15 percent profits between downside direction and premium collection. However, if you were in a bear spread position, one that has a limited loss scenario, you may have been able to hold on because you would not be in a position to lose all of your profits due to the limited loss profile of the bear spread. Controlling/limiting risk as the bear spread does can provide time to allow the stock to move.

Example 3: Johnson & Johnson

Figure 12.5 shows the Johnson & Johnson (JNJ) daily chart.

Notes

Vertical Bear Spread

1. During the month of April, Johnson & Johnson ends a long run by turning over and starting to trade down in a gradual, consistent manner over the course of a five-month period through September.

FIGURE 12.5 JNJ Daily Chart
Source: Courtesy of Think or Swim (www.thinkorswim.com)

2. This slow and gradual movement offers an opportunity for an investor to capture some time premium decay as well as the downward movement of the stock. The sell-write is an excellent strategy here; however, not everyone can be in a position to short a stock at all, let alone a $70.00 stock.

3. The use of a long vertical put spread (bear spread) offers an alternative. The vertical spread allows investors to play the short side in terms of direction but, when constructed properly, the bear spread will allow for premium collection in situation like this one, where the stock has a slow, consistent, gradual movement.

4. As the months go by, the spread can be rolled down to take advantage of further downside movement and can be rolled out to the next month in order to continue the position over time.

5. The spread will expand in price as the stock continues down. So, as each spread maxes out in price, the spread will be primed to be rolled up, out, or up and out. These spreads will not only be directional trades, but by being short the at-the-money option, they can also collect premium.

Example 4: Symantec

Figure 12.6 shows the daily chart from Symantec (SMYC).

Notes

Vertical Bear Spread

1. After trading up aggressively for several years and having two 2-for-1 stock splits, Symantec breaks down out of a near-vertical trading channel with a gap down opening in late November.

2. After another gap down opening, Symantec starts a slow, gradual decline from around $26.00 at the beginning of December to about $20.00 by the end of May, six months later.

3. This slow, gradual decrease can be taken advantage of by use of a sell-write. However, with the difficulties of shorting stock (regulation and margin), a long vertical put spread might be a better bet.

4. During this period, a long vertical put spread constructed by purchasing an in-the-money put and selling an at-the-money or slightly out-of-the-money put would allow for profit from the directional movement of the stock plus profit from the capture of premium by virtue of selling an at-the-money option.

FIGURE 12.6 SMYC Daily Chart
Source: Courtesy of Think or Swim (www.thinkorswim.com)

5. The use of the vertical put spread would require less capital and provide a limited potential loss scenario and a better return than the sell-write.

6. Further, the put spread can easily be morphed into a more aggressive premium collection strategy when the stock bottoms out and consolidates into a potential sideways trading pattern, as Symantec does in mid-May.

BULL SPREAD SYNOPSIS

Construction. Long one call while simultaneously short one call with a higher strike in the same month. Or short one put while simultaneously long one put with a lower strike in the same month.

Function. Low-cost stock directional play, which allows you two choices to put on the same trade: long vertical call spread or short vertical put spread.

Bias (Lean). Bullish.

When to Use. Use when you feel the stock is likely to rise but not too quickly or explosively, as this strategy has a limited profit potential. Also, when constructed properly, this spread can be used as a premium collection strategy.

Profit Scenario. If the stock rises, profit will be defined by the increase in value of the long vertical call spread or, in the case of a short vertical put spread, its decrease in value.

Loss Scenario. If the stock declines, loss will be defined by the decrease in value of the long vertical call spread or, in the case of a short vertical put call spread, its increase in value.

Key Concepts. The maximum value of a vertical spread will be equal to the difference between the two strikes. Therefore, both the buyer and the seller will have a limited profit and a limited loss scenario. Depending on which strikes you use, time decay can help or hurt the position. Thus, some vertical spreads can make money over time even if the stock stays stagnant.

BEAR SPREAD SYNOPSIS

Construction. Long one call while simultaneously short one call with a lower strike in the same month. Or short one put while simultaneously long one put with a higher strike in the same month.

Function. Low-cost stock directional play, which allows you two choices to put on the same trade: short vertical call spread or long vertical put spread.

Bias (Lean). Bearish.

When to Use. Use when you feel the stock is likely to decline but not too quickly or explosively, as this strategy has a limited profit potential. Also, when constructed properly, this spread can be used as a premium collection strategy.

Profit Scenario. If the stock declines, profit will be defined by the decrease in value of the short vertical call spread or, in the case of a long vertical put spread, its increase in value.

Loss Scenario. If the stock rises, loss will be defined by the increase in value of the short vertical call spread or, in the case of a long vertical put spread, its decrease in value.

Key Concepts. The maximum value of a vertical spread will be equal to the difference between the two strikes; therefore, both the buyer and the seller will have a limited profit and limited loss scenario. Depending on which strikes you use, time decay can help or hurt the position. Thus, some vertical spreads can make money over time even if the stock stays stagnant.

CHAPTER 13

Time Spreads

*T*ime spreads, also known as *calendar spreads*, are an ideal way to take advantage of time decay and changes in implied volatility. The time spread strategy focuses on the movement of time and volatility more than on the movement of the stock. Therefore, this strategy is ideal for use when you anticipate either stagnant or explosive periods in a stock.

The time spread, like other spreads, has its risks and rewards. The risk is very limited for the buyer but substantial for the seller. The seller's risk can be avoided or contained with due diligence at the expiration of the near month's option. Also, a variety of strategies can affect the seller's risk.

The advantage of this strategy is that the investor can pursue a time decay or volatility position without the large capital outlay necessary for the purchase of the stock.

CONSTRUCTION OF THE TIME SPREAD

The construction of the time spread involves the purchase of one option and the sale of another in different months, but with both having the same strike. You can construct a time spread using either two calls or two puts.

A long time spread is constructed by purchasing the out month option and selling the nearer month option. For example, you buy September 45 calls and sell August 45 calls or buy April 30 puts and sell February 30 puts. A short time spread is constructed by selling the farther-out month and buying the nearer month. For instance, sell July 50 calls and buy May 50 calls.

The four important elements in the construction of the time spread are:

1. Use two call or two put options on the same stock.
2. Use the same strike for both.
3. Choose different months for each.
4. Use a one-to-one ratio.

A time spread can utilize any two months as long as it has the same strike price and the trade is done in a one-to-one ratio.

Most time spreads are executed at the money because at-the-money options have the greatest amount of extrinsic value. An option's extrinsic value is what decays over time and is the basis of the time spread's strategy. Since the time spread is built to take advantage of time decay, it is naturally better suited for at-the-money options.

This does not mean that the time spread cannot be used effectively with in-the-money or out-of-the-money options, both of which have less extrinsic value than at-the-money options.

However, the rate of decay (to be discussed) of an in-the-money or out-of-the-money option with one month until expiration is still greater than that of an in-the-money or out-of-the-money option of the same strike that has three months to go before expiration. This being said, the time spread can be constructed using any option regardless if it is in, out, or at the money.

BEHAVIOR OF THE SPREAD

Time spreads can be a profitable investment strategy if you understand the concept of time decay. A time spread is designed to take advantage of the fact that an option's decay curve is nonlinear; that is, an option's value does not decay evenly over time. As an option gets closer to expiration, its rate of decay increases, meaning the option loses value more quickly. That decay rate increases progressively day after day until expiration.

As I explained in an earlier chapter, an option's decay rate begins to accelerate when the option is about 45 days out. It picks up steam at 30 days out, really comes under decay pressure at about 15 days out, and rapidly decays as it approaches expiration. In time spreads, both options have the same strike price, which remains constant.

However, each option's value decays at different rates and over different lengths of time. The option with one month until expiration experiences value decay at a faster rate than an option that has three months until expiration.

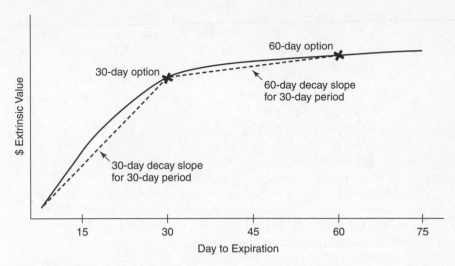

FIGURE 13.1 Time Decay

If you buy an option with three months to go and sell an option with the same strike but with one month to go, you have set up a spread between the two options values (prices). As time passes, your short option loses value more quickly than your long option, which decays more slowly. The value of the spread widens, and you profit from that spread's expansion. This is the fundamental behavior of the time spread.

Figure 13.1 shows an option decay graph. The numbers across the bottom represent days to expiration. Along the decay line, you will notice an "X" at the 30-days-to-expiration line and another "X" at the 60-days-to-expiration line. The first "X" represents a 30-day option; the second "X" represents a 60-day option. If you look closely at the chart, you will see the nature of the time spread.

Let's say you are long the 60–30 day time spread. That means you are long the 60-day option and short the 30-day option. Further, we will assign a price of $3.00 to the 60-day option and $2.00 to the 30-day option. Since you pay for the one and receive payment for the other, the bottom-line cost of what you put out for the spread is $1.00.

Now look at the slope of the line (representing decay) drawn from the 60-day option to the 30-day option. Compare the slope of that line to the slope of the line drawn from the 30-day option to expiration (Day 0). As you can see, there is a big difference in the steepness of the slope of the two lines.

The slope of the line drawn between the 30-day option to expiration is much steeper than the slope of the line drawn from the 60-day option to the 30-day option.

These slopes show how the time spread works. During the first 30-day period, the 30-day option has a steeper slope, meaning a higher rate of decay. During that 30-day period, this option will go from $2.00 to $0. Meanwhile, the 60-day option, having a flatter slope, will not decay as quickly.

During the same 30-day period, the option goes from $3.00 to $2.00. Remember, the spread's bottom-line cost was $1.00. The 30-day option (now expired) will be worth $0 while the 60-day option (now a 30-day option) will be worth $2.00. If you had invested in this spread, after 30 days of decay you would be holding one option worth $2.00. The investment has provided a nice return.

However, this is an ideal situation. The stock price and volatility remain constant, and you capture the decay. The time spread has worked just as it should, and it does work that way sometimes. But nothing works as it should all the time. As we know, stock prices and volatility levels do not remain constant.

They are always changing. In the time spread strategy, the investor must choose opportunities carefully. In addition to picking a stock that will be in a stagnant period, the investor should look for two other situations where the spread has profit possibilities: changes in volatility and, to a lesser degree, stock price movements.

EFFECTS OF STOCK PRICE ON THE TIME SPREAD

The price of a time spread will fluctuate with movements in stock price. A time spread will be at its widest when the stock price and the strike price of the spread are identical (i.e., at the money).

As the stock moves away from the strike in either direction, the value of the time spread will decrease. As the stock moves in either direction away from the spread's strike, the closer month will experience a quicker price change due to the front month's higher gamma.

Gamma shows the rate of change of an option's delta in relation to movements in the price of the stock. It is the delta of the delta. Gamma is highest in at-the-money options and in the front month. It decreases as you move away from the at-the-money strike and as you move out over time.

In the same way that a time spread loses value as the stock price moves away from the strike price, the opposite is true also. As the stock price moves closer to the strike price, the value of the time spread increases.

For example, let's examine the June/July 65 call time spread. With the stock priced at 65 (directly at the strike), the spread is at its widest point (highest value). As the stock climbs away from 65 and pushes toward 70,

TABLE 13.1 Spreads with 50 Volatility

Stock Price	June/July 65	June/July 70
57.50	1.14	0.67
59.50	1.40	0.93
61.50	1.59	1.19
63.50	1.74	1.44
65.50	1.77	1.65
67.50	1.73	1.79
69.50	1.65	1.89
71.50	1.51	1.93
73.50	1.33	1.86
75.50	1.20	1.72
77.50	0.80	1.57

the June/July 65 spread loses value. Table 13.1 shows prices of two spreads with a volatility level of 50.

However, at the same time the June/July 65 spread loses value, the June/July 70 spread gains in value as the stock approaches the 70 strike. When the stock reaches 67.50—the point equidistant (midpoint) between the two strikes—both spreads will be trading at approximately the same value.

Look at Table 13.1. Notice that as the stock increases from $57.50, both the June/July 65 and then June/July 70 spreads increase in value. Their increases continue until they reach their strike price, at which time they both begin to lose value.

This table demonstrates that the spread with the strike price that the stock is moving toward will increase in value while the spread with the strike price that the stock is moving away from will simultaneously lose value.

EFFECTS OF VOLATILITY ON THE TIME SPREAD

When purchasing a time spread, investors should pay attention not only to the movement of the stock price but especially to the movement of volatility.

Volatility plays a very large role in the price of a time spread. As stated, the time spread is an excellent way to take advantage of anticipated volatility movements in a hedged fashion.

Since the time spread is composed of two options, you should understand the role of volatility in options to understand its role in time spreads. Let's review option volatility.

An option's volatility component is measured by vega. Vega, one of the components of the pricing model, measures how much an option's price will change with a one-point (or tick) change in implied volatility. Based on current data, the pricing model assigns the vega for each option at different strikes, different months, and different prices of the stock.

Vega is always given in dollars per one-tick volatility change. If an option is worth $1.00 at a 35 implied volatility and it has a .05 vega, then the option will be worth $1.05 if implied volatility were to increase to 36 (up one tick) and $0.95 if the implied volatility were to decrease to 34 (down one tick).

Remember, vega is given in dollars per one tick volatility change.

As we continue to discuss vega, keep these five facts in mind:

1. Vega measures how much an option price will change as volatility changes.
2. Vega increases as you look at future months and decreases as you approach expiration.
3. Vega is highest in the at-the-money options.
4. Vega is a strike-based number—it applies whether the strike is a call or a put.
5. Vega increases as volatility increases and decreases as volatility decreases.

It is important to note that an option's volatility sensitivity increases with more time to expiration. That is, options that are farther out in months have higher vegas than near-term options have. The farther out you go over time, the higher the vegas become.

Although vegas are increasing, they do not progress in a linear manner. When you check the same strike price out over future months, you will notice that vega values increase as you move out.

The at-the-money strike in any month will have the highest vega. As you move away from the at-the-money strike, in either direction, the vega values decrease and continue to decrease the farther away you get from that strike.

Remember, vega, an option's volatility component value, is highest in at-the-money, out-month options. Vega decreases the closer you get to expiration and the farther away you move from the at-the-money strike. Table 13.2 shows vega values for QUALCOM, Inc. (QCOM) options.

TABLE 13.2 Vega's Effect (Stock 67.50), Volatility 40

Strike Price	June	July	October	January
50	0	.008	.064	.114
55	.004	.030	.102	.153
60	.023	.063	.135	.184
65	.053	.090	.157	.205
70	.056	.094	.165	.215
75	.032	.077	.154	.213
80	.011	.052	.142	.203

As you look at the table, observe the important elements: The stock price is constant at 67.50; volatility is constant at 40; time progresses from June to January; and the strike price changes from 50 through 80. Notice the increasing pattern as you go out over time. Also notice how the value decreases as you move away from the at-the-money strike.

Another important fact about vega is that it is a strike-based number. That means that the vega number does not differentiate between put and call. Vega tells the volatility sensitivity of the strike regardless of whether you are looking at puts or calls. So, the vega number of a call and its corresponding put are identical.

Vega can also be used to calculate how much a specific option's price will change with a movement in implied volatility. You simply count how many volatility ticks implied volatility has moved. Multiply that number times the vega, and either add it (if volatility increased) to the option's present value or subtract it (if volatility decreased) from the option's present value to obtain the option's new value under the new volatility assumption. The calculation works on individual options and can be used to calculate the value of the time spread.

Now let's apply the concepts of vega to the time spread. When you do so, you see that as implied volatility increases, the value of the time spread increases. This is because the out-month option with the higher vega will increase more than the closer-month option with the lower vega—that widens or increases the spread.

Table 13.3 shows a time spread and its reaction to increasing volatility. As you can see, each time implied volatility increases, the value of the time spreads increase. This increase would naturally favor the buyer. In this table, volatility is increased to 70.

As you can see, if an investor bought the time spread at low volatility and within a few weeks volatility had increased and pushed the spread price higher, the investor could sell the spread at a profit even before expiration.

TABLE 13.3 Time Spread Affected by Increased Volatility

| Stock Price | June/July 65 | | June/July 70 | |
	Volatility 50	Volatility 70	Volatility 50	Volatility 70
57.50	1.14	1.19	0.67	1.47
59.50	1.40	2.12	0.93	1.75
61.50	1.59	2.27	1.19	2.02
63.50	1.74	2.41	1.44	2.23
65.50	1.77	2.46	1.65	2.42
67.50	1.73	2.47	1.79	2.56
69.50	1.65	2.41	1.89	2.63
71.50	1.51	2.31	1.93	2.66
73.50	1.33	2.14	1.86	2.61
75.50	1.20	2.00	1.72	2.56
77.50	0.80	1.90	1.57	2.39

Of course, the vega can also demonstrate the opposite effect. As implied volatility decreases, the spread tightens, or decreases in value. As volatility comes down, the out-month option with its higher vega will lose value more quickly than will the nearer-month option with its lower vega. In Table 13.4, you see how the time spread's value is affected by decreasing volatility. In the table, volatility is decreased to 30.

Compare Tables 13.3 and 13.4 and note that the stock price is constant. The changes in the price of the spreads are due to the change in volatility. We discussed how to use vega to calculate an option's price when volatility

TABLE 13.4 Spread Prices Decrease as Volatility Decreases

| Stock Price | June/July 65 Prices | | June/July 70 Prices | |
	Volatility 50	Volatility 30	Volatility 50	Volatility 30
57.50	1.14	0.37	0.67	0.09
59.50	1.40	0.60	0.93	0.19
61.50	1.59	0.86	1.19	0.35
63.50	1.74	1.02	1.44	0.59
65.50	1.77	1.09	1.65	0.82
67.50	1.73	1.01	1.79	1.04
69.50	1.65	0.85	1.89	1.16
71.50	1.51	0.66	1.93	1.13
73.50	1.33	0.47	1.86	1.04
75.50	1.20	0.40	1.72	0.85
77.50	0.80	0.30	1.57	0.66

changes. The same calculation method works for time spreads, but the calculation is slightly more difficult.

Spread traders need to understand and properly calculate accurate volatility levels. In order to get accurate volatility levels, you must first determine a base volatility for the two options involved in the spread.

You must get a base volatility because different volatilities in different months cannot, and do not, get weighted evenly mathematically.

Since they are weighted differently, you cannot simply take the average of the two months and call that the volatility of the spread; the situation is more complicated than that.

The problem is related to calculating the spread's volatility with two options in different months. Those different months are usually trading at different implied volatility assumptions. You cannot compare apples with oranges; nor can you compare two options with different volatility assumptions.

It is important to know how to calculate the actual and accurate volatility of the spread. The current volatility level of the spread is one of the best ways to determine whether the spread is expensive or cheap in relation to the average volatility of the stock.

There are several ways to calculate the average volatility of a stock and to determine the average difference between the volatility levels for each given expiration month. Volatility cones and volatility tilts are very useful tools that aid in determining the mean, mode, and standard deviations of a stock's implied volatility levels and the relationship between them.

You then can compare the current volatility level of the spread to those average values and determine the worthiness of the spread. If you determine that the spread is trading at a high volatility, you can sell it. If it is trading at a low volatility, you can buy it. But first you must know the current trading volatility of the spread.

The key to accurately calculating volatility levels for pricing and evaluating a time spread is to get both months on an equal footing. You need to have a base volatility that you can apply to both months. For instance, say you are looking at the June/August 70 call spread. June's implied volatility is currently at 40 while August's implied volatility is at 36. You cannot calculate the spread's volatility using these two months as they are. You must either bring June's implied volatility down to 36 or bring August implied volatility up to 40. You may wonder how you can do this.

Actually, you have the tools right in front of you. Use the June vega to decrease the June option's value to represent 36 volatility or use August's vega to increase the August option's value to represent 40 volatility. Both ways work; it doesn't matter which one you choose.

Let's use some real numbers so that we can work through an example together. Let's say the June 70 calls are trading for $2.00 and have a .05 vega at 40 volatility. The August 70 calls are trading for $3.00 and have a .08 vega at 36 volatility. Thus the August/June 70 call spread will be worth $1.00.

To calculate the volatility of the spread, we must equalize the volatilities of the individual options.

First, let's move the June calls by moving June's implied volatility down from 40 to 36, a decrease of four volatility ticks. Four volatility ticks multiplied by a vega of .05 per tick gives us a value of $0.20. Next we subtract $0.20 from the June 70 option's current value of $2.00, and we get a value of $1.80 at 36 volatility. Now the two options are valued at an equal volatility basis.

Looking at this first adjustment, where we moved the June 70's volatility down to 36 from 40, we have a value of $1.80 at 36 volatility. The August 40 call has a value of $3.00 at 36 volatility. So the spread will be worth $1.20 at 36 volatility.

If you wanted to move the August 70 calls instead, you would take the August 70 call vega of .08 and multiply it by the four-tick implied volatility difference.

This gives you a value of $0.32, which must be added to the August 70 call's current value to bring it up to an equal volatility (40) with the June 70 call. Adding the $0.32 to the August 70 call will give it a $3.32 value at the new volatility level of 40, which is the same volatility level as the June 40 calls.

Now our spread is worth $1.32 at 40 volatility. August 70 calls at $3.32 minus the June 70 calls at $2.00 gives the price of the spread at 40 volatility.

It does not make any difference which option you move. The point is to establish the same volatility level for both options. Then you are ready to compare apples to apples and options to options for an accurate spread value and volatility level.

Since we now have an equal base volatility, we can calculate the spread's vega by taking the difference between the two individual options' vegas. In the last example, the spread's vega is .03 (.08 − .05). The vega of the spread is calculated by finding the difference between the vegas of the two individual options because in the time spread, you will be long one option and short the other option.

As volatility moves one tick, you will gain the vega value of one of the options while simultaneously losing the vega value of the other. Thus the spread's vega must be equal to the difference between the vegas of the two options. So our spread is worth $1.20 at 36 volatility with a .03 vega or $1.32 at 40 volatility with a .03 vega.

Going back to our original spread value of $1.00 with a vega of .03, we can now calculate the volatility of that spread. We know the spread is worth $1.20 at 36 volatility with a vega of .03. So, we can assume that the spread trading at $1.00 must be trading at a volatility lower than 36.

To find out how much lower, we first take the difference between the two spread values, which is $0.20 ($1.20 at 36 volatility minus $1.00 now also at 36 volatility). Then we divide the $0.20 by the spread's vega of .03, and we get 6.667 volatility ticks. We then subtract 6.667 volatility ticks from 36 volatility, and we get 29.33 volatility for the spread trading at $1.00.

We can also determine the volatility of the spread as the spread's price changes. Let's fix the spread price at $1.30. To calculate this, we must first take the value of the spread ($1.20 at 36 volatility) and find the dollar difference between it and the new price of the spread ($1.30). The difference is $0.10. This dollar difference must now be divided by the vega of the spread. The $0.10 difference divided by the .03 vega gives you a value of 3.33 volatility ticks. Then add the 3.33 ticks to the 36 volatility, and you get 39.33 as the volatility for the spread trading at $1.30.

Let's double-check our work by calculating the volatility the other way.

This time we will do the calculation by moving the August 70 calls up to the equal base volatility of the June 70 calls. As calculated earlier, the August 70 calls will have a value of $3.32 at 40 volatility. The June 70 calls are worth $2.00 at 40 volatility. Thus the spread is worth $1.32 at 40 volatility.

Now let's again move the spread price to $1.30, $0.02 lower than the value of the spread at 40 volatility. As before, we take the difference in the prices of the spread. The result is $0.02 ($1.32 – $1.30). Then we divide $0.02 by our spread's vega of .03 (remember that the vega of the spread is equal to the difference between the vega of the two individual options). $0.02 divided by .03 gives us a value of .67. That .67 must be subtracted from our base volatility of 40. That gives us a 39.33 (40 – .67) volatility for the spread trading at $1.30. This volatility matches our previous calculation perfectly.

At first glance, you might be wondering why we went through all of these calculations.

With the June 70 calls at 40 volatility, price $2.00, vega .05 and the August 70 calls at 36 volatility, price $3.00, vega .08, why not just take an average of the volatility? This would give us a 38 volatility for the spread with a price of $1.00 when $1.00 in the spread actually represents a 29.33 volatility.

This would be almost a nine-tick difference, which represents a whopping 30 percent mistake! Remember, vega is not linear; you cannot weigh each month evenly and just take an average of the two months. For argument's sake, though, suppose you did.

Let's say you found the difference of the vegas of the options and came up with a spread vega of .03, which is correct. However, when you try to calculate the spread's volatility and price, you would have difficulty. Now recalculate the spread with the trading price of $1.30, or $0.30 higher than your value at 38 volatility. Divide that $0.30 higher difference by the spread's vega of .03.

You get a 10-tick volatility increase. Add that increase to the base 38 volatility. That would mean you feel the spread is trading at 48 volatility instead of a 39.33 volatility.

This type of mistake could be very, very costly. Remember, apples to apples, oranges to oranges. It doesn't matter which option's volatility of the spread you move as long as you get both options to an equal base volatility.

BUYER RISK AND REWARD

Like most trades, time spreads have a maximum loss for the buyer. As a buyer, you can lose only what you have spent. If you paid $1.00 for the spread, then your maximum potential loss is that $1.00. If you bought the spread for $2.00, then $2.00 is your maximum potential loss.

The buyer of a time spread will be purchasing the out-month option while selling the nearer-month option of the same strike in a one-to-one ratio. Since the out-month option will have more time until expiration than the nearer-month option, the out-month option will cost more. This means the buyer will be putting out money (debit spread), which makes sense. The buyer can lose only the amount of money spent to purchase the spread. Thus the buyer's maximum risk is the cost of the spread.

The buyer can profit in several ways. First and foremost, being a time spread, the buyer can profit by the passage of time. Options are wasting assets. So as the nearer-month option decays away more quickly than the outer-month option, the spread widens (increases in value) and the buyer sees a profit.

Second, implied volatility can increase. As it increases, the out-month option, which the buyer is long, increases in value more quickly (due to its higher vega) than the nearer-month option, which the buyer is short. This will force the spread to widen or increase in value, which again is profitable for the buyer.

Third, the buyer can make money due to stock price movement. As stated before, a time spread's value is at its maximum when the stock price and the spreads strike price are identical (at the money). You could have an increase in value if you owned an out-of-the-money or in-the-money time spread, and the stock moved either up or down toward your strike. As the stock moves closer to your strike, the spread will expand and increase in value, creating a profit for you, the buyer.

The buyer's risks are obviously the opposite of the rewards. You cannot stop or reverse time so time can never hurt the buyer of the spread.

Implied volatility, however, can decrease as easily as it can increase. A decrease in implied volatility will decrease the value of the out-month option (which the buyer is long) faster than it will decrease the value of the nearer-month option (which the buyer is short) due to the higher vega of the out-month option. This will narrow the spread, thereby creating a loss for the buyer.

Just as stock movement in the right direction can be profitable for the buyer of a time spread, stock movement in the wrong direction can be costly. As the stock moves away from the spread's strike, the spread decreases in value. That will create a loss for the buyer of the spread.

SELLER RISK AND REWARD

The seller of a time spread buys the nearer-month option and sells the outer-month option in a one-to-one ratio. In order to profit from the sale of the time spread, as the seller, you are looking basically for two things.

First is a decrease in implied volatility. As volatility decreases, the out-month option (which you are short) loses money faster than the nearer-month option (which you are long) because of the higher vega in the out-month option. This will cause the spread to contract or lose value. That will be profitable for the time-spread seller.

Second, the stock can move. As stated before, a time spread is at its widest, most expensive point when it is at the money.

A movement away from the strike in either direction decreases the value of the spread. So, as long as the stock moves in either direction away from the strike, the seller's position could be profitable, provided that time decay does not outperform the stock movement.

Time, unfortunately, never works in favor of the time-spread seller. The passage of time hurts the seller because the nearer-month option (which the seller is long) naturally decays at a faster rate than does the out-month option (which the seller is short). These differing decay rates cause the spread to expand and increase in value. That obviously produces a loss for the time-spread seller. Time can neither be stopped nor turned back; it only moves forward, which always hurts the time-spread seller.

Increases in implied volatility are also detrimental to the potential profits of the time-spread seller. When implied volatility increases, the out-month option (which the seller is short) increases in value faster than the nearer-month option (which the seller is long) due to the out-month option's higher vega. This creates an expansion in the spread and increases its value, resulting in a negative for the spread seller.

The time-spread seller, in theory, has an unlimited loss potential. For the seller, the maximum loss potential is not determined so much by the stock price movement but by the movement in implied volatility. As the seller, you will be long the front-month call and short the out-month call.

As we know, the out-month call will be more sensitive to movements in implied volatility due to a higher vega or volatility sensitivity component. If implied volatility increases, then the seller's short out-month option will increase more in value than will the seller's long, front-month option. This will cause the spread to widen or increase in value; that is negative for the seller.

The risk is that the option the seller is long is going to expire approximately 30 days prior to the option the seller is short. If volatility does not decrease or the stock does not move away from the strike significantly before the seller's long option expires, he or she will be left short a naked or unhedged option and a loss on the position. If the seller can wait out the position, the lost extrinsic value of the short option can be recaptured. As we know, this option too has a limited life and must shed its extrinsic value, no matter how much, by its expiration. The problem is that the position is no longer hedged so the seller now faces unlimited risk.

Once the long option expires and the seller is left short a now-naked call, stock price movement in the wrong direction is a substantial risk and, under the circumstances just described, a big problem.

While the seller can wait out an implied volatility movement that created an increase in extrinsic value, he or she probably will not be able to wait out a large, negative stock movement creating an increase in intrinsic value. In that case, the seller must take action to prevent substantial losses once the front month expires. Attention to the implied volatility in the farther-out option when the nearer-month option expires can save the seller from a large loss.

ROLLING THE POSITION

Time spreads are unlike all the other strategies discussed earlier when I discussed rolling or continuing the position. In other strategies, the option component is limited to a single month. At expiration, the position disappears. It either transforms into stock or expires worthless, leaving you with no option position. In a time spread, however, you are dealing with two different expiration months.

After the front month expires, in addition to a potential stock position, you will still have an option position—the out-month option still will have time until expiration. To roll that position properly, first you must understand the new position you have inherited.

Rolling the Call Spread

Let's look at the call time spread first. For the purposes of our example, let us pretend we are long the September/October 25 call spread. If the stock were to close below $25.00 on expiration Friday of September, the September 25 calls would expire worthless and you would be left with a long October 25 call position. There are several things you can do from this position.

First, you could just sell out the October 25 call. The hope is that the combination of the expiration of the September 25 calls and their subsequent worthlessness along with the proceeds gained from the sale of the October 25 calls after September expiration might make a profitable trade.

You could keep the position open and continuing in several ways. You could stay long the October 25 call naked. You could sell the October 30 call and become long the October 25/30 vertical call spread if you are bullish. You could sell the October 20 call and become short the October 20/25 vertical call spread if bearish.

You could buy the October 25 puts and become long the October 25 straddle if you felt the stock would become volatile. You could even sell the stock and create a synthetic put if you were very bearish. There are ways to create a new position that reflects any possible future outlook an investor can have.

If the stock were to close above $25.00, then the September 25 call would close in the money. At that time, you would be assigned your short September 25 call, and that would translate into a short stock position. That short stock position that you received from the assignment of your short September 25 call along with the remaining October 25 long call position is the equivalent of a synthetic put. At this time, you could close out the position or keep it.

The position is a bearish one so if you felt the stock would be heading down, you could keep the position on. You could sell another option of a different strike to set up either a bull or bear put spread. You could buy the October 25 call to create a long straddle.

As you see, many different combinations could be created.

If you were short the September/October 25 call time spread and the stock expired under $25.00 on expiration Friday in September, you would have a remaining position of a short October 25 call naked. Again, there are many potential ways of continuing the position. Of course, you could always buy back the naked call and close the position if you no longer wanted to maintain a position in the stock.

If you did, you could buy a call in the same month and create a vertical spread, sell the corresponding put and create a short straddle, or buy the stock one to one and create a buy-write or other combination based on what you felt the stock would do.

If the stock closed above $25.00 and you were short the call time spread, then you would be left with a long stock position from your long September 25 call and short the October 25 call against the long stock position. The position you would be left with is a buy-write. Depending on your outlook for the stock, you could keep the buy-write on, take it off, or use other options to change the position.

Rolling Put Spreads

As far as put spreads, let's take an example and see where we are when the front-month option expires. We will use the September/October 25 put spread for our example.

When long the spread and the stock closes above $25.00, the September 25 puts, which you are short, will expire worthless, leaving you with a long naked put position.

From that position, you can close it or combine it with other option or stock to create a different position. Again, there are many different possibilities.

If you were short the put time spread, and the stock closed above $25.00, then the September 25 put, which you are long, will expire worthless, leaving you with a short naked put position in the October 25 puts. This position can be closed out or combined with other options or stock to create a strategy that will take advantage of the outlook you have on the stock.

When the stock closes below $25.00, the scenario is different. When long the spread with the stock closing lower than the strike price, the front-month put, which you are short, will be assigned to you, thus making you long stock in addition to your long October 25 put. This position is known as a synthetic call.

As before, there are many ways to combine other options and/or stock to change the position so that it is in line with what you want it to be going forward.

If you were short the spread, and the stock closed below $25.00, then you would exercise your long September 25 put, making you short stock and short the October 25 put. That position, which is called a sell-write (the sister strategy to the buy-write), can be kept as is, closed out, or changed in different ways by combining it with stock or other options, based on your expectations of the stock's future movements.

Closing the Time Spread Position

It is important to remember that the time spread will leave you with several potential positions that can be altered by other options or stock in numerous ways. You must make three decisions to clarify your understanding and goals:

1. It is important to understand what position you are going to be left with when the near-month option expires.
2. You must form your opinion of what you think the stock is going to do (formulate a bullish or bearish lean) and then figure out the best way to take advantage of that opinion.
3. You must determine how to adjust your present position and change it into an advantageous position for a profitable outcome. That might mean selling out of the position totally. Not only must your changes to the position be correct; they also must be done in the most efficient, cost-effective manner, including keeping commission prices down.

Also note that you should make sure to go from a hedged position to another hedged position to ensure proper risk management.

CONCLUDING THOUGHTS

The time spread is an excellent strategy for premium sellers who want to capture premium in a hedged way. It is best used in stagnant periods when a stock is likely to remain in a tight price range. It is less expensive and less risky than most other premium collecting strategies; thus it is friendlier to investors who are short on capital and experience. It can also be used to take advantage of volatility changes and even some directional stock movements.

The time spread can leave you with a residual naked position that needs to be managed for risk at the expiration of the front-month option. As always, it is important to fully understand the risks and rewards of the strategy and the potential risks and solutions of the residual position before executing the strategy.

The residual position does allow you many choices, including closing out the position totally or continuing the position by combining it with either stock or another option to create a new position that fits the investor's new expectations for the stock.

EXAMPLES

Review these examples of time spreads and see how the daily movement of stock can be interpreted for opportunities.

FIGURE 13.2   XOM Daily Chart
Source: Courtesy of Think or Swim (www.thinkorswim.com)

Example 1: Exxon Mobil

Figure 13.2 shows the Exxon Mobil (XOM) daily chart.

Notes

Time Spreads

1. Starting in early June and lasting through August, Exxon Mobil begins a trading pattern around the $60.00 range. Prior to that, although volatile, the stock often traded in the $60.00 range with a decent amount of large deviations away from the $60.00 level.

2. Even with the couple of movements away from the $60.00 price, the stock seems to return to the $60.00 level and hangs in an even tighter, more disciplined range from early June through August. This seems to be a very good opportunity for premium collection. But both the short straddle and the short strangle have unlimited loss profiles above the upper break-even and below the lower break-even. This, however, is a long time spread. That means you purchased it. Remember, when purchasing a time spread, you can lose only what you spent, which means limited risk.

3. With a stock like Exxon Mobil, which can have big movements, the short straddle and the short strangle may have a little too much risk

for some investors because they have an unlimited loss scenario. Those who cannot tolerate this risk may want to use the time spread for premium collection.

4. The time spread is a premium collection strategy that limits a buyer's potential loss only to the price paid for the spread. Meanwhile, as the stock stays around the $60.00 level, that short front-month option will decay at a faster rate than the outer-month option, which you are long. This will expand the value of the spread and profit the buyer.

Example 2: Raymond James Financial

Figure 13.3 shows the daily chart for Raymond James Financial (RJF).

Notes

Time Spreads

1. Raymond James breaks down out of an uptrending trading channel in a reasonably aggressive fashion in mid-April. This movement (chart break-down) could have been played with the synthetic put strategy.

2. Raymond James then bottoms out in late April at around $26.50 and then starts a slow, gradual recovery through early July before a small break-out to a new, higher trading range.

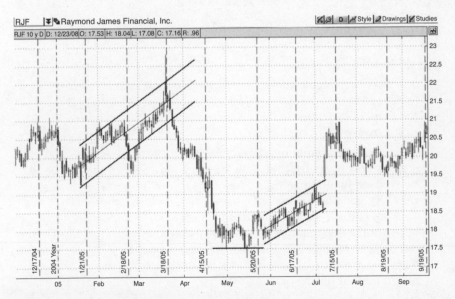

FIGURE 13.3 RJF Daily Chart
Source: Courtesy of Think or Swim (www.thinkorswim.com)

3. Once arriving in that trading range in early July, Raymond James begins to consolidate around the $30.00 mark, and the range begins to tighten. This is an excellent opportunity to use a time spread.

4. While the stock is trading in a sideways pattern, it is a good idea to employ a premium collection strategy, such as the time spread. The short front-month option will decay at a much faster rate than the out-month option that you are long. The longer the stock stays in that sideways pattern and stays near the strike of the time spread, the better for the collection of premium.

Example 3: Raytheon

Figure 13.4 presents the daily chart of Raytheon (RTN).

Notes

Time Spreads

1. After trading up into the $39.00 price range in March and April, Raytheon gives back the gain of mid-April only to rally back into its previous trading pattern.

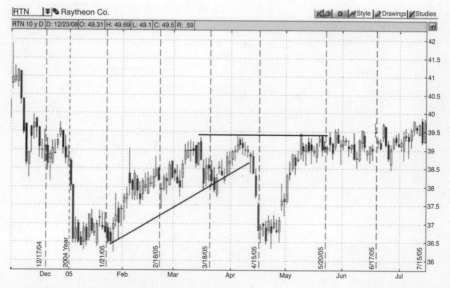

FIGURE 13.4   RTN Daily Chart
Source: Courtesy of Think or Swim (www.thinkorswim.com)

2. This trading pattern (barring the mid-April aberration) seems to be a slow, steady uptrending pattern that is not starting to consolidate in the $39.00 area. This pattern seems to be capable of being a longer-term pattern around $40.00.

3. A 40 strike time spread would be a good premium collection strategy that is a low cost and fixed risk alternative strategy to a straddle or strangle. In this strategy, the largest potential loss is only the amount of money spent on the purchase of the time spread.

4. The time spread takes advantage of the nonlinear rate of decay of options. The front-month option, which you are short in the time spread, will decay at a much faster rate than the outer-month option, which you are long. In this way, if the stock trades sideways, time will pass and you will capture the decay-rate difference between the quicker rate of decay of the front-month options than the slower decay of the long out-month options.

TIME SPREAD SYNOPSIS

Construction. Long one call in a farther-out month while simultaneously short one call with the same strike but in a closer expiration month.

Function. Collect time premium by taking advantage of options non-linear rate of decay.

Bias (Lean). Neutral.

When to Use. Best used during stagnant periods in order to collect premiums due to time decay. Unlike other premium collection strategies, the time spread offers a limited loss scenario in both directions.

Profit Scenario. If the stock remains stagnant, the position will profit by the nearer-month option (which you are short) decaying at a faster rate than the farther-out-month option (which you are long). When this occurs, the spread will widen, thus creating a profit. Profit can also be attained if implied volatility increases.

Loss Scenario. If the stock moves away from the strike by rising or falling, the spread will tighten, thus losing value and creating a loss.

Key Concepts. Time spreads are best done in at-the-money options where the extrinsic value is the highest, which accentuates the rate of decay. Best results are found in stocks that are in a stagnant period, as stock movement away from the strike will lead to losses.

CHAPTER 14

The Stock Replacement/ Covered Call Strategy (Diagonal Spread)

Now that we have discussed vertical spreads and time spreads, we come to a spread that combines both the vertical spread and the time spread into one: the *diagonal spread*. Sometimes it is called the stock replacement/covered call because the diagonal spread, at least the long diagonal spread, functions very much like the covered call strategy.

When you look at the covered call, you see that you are long a stock and short the call where you are collecting premium. If you substitute an option position for your stock, you have a long deep in-the-money, out-month option and a short at-the-money, front-month option. Looking at that carefully, you see you have a diagonal spread.

A long diagonal spread looks very much like either the covered call in the call version or a covered put in the put version. If you ever hear someone refer to a stock replacement covered call, understand that they are talking about the diagonal spread.

In general, a diagonal spread is constructed long an out-month, deep in-the-money option and short a nearer-term option. Obviously, the diagonal spread (stock replacement covered call) is constructed with options in different months and different strikes.

When can this strategy be advantageous for use by an investor?

Let's assume that you wanted to take advantage of an opportunity but are unable to participate due to capital requirements. The stock you are interested in is trading at $58.90, and you do not have sufficient funds to support buying the stock at that price. In many instances, an insufficient amount of funds in an investor's account can mean the loss of a golden opportunity when dealing with high-dollar stocks.

This is the time to consider using the stock replacement/covered call strategy.

The alternative to purchasing the stock outright is to find a way to **replace the actual stock with something else that is not as expensive. In this case, a deep-in-the-money call would do just that.**

When a call is deep in the money, meaning that the strike price of the call is much lower than the current stock price, the delta of the call approaches 100. This means there is close to a 100 percent chance that this option will expire in the money.

Because of this, the option will trade just like the stock; penny for penny, dollar for dollar (in a theoretical 100 delta scenario.) If you recall, the term *delta* was mentioned when describing the option in question. Delta is the first derivative of the call's price with respect to the stock's price, and it has a three-pronged definition. Let's now take a closer look at these definitions for delta.

- The first is *percentage change*. Delta can be interpreted as the *percentage change*, which simply shows the expected percent increase in the option's price for a $1.00 change in the stock's price. **For example, a 50 delta option will move 50 percent the amount the stock does.** If the stock moves $1.00, then the option moves $0.50. A 30 delta option, however, would move only $0.30 for the same $1 change in the stock's price.

- Delta can also be defined as *percent chance*. This term is used to describe the percent chance that the option will expire in the money. **A 90 delta option has a 90 percent chance of finishing in the money at expiration.**

- Finally, delta can also be defined as *hedge ratio*, which is the amount of deltas needed to hedge a position properly. For example, if you own 100 shares of stock and wish to fully hedge the position with a 50 delta option, then you would need to buy two puts, since each put is effectively behaving like 50 shares of stock.

It was important to understand delta so that you recognize that the deep in-the-money call performs and acts just like the stock. One way to determine if the call you will select is in the money enough for your purpose is to check the delta.

A delta in the mid- or high 80s is an ideal candidate. The selection of the proper in-the-money call to use is a critical element in the success of this strategy. In order to obtain an accurate delta of all options under consideration for stock replacement use, you can go to any number of web sites or visit your online broker.

If all else fails, you can use a little trick of the trade to aid in selecting a call that is deep enough in the money to suit the stock replacement criteria. **If there is little to no bid quoted for the put, then the call is deep enough in the money to consider it for a stock surrogate.** There are several reasons for this call being an adequate selection, which we won't cover here. But for the purposes of this discussion, it is enough to know that this method does work.

WHEN TO USE THE DIAGONAL SPREAD

Let's look back in time to 2003 for a scenario that would be good for the replacement strategy. In October and November of that year, the giant biotech Amgen (AMGN) came under some intense pressure, trading down about $12.00 or so before it found what appeared to be a decent level of support and began to consolidate. At that level, anyone interested in going long Amgen at a discounted price planned to do so. Implied volatility was high coming off the precipitous drop, which caused premiums in the options to increase considerably.

This scenario was very attractive for a covered call seller (buy writer). On December 2, 2003, Amgen was trading at $58.90, the December 60 call was trading at $1.30, and there were only two weeks left until expiration.

Meanwhile, the May 45 calls met the criteria for stock replacement. The call had a mid- to high 80 delta and its corresponding put had only a $1.00 bid. The May 45 call was trading at $15.00, or $1.10 over parity. Purchasing this option, you would be equivalently buying the shares for $60.00 (strike price + option price). In other words, if you bought the call and exercised it, you would pay the $45.00 strike price for the shares. Because you paid $15.00 for the call, your total cost is effectively $15.00 + $45 = $60.00 for the shares.

Why purchase the $45 strike that effectively increases your cost basis by $1.10 over the current stock price? The benefit is that you are paying only $15.00 for an asset ($45 call) that behaves like shares costing $58.90. That's a substantial reduction in cost that allows many investors an opportunity they may not have been able to consider.

Let's say that you bought 10 May 45 calls for $15.00. Your total cost to fulfill your stock requirement on this stock replacement is $15,000. If you had purchased the stock outright (1,000 shares), you would have spent $58,900. **The difference between the capital needed to purchase the stock outright ($58,900) and the capital needed to buy the in-the-money call ($15,000) is the key to this strategy.**

Now that you have your stock (via the 45.00 strike calls you purchased), it is time to **sell covered calls against this position** (this creates a "spread"), which would be the December 60 calls, which were trading for $1.30. If the stock stays at its current level until expiration, you would then capture the $1.30 premium that you sold the December 60 calls for because they would have expired out of the money at expiration.

This scenario represents an 8.6 percent return in just two weeks. This well outperforms the return garnished on a $58,900 investment, which would be only a 2.2 percent return in the two weeks, if you purchased the actual stock.

As you can see, you are getting the same dollar return on fewer dollars invested, which creates a much higher percentage rate of return. **This is one of the positive leverage effects** that the proper usage of options can provide.

When you initiate this trade, you are buying and selling two different options simultaneously, which is known as a spread. As you'll recall, a spread is a trade that involves the buying of one option against the sale of a different option simultaneously.

By purchasing the May 45 calls for $15.00 and then selling the December 60 calls at $1.30, you are buying the May 45–December 60 call spread for $13.70. This is a diagonal spread because the options involved are of different months and different strikes. Remember, a spread involving different strikes but the same month is a vertical spread. Meanwhile, a spread involving different months but the same strike is a time spread. So, different months and different strikes is a diagonal spread.

 KEY POINT

The fact that you are creating the covered call strategy (buy-write) by doing the diagonal spread is very important to note. For margin purposes, the diagonal spread will be margined at a much more favorable rate than the traditional buy-write because you do not own the actual stock and therefore do not have as much to lose. This is especially important for those who trade on margin, or borrowed funds.

This scenario includes another value-added benefit. **When you purchase a spread, the most you can lose is the amount you paid for the spread,** which in this case is $13.70.

As you already know, the biggest risk in a covered call strategy is a large downward move in the stock. If you had done this trade with the actual stock and the stock traded all the way down to $20.00 from $60.00 (although unlikely) we would stand to lose almost $40,000.00.

However, if you did the trade with the $45 calls in place of the stock via the diagonal call spread, the maximum loss is what you spent on the trade. Remember, you purchased the diagonal call spread for $13.70. If you traded the spread an equivalent amount of times to equal 1,000 shares, you would have bought a total of 10 spreads.

The total dollar amount of your investment would be $13,700.00, as opposed to $57,600.00 had you bought 1,000 shares of Amgen outright. Your loss will be maximized at $13,700.00 if the stock traded down to $20.00 as opposed to a $37,600.00 loss in the case of outright stock ownership. Even if the stock became worthless, your maximum loss would still be $13,700.00.

This is because once the stock gets below a certain price, May 45 calls will become worthless; thus, the calls cannot lose any more money no matter how much more the stock trades down.

ROLLING THE POSITION

In order to continue, or "roll," this position, you will have to roll your short front-month option into the next month or in the same month if you get a quicker stock movement. In a traditionally structured covered call strategy (long stock, short call), you are dealing with only one option.

However, in the stock replacement strategy, you have a second option series (the call you purchased to replace the stock) to roll. This may incur an additional commission, but the trade is obviously well worth it when you look at the risk/reward scenarios and the size of the capital outlay needed to initiate the position. This call (the long May 45) can be rolled up with a climbing stock to maintain the position while locking in profits; it also can be rolled out in case you need more time due to the upward stock pattern continuing past May.

CONCLUSION

As detailed here, the stock replacement version of the covered call (buy-write) strategy is an example of the proper use of option leverage. **It offers the investor a bigger percentage return, less risk, and less capital requirement than the traditional covered call.**

Anytime you are interested in a high-dollar stock, first look to see if any deep in-the-money calls fit this replacement scenario. Evaluate whether they might be a better solution.

CHAPTER 15

Straddles

I n previous chapters, I discussed option strategies that feature the use of options in combination with stock (like the buy-write) and the use of options against each other in the form of spreads. Now I will focus on the straddle, which uses options in unison with each other.

Unlike a spread, which features a long option versus a short option, the straddle features one position (either long or short) and two options: a call and its corresponding put. Two options are said to be corresponding when they have the same month and same strike. In order for two options to have the same month and strike, one must be a call and the other must be a put.

WHAT IS A STRADDLE?

A *straddle* is a strategy composed of a long (or short) call and a long (or short) put where both options have the identical strike price and expiration month.

When putting together a straddle, the construction should be:

- Different options (call and its corresponding put)
- Same stock
- Same strike
- Same expiration
- One-to-one ratio

TABLE 15.1   Straddle Construction

Position	Calls	Puts
Long 1 Jan 25 straddle	+1 Jan 25	+1 Jan 25
Long 5 March 40 straddles	+5 Mar 40	+5 Mar 40
Long 10 Jul 70 straddles	+10 Jul 70	+10 Jul 70
Long 25 Nov 35 straddles	+25 Nov 35	+25 Nov 35
Short 1 Jan 25 straddle	−1 Jan 25	−1 Jan 25
Short 5 March 40 straddles	−5 Mar 40	−5 Mar 40
Short 10 Jul 70 straddles	−10 Jul 70	−10 Jul 70
Short 25 Nov 35 straddles	−25 Nov 35	−25 Nov 35

Straddle positions are referred to as long straddle or short straddle, depending on whether you purchase the call and its corresponding put (long) or sell the call and its corresponding put (short).

For example, the long straddle is constructed by purchasing both the July 60 call and the July 60 put. Meanwhile, the short straddle is constructed by selling both the July 60 call and the July 60 put. It is important to note that the straddle is a one-to-one ratio strategy. For every call that you buy (or sell), you must purchase (or sell) exactly one corresponding put to properly construct a straddle. Table 15.1 shows the proper straddle constructions.

STRADDLE SCENARIOS

The straddle is a strategy that relies on movements in stock price or in implied volatility to establish profit opportunities. The straddle buyer is looking for the stock to move aggressively in either direction or for the anticipated perception of possible aggressive moves that will bring about an increase in implied volatility.

Sellers of the straddle will be hoping for the opposite scenario. A lack of stock movement, or a perceived lack of movement, causing implied volatility to decrease, will create profitable scenarios for the straddle seller.

HOW IT WORKS

As a first step in understanding the straddle, let's look at how one works. In our illustration, we will look at the July 65 straddle. We can either buy or sell the straddle.

If we purchase both the July 65 call and the July 65 put simultaneously in a one-to-one ratio, we have a long straddle. To construct a short straddle,

TABLE 15.2   Straddle Value at Expiration (Strike 65)

Strike	Call Price	Put Price	Straddle Price	P&L
50	15.00	0.00	15.00	+9.40
55	10.00	0.00	10.00	+4.40
60	5.00	0.00	5.00	−0.60
65	0.00	0.00	0.00	−5.60
70	0.00	5.00	5.00	−0.60
75	0.00	10.00	10.00	+4.40
80	0.00	15.00	15.00	+9.40

we would sell both the July 65 call and July 65 put simultaneously in a one-to-one ratio.

Continuing with our illustration, we will set the price for each of the options. With our imaginary stock trading at $65.50, the July 65 call trades at $3.13 and the July 65 put trades at $2.47. The combination of these two prices accounts for the $5.60 cost of the straddle.

Now fast forward to expiration and observe what happens to the value of the straddle at different stock prices at expiration (Table 15.2).

As you can see, the straddle's value increases the farther the stock moves away from the strike. The closer the stock is to the strike, the lower the value of the straddle at expiration. The chart clearly shows that the more the stock moves away from the strike, the higher the straddle's value becomes.

Conversely, the closer the stock finishes to the strike, the lower the value of the straddle.

Owners of straddles want and need movement while sellers of straddles want and need stagnation.

How does this example impact your investment strategy? If you feel a stock is likely to move aggressively in either direction or if you feel that implied volatility is expected to increase possibly due to impending news (such as earnings, Food and Drug Administration approval, etc.), you should look into the purchase of a straddle.

However, if you feel that a stock is likely to enter a stagnant phase or if you feel that implied volatility is likely to decrease, then the sale of a straddle could be a very profitable trade for you.

FACTORS THAT AFFECT STRADDLE PRICES

Since the straddle's profit potential is dependent on its price from purchase time to expiration, investors should be aware of the several factors that affect its price.

The first factor is, of course, stock price.

The stock's price dictates the value of both components of the straddle—the call and the put thus affect the straddle price as a whole. As the stock price moves, the prices of the call and the put will fluctuate via the current deltas of the options and thereby will affect the price of the straddle.

As the stock moves higher, the price of the call increases while the price of the put will decrease. However, they do not move linearly; as the stock continues higher, the call's value increases progressively more while the put's value decreases progressively less. This nonlinear effect is caused by the option's changing delta.

As the stock goes up, the call delta increases while the put delta decreases. This opposing effect continues until finally the call gains value dollar for dollar with the stock (once its delta reaches 100) indefinitely. At the same time, the put value loss stops because the put now has no value (as put delta approaches zero).

Of course, the opposite is true if the stock trades down. The call loses value progressively slower until it reaches $0 while the put gains value at an increasing rate until the delta becomes 100; then the put gains dollar for dollar with the stock indefinitely. The effect of stock movement on the dollar value and delta value of the straddle is seen in Table 15.3.

This time we use the June 65 straddle as an example. The straddle is worth $5.82 ($3.19 for the call, $2.63 for the put). Table 15.3 shows the value of the June 65 straddle at a 50 volatility through a range of different stock prices.

A second factor that affects the pricing of a straddle is implied volatility. As implied volatility increases, the value of the straddle increases.

TABLE 15.3 June 65 Value: Different Stock Prices, Same Volatility (50)

Stock Price	Call Price	Delta	Put Price	Delta	Straddle Price
57.50	0.47	16	7.92	−84	8.39
59.50	0.85	24	6.29	−76	7.14
61.50	1.42	34	4.87	−66	6.29
63.50	2.18	45	3.62	−55	5.80
65.50	3.19	55	2.63	−45	5.82
67.50	4.40	65	1.84	−35	6.24
69.50	5.80	74	1.24	−26	7.04
71.50	7.37	82	0.81	−18	8.18
73.50	9.07	87	0.51	−13	9.58
75.50	10.80	91	0.31	−9	11.11
77.50	12.70	95	0.18	−5	12.88

As stated, the price of both calls and puts increases as implied volatility increases. A straddle will feel a double effect when volatility increases because the strategy employs two options working together, not against each other.

When a strategy uses two options working against each other, the effect of implied volatility on the strategy is the difference of its effect on each option. This is different with a straddle. With a straddle, the two options are working together so the effect of implied volatility on each option is added together. Implied volatility movement affects an individual option to an exact dollar amount as indicated by the option's volatility sensitivity component, or vega.

An option with a $0.05 vega will increase $0.05 in value for every tick that implied volatility increases; likewise, it will decrease in value $0.05 for every tick that implied volatility decreases.

I have discussed previously that a call and its corresponding put will have the same vega. That is, if the June 65 call has a .05 vega, then the June 65 put will also have a .05 vega. Remember, vega is calculated by the strike price and does not differentiate put or call.

Now that we have reconfirmed this concept, we can use it to calculate how much our straddle price will change with a movement in implied volatility. Because the straddle combines a call and its corresponding put, the vega effect is doubled in the straddle. This means that the vega of a straddle is the addition of the vega of the call and the vega of the put. Since the put and call vega are the same, we simply multiply the vega of the strike by 2.

Look back at our example. If the June 65 call has a .05 vega, then the June 65 put must also have a .05 vega, and thus the June 65 straddle will have a .10 vega. For every tick that implied volatility increases, the June 65 straddle will increase $0.10 in value.

Conversely, for every tick that volatility decreases, the July 65 straddle will decrease in value. Table 15.4 shows how the straddle's value changes when volatility decreases to 30.

When you study Table 15.4, you can see that as implied volatility increases or decreases, the value of the straddle increases or decreases by the amount of the straddle's vega multiplied by the amount of tick change in implied volatility.

Finally, time is another major factor affecting the price of a straddle. As you have learned from our previous strategies, time takes a toll on all options. Its effect is even more pronounced on this strategy, which combines two options for the same time period.

A straddle will see twice the rate of decay that a single option will. From previous discussions, you should be familiar with the option decay chart and its nonlinear curve. As time goes by, the straddle will

TABLE 15.4 Volatility Effect on Straddle Price

Stock Price	Call Price Volatility		Delta Volatility		Put Price Volatility		Delta Volatility		Straddle Price Volatility	
	50	30	50	30	50	30	50	30	50	30
57.50	0.47	0.05	16	3	7.92	7.52	−84	−97	8.39	7.57
59.50	0.85	0.18	24	10	6.29	5.64	−76	−90	7.14	5.82
61.50	1.42	0.49	34	22	4.87	3.94	−66	−78	6.29	4.43
63.50	2.18	1.09	45	38	3.62	2.53	−55	−62	5.80	3.62
65.50	3.19	2.04	55	56	2.63	1.48	−45	−44	5.82	3.52
67.50	4.40	3.34	65	72	1.84	0.77	−35	−28	6.24	4.11
69.50	5.80	4.92	74	85	1.24	0.36	−26	−15	7.04	5.28
71.50	7.37	6.71	82	92	0.81	0.15	−18	−8	8.18	6.86
73.50	9.07	8.62	87	97	0.51	0.05	−13	−3	9.58	8.67
75.50	10.80	10.50	91	99	0,31	0.02	−9	−1	11.11	10.52
77.50	12.70	12.50	95	100	0.18	0.00	−5	0	12.88	12.50

decay, day after day, at an ever-increasing rate until expiration Friday at 4:00 P.M.

The implication to the buyer and seller should be obvious. The passage of time decreases the value of the straddle and thus always favors the seller. Time works against the buyer. The buyer has only until expiration to get either a large stock or implied volatility movement to offset the price paid for the straddle.

RISKS AND REWARDS

The buyer of the straddle has the same risk/reward scenario as a buyer of an individual option. That is, **the straddle buyer has an unlimited reward and a limited risk.**

As stated earlier, the farther the stock moves away from the strike, the higher the value of the straddle. This creates an unlimited potential profit for the buyer. A straddle buyer's risk, however, is fixed and limited to the amount spent to purchase the straddle.

The risk/reward scenario for the seller of a straddle is the same risk/reward scenario as a seller of an individual option. That is, **the straddle seller has a limited reward and an unlimited risk.**

The seller can gain only what was collected in premium from the sale of the straddle (limited reward). As far as the risk to the seller, the straddle value can increase as much as the stock price can go up or down. Since the stock has an infinite upside, in theory, so does the straddle. This is why the straddle seller is said to have an unlimited risk.

BREAK-EVEN, MAXIMUM REWARD, AND MAXIMUM RISK

When you are contemplating your possibility for profit with a particular straddle, you must establish your break-even point. The straddle is unique in that it has two break-even points. It is important to calculate both to determine how much the stock must move (either up or down) to close at a price that is profitable for the buyer/seller of the straddle.

Break-even is defined as the stock price, at expiration, where the position neither makes nor loses money. Because the straddle involves both a call and a put, the position can make money with a stock movement in either direction, up or down.

Therefore, a straddle has to have two break-even points. One is at a stock price above the strike of the straddle; the other is at a stock price below the strike of the straddle.

In order to calculate the break-even for a straddle, take the strike price and then add the price of the straddle to it to determine the upper break-even price. To determine the lower break-even price, subtract the straddle price from the strike price.

Let's look at an example. We will use the May 30 straddle trading at $3.00 with the stock price directly at $30.00. For simplicity, let's assign a price of $1.50 for the calls and $1.50 for the puts. As defined by the formula, in order to calculate the downside break-even of the straddle, we take the straddle's strike (30) and subtract the straddle's price ($3.00). We get a price of $27.00 as our downside break-even. Let's see how this works.

At expiration, with the stock at $27.00, the May 30 call will be worthless, losing all $1.50.

Meanwhile, the May 30 put will be worth $3.00, gaining $1.50. The loss in the call was offset exactly by the gain in the put. So, at expiration, the straddle is still worth $3.00 (May 30 call $0 plus May 30 put $3.00).

As for the upside break-even, we follow the same formula, but this time we add the price of the straddle ($3.00) to the strike price of the straddle (30) and get a price of $33.00 for the upside break-even. This checks out because at expiration, the May 30 puts will be worthless, losing $1.50.

Meanwhile, the May 30 call will be worth $3.00, gaining $1.50 which offsets the put loss exactly. The straddle started out worth $3.00 ($1.50

May 30 call and $1.50 May 30 put). With the stock at $33.00 at expiration, the straddle will still be worth $3.00 (May 30 call $3.00, May 30 put $0).

It is important to calculate break-evens to determine where the stock has to close to profit the buyer or seller of the straddle. A simple rule of thumb can be applied once the break-evens are properly calculated. This rule of thumb works every time: The straddle is profitable when the stock closes outside the range between the two break-even prices.

Using our previous example of the May 30 straddle and our two break-even prices of $27.00 and $33.00, Table 15.5 shows a range of possible stock closing prices at expiration and the profit/loss associated with those prices for the buyer. The break-even prices are marked with an asterisk (∗). The buyer's profitable areas are outside of the two break-even prices.

Notice that the buyer's profit starts at the first price outside of the break-even range and increases dollar for dollar with the stock as the stock continues to move away from the strike (Figure 15.1).

Also notice that the buyer's loss is at its maximum when the stock closes directly on the strike. Of course, the buyer can sell out of the straddle prior to expiration if he or she felt that the straddle was priced at a level worthy of a sale for either profit or for minimizing a loss. Investors never have to hold a position all the way to expiration if they do not want to.

A profit can be taken at any time during a position's life. Likewise, a loss can be taken at any time during a position's life in order to minimize a future larger loss. **Positions do not need to be held until expiration.** This is normally more important to buyers of option positions as opposed to sellers of option positions.

For a buyer of a straddle, time decay starts to erode its price immediately. Time decay does not sleep and increases progressively over the

TABLE 15.5 Buyer Profits in May 30 Straddle

Stock Price	Call Price	Put Price	Straddle Price	P&L
25	5.00	0.00	5.00	+2.00
26	4.00	0.00	4.00	+1.00
*27	3.00	0.00	3.00	0.00
28	2.00	0.00	2.00	−1.00
29	1.00	0.00	1.00	−2.00
30	0.00	0.00	0.00	−3.00
31	0.00	1.00	1.00	−2.00
32	0.00	2.00	2.00	−1.00
*33	0.00	3.00	3.00	0.00
34	0.00	4.00	4.00	+1.00
35	0.00	5.00	5.00	+2.00

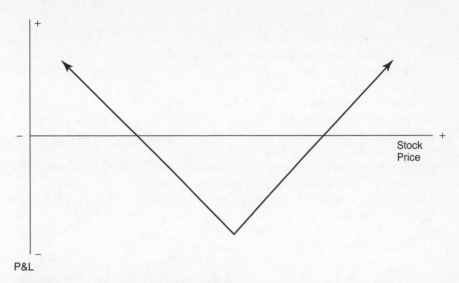

FIGURE 15.1 Long Straddle P&L Chart

course of the position. The buyer is faced with a large premium decay because the straddle features the owning of not one but two options, hence double the decay. With decay working against the long straddle, the buyer is best served taking profits a little more quickly or at least being much more diligent in monitoring the position and reacting quickly to changing prices.

If the straddle was purchased in front of an expected news release (as most straddles are) that could move the stock dramatically, buyers are advised to be ready to take profit or limit losses shortly after the news is out. Further delay will cost time decay dollars.

The seller of the straddle has a potential profit when the stock closes inside of the range formed by the two break-even prices (Figure 15.2).

Again, using our May 30 straddle example and our two break-even prices of $27.00 and $33.00, Table 15.6 shows a range of possible stock closing prices at expiration and the profit/loss associated with those prices for the seller. The break-even prices are marked with an asterisk (∗) and the seller's profitable areas are in bold. Notice how the seller's profit area is located in between the two break-evens.

Notice that the seller's profit starts at the first price inside the range of stock prices defined by the break-even prices and increases as we move to the strike price of the straddle from both break-even prices.

The maximum profit of the straddle for the seller is obtained when the stock closes exactly at the strike price at expiration. Outside the range

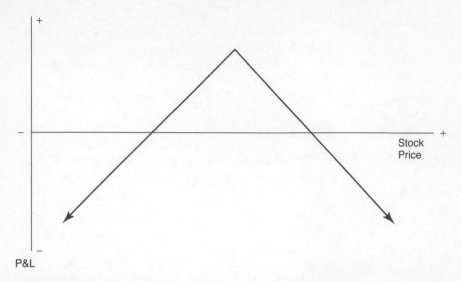

FIGURE 15.2   Short Straddle P&L Chart

of the break-even prices, the straddle loses money for the seller at a dollar-for-dollar pace with the movement of the stock away from the break-even range.

Of course, the seller does not have to carry the position all the way to expiration. At any time prior to expiration, the position may be bought back when it is deemed prudent by the seller. Normally, however, the longer the seller waits to take the position off, the better.

TABLE 15.6   Sellers Profits in May 30 Straddle

Stock Price	Call Price	Put Price	Straddle Price	P&L
25	5.00	0.00	5.00	−2.00
26	4.00	0.00	4.00	−1.00
*27	3.00	0.00	3.00	0.00
28	**2.00**	**0.00**	**2.00**	**+1.00**
29	**1.00**	**0.00**	**1.00**	**+2.00**
30	**0.00**	**0.00**	**0.00**	**+3.00**
31	**0.00**	**1.00**	**1.00**	**+2.00**
32	**0.00**	**2.00**	**2.00**	**+1.00**
*33	0.00	3.00	3.00	0.00
34	0.00	4.00	4.00	−1.00
35	0.00	5.00	5.00	−2.00

For the seller, time decay is welcome. The more time that goes by with stagnation, the lower the straddle's value becomes, thus the more profit there is to be had. Sellers of straddles need to be patient and to allow time to do its thing. However, that being said, a straddle seller does not have to wait until expiration either.

The straddle does not have to go to $0 in order for the seller to make money.

If the straddle loses value quickly, as in the case of a decrease in implied volatility, there may be a big enough profit in the trade to justify the seller locking in the profit before expiration. There is nothing wrong with taking profits and eliminating risk at the same time. That is how money is made and kept.

CONCLUSION

In conclusion, the straddle is an ideal strategy for playing large stock movements, movements in implied volatility and time decay. It is constructed by the purchase or sale of a call and a put in the same stock, same month, and same strike.

The buyer has an unlimited profit potential and a limited loss scenario. The seller has a limited profit potential and an unlimited loss scenario. The price of a straddle can be influenced by stock price, implied volatility, and time decay. It is a position that requires large stock or volatility movements for the buyer and, of course, a lack of movement for the seller.

As always, investors should complete their due diligence research on the stock, formulate an opinion, then weigh the strategies available. They should choose to execute the straddle based on their judgment that it is the safest and most efficient way to profit from the stock's future movement.

EXAMPLES

Here are some examples of scenarios that signal straddle use.

Example 1: Research in Motion

Figure 15.3 presents the daily chart for Research in Motion (RIMM).

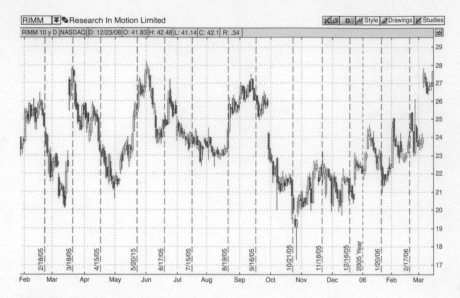

FIGURE 15.3   RIMM Daily Chart
Source: Courtesy of Think or Swim (www.thinkorswim.com)

Notes

Long Straddle

1. Since the beginning of 2005, Research in Motion has been trading in a fairly volatile fashion, including an opening gap down day of around 10 percent.

2. Besides the up and down monthly ranges, the stock has many long candles, indicating large intraday movements. There are as many large downside days as upside days, and even though the stock has an incredible range, it is actually in a sideways trading pattern.

3. In this case, a long straddle could be used to acquire a long gamma position. The long gamma position could be traded effectively on a daily basis to offset the decay of the position. Further, the long gamma position will benefit from gap openings and the large intraday moves.

4. The long gamma position benefits from movement, whether intraday, weekly, back and forth, or in a single direction. But, like all strategies, there is a downside: decay. You must offset the decay of the position by trading the stock back and forth, hoping for some large intraday ranges and a few gap openings, as Research in Motion demonstrates here.

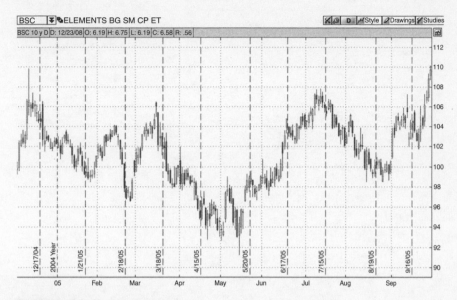

FIGURE 15.4 BSC Daily Chart
Source: Courtesy of Think or Swim (www.thinkorswim.com)

Example 2: Bear Stearns

Figure 15.4 presents the daily chart for Bear Stearns (BSC).

Notes

Long Straddle

1. Starting back in late December, Bear Stearns looks as if it has had a pretty wide trading range with the stock as low as 93 and as high as 110.

2. These volatile movements are very consistent throughout the viewing period. There does not seem to be a substantial consolidation period in the course of these nine months. Further, there are many long candlesticks, indicating many large-range days. This benefits long gamma positions like the long straddle.

3. The purchase of a well-positioned straddle, in this case, will not only allow for profit potential from gamma trading the range (for professional traders) but also allows traders to profit from the gap openings and high-low ranges of the stock.

4. Volatility or the passage of time. So, you must be wary of the level of implied volatility. If implied volatility is not too high compared to the

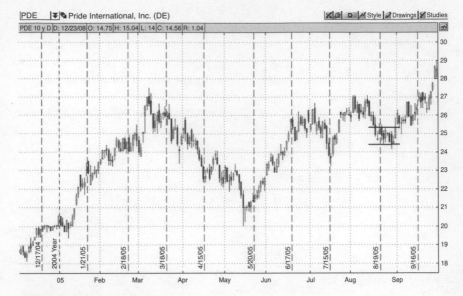

FIGURE 15.5   PDE Daily Chart
Source: Courtesy of Think or Swim (www.thinkorswim.com)

actual volatility of the stock, then the gamma/theta ratio probably will
be advantageous for gamma trading a long straddle, as in the case of
Bear Stearns here.

Example 3: Pride International

Figure 15.5 presents the Pride International (PDE) daily chart.

Notes

Short Straddle

1. Pride International (PDE) breaks out of a trading range in January 2005
   and proceeds to trade up around the $27.00 level. After trading back
   down to around $20 (in a style that would also be perfect for a sell-
   write), the stock trades back up to the $25.00 range.

2. At this price, Pride begins to consolidate in this $25.00 area. This
   consolidation begins around mid-June and extends through August
   and into September. This consolidation around the $25.00 stock price
   presents an excellent opportunity for premium collection via the short
   straddle.

3. By selling both the 25 strike call and put, which are both at-the-money options, you will have the opportunity to capture a large amount of premium.

4. The straddle will set up break-evens both above and below the strike in the amount of proceeds brought in by the sale of the straddle. If the stock closes near the 25 strike at expiration, the stock will more than likely finish inside of the break-even parameters, profiting the straddle seller.

Example 4: Red Hat Inc.

Figure 15.6 presents the Red Hat Inc. (RHAT) daily chart.

Notes

Short Straddle

1. After running up from the $6.00 to $8.00 range, Red Hat Inc. reaches a high of about $28.00 before breaking down to a lower trading range in the $15.00 area.

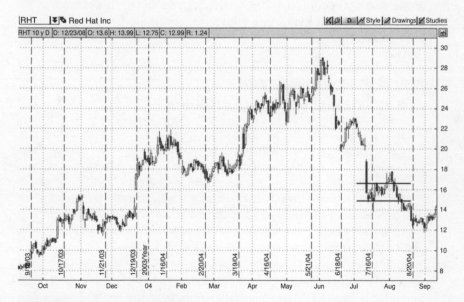

FIGURE 15.6 RHAT Daily Chart
Source: Courtesy of Think or Swim (www.thinkorswim.com)

2. Once falling into the new trading range in early July, Red Hat starts to develop a new range around $15.00. The range starts out relatively wide but appears to tighten as time goes on. This consolidation is an ideal time to sell a straddle.

3. The short straddle involves the simultaneous selling of an at-the-money call and its corresponding at-the-money put. For this, you will have a position that collects money as time passes. The short call and short put will provide break-even prices above the call strike and below the put strike. If the stock stays between these two break-evens between now and expiration, you will collect the value of your short straddle.

4. As the stock continues to consolidate and the range tightens, there is a chance that a short straddle will be better in the future as the stock's range tightens.

LONG STRADDLE SYNOPSIS

Construction. Long one call and one put with the same strike price, in the same expiration month, and in a one-to-one ratio. The strike price used is normally at the money.

Function. Take advantage of large potential stock movements in either direction or if you anticipate an upward movement in implied volatility.

Bias (Lean). Volatile in either direction.

When to Use. Normally around news release time (i.e., earnings) when you feel that the news can affect the stock aggressively but are not sure in which direction. Also, it is good to use when you feel implied volatility is likely to increase sharply.

Profit Scenario. Profit will be obtained in a dollar-for-dollar fashion if the stock closes outside of the parameters of the break-evens set forth by first adding the strike price to the amount paid for the straddle then subtracting the amount paid for the straddle from the strike price. Theoretically it offers unlimited potential reward.

Loss Scenario. Loss occurs if stock closes between break-even points, as defined. Maximum loss occurs if stock closes directly at the strike and lessens as stock closes closer to either of the break-even points. Maximum loss is limited to price paid for straddle.

Key Concept. Because of large decay associated with this position, time sensitivity is critical. Once anticipated movement occurs, it is critical to close down the position in order to secure profit and eliminate further risk of substantial decay.

SHORT STRADDLE SYNOPSIS

Construction. Short one call and short one put with the same strike price, in the same expiration month, in a one-to-one ratio. Strike price used is normally at the money.

Function. Take advantage of a stock entering a stagnant or low-volatility trading range.

Bias. Stagnant.

When to Use. Normally a time outside of expected news releases (i.e., earnings), when you feel that the lack of news can lead to a period of stagnation or lack of movement of the stock without directional bias. Also it is good to use when you feel that implied volatility is likely to decrease sharply.

Profit Scenario. Profit will be obtained if the stock closes inside of the parameters of the break-evens set forth by first adding the strike price to the amount paid for the straddle, then subtracting the amount paid for the straddle from the strike price. This strategy has a potential reward limited to the amount received from the sale.

Loss Scenario. Loss occurs if the stock closes outside break-even points, as defined. Maximum loss occurs once the stock closes outside either of the break-even points and increases as stock moves farther away beyond either of the break-even points.

Key Concept. Because of the large decay associated with this position, time sensitivity is critical. The longer the stock remains stagnant or between the two break-even points, the better for the seller. The passage of time aids this strategy. Due to the nature of the position, maximum loss is theoretically unlimited.

CHAPTER 16

Strangles

The strangle is another option strategy that features the use of options in unison with each other. The strangle is philosophically identical to its cousin, the straddle. However, the straddle has a single strike as its focal point, whereas the strangle has its focal point spread out over two strikes.

Compared to the straddle, the strangle will produce wider break-even points and lower prices. The widening of the break-even points changes the risk/reward scenarios for both the buyer and the seller of the strangle as opposed to the straddle.

The benefit to the buyer of the strangle is that it will cost less than a straddle (thus less risk). But, like all risk/reward scenarios, less risk equals less reward. The buyer's trade-off for lower cost and less risk is that the stock will have to move significantly more than if the buyer had purchased a straddle.

The benefit to the seller of the strangle is that the strangle offers a larger margin of error in terms of the anticipated stock movement. The wider range of the break-even prices allows the stock to have more movement while still allowing the seller to profit. The seller's trade-off for this luxury is price. The seller will not bring in as much premium from the sale of a strangle as from the sale of a straddle.

That being said, let's take a close look at the strangle.

WHAT IS A STRANGLE?

The *strangle*, like the straddle, consists of two options. In the strangle, however, the two options are not at-the-money options of the same strike (straddle) but out-of-the-money options (both a call and a put) of different strikes. The strangle features one position (either long or short) and two options: an out-of-the-money call and an out-of-the-money put. (See Figures 16.1 and 16.2.)

Construct a strangle in this way:

- Different options (out-of-the-money call and out-of-the-money put)
- Same stock
- Same expiration
- One-to-one ratio

Strangle positions are referred to as long strangle or short strangle, depending on whether you purchase the call and the put (long) or sell the call and the put (short).

For example, with the stock trading at $57.50, the long strangle will be constructed by purchasing both the July 60 call and the July 55 put. Meanwhile, the short strangle will be constructed by selling both the July 60 call and the July 55 put.

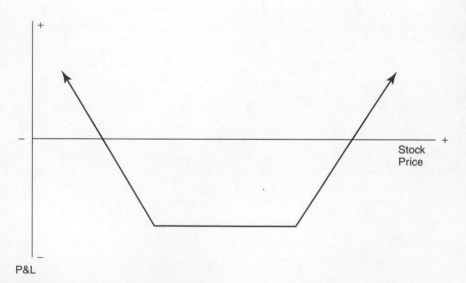

P&L

FIGURE 16.1   Long Strangle P&L Chart

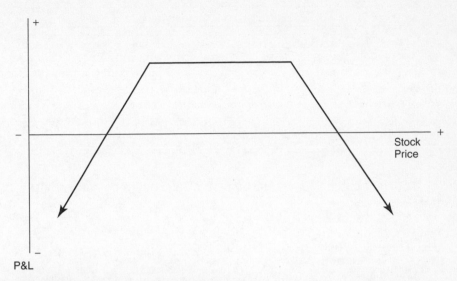

FIGURE 16.2 Short Strangle P&L Chart

It is important to note that the strangle is a one-to-one ratio strategy. For every call that you buy (or sell), you must purchase (or sell) exactly one put to construct a strangle properly.

STRANGLE SCENARIOS

The strangle is a strategy that relies on movements in stock price or in implied volatility to establish profit opportunities. The strangle buyer is looking for the stock to move aggressively in either direction or for the anticipated perception of possible aggressive moves, which will bring about an increase in implied volatility.

Sellers of the strangle are hoping for the opposite, of course. A lack of stock movement or a perceived lack of movement causing implied volatility to decrease will create profitable scenarios for the strangle seller.

HOW IT WORKS

As a first step in understanding the strangle, let's look at how a strangle works. In our illustration, we will look at the July 60/65 strangle. We can either buy or sell the strangle.

If we purchase both the July 65 call and the July 60 put simultaneously in a one-to-one ratio, we have a long strangle. To construct a short strangle,

TABLE 16.1 Value of Strangle July 60/65 at Expiration

Stock Price	Call Price	Put Price	Strangle Price	P&L
50	0.00	10.00	10.00	6.69
55	0.00	5.00	5.00	1.69
60	0.00	0.00	0.00	−3.31
65	0.00	0.00	0.00	−3.31
70	5.00	0.00	5.00	1.69
75	10.00	0.00	10.00	6.69

we would sell both the July 65 call and July 60 put simultaneously in a one-to-one ratio.

Continuing with our illustration, we will set the price for each of the options. With our imaginary stock trading at $63.50, the July 65 call trades at $2.11 and the July 60 put trades at $1.20. The combination of these two prices accounts for the $3.31 cost of the strangle.

Now fast forward to expiration, and observe what happens to the value of the strangle at different stock prices at expiration (Table 16.1).

As you can see, the strangle's value increases the farther the stock moves below the lower strike or above the upper strike. The closer the stock is to the area defined by the inner border between the two strikes, the lower the value of the strangle at expiration. The table clearly shows that the more the stock moves away from the inside of the strikes, the higher the strangle value becomes.

Conversely, the closer the stock finishes to the area in between the strikes, the lower the value of the strangle. Owners of strangles want and need movement while sellers of strangles want and need stagnation.

How does this example impact your investment strategy? If you feel a stock is likely to move aggressively in either direction or if you feel that implied volatility is expected to increase possibly due to impending news (such as earnings, Food and Drug Administration approval, etc.), you should look into the purchase of a strangle.

However, if you feel that a stock is likely to enter a stagnant phase or if you feel that implied volatility is likely to decrease, then the sale of a strangle could be a very profitable trade for you.

FACTORS THAT AFFECT STRANGLE PRICES

Since potential profit of the strangle is dependent on its price from purchase time to expiration, the investor should be aware of the several factors that affect the strangle's price. The first factor is, of course, stock price.

The stock's price will dictate the value of both components of the strangle—the call and the put thus affecting the strangle price as a whole. As the stock price moves, the prices of the call and the put will fluctuate via the current deltas of the options and thereby affect the price of the strangle.

As the stock moves higher, the price of the call will increase while the price of the put will decrease. However, they do not move linearly; as the stock continues higher, the call's value increases progressively more while the put's value decreases progressively less. This nonlinear effect is caused by the option's changing Delta.

The call delta increases as the stock goes up while the put delta decreases as the stock goes up. This opposing effect continues until finally the call gains value dollar for dollar with the stock (once its delta reaches 100) indefinitely. At the same time, the put value loss stops because the put now has no value (as put delta approaches zero). Of course, the opposite is true if the stock trades down.

The call will lose value progressively slower until it reaches $0 while the put will gain value at an increasing rate until the delta becomes 100. Then the put will gain dollar for dollar with the stock indefinitely. The effect of stock movement on the dollar value and delta value of the strangle is seen in Table 16.2.

Again, we will use the July 60/65 strangle as an example. The strangle will be worth $3.31 ($2.11 for the call, $1.20 for the put). For clarification, these prices are not expiration prices. This strangle has three weeks to go before expiration.

A second factor that affects the pricing of a strangle is implied volatility. As implied volatility increases, the value of the strangle increases. As stated, the price of both calls and puts increase as implied volatility increases.

A strangle will feel an increased effect when volatility increases because the strategy employs two options working together and not against each other. When a strategy uses two options working against each other,

TABLE 16.2 Effect of Stock Movement on Delta and Strangle Price

Stock Price	Call Price	Delta	Put Price	Delta	Strangle Price
57.50	0.42	15	3.86	−62	4.28
59.50	0.78	24	2.74	−50	3.52
61.50	1.35	34	1.85	−38	3.20
63.50	2.11	45	1.20	−28	3.31
65.50	3.13	56	.74	−19	3.87
67.50	4.35	66	.44	−13	4.79
69.50	5.77	75	.25	−08	6.20

the effect of implied volatility is the difference of its effect on each option. This is not the case with a strangle. With a strangle, the two options are working together so the effect of implied volatility on each option is added together.

Implied volatility movement affects an individual option to an exact dollar amount, as indicated by the option's volatility sensitivity component, or vega. An option with a .05 vega will increase $0.05 in value for every tick that implied volatility increases and likewise will decrease in value $0.05 for every tick that implied volatility decreases.

Because the strangle combines a call and a put, the vega value of the call is added to the vega value of the put. This means that the vega of a strangle is the sum of the vega of the call plus the vega of the put.

Look back at our example. If the July 65 call has a .10 vega and the July 60 put has a .07 vega, then the July 60/65 strangle will have a .17 vega. This means that for every tick that implied volatility increases, the July 60/65 strangle will increase $0.17 in value.

Conversely, for every tick that volatility decreases, the July 60/65 strangle will decrease in value. Table 16.3 shows how the strangle's value changes at different implied volatility levels.

When you study Table 16.3, you can see that as implied volatility increases or decreases, the value of the strangle increases or decreases by the amount of its vega multiplied by the amount of the tick change in implied volatility.

Finally, time is another major factor affecting the price of a strangle. As you have learned from previous strategies, time takes a toll on all options. Its effect is even more pronounced on this strategy, which combines two options for the same time period.

A strangle will see a much higher rate of decay than a single option. From previous discussions, you should be familiar with the option decay chart and its nonlinear curve.

As time goes by, the strangle will decay, day after day, at an ever-increasing rate until expiration Friday at 4:00 P.M. The implication to the buyer and seller should be obvious. The passage of time decreases the

TABLE 16.3 Strangle Value Changes at Different Volatilities

Stock Price	Volatility	Call Price	Put Price	Strangle Price	Strangle Vega
63.50	30	2.11	1.20	3.31	.168
63.50	40	3.02	1.97	4.99	.173
63.50	50	2.92	2.80	6.72	.174
63.50	60	4.83	3.63	8.46	.174
63.50	70	5.73	4.46	10.19	.174

value of the strangle and thus always favors the seller. Time works against the buyer. The buyer has only until expiration to get either a large stock or large implied volatility movement to offset the price paid for the strangle.

RISKS AND REWARDS

The buyer of the strangle has the same risk/reward scenario as a buyer of an individual option. That is, **the strangle buyer has an unlimited reward and a limited risk.**

As stated earlier, the farther the stock moves away from the strike, the higher the value of the strangle. This creates an unlimited potential profit as a reward for the buyer. On the other hand, a strangle buyer's risk is fixed and limited to the amount spent to purchase the strangle.

The risk/reward scenario for the seller of a strangle is the same risk/reward scenario as a seller of an individual option. That is, **the strangle seller has a limited reward and an unlimited risk.**

The seller can gain only what was collected in premium from the sale of the strangle (limited reward). As far as the risk to the seller, the strangle value can increase as much as the stock price can go up or down. Since the stock has an infinite upside, in theory, so does the strangle. This is why the strangle seller is said to have an unlimited risk.

BREAK-EVEN, MAXIMUM REWARD, AND MAXIMUM RISK

When you are contemplating your possibility for profit with a particular strangle, you must establish your break-even point. The strangle is unique in that it has two break-even points. It is important to calculate both to determine how much the stock must move (either up or down) to close at a price that is profitable for the buyer/seller of the strangle.

Break-even is defined as the stock price, at expiration, where the position neither makes nor loses money. Because the strangle involves both a call and a put, the position can make money with a stock movement in either direction, up or down.

Therefore, a strangle will have two break-evens. One is at the stock price above the higher strike of the strangle; the other is at the stock price below the lower strike of the strangle.

In order to calculate the break-even for a strangle, you take the strike price of the call and then add the total price of the strangle to it to determine the upper break-even price. To determine the lower break-even price, subtract the total price of the strangle from the strike price of the put.

Let's look at an example. We will use the May 55/60 strangle trading at $3.00 with the stock price directly at $57.50. For simplicity, let's assign the May 60 calls a price of $1.50 and $1.50 for the May 55 puts. As defined by the formula, in order to calculate the downside break-even of the strangle, we take the put's strike price (55) and subtract the strangle's total price ($3.00). We get a price of $52.00 as our downside break-even.

Let's see how this works. At expiration, with the stock at $52.00, the May 55 put will be worth $3.00, a net gain of $1.50. Meanwhile, the May 60 call will be worthless, incurring a net loss of $1.50. The loss in the call was offset exactly by the gain in the put.

So, at expiration, the strangle is still worth $3.00 (May 60 call $0 + May 55 put $3.00). As for the upside break-even, we take the call's strike price (60) and add to it the total price of the strangle ($3.00) and get $63.00 as our upside break-even. This checks out because at expiration, with the stock at $63.00, the May 55 puts will be worthless, losing $1.50.

Meanwhile, the May 60 call will be worth $3.00, gaining $1.50, which offsets the put loss exactly. The strangle started out worth $3.00 ($1.50 May 60 call and $1.50 May 55 put). With the stock at $63.00 at expiration, the strangle will still be worth $3.00 (May 60 call $3.00, May 55 put $0).

The importance of calculating break-evens is to determine where the stock has to close at expiration to profit the buyer or seller of the strangle. A simple rule of thumb can be applied once the break-evens are properly calculated. This rule of thumb works every time: The buyer of the strangle profits when the stock closes outside the range between the two break-even prices at expiration. The seller of the strangle profits when the stock closes inside the break-even prices.

Using our previous example of the May 55/60 strangle and our two break-even prices of $52.00 to the downside and $63.00 to the upside, Table 16.4 shows a range of possible stock closing prices at expiration and the profit/loss associated with those prices for the buyer of the strangle. Break-even prices are marked with an asterisk (*). Lines in bold indicate profit.

Notice that the buyer's profit starts at the first price outside of the break-even range and increases dollar for dollar with the stock as the stock continues to move away from the higher and lower strikes respectively.

Also notice that the buyer's loss is at its maximum when the stock closes anywhere between the two strikes. Of course, buyers can sell out of the strangle at any time prior to expiration if they feel it is wise to move, either for profit or to minimize a loss.

Investors never have to hold a position all the way to expiration if they do not want to.

TABLE 16.4 Buyer of the Strangle Profit and Loss

Stock Price	Call Price	Put Price	Strangle Price	P&L
50	**0.00**	**5.00**	**5.00**	**+2.00**
51	**0.00**	**4.00**	**4.00**	**+1.00**
*52	0.00	3.00	3.00	0.00
53	0.00	2.00	2.00	−1.00
54	0.00	1.00	1.00	−2.00
55	0.00	0.00	0.00	−3.00
56	0.00	0.00	0.00	−3.00
57	0.00	0.00	0.00	−3.00
58	0.00	0.00	0.00	− 3.00
59	0.00	0.00	0.00	−3.00
60	0.00	0.00	0.00	− 3.00
61	1.00	0.00	1.00	−2.00
62	2.00	0.00	2.00	−1.00
*63	3.00	0.00	3.00	0
64	**4.00**	**0.00**	**4.00**	**+1.00**
65	**5.00**	**0.00**	**5.00**	**+2.00**

A profit can be taken at any time during a position's life. Likewise, a loss can be taken at any time during a position's life in order to minimize a future larger loss. Positions do not need to be held until expiration—this is normally more important to buyers of option positions than to sellers because buyers of premium are hurt by the passage of time while sellers are aided by it.

For a buyer of a strangle, time decay starts to erode the strangle's price immediately. Time decay does not sleep and increases progressively over the course of the position. Buyers are faced with a large premium decay because the strangle features the owning of not one but two options, hence double the decay.

With decay working against the long strangle, buyers are best served taking profits a little more quickly or at least being much more diligent in monitoring the position and reacting quickly to changing prices.

If the strangle was purchased in front of an expected news release (most strangles are) that could move the stock dramatically, buyers are advised to be ready to take profit or limit losses shortly after the news is out. Delay will cost time decay dollars and probably expand losses by a decrease in implied volatility once the news event is over.

The seller of the strangle has a potential profit when the stock closes inside of the range formed by the two break-even prices. Again, using our May 55/60 strangle example and our two break-even prices of $52.00 and $63.00, Table 16.5 shows a range of possible stock closing prices at

TABLE 16.5 Profit and Loss for Seller of the Strangle

Stock Price	Call Price	Put Price	Strangle Price	P & L
50	0.00	5.00	5.00	−2.00
51	0.00	4.00	4.00	−1.00
*52	0.00	3.00	3.00	0.00
53	**0.00**	**2.00**	**2.00**	**+1.00**
54	**0.00**	**1.00**	**1.00**	**+2.00**
55	**0.00**	**0.00**	**0.00**	**+3.00**
56	**0.00**	**0.00**	**0.00**	**+3.00**
57	**0.00**	**0.00**	**0.00**	**+3.00**
58	**0.00**	**0.00**	**0.00**	**+3.00**
59	**0.00**	**0.00**	**0.00**	**+3.00**
60	**0.00**	**0.00**	**0.00**	**+3.00**
61	**1.00**	**0.00**	**1.00**	**+2.00**
62	**2.00**	**0.00**	**2.00**	**+1.00**
*63	3.00	0.00	3.00	0
64	4.00	0.00	4.00	−1.00
65	5.00	0.00	5.00	−2.00

expiration and the profit/loss associated with those prices for the seller of the strangle. The break-even prices are marked with an asterisk (∗). Bold lines indicate area of profit.

Notice that the seller's profit starts at the first price inside the range of stock prices defined by the break-even prices and increases as you move to the middle of the strike prices (call and put) of the strangle from both break-even prices.

The maximum profit of the strangle for the seller is obtained when the stock closes, anywhere between the strike prices at expiration.

Outside the range of the break-even prices, the straddle loses money for the seller at a dollar-for-dollar pace with the movement of the stock away from the break-even range in either direction. Of course, sellers do not have to carry the position all the way to expiration.

At any time prior to expiration, sellers may buy back the position when deemed prudent. Normally, however, the longer sellers wait to take the position off, the better. The passage of time works in favor of sellers. As more time goes by without a stock or implied volatility movement, the bigger the profit grows for sellers.

Remember, however, the seller's profit is always limited to the total price received for the sale of the strangle.

Sellers welcome time decay. The more time that goes by with stagnation, the lower the strangle's value becomes, thus the more profit there is to be had. Sellers of strangles need to be patient and to allow time to do its thing. However, that being said, strangle sellers do not have to wait until expiration.

The strangle does not have to go to $0 in order for sellers to make money. If the strangle loses value quickly, as in the case of a decrease in implied volatility, there may be a big enough profit in the trade to warrant sellers locking in the profit before expiration. There is nothing wrong with taking profits and eliminating risk at the same time. That is how money is made and kept.

CONCLUSION

In conclusion, the strangle is an ideal strategy for playing large stock movements, movements in implied volatility, and time decay. It is constructed by the purchase or sale of an out-of-the-money call and an out-of-the-money put in the same stock and the same month. **The buyer has an unlimited profit potential and a limited loss scenario.**

The seller has a limited profit potential and an unlimited loss scenario. The price of a strangle can be influenced by stock price, implied volatility, and time decay. It is a position that requires large stock or volatility movements for buyers and, of course, a lack of movement for sellers.

As always, the strangle should be executed only after investors complete due diligence research on the stock, formulate an opinion, then weigh the strategies available. They should choose the strangle based on their judgment that it is the safest and most efficient way to profit from the stock's future movement.

EXAMPLES

Example 1: Goldman Sachs

Figure 16.3 presents the Goldman Sachs (GSCO) daily chart.

Notes

Long Strangle

1. Aside from a roughly one-and-a-half-month period where Goldman Sachs traded sideways from mid-December to late January, the stock showed a propensity for volatile movements
2. These movements, both up and down, are easily seen by the displayed candlestick chart in Figure 16.3. The chart is filled with large-size

FIGURE 16.3 GSCO Daily Chart
Source: Courtesy of Think or Swim (www.thinkorswim.com)

candles, both up and down. This indicates a lack of a consistent pattern but indicates a good amount of nondirectional volatility. This is an excellent time to apply a long strangle position. A long strangle will provide a long gamma position, which allows for a gamma trading position. Gamma trading positions allow traders to trade the stock back and forth in a hedged fashion.

3. The long strangle is constructed by the simultaneous ownership of both an out-of-the-money call and put in the same month and in a one-to-one ratio. This not only provides protection for swing and day traders but also allows for increased profitability in cases where the stock makes quick, aggressive movements in either direction. Here, Goldman Sachs demonstrates the downside in April–May and on the upside during mid-June to mid-July. Further, this strategy allows the trader to prosper from gap openings and increases in volatility.

4. Volatility decreases and stagnation are detrimental to the long strangle. Other than from mid-December to late January, Goldman Sachs shows little of this type of movement.

Example 2: Enbridge Energy Partners LP

Figure 16.4 presents the Enbridge Energy Partners LP (EEP) daily chart.

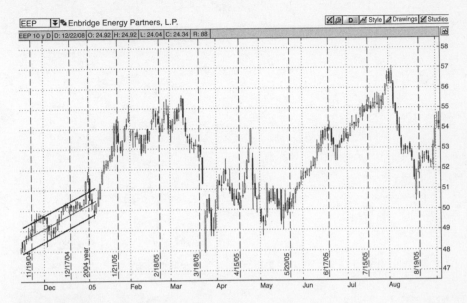

FIGURE 16.4 EEP Daily Chart
Source: Courtesy of Think or Swim (www.thinkorswim.com)

Notes

Long Strangle

1. After trading up out of a slow, uptrending trading pattern, Enbridge Energy Partners seems to break out in late December. It then pulls in sharply, which appears to be a false break-out.

2. However, instead of breaking down, Enbridge rebounds and breaks out nicely. This action seems to ignite its volatile side, and the stock begins to trade in a much bigger daily range. This increase in intraday volatility should provide traders with an excellent opportunity for gamma trading using a long strangle.

3. As we've covered, the long strangle involves the simultaneous purchase of both an out-of-the-money call and an out-of-the-money put in the same month, in a one-to-one ratio. This allows the trader to both buy and sell the stock back and forth, making money in a hedged fashion.

4. Because the trader is hedged, and also due to the nature of long gamma, the trader can trade a single side of the market repeatedly without incurring directional overexposure. Gap openings are also a profitable situation for the long strangle owner.

5. The major downside is decay. This position will decay daily, so the trader must offset the decay by flipping.

FIGURE 16.5 IMCL Daily Chart
Source: Courtesy of Think or Swim (www.thinkorswim.com)

Example 3: Imclone Systems Inc.

Figure 16.5 presents the Imclone Systems Inc. (IMCL) daily chart.

Notes

Short Strangle

1. ImClone broke down out of a higher trading range and began to form a new, lower trading range. During this period, ImClone goes into a period of consolidation.

2. Due to ImClone's nature and the fact it is a biotech company, it carries a reasonably higher volatility than most. Combine this with the fact that ImClone just had a technical breakdown, which is a high-volatility event, and it stands to reason that volatility is probably on the high end for this stock at the present time.

3. With volatility high and the stock starting to consolidate, this would be an excellent time to collect premium via a short strangle.

4. When the stock bottoms out in mid-April, it begins a new trading range that lasts through September with a high of 37 and a low of 30. This five-month period would be good for selling the 30–35 strangle and

occasionally the 32.5–35 or 32.5–37.5 strangle, depending on the stock price at the time. The short strangle allows for premium collection while still allowing the stock room to move a little. It does not cause strangle sellers the anxiety they ordinarily might feel in a volatile stock like this.

Example 4: XILINX Inc.

Figure 16.6 presents the XILINX Inc. (XLNX) daily chart.

Notes

Short Strangle

1. After trading up for the better part of two years, XILINX tops out around $43.00 in January 2004 but cannot hold the new level and begins a precipitous drop, which lasts through August 2004 and takes the stock as low as $25.00. Here it begins to consolidate around $27.50, trading between $25.00 and $33.00.

2. During this period, we see that the range on XILINX begins wide but slowly and steadily tightens in a classic consolidating formation.

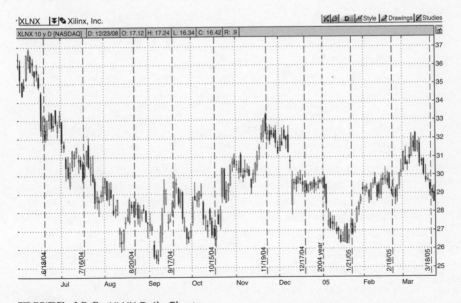

FIGURE 16.6 XLNX Daily Chart
Source: Courtesy of Think or Swim (www.thinkorswim.com)

3. The sale of the 25–30 strangle turns out to provide an excellent premium collection strategy. It comes equipped with a significantly wide break-evens, which aid in lessening risk but do not eliminate it.

4. With a reasonably higher volatility-per-dollar price of this stock, the short strangle should provide enough premium to offset its riskiness.

LONG STRANGLE SYNOPSIS

Construction. Long one call and one put with different strike prices but in the same expiration month in a one-to-one ratio. Both options are usually out of the money.

Function. To take advantage of large potential stock movements in either direction or if you anticipate an upward movement in implied volatility.

Bias. Volatile in either direction.

When to Use. Normally around news release time (i.e., earnings) when you feel that the news can affect the stock aggressively but aren't sure in which direction. Also it is good to use when you feel implied volatility is likely to increase sharply.

Profit Scenario. Profit will be obtained in a dollar-for-dollar fashion if the stock closes outside of the parameters of the break-evens set forth by first adding the strike price of the call to the amount paid for the strangle then subtracting the amount paid for the strangle from the strike price of the put. Theoretically, it offers unlimited potential reward.

Loss Scenario. Maximum loss occurs if the stock closes between the break-even points, as defined. Maximum loss is limited to the price paid for the strangle.

Key Concept. Because of large decay associated with this position, time sensitivity is critical. Once anticipated stock or volatility movement occurs, it is critical to close down the position in order to secure profits and eliminate further risk of substantial decay. Philosophically identical to the straddle except the strangle's wider break-evens require a larger stock movement. The trade-off for this is the lower cost of the strangle.

SHORT STRANGLE SYNOPSIS

Construction. Short one call and short one put with different strike prices, in the same expiration month and in a one-to-one ratio. Both options are usually out of the money.

Function. To take advantage of a stock entering a stagnant or low-volatility trading range.

Bias. Stagnant.

When to Use. Normally a time outside of expected news releases (i.e., earnings) when you feel that the lack of news can lead to a period of stagnation or lack of movement of the stock without directional bias. Also good to use when you feel implied volatility is likely to decrease sharply.

Profit Scenario. Profit will be obtained if the stock closes inside of the parameters of the break-evens set forth by first adding the strike price of the call to the amount paid for the strangle, then subtracting the amount paid for the strangle from the strike price of the put. This strategy has a potential reward limited to the amount received from the sale.

Loss Scenario. Loss occurs if the stock closes outside break-even points, as defined. Maximum loss occurs as the stock continues to trade farther outside and away from either break-even point. Potential loss is theoretically unlimited.

Key Concept. Because of large decay associated with this position, time sensitivity is critical. The longer the stock remains stagnant or between the two break-even points, the better for the seller. The passage of time aids this strategy, as do decreases in implied volatility. Due to the nature of the position, maximum loss is theoretically unlimited.

PART IV

Combination Strategies

I have discussed strategies that use options with stock and options with options. Now I will focus on option strategies that combine strategy with strategy. While the basis of each of these strategies is options combined with options, both the butterfly and condor can be broken down to reveal a strategy with a strategy.

Investors interested in the strong premium collection of the short straddle and short strangle may be hesitant to commit to those strategies because of their risk of unlimited loss. The butterfly and condor are perfect for those scenarios because they are almost as strong in premium collection as the short straddle and short strangle, but they are fully hedged. That hedge sacrifices some premium but in return limits the substantial loss that may happen with the short straddle or short strangle.

If the opportunity seems good for the short strangle or short straddle, investigate the butterfly and condor to protect your bottom line.

CHAPTER 17

The Butterfly

The *butterfly* is often touted as a sophisticated, advanced strategy. While it is true that it is more sophisticated than our previous strategies, if you have done your homework and have learned option basics properly, then the butterfly, while complex, is just a combination of already-familiar, basic strategies. Let's take a closer look and uncover the secrets of the mysterious butterfly.

CONSTRUCTING THE BUTTERFLY

The first thing you must understand about the butterfly is that it is constructed by using either all calls or all puts. The exception, called the iron butterfly, will be explained later.

Whether you choose to use calls or puts, butterflies are always constructed in a 1-2-1 arrangement. For the long butterfly, you would buy one low strike, sell two medium strikes, and buy one high strike with the strike prices equally spaced. The center strike typically matches the current price of the stock. As you can see, its construction is the complex part.

For example, if the stock is 55 and you decide to create a long butterfly by using calls, you could buy a 50 call, sell two 55 calls, and buy one 60 call. If you decided to use puts, you could buy a 50 put, sell two 55 puts, and buy one 60 put. The long butterfly is always long the outer strikes and short the center strike.

The short butterfly is constructed in the opposite way. The short butterfly is always short the outer strikes and long the center strike. For

299

example, to create a short butterfly, you could sell a 50 call, buy two 55 calls, and sell one 60 call. The short butterfly trader is simply taking the opposite side of the long butterfly trader.

The trick to the construction is to understand that while there are three strikes to a butterfly, there are a total of four options involved.

I know the construction will be hard to associate with long or short at the start, so here is a little trick to help you remember how to differentiate a long butterfly from a short one.

When I try to determine whether a butterfly is long or short, I always look at that first strike. If that first strike is long, then it is a long butterfly—it is as simple as that. Some people find it easier just to focus on the center strike, where you have the two option positions. You are long the butterfly if you are short the center strike.

The opposite would be true for short butterflies. These are just two ways that you can determine whether a butterfly is long or short until you become so familiar that you automatically know which butterfly is which.

But until you get to that point, you will want to use little tricks. Use whichever one is most comfortable for you. I suggest you focus on only one trick and use only it until you become so familiar with butterflies that you don't need tricks to recognize which butterfly you have. Make your choice and stick with it!

Table 17.1 shows the long and short butterfly construction.

Notice that the strike prices are equally spaced. This is a necessary aspect of all butterflies. However, while the strikes must be equally spaced, they do not need to be spaced by $5.00 as in this example.

They can be spaced by $10.00. That butterfly is created by purchasing the 45 call, selling two 55 calls, and buying one 65 call. You just have to understand that the strikes must be set up in an equidistant manner, and they must be either all calls or all puts in the proper 1-2-1 ratio.

From a terminology standpoint, we refer to the butterfly in Figure 17.1 as the 50/55/60 butterfly or, more simply, the 55 butterfly, taking the lead from the butterfly's middle strike.

We add to that term whatever month we are dealing with. If we are looking at the June expiration cycle, for example, this would be called

TABLE 17.1 Butterfly Construction

Strike Price	Long Butterfly	Short Butterfly
50	+1	−1
55	−2	+2
60	+1	−1

the June 55 butterfly. If we were in April, it would be called the April 55 butterfly.

WHY USE BUTTERFLIES?

The butterfly's primary objective is premium collection. Much like the short straddle and the short strangle, the butterfly is a premium-collection strategy except for a significant difference. The difference is that the butterfly is a hedged premium-collection strategy. The long butterfly (short iron butterfly) is the most common of the butterflies used by individual investors due to its limited risk scenario.

This limited risk is what separates it from most of the other premium-collection strategies. Because the butterfly is hedged, it has a fixed loss profile. As a premium-collection strategy, it is not as aggressive or risky as the straddle or the strangle. However, as with any investment, if you take less risk, you get less reward.

The butterfly's primary goal is premium collection, which comes through the sale of the center strike options. But in order to hedge, you must somewhere, somehow, give up a little something, and that something is going to be a portion of the total potential premium collected. In other words, a portion of the premium we collect from selling the center strikes will be used to buy the outer strikes. These outer strikes protect us from losses at the expense of reducing our potential profit.

The butterfly will not be as big a moneymaker as a straddle or strangle, but it will not expose you to as much loss either. Figure 17.1 shows the profit and loss profile for the long butterfly.

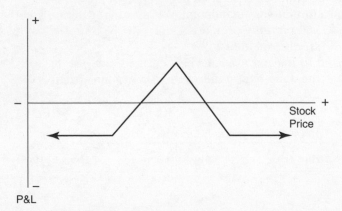

FIGURE 17.1 Long Butterfly P&L Chart

For any profit and loss diagram, the bends in the chart always occur at a strike price.

For the long butterfly, points A and C represent the long strikes. Point B is the short position located at the center strike. By looking at the profit and loss diagram for the long butterfly, you can see that the trader wants the stock price to stay still at the center strike (point B), since that is the point of maximum profit.

As the stock moves to the right or left from the center peak, profits are reduced until the position breaks even. If the stock price moves beyond the break-evens, the ensuing loss will last only for a little while before the graph flattens out at strikes A and C and the red line heads sideways.

That is why the arrows point sideways. You can clearly see the reason for buying the outer strikes A and C; they hedge us against unlimited losses. This means that once the stock price moves beyond a certain point, either up or down, your losses stop accruing. Any further stock price movement in that direction will incur no further dollar loss.

Now let's take a look at the profit and loss diagram for the short butterfly in Figure 17.2.

This profit and loss diagram tells a different story. While the long butterfly trader wants the stock to stay at the center strike, the short butterfly trader wants the stock price to move far away from the center strike. This should make intuitive sense because I said earlier that the short butterfly trader is simply taking the opposite side of the long butterfly trader. This means that the profits to the long butterfly trader are exactly the losses to the short butterfly trader, and vice versa.

We know now to classify the butterfly as a premium-collection strategy with risk protection.

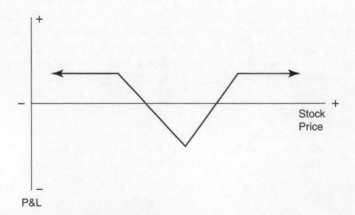

FIGURE 17.2   Short Butterfly P&L Chart

We also know how the butterfly is constructed: either all calls or all puts with three equidistant strikes in a 1-2-1 format. Now let's dive deeper and see how the butterfly works.

BUTTERFLY AND SYNTHETIC POSITIONS

The best way to see how anything works is to break it down into smaller components. From there, it is much easier to understand how each part contributes to the overall arrangement. In the case of option strategies, we want to break more complex positions down into synthetic positions to get a different perspective. Remember our synthetics from earlier chapters.

Just about everything can be broken down synthetically. The butterfly is no exception. New traders are often overwhelmed by the butterfly. They grumble, "I'm long this option, I'm long two of these, I'm long this other one, and there are three different strikes and four options." It is not overwhelming, and it definitely is not that complicated if you step back and look at it synthetically. The left side of Table 17.2 shows the construction of a long May 55 butterfly.

We can break this complicated-looking structure down in just one simple step. Rather than view the long butterfly as long one 50 call, short two 55 calls, and long one 60 call, as we have done in the column headed "Long Butterfly," let's pair them in a different way. Let's pair the long 50 call with one of the short 55 calls. Then let's pair the other short 55 call with the long 60 call, as we have done in the column headed "Long Butterfly (Broken Down)" and see what we have.

First, let's just look at the left side of the column labeled Long Butterfly Broken Down. We are long one May 50 call (+1), and short one May 55 call (−1). This is simply a long vertical call spread or, more specifically, a bull call spread. In the next column, look at the bold numbers. We are short one May 55 call (−1) and long one May 60 call (+1).

This is a short vertical call spread, or a bear call spread. When you break down the long butterfly, you end up with two vertical call spreads

TABLE 17.2 May 55 Butterfly

Strike Price	Long Butterfly	Long Butterfly (Broken Down)	
50	+1	+1	
55	−2	−1	**−1**
60	+1		**+1**

(as seen under the "broken down" column) that are converging against each other. In other words, the butterfly is nothing more than a bull spread and a bear spread acting together. The May 50–55 call spread maximizes its profits if the stock rises to 55 or higher.

We know that the profit potential is maximized out at a stock price of $55.00 at expiration. Anything above $55.00 is just added security; that's our ability to sleep at night. Meanwhile our short May 55–60 call spread to the right maximizes its profits if the stock falls to $55.00 or below. So if the bull spread maximizes at $55.00 or higher and the bear spread maximizes at $55.00 or lower, a stock price of $55.00 will maximize both spreads.

Both of these converging spreads want the stock to go to the butterfly's middle strike, and that's exactly what you want to happen when you are in a long butterfly. You want that stock price to finish directly at the middle strike; in this case, the 55 strike. That is your goal, because if it does, your vertical call spread maxes out on a positive side and your short vertical call spread maxes out on the negative side. You want this position to close at 55.

I stated earlier that most butterflies are initially set up with the short center strikes at the money. Once again, the reason is because butterflies are premium-collection strategies, and we want to be short at-the-money options because that is where the biggest extrinsic value is. Too many people forget that the butterfly is a premium-collection strategy. We aren't looking for big stock movement. We are looking for stagnation. We are going to use our two short at-the-money options, which are rich with decay. They have big extrinsic value, and we want to collect that extrinsic value. We capitalize on this by shorting *two* of them.

Now remember, the difference with the butterfly is that it is a premium-collection strategy that has a hedge. The hedge is derived from the outer strikes, or the 50 call and the 60 call in this example. We know from a reward standpoint that vertical spreads provide a limited reward for both buyers and sellers. And from a risk standpoint, buyers and sellers have limited risk.

So let's take a look first at the last column on Table 17.2: the long 50–55 call spread. If you own the 50 call and sold the 55 call, what is the worst that can happen? Think back to your basic rights and obligations with options. You have the right to buy stock for 50 and the obligation to sell it for 55, which means the most the spread will ever be worth is the difference in strikes, or $5.00 in this example, if the stock rises to 55 or higher. If the stock is at 55, that's great; we maxed out the spread.

But if the stock trades down to 50, we are going to lose everything. But—and it is a big but—we are not going to lose any more than what we spent. That is the risk scenario of a vertical call spread: Because you can lose only what you spent to enter the vertical spread, it is a limited risk strategy.

Therefore, using our butterfly, if the stock starts trading down, our risk is limited to 50. If the stock continues to fall below 50, it doesn't matter since our risk is fixed at 50.

Let's take a look at the other half of the butterfly, the short 55–60 call spread. If we are short the 55 call and long the 60 call, then we have the right to buy stock for 60 and the obligation to sell it for 55, which results in a $5.00 loss if the stock is 60 or higher at expiration. So we obviously want the stock to close at 55 or below.

As a seller, we have maxed out our spread and our profit in the spread. But remember, if the stock were to run up above 60, our loss is limited because the vertical spread has a limited loss scenario for both buyers and sellers.

The butterfly therefore consists of two conflicting spreads: One spread wants the stock to move higher while the other wants it to move lower. Both spreads ideally want the stock to move to or, better yet, if we put it on properly, stay at 55. And if by chance the stock moves in either direction against this, we have a limited loss scenario. There is your premium collection and your hedge.

WHAT WILL A BUTTERFLY COST?

The 55 strike in this case, the one we are short two contracts, is where we collect our premium. Remember, it is an at-the-money strike; it will have much more extrinsic value than either the 50 or 60 strike. So we will be collecting more extrinsic value with two short 55 strikes than we are spending on the 50 strike or the 60 strike.

The 50 strike, which is an in-the-money call, will have intrinsic value and very little extrinsic value. The 60 call, which is out of the money, has only a little extrinsic value.

So we are putting out a little extrinsic value to protect our short extrinsic value exposure in the 55 strikes. The net effect is that we are receiving more extrinsic value than we are spending; in short, we are *collecting premium*.

Now, in total, we will spend more than we receive, largely due to the fact that one of the outer strikes is an in-the-money option; thus, it will cost more due its intrinsic value. This means that butterflies will always have net cost; they are a debit transaction. Don't ever pass up the chance to execute a long butterfly for a net credit because that would be an arbitrage—a risk-free trade!

The bottom line is this: When you are long a butterfly, you have two conflicting vertical spreads. That being the case, you want the stock to finish dead-bang in the center where the long butterfly will be most profitable.

Of course, the short butterfly is going to work the opposite way. Instead of being short two 55 strikes, you are long the 55 strike. Instead of being long one 50 and one 60, you are short a 50 and a 60. In this case, you want the stock to trade away from the 55 strike and move toward either the 50 strike or the 60 strike.

That is because you have created two vertical spreads that are no longer converging at 55; they are now pushing away from 55. Think about two magnets. You can get two magnets to stick together quickly: you hold one in each hand, bring them close, and then, "bang," they attract each other and stick together.

That is like the long butterfly, both short options sticking together right in the middle at the 55 strike. With the short butterfly, turn one of those magnets to the other side and try pressing them together. Now they push against each other.

The short butterfly wants the stock to trade away in either direction, either to 50 (or below) or to 60 (or above), to maximize our short butterfly profitability. The short butterfly needs stock price movement to be profitable.

Despite its overwhelming first appearance, the butterfly is nothing more than two vertical spreads working in coordination with each other. Long butterflies need a lack of movement while short butterflies need price movement away from the center strike. Regardless of what happens, both trades, long and short, are automatically hedged, thus making the butterfly a more secure premium-collection strategy.

How much premium can you collect? Look at the price for the July 60, 65, 70 butterfly (Table 17.3) at 50 volatility from early to expiration. Notice cost to buy and price at expiration, and you can determine your loss/gain.

TABLE 17.3 July 60, 65, 70 Butterfly Prices

Stock Price	Butterfly	Butterfly at Expiration
$59.50	$0.71	$0.00
$61.50	$0.80	$1.50
$63.50	$0.84	$3.50
$65.50	$0.86	$4.50
$67.50	$0.85	$2.50
$69.50	$0.78	$0.50
$71.50	$0.75	$0.00

BUTTERFLY AND THE GREEKS

Now that we have covered the basic elements of the butterfly and how it is constructed, let's talk about the Greeks. What are the positions of the Greeks in a butterfly?

First, remember that the butterfly is a hedged premium-collection strategy. When we discussed the straddle and strangle (also premium collecting strategies), I stated that you should execute those at the money, especially if you were going to sell them, because you want to collect as much premium as possible.

The same reasoning applies to the butterfly. You do not want, nor should you have, a delta position. Luckily, the way the butterfly is constructed with those converging vertical spreads, if the stock is directly at the money, you will have no delta. You can easily verify this by checking your butterfly deltas against your trading sheets.

You will find the 50 strike is about a 75 delta, the 55 strike will be 50 delta, and the 60 strike is about 25 delta. The long butterfly is four options: +1 (50 strike), −2 (55 strike), +1 (60 strike). That converts to deltas of +75, −50, −50, +25. Putting the like signs together, we have +100 and −100, which means you have no delta.

In fact, you are not going to have delta in a properly constructed butterfly. In the real world of trading, you will most likely have some deltas if due only to the fact that the stock's price will rarely be exactly the same as the center strike. But just remember that delta is not the play here; premium collection is.

And when we are collecting premium, we normally do not want to take a delta lean. If we did, there are other strategies for that. We could do a single vertical spread, a buy-write or a sell-write. The butterfly is ideally set up as a delta-neutral position; it will generate deltas if the stock should move.

For example, if the stock rises in a long butterfly, deltas will become negative, which indicates that the position now needs the stock to move *down* in order to be profitable.

Conversely, if the stock price should fall, the butterfly deltas will become positive, signifying that the position needs the stock price to rise to become profitable.

Now let's look at gamma. We know that gamma is always the largest with at-the-money options. It follows that out-of-the-money and the in-the-money options must have fewer gammas than at-the-money options. In the long butterfly, we are short two at-the-money options so we will be short a great deal of gamma.

We will also be long an in-the-money call and an out-of-the-money call so will have a relatively small amount of long gamma. The net effect is that we will have negative gamma for the overall long butterfly. This should make intuitive sense once you understand that gamma measures the speed or pace that the stock must move.

A long butterfly does *not* want the stock to move—it must have negative gamma.

The reverse is true for the short butterfly, but let's go through the motions to be sure you understand. For the short butterfly, we will be long the two at-the-money strikes, which will definitely have more gammas than the in-the-money and out-of-the-money options, so we will be in an overall long gamma position.

This should make sense because we *do* want stock price movement for a short butterfly. Remember, we want the stock to move away from that middle strike, whether up to the 60 strike or down to the 50 strike. We want movement, so it makes perfect sense that the construction of the short butterfly will create a long gamma position. See how that came together? It makes perfect sense once you understand the theory behind options.

What about the vega positions? As with delta and gamma, vega is largest for the at-the-money strikes. Since the long butterfly is short the two at-the-money strikes, we know that the overall vega will be negative. Think about it intuitively. If the long butterfly is seeking stock price stagnation, we don't want volatility. That means we want *negative* vega. Any strategy with negative vega will decrease in value if volatility increases, and the long butterfly will decrease in value as the stock gains volatility.

Negative vega tells us that we want the stock's price to sit quietly right where it is. We do not want volatile stock prices—we want negative vega.

Meanwhile, the short butterfly is long the middle strikes, so you are going to have a long vega position. Those two at-the-money strikes will have much more vega than the 50 and 60 combined. Again, this should make intuitive sense because the short butterfly wants the stock's price to move far away from the center strike. It needs high volatility. It needs positive vega. As long as you understand your Greek positions, this all comes together for you. That's why we went over the Greeks.

Next we'll look at theta. As with the previous Greeks, theta is highest for at-the-money strikes. But we must remember that theta is always represented by a minus sign to denote that it subtracts from an option's value. If we are short a lot of negative theta, then the overall butterfly must have positive theta.

Are you starting to see the connections? The butterfly is a premium-collection strategy—we are collecting time premium. In other words, we are collecting theta. And that means we must be long theta. For the long butterfly, the passage of time helps us.

We are long theta in the long butterfly because we are collecting premium. We want time to go by with nothing else happening. The more time that goes by, the more time premium we collect. Each and every day that goes by, we collect progressively more and more. So to the long butterfly, time is a friend, which means it must be long theta.

The short butterfly is obviously the opposite situation. For the short butterfly, we are long the two middle strikes, which will have value bleeding out every day. We need the stock to move because we are short theta. The position is decaying; we need to get some stock price action.

The short butterfly trader spends net time premium and is therefore short theta. The short butterfly is long those two at-the-money options that are bleeding every day. Time does not help the short butterfly.

The short butterfly is running out of time; it needs to get movement away from that strike before its time runs out.

When you look at the construction of the butterfly and its Greek positions, ask yourself what the goals and the objectives are. Then compare your answer to what your Greek positions actually are, and see if it makes sense—if it matches and comes together for you.

IRON BUTTERFLY

At the beginning of this discussion I mentioned that there was an exception to the rule about butterflies always being constructed with all calls or all puts. That exception is the *iron butterfly*.

The iron butterfly's construction is very similar to the regular butterfly's in that it consists of three different equidistant strikes in the 1-2-1 ratio. For the iron butterfly, we will buy a low strike, sell two middle strikes, and buy a high strike just as we did for the regular butterfly.

However, rather than using all calls or all puts, the iron butterfly uses a combination of the two. Table 17.4 shows the construction for an iron butterfly.

Specifically, it is a "short" iron butterfly. You will find out why it's considered short once you understand its construction. Notice its components. You see it is long one May 50 put, short one May 55 call, short one May 55

TABLE 17.4 May 55 Iron Butterfly

Strike Price	Call Position	Put Position
50		+1
55	−1	
55		−1
60	+1	

TABLE 17.5 May 55 Iron Butterfly (Broken Down)

Strike	Short Straddle	Long Strangle
50 Put		+1
55 Call	−1	
55 Put	−1	
60 Call		+1

put, and long one May 60 call. That looks just a mess! However, it is not really a mess if you look at it synthetically, as we've done in Table 17.5.

Look at the center strikes—short one May 55 call, short one May 55 put. What is that? That is one short May 55 straddle, which we know is a premium-collection strategy. But we are also left with something else.

We have a long strangle which is one long May 50 put and one long May 60 call. So our synthetic analysis shows that the iron butterfly is nothing more than a short straddle combined with a long strangle.

We have a short straddle (short one 55 put, short one 55 call). Because it is at the money, we know it will have more extrinsic value when compared to either the 50 or 60 strikes. That at-the-money straddle is rich in premium; it is our goal to collect that premium.

However, as we well know, short straddles present unlimited upside and downside risk. Because the iron butterfly has a long strangle around it, we are protected from these unwanted risks.

In essence, with the iron butterfly, we are strangling a straddle. The straddle is collecting the premium, and the strangle is hedging our upside and downside risks—exactly like the regular butterfly. If the stock closes at exactly the center strike, the short straddle and long strangle expire worthless, and the trader keeps the entire premium.

However, if the stock's price makes a large move up or down, the straddle begins to lose money. It would continue to lose money in an unlimited fashion if it weren't for the long strangle.

While the ideas behind the iron butterfly and the regular butterfly are the same, their construction is what separates them. The regular or conventional butterfly is a combination of two vertical spreads. The iron butterfly is a combination of a short straddle plus a long strangle. Both strategies are doing the same thing: offering premium collection and risk protection.

Just for the record, if you take another look at the iron butterfly, you will notice that you can see the combination of the straddle surrounded by the strangle. However, you may also notice that there is another breakdown here. A breakdown into . . . yep, you guessed it . . . two vertical spreads. Unlike the conventional butterfly, which breaks down into either two call spreads (conventional call butterfly) or two put spreads (conventional put spreads), the iron butterfly breaks down into one vertical call spread and one vertical put spread.

If we were to draw a profit and loss diagram for the short iron butterfly, we would see that it looks exactly like the regular long conventional butterfly.

Now that you understand how an iron butterfly is constructed, I explain why the long butterfly equals a short iron butterfly. The reason has to do with an industry standard in that long assets are purchased (your account is debited) while short assets create credits. If you buy an asset, your account is *debited* the amount of the trade, and you are long the asset.

However, if you short an asset, you receive a *credit.* For example, if you buy a call option, you are long the call since you paid money for it. Your account is debited for the trade. But if you short a call, you receive a credit and have the obligation to sell shares of stock.

In the same way, if you place a long butterfly trade, you will pay to do so; in other words, your broker will debit your account. Remember, a long butterfly created for a credit is an arbitrage; so don't expect it to happen. However, if you place the iron butterfly, you will receive a credit to your account. That is because you are selling the straddle and buying the strangle. Since the straddle is at the money, it has far more value than the out-of-the-money strikes of the strangle.

This means you receive more money for selling the straddle than you spend on buying the strangle, which means your account is credited when placing this trade. It is therefore a short iron butterfly. So a long butterfly equals a short iron butterfly. The reverse is also true: A short butterfly equals a long iron butterfly.

If we investigate the Greek positions in the iron butterfly, we would find that they are the same as those in the regular butterfly. Let's run through a quick example using delta.

Look at delta in the short iron butterfly on Table 17.5; what is it?

The delta is zero (or very close to zero). You know your middle straddle here—short the 55 call and short the 55 put—will have no delta, because you know from our previous discussions on straddles that straddles have no deltas.

On the outside, we are long the strangle—long the May 60 call and long the May 50 put—and we also probably have no delta. If we set up this short iron butterfly with the stock directly at the money (55), the 50 put and the 60 call (equidistant from the middle) are probably going to have two deltas that will cancel each other out.

For example, the out-of-the-money 60 call may have 25 deltas. The out-of-the-money 50 puts may also have –25 deltas. The strangle will be long 25 deltas from the call and short 25 deltas from the put, or +25 and –25, which means the total delta is zero. Since the two components of the iron

TABLE 17.6 May 55 Long Iron Butterfly

Strike	Calls	Puts
50		−1
55	+1	+1
60	−1	

butterfly, the straddle and the strangle, have zero deltas, the iron butterfly has no deltas.

That matches the delta position of the regular butterfly. The other Greeks also perform the same in the iron butterfly as they do in the regular butterfly. The iron butterfly also responds in the same way to outside influences: time, volatility, and stock price movement.

LONG IRON BUTTERFLY

If we were looking at the opposite trade, we would be looking at the *long iron butterfly*. Table 17.6 shows the long iron butterfly. If we are short the 50 put, long the 55 call and the 55 put, and short the 60 call, then we are looking at the same thing as a short regular butterfly. Synthetically, the short conventional butterfly and the long iron butterfly are identical.

What you need to know about the regular butterfly and the short iron butterfly is that synthetically they are the same. They look for the same thing, they want the stock to go to the same place, they want to have everything the same, and they are identical strategies but just different constructions—kind of like a regular call and a synthetic call.

We have proved that regular calls and synthetic call positions are equal: same risk; same reward; same delta, gamma, vega, and theta; just different construction. That also holds here with the regular butterfly and the short iron butterfly; they are the same thing, their construction is just different.

USING THE BUTTERFLY

You might ask yourself why a butterfly is important today. Obviously in days gone by, when people didn't really understand the volatility smile and volatility tilts, a lot of these different strategies could exploit mispricings, and you could make money with them as trades. Nowadays butterflies are used in more of a position play. Most traders use butterflies (or iron butterflies) to create a hedged time-decay play.

Suppose you encounter a high-volatility stock, which means it is capable of very large price moves. You might consider a straddle, but feel that it is so high priced that it is going to be tough for this stock to exceed the break-evens of the straddle. In that case, you might think that the short straddle makes more sense. But because the stock is so volatile, it still has a chance to rise above the break-even points, and that is scary. Instead of executing a high-risk short straddle, you may wish to short the iron butterfly to collect time decay. Short the straddle to collect the high premium but then put the strangle around it for protection so you don't get blown away if the stock moves against you. That's what the short iron butterfly is about.

There are a couple of other ways to trade the butterfly in today's markets. The butterfly can be used to trade the volatility smile (which is a topic for another time). It also allows us to hedge spreads, straddles, and strangles.

That's the butterfly. What at the beginning appeared a complex and mysterious strategy is really a simple hedged premium-collection strategy. It is not that complicated. If you understand synthetics and the Greeks, you can easily break the butterfly down into simpler components to understand how it works. Once that is accomplished, you will see many uses, including the ability to trade the smile, hedge, or close exiting positions.

LONG BUTTERFLY SYNOPSIS

Construction. Short two calls (puts) of the same month and strike while long a call (put) above and long a call (put) below both equidistant from the strike of the two short calls (puts). In the case of an iron butterfly, short a straddle while long a strangle around it.

Function. Premium-collection strategy with upside and downside protection. Also, short volatility play.

Bias. Stagnant.

When to Use. When you feel the stock will trade in a very tight range near a strike price and stagnate there. Also if you feel the stock has a likelihood of a decrease in implied volatility. The butterfly allows you to take advantage of these potential situations while offering a hedged position.

Profit Scenario. Maximum profit occurs when the stock closes directly at the strike of the two short options and decreases as the stock moves in either direction away from the strike.

Loss Scenario. Maximum loss occurs when the stock closes at either strike of the long options. Maximum loss is limited.

Key Concepts. Long butterflies are ideal strategies for premium collectors who seek to minimize potential losses in the event the stock moves adversely. This strategy can also take advantage of expected decreases in implied volatility. The strategy can be viewed as two separate trades. A traditional butterfly can be broken down into two vertical spreads, one long and one short, with each sharing the same short strike and having different but equidistant long strikes. The iron butterfly can be broken down to a short straddle surrounded by a long strangle. Butterflies are best entered into in farther-out months.

SHORT BUTTERFLY SYNOPSIS

Construction. Long two calls (puts) of same month and strike while short a call (put) above and short a call (put) below both equidistant from the strike of the two long calls (puts). In the case of an iron butterfly, long a straddle while short a strangle around it.

Function. Limited directional stock movement play. Also long volatility play.

Bias. Limited directional movement but in either direction.

When to Use. When you feel the stock will trade away from a strike but not aggressively. Also if you feel the stock has a likelihood of an increase in implied volatility. The short butterfly allows you to take advantage of these potential situations while offering a hedged position.

Profit Scenario. Maximum profit occurs when the stock closes at or above the highest of the short strikes or at or below the lowest of the short strikes. The trade will also be profitable in event of increasing implied volatility.

Loss Scenario. Maximum loss occurs when the stock closes at the center strike. Maximum loss is limited.

Key Concepts. Short butterflies are an ideal strategy for long-volatility players who seek minimizing potential loss in the event the stock moves adversely. The strategy can be viewed as two trades. A traditional butterfly can be broken down into two conflicting vertical spreads, one long and one short, with each sharing the same short strike and different but equidistant long strikes. The iron butterfly can be broken down to a long straddle surrounded by a short strangle. Butterflies are best entered into in farther-out months.

CHAPTER 18

The Condor

The final strategy that we are going to discuss is the condor. The condor's relationship to the butterfly is very much like the relationship between the straddle and the strangle.

The straddle uses one strike while the strangle uses two. Aside from that small difference, the straddle and the strangle are virtually the same strategy. In a similar way, the butterfly uses one central strike while the condor uses two. The butterfly and condor are nearly the same strategy in all other ways.

LONG CONDOR

The condor, much like the butterfly, is a premium-collection strategy that is hedged. It's a hedged time decay play. Let's take a look at the construction of the long condor by using the four strikes shown in Table 18.1.

Remember, to set up a condor, we must use *four* strikes. We will be using two strikes at the center rather than the one center strike we used for the butterfly.

How do we set up a condor? We must start by considering either *all calls* or *all puts* with four strikes that are *equally* spaced. In this example, all strikes are separated by $5.00. Just to be clear, we do not need $5.00 increments to set up condors but rather equal distance between the strikes.

Stocks that are priced between $25.00 and $200.00 will have $5.00 increments between strikes so a $5.00 strike separation will be the most common. However, stocks priced below $25.00 will have options with $2.50

315

TABLE 18.1 Long Condor Construction

Strike Price	Long Condor
50	+1
55	−1
60	−1
65	+1

increments between strikes. Stocks over $200.00, as well as many index options, will have $10.00 increments (or higher) between strikes. All of these increments are acceptable for condors as long as we use equal spacing between the strikes. You cannot construct the condor using $22\frac{1}{2}$, 25, 30, 35. That doesn't work. All strikes must be equidistant.

When setting up a long condor, buy the lowest strike, sell the next two higher strikes, and then buy the highest strike. In our example, we are using the 50, 55, 60, and 65 strikes so you would buy the 50 strike, sell the 55 strike, sell the 60 strike, and buy the 65 strike. Our long condor ratio is +1, −1, −1, +1. Just like the butterfly, we can refer to this condor by the center strikes; professional traders would refer to this as the 55–60 condor. Because we are referring to the center strikes, any professional trader seeing a long 55–60 condor would automatically know that the trade must also be long the 50 strike and the 65 strike.

New traders often wonder how to tell the difference between a long and a short condor. Use the simple little trick from the butterfly to remember. Look at the lowest or the highest strike, which are the 50 and 65 strikes in our example. If those are long, you are long the condor. If they are short, you are short the condor.

SHORT CONDOR

Let's take a look at the short condor (Table 18.2). The short condor is just the opposite side of the trade of the long condor so its construction

TABLE 18.2 Short Condor

Strike Price	Short Condor
50	−1
55	+1
60	+1
65	−1

TABLE 18.3 A Condor Equals Two Butterflies

Strike Price	55 Butterfly	60 Butterfly	Combination (Condor)
50	+1		+1
55	−2	+1	−1
60	+1	−2	−1
65		+1	+1

obviously is the opposite of a long condor. If you are long a condor, the trader on the other side of the trade is short the condor.

Using our same example, the short condor would be created by selling the lowest strike, buying the next two higher strikes, and then selling the highest strike. So our short condor ratio is −1, +1, +1, −1. Use the trick that worked for you to remember the long condor, and you will automatically know that the *opposite* must be the short condor.

As you can see, the condor is very similar to the butterfly, except that the condor has two middle strikes rather than one. Despite the differences in strikes between the butterfly and condor, the overall *ratios* are the same. In other words, while the butterfly uses only three strikes, it does make use of *four* contracts.

For example, if we were to use the previous strikes to create a butterfly, we might buy the 50, sell the 55, sell the 55, and then buy the 60. Notice that the ratios are +1, −1, −1, +1 if we look at the butterfly on a per-contract basis. The condor uses these same ratios but across a wider range of strikes; that's the only difference between the two strategies.

In fact, we can show that the condor is really two butterfly spreads in disguise. Assume we placed a butterfly spread with the 50, 55, and 60 strikes and then placed another butterfly using the 55, 60, and 65 strikes as shown in Table 18.3.

The vertical summations of each strike results in a condor. In other words, a 55 butterfly plus a 60 butterfly equals a 55–60 condor.

WHY USE CONDORS?

Like the butterfly, the condor's primary objective is *premium collection*. Much like the short straddle and the short strangle, the condor is a premium-collection strategy except for a significant difference. The difference is that the condor, like the butterfly, is a *hedged* premium-collection strategy. Because the condor is used mostly for premium collection, the

TABLE 18.4 Condor Prices from Start to Expiration, −50 Volatility

Stock Price	Condor Price	Condor at Expiration
$59.50	$1.21	$0.00
$61.50	$1.37	$1.50
$63.50	$1.48	$3.50
$65.50	$1.58	$5.00
$67.50	$1.62	$5.00
$69.50	$1.56	$5.00
$71.50	$1.51	$3.50
$73.50	$1.40	$1.50
$75.50	$1.31	$0.00

long condor (short iron condor) is the most common of the condors used by individual investors due to its limited risk scenario.

That is what separates it from most of the other premium-collection strategies. Because the condor, like the butterfly, is hedged, it has a fixed loss profile. As a premium-collection strategy, it is not as aggressive or risky as the straddle or the strangle. However, as with any investment, if you take less risk you get less reward. Table 18.4 shows the prices paid for the July 60, 65, 70, 75 condor and the price of that same condor at expiration.

The condor's primary goal is premium collection, which comes through the sale of the center strike options. But in order to hedge, you must somewhere, somehow, give up a little something, and that something is going to be a portion of the total potential premium collected. In other words, a portion of the premium we collect from selling the center strikes will be used to buy the outer strikes. These outer strikes protect us from losses at the expense of reducing our potential profit.

The condor is not going to be as big a moneymaker as a straddle or strangle, but it will not expose you to as much loss either. Figure 18.1 shows the profit and loss profile for the long condor.

For any profit and loss diagram, the bends in the chart always occur at a strike price.

For the long condor, points A and D represent the long strikes. Points B and C is the short position located at the center strike. By looking at the profit and loss chart for the long condor, you can see that the trader wants the stock price to stay still in between the two center strikes (points B and C) since that is the area of maximum profit.

As the stock moves to the right or left from the two center strikes, profits are reduced until the position breaks even. If the stock price moves beyond the break-evens, the ensuing loss will last only for a little while

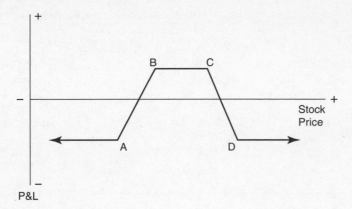

FIGURE 18.1 Long Condor P&L Chart

before the graph flattens out at strikes A and D and the dotted line heads sideways.

That is why the arrows point sideways. You can clearly see the reason for buying the outer strikes A and D; they hedge us against unlimited losses. This means that once the stock price moves beyond a certain point either up or down, your losses stop accruing. Any further stock price movement in that direction will incur no further dollar loss.

Now let's take a look at the profit and loss diagram (Figure 18.2) for the short condor.

This profit and loss diagram tells a different story. While the long condor trader wants the stock to stay in between the two center strikes, the

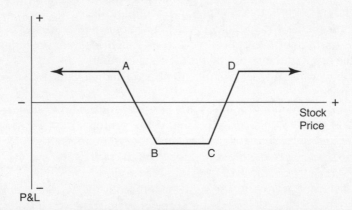

FIGURE 18.2 Short Condor P&L Chart

short condor trader wants the stock price to move far away from the center strikes. This should make intuitive sense because we said earlier that the short condor trader is simply taking the opposite side of the long condor trader. The profits to the long condor trader are exactly the losses to the short condor trader, and vice versa. We know to classify the condor as a premium-collection strategy with risk protection.

Last, we know how the condor is constructed. It is either all calls or all puts with four equidistant strikes in a 1-1-1-1 ratio format. Now let's dive deeper and see how it works.

HOW IT WORKS

Let's break down the condor into its nuts-and-bolts components. We do that by looking at our synthetics. Let's take apart the condor by looking at Table 18.5.

The column headed "Long Condor" shows our basic long condor construction: long one 50 contract, short one 55 and 60 contract, and then long one 65 strike. That is the traditional long condor setup.

Now let's break it down a little bit. In the column headed "Long Condor (Broken Down)," I've broken the condor down into two separate spreads, just as I did in the butterfly. You can see that we are long a 50 and short a 55. What does this mean? We are long the 50–55 vertical call spread. We want the stock to run up and close at either 55 or above. Keep that in mind.

Meanwhile, the next part of the chart is also a vertical call spread. We are short a 60 and long a 65. That is a short 60/65 call spread. That spread is most valuable if the stock closes below 60 at expiration. The long 50–55 call spread needs the stock to close above 55 for maximum profit and the 60–65 short call spread needs the stock to close below 60. Therefore, the condor will produce its maximum profit if the stock is above 55 and below 60 at expiration.

TABLE 18.5 May 55–60 Condor

Strike	Long Condor	Long Condor (Broken Down)	
50	+1	+1	
55	−1	−1	
60	−1		−1
65	+1		+1

CONDORS VERSUS BUTTERFLIES

If condors are so similar to butterflies, how do we decide which one to use? I said at the beginning of this discussion that the condor is related to the butterfly in much the same way that a strangle is related to a straddle. Let's back up to the discussion on how we decide between using straddles and strangles. Then it will be much easier to understand when to use a condor over a butterfly.

Assume a stock is trading at or very close to one of the available strike prices, say $55. In this case, we would use the straddle by purchasing the 55 call and put. But if the stock's price is between two strikes, say $57.50, we would use the strangle. The same reasoning determines whether we use the condor or the butterfly.

For example, say the stock is $55, and we are thinking about selling a straddle but were afraid to because it is a very volatile stock. We could do the butterfly instead. The butterfly would focus on that one center strike of 55, and the 50 and 60 calls would hedge us from the potentially devastating large moves up or down.

But if the stock was $57.50 and we wanted to sell the 55/60 strangle, then we might decide to put on a condor to hedge us from the unwanted large moves that might occur.

As you can see with the condor, its "center" really lies over the middle strike range, which is 55 and 60 in this example. Our exact focal point is really 57.50; since there is no 57.50 strike, we would sell the 55 and 60 as substitutes.

If the stock is $57.50, is there anything wrong with buying the 55 butterfly? Not necessarily. We might decide to do that if we thought the stock price was going to fall and then stagnate. However, doing so introduces a directional bias, or lean, in the strategy, and butterflies and condors are not directional strategies. They are neutral.

They are intended to be used as premium-collection strategies rather than to take advantage of a directional move in the stock. With the stock at $57.50, the 55 butterfly would have negative delta; that is, the strategy would need the stock to fall in order to produce maximum profit. The 60 butterfly, however, would have positive delta. We would need the stock price to rise to 60 and then stagnate.

However, in most cases, we do not want to have any delta because this is not a delta play. We might want to play time decay or volatility, but we don't want to play delta.

But if the stock's price is between two strikes, then the straddle would give us positive or negative delta, depending on which butterfly you choose.

So, if the stock is in between strikes, do the condor. The choice of which of the two strategies to use is just a matter of where the stock is located in relation to the strike prices. In all other aspects, the condor and the butterfly are the same just as the straddle and the strangle are very much the same. The strategy you choose is predicated on where the stock is located. Yes, each strategy will have different break-even points, but that is a direct result of having different strike prices.

Other than that, the butterfly and condor are basically the same. The key is to have a strike price representing the current stock price. But if that strike price is not available, use the condor and split the difference. That will keep the delta component out of it.

When we look at the components of the condor, we discover it is really two vertical spreads. When we look at a long condor, the two vertical spreads are converging on each other. They are going to meet at a center area that is located not at the strike, like a butterfly, but in between two strikes. The focal point, or convergence point, of the two spreads we just described is $57.50. That stock price ($57.50) would be directly between the two condor strikes, the 55 and 60.

If we were short the condor and we spun these numbers around, instead of having two spreads converging on that middle, we would have two spreads that were moving away from the middle. Go back and take a look at your short condor construction. It is made up of two vertical spreads, the short 50/55 vertical and the long 55–60 vertical. Let's look at these individually.

If you are short the 50–55 call spread, where do you want the stock to go? You want the stock to go down below 50. Meanwhile, you are long the 60/65 call spread, which means you want the stock to go up above 65. So, with a short condor, you want the stock to go down below 50 or up above 65. Again, the two spreads are working in a diverging sense, moving away from each other.

Just think about the magnet analogy that we talked about with the butterfly. With a long condor, imagine that you have two magnets, one in each hand. Slowly bring them close together and suddenly—boom!—they stick together. They are attracted to each other right at that middle focal point.

In the short condor, it's the opposite. Take those two magnets and turn one around. Now all of a sudden, as you try to push them together, what are they doing? They are now pushing away from each other.

Basically, the condor, just like the butterfly, is two vertical spreads—either two vertical call spreads or two vertical put spreads, depending on whether you did the put condor or the call.

Long condors converge on a center point while short condors push away from that center point. And that center point is not defined by a strike price, as it is in the butterfly. That center point is defined by two separate strikes because the stock is located in between them.

CONDORS AND THE GREEKS

Let's talk about the Greek sensitivities of the condor. If you think it would be just like the Greek position of the butterfly, you are absolutely correct.

Remember that these strategies are the same philosophy. There will be some price differences because we are dealing with two strikes with the condor, but the philosophy of the trade remains identical. Thus, the condor's Greeks are going to be pretty close to those of the butterfly.

Let's start with the delta. What's the delta of a condor? Well, first what should it be? Are we trying to play delta in a condor? No, we are not trying to play delta. There are better ways of playing delta than a condor. What do you think the delta position of the condor is going to be? If you said flat or close to flat, you are right. Condors and butterflies don't have much delta. They are not supposed to.

We set up a condor because the stock was trading at $57\frac{1}{2}$ or so. We didn't want to do the 55 butterfly because it would leave us with a positive delta, since the 55 call would be $2.50 in the money; the 55 put would be $2.50 out of the money. There was going to be a major delta difference between those two options, leaving us with a delta that we did not want.

Remember, we said the whole reason for choosing the condor over the butterfly is because we don't want any delta; the only way to avoid delta is to use two strikes at the center. So the condor has little to no delta at all.

What about gamma? Look at the setup of our position and think about where the stock is in this example. The stock is at $57.50. We know that gamma is highest at the at-the-money strikes and then tapers off. This means that the gamma of the 55 strike and the 60 strike—the center strikes—is going to be much greater than that of the 50 strike and the 65 strike, since those strikes are farther away from at the money. Because those center strikes are short, what will that leave us for gamma?

Obviously, short gamma! The long condor has a short gamma position.

The short condor, being on the opposite side of the trade, must have long gamma for the same reason. For a short condor, we would be long the 55 and 60 strikes, which we just said contained more gamma than the other two strikes. If we are long those two strikes and they are our heavy influence on gamma, we are going to be long gamma in the short condor. So in the long condor, we are short gamma. In the short condor, we are long gamma. This should make intuitive sense when you think about gamma.

Gamma dictates the speed or pace component to an option. If you have positive gamma, that means you need the stock's price to move in order to make money. For example, if you buy a call option, you will have positive gamma because you paid a premium for the option and *must* have the stock's price move before you can make any money. However, if you short a call option, you receive a credit and do not need the stock's price to move. In fact, you want it to stay still.

That is negative gamma. Once you understand the function of the long and short condors, you will have no trouble figuring out the gamma. Long condors need the stock to stay still at the center; they have negative gamma. Short condors, however, need the stock's price to move away from the center; they have positive gamma.

What about vega? Let's approach it the same way as gamma. Where is vega the largest? The answer is in the at-the-money strike. Again, with the stock at $57.50, the 55 and 60 strikes are closest to at the money. Because those strikes are short, we know the long condor must have negative vega. The short condor will have positive vega.

Finally, what about theta? First of all, remember that theta is negative for long positions. The reason is that you pay a premium for long options and that premium decays a little every day. Long options are adversely affected by time. So long options have negative theta. If long options have negative theta, then short options must have positive theta.

Next, ask yourself where theta is the heaviest. It is heaviest at the at-the-money strikes. Because the long condor is *short* the strikes closest to at the money, the long condor must be long theta.

Another way to understand this is to think about what the time premium in the option actually represents. It represents a cash value for *time*. As a convention, cash outflows are represented by minus signs (since cash is being debited from your account) while cash inflows are represented as positive (because cash is being credited to your account). Since the long butterfly collects more time premium than it costs, it must have positive theta.

I hope you are starting to see how all the Greeks are tied together. We figured out that we were going to be short gamma. That means we want the stock to sit still, and the only time that happens is if you are long theta. Meanwhile, for the short condor, we know the opposite is happening. We are long gamma since we are long the two at-the-money options. We have to be short theta. We are decaying. We need movement.

Those are the Greek positions for the condor. And because we know our Greek positions, we now know what the position is going to do in response to changes in the different variables.

People always ask me why the Greeks are important. The reason is that once you understand the Greeks, you know what a position is going to do no matter what happens. Now, does that mean I can stop it from doing those things? No. But I now know my risk. I know where I may get hit and will not get blindsided. I know the risks *before* I put my money into the trade and can make a more informed decision. For example, you might wonder how the condor will respond to changes in some of the major variables. Let's start with the long condor and see how stock movement will affect it.

Well, let's see. We are short the 55 and 60 strikes in the middle. We don't want the stock to move, do we? We want that stock to finish and close where it is right now, $57.50. If they could just shut the exchange down for four weeks, we would be in perfect position. We don't want a stock movement in the long condor. In actuality, that is the general idea and the major objective of a long condor.

That's why 99 percent of condors are traded as premium-collection strategies. What is the best way of collecting premium? Have the stock stay still, stagnation. We don't want stock movement since that is a negative action for a condor.

We could have arrived at that answer immediately by noting that the long condor has negative gamma. If you have any option position with negative gamma, stock movement is a bad thing.

If stock price movement is a bad thing for a long condor, then it must be a good thing for a short condor, which is what we found out earlier. Remember, with the short condor, you are long the middle strikes, so you do not want the stock near those two strikes. You want the stock to either go below 50 or above 65. And that makes perfect sense because the short condor has long gamma. Long gamma positions need stock price movement.

How will movement in volatility affect the condor? Well, since we know our Greeks, we know that we are short vega with a long condor. Remember, with the long condor, we are short the center strikes, which have more vega than the outer strikes. That is going to create a short vega position. And when you are short vega, what do you want volatility to do? You want volatility to hold still or go down.

Some of you might say wait a minute, why would we want volatility to stay still? When you are short vega and volatility holds, you are going to collect premium. This corresponds to the fact that we are also short gamma and long theta. Short gamma tells us that we don't want stock price movement. If we don't want stock price movement, we definitely don't want volatility to increase. Long theta tells us that we will make money from time decay since we have sold the option premium. If we are the seller of option premium, we don't want stock price movement.

So at least if volatility doesn't increase, this position will decay. Once again, this is easy to determine if we know our Greeks. In the long condor, your short vega tells you that you want volatility to stay still or go down (go down, of course, is optimal).

In the short condor, we can tell the opposite occurs with a movement in volatility just by looking at vega. We said that you were long vega in the short condor. Why? Because, in this position, you are long the 55 and 60 strikes. If you are long the 55 and 60 strikes, you will benefit if volatility rises. Remember, the position will also decay over time. However, if volatility rises, it will offset the time decay. So a rise in volatility helps the short condor but hurts the long condor.

The last thing is the passage of time. Because we are long theta in our long condor, the passage of time is a benefit. Heck, let's get some four-day weekends in here. Let's get that stock to stay still and let time go by. Let's collect premium. Passage of time helps the long condor because of those two short strikes, the 55 and 60 that are nearly at the money. However, in the short condor, the opposite happens.

In the short condor, we are long the 55 and 60 strikes—we are short theta. We need movement; we need it now because we are short theta. Time is passing by and money is wasting. We have to get the stock to move. The passage of time helps the long condor; it hurts the short condor.

Once again, notice how quickly you can determine each of these scenarios just by looking at the Greeks. You don't need to take the long way by considering which strikes are long or short and then figuring out how those will be affected by the variables in question. All you need to do is look at the Greeks—a simple plus or minus sign—to get the answer.

Of course, you can take it a step further and look at the actual Greek number to find out to what degree that variable will be affected. For example, if you see that your position has a theta of −.10, then you know that time works against you since theta is negative. To what degree does it work against you? In this case, it is going to cost you $0.10 a day. It is imperative that you understand the Greeks in order to trade options well.

IRON CONDORS

Just in the same way that we had an iron butterfly, we have an iron condor. I said the iron butterfly is the combination of a long strangle and short straddle. In other words, I was putting a protective strangle around a short straddle in the butterfly.

But remember that the condor does not have a central strike, as the butterfly has. In the condor we have split strikes, just like the strangle. So in the iron condor we have strangles, one short and one long—a big wide long one strangling a tighter short one.

TABLE 18.6 May 55 Iron Condor

Strike	Call Position	Put Position
50	+1	
55		−1
60		−1
65	+1	

The iron butterfly strangled the straddle. The iron condor is strangling another strangle.

Let's take a look at the iron condor in Table 18.6, which shows the classic short iron condor setup.

We are selling the center-strike strangle and buying the outer-strike strangle. Center strikes are more valuable than outer strikes; that means we are bringing in more money than we're spending to trade this position. Therefore, it produces a credit to your account; it is a "short" iron condor.

We are starting with the short iron condor because it produces exactly the same profit-and-loss diagram as a long condor. A long condor equals a short iron condor from a profit-and-loss standpoint.

If you are having trouble seeing the two strangles, I've broken them down a little bit in Table 18.7. In the column headed "Short Strangle," we can group the two center strikes together, the short 55 put and the short 60 call. What do we have there? Short one May 55 put; short one May 60 call.

That is a short May 55–60 strangle. So with this May 55 iron condor, you have a short strangle on the inside. What about on the outside? There you are long one May 50 put and long one May 65 call. What do you have there? You have a long strangle.

So the iron condor, just like the condor, is a hedged time-decay position. The interior short strangle is definitely a time-decay play. We want the stock price to stay still so we can collect the two option premiums. However, we have risk. We know that if the stock explodes in either direction and we are short this strangle, we are at big risk.

TABLE 18.7 May 55 Iron Condor (Broken Down)

Strike	Short Strangle	Long Strangle
50 Put		+1
55 Put	−1	
60 Call	−1	
65 Call		+1

But we decide that we are not just going to do the short strangle. We are going to do the iron condor, and we are going to put another strangle around that short strangle. Sure, we are giving up some of our profit potential, but we are not going to get blown out of the water if, by chance, our execution of that short strangle was the wrong trade at the wrong time.

By purchasing this outer strangle, we have reduced our potential profit, but we have also limited our potential losses. If the stock opened at $80.00 one day on a takeover rumor or opened down at $30.00 because the new drug the company was expecting to put on the market to cure hemorrhagic fever killed test patients, we are okay. Our principal is protected. Those are the reasons we decided to buy the long strangle. The long strangle covers—hedges—our short strangle from catastrophic events. If the stock were to stay directly at $57.50, our short premium in the tight 55–60 strangle will surpass the smaller amount of extrinsic value that's located in the wider 50 put and the 65 call.

We won't ever see the full value of the interior strangle because we gave up some of it to buy the 50–65 strangle for protection. But if the stock stays at $57.50, we are going to have a nice profit. And we are protected. So, the short iron condor performs the same way as the regular condor. Philosophically it's the same thing. It's just constructed differently.

That is one of the most remarkable properties of options: We can achieve the same risk/reward profiles in different ways. So another motivation for considering iron condors over regular condors could be due to costs or implied volatility differences. We may, for example, be better off selling the call and put center strikes (short iron condor) rather than selling two calls in the center (regular condor). Two strategies may have the same profit-and-loss profile, but one might have a higher probability of winning because it is more effective at the time the trade is executed.

Obviously the long iron condor is constructed in the opposite manner. It would be short one May 50 put, long one May 55 put, long one May 60 call, and short one May 65 call.

The short and long iron condors are just opposite sides of the same trade.

Short Iron Condor

Now, I said that the long conventional condor is a premium-collection strategy, which is readily seen once you understand the profit-and-loss diagram in Figure 18.3.

Let's start by looking at the break-even points, which are defined by the intersection of the dotted line and the black horizontal line. Remember, the black horizontal line represents zero profit or loss; any time the profit-and-loss diagram crosses the horizontal line that represents a break-even point.

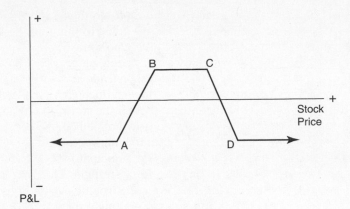

FIGURE 18.3 P&L Chart for Short Iron Condor

Notice that for the condor (iron or regular), there are two break-even points: an upside one and a downside one. If the stock finishes in the middle, as you can see, you are going to have a profit. If the stock finishes outside of either break-even point, you are going to lose money.

However, unlike the strangle, which would show two arrows continually heading straight down as the stock moves away from that middle area in either direction, the condor flattens out. That is your protection from the hedge. Where does the hedge come from? In the case of an iron condor, it comes because you are long an outside strangle that is offsetting the losses from the inside strangle if the stock rises or falls too far. In the case of a regular condor, it's due to both vertical spreads limiting out.

To demonstrate, assume we have a 55–60 regular condor spread. If the stock is above 65 at expiration, the 50–55 vertical spread is worth exactly $5.00 while the short 60/65 spread is worth −$5.00, which is a wash. Your only loss is what you paid for the condor. That is why the profit-and-loss line flattens out on the far right side for a regular condor since both spreads are limiting out to +$5.00 and −$5.00.

Incidentally, butterflies and condors get their names from the shape of their respective profit-and-loss diagrams, which, after using a lot of artistic freedom, represent the body and the wings of these animals. Now let's take a look at the profit-and-loss diagram for a long iron condor, which is shown in Figure 18.4.

Obviously, it is the opposite of your long condor. Whatever represents a gain in the short condor must be a gain for the long condor, and vice versa. In your short condor, you definitely want that stock to move because if the stock stays constant you lose money.

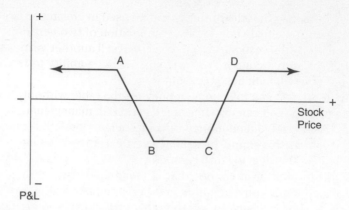

FIGURE 18.4   P&L for Long Iron Condor

You need that stock to go in either direction away from that middle area. Again, your break-evens are defined by the intersection of the black line and the dotted line. There are two intersections; one to the upside and one to the downside. You need the stock to move to the outside of that area, as defined by the two break-evens. Again, in a regular strangle, you would see those two dotted lines pointing straight up with the arrows straight up. Here you see them flatten out and point away, showing your hedge. You are limited.

You have limited loss, but you have a limited return.

HOW DO WE USE CONDORS?

How do we use condors in today's market? For starters, what about trading the smile?

The condor can be used to trade the volatility smile just in the same way the butterfly is used. What's the difference? Once again, it depends on the stock's price relative to the strikes at the time you place the trade. As with the butterfly, the use of the condor with the smile is an advanced strategy that is not discussed here.

However, because the condor and butterfly are the same philosophically, we can certainly use condors for the same reasons we would use butterflies. The location of the stock price relative to the strike prices dictates which strategy to use.

As mentioned before, if the stock is located between two strikes, use the condor. If the stock is located directly on the strike, use the butterfly. Remember, if the stock is located in between two strikes, use the condor.

Now, I also said that the butterfly can be used in closing or exiting positions. First off, the plain condor is a combination of two vertical spreads. So if you are long the vertical spread, you could sell another vertical spread to put yourself into a condor. You will still have the ability to make some money, but you will lock in some profit.

This means you can take some money off the table without totally exiting the position. You can practice some good risk management by taking off some risk, putting some money in your pocket, and still remain in the game. You can do this simply by selling a vertical spread against your long vertical spread, thus legging into a condor.

We also have an iron condor that is made up of two strangles. So if you are in a strangle, you can put on another strangle. Obviously if you are long one strangle, you have to sell the other strangle. If you are short one strangle, you have to buy the other strangle. You have to do the opposite, but you can set up a condor from a strangle by trading another strangle.

Again, either of these trades will put some money in your pocket, take away some risk, but still keep you in the game with the ability to make some more money. This is not to say that you should always leg into a condor every time you place a strangle or vertical spread. Instead, keep the condor in the back of your mind as an alternative way to hedge or exit a position, depending on the situation at the time.

Although the condor's main goal is a hedged time-decay play, it can be used in today's market. Other alternative ways of using the condor include trading the volatility smile and in helping close or exit positions without completely taking the position off. The condor has several functions. Obviously its main goal and objective is to collect time premium, but it can also be used in other ways.

Remember, it is good to have choices. Always explore all of your potential choices, your potential alternatives before making a trade. Choose whichever strategy is best for you at that moment in time. Understanding options opens a world of possibilities. It provides tools for you to use to implement strategies that will protect your portfolio, increase profitability, and reduce risk.

LONG CONDOR SYNOPSIS

Construction. Short two calls (puts) of the same month and adjacent strikes while long a call above the highest of the short call (put) strikes and long a call (put) below the lowest of the short call (put) strikes. Both short-call (put) strikes must be equidistant from the strike of the two short calls (puts). In the case of an iron condor, short an interior strangle while long an exterior strangle around it.

Function. Premium-collection strategy with upside and downside protection. Also a short volatility play.

Bias. Stagnant.

When to Use. When you feel the stock will trade in a very tight range between two strike prices and stagnate there. Also use if you feel the stock has a likelihood of a decrease in implied volatility. The long condor allows you to take advantage of these potential situations while offering a fully hedged position.

Profit Scenario. Maximum profit occurs when the stock closes anywhere between the two short strikes and decreases as the stock moves in either direction outside and away from the two short strikes.

Loss Scenario. Maximum loss occurs when the stock closes at or above the highest strike of the long strikes or at or below the lowest of the long strikes. Maximum loss is limited.

Key Concepts. The long condor is an ideal strategy for premium collectors who seek to minimize potential losses in the event the stock moves adversely. This strategy can also take advantage of expected decreases in volatility. The strategy can be broken down and viewed as two trades. In the case of a traditional condor, the position can be broken down into two conflicting vertical spreads, one long and one short. In the case of an iron condor, the position can be broken down to a short interior strangle surrounded by a long exterior strangle. Condors are best entered into in farther-out months.

SHORT CONDOR SYNOPSIS

Construction. Long two calls (puts) of the same month and adjacent strikes while short a call (put) above the highest of the short call (put) strikes and short a call (put) below the lowest of the short call (put) strikes. Both short-call (put) strikes must be equidistant from the strike of the two short calls (puts). In the case of an iron condor, short an interior strangle while long an exterior strangle around it.

Function. Limited directional stock movement play. Also long volatility play.

Bias. Limited directional but in either direction.

When to Use. When you feel the stock will trade away from a range between two strikes but not aggressively. Also use if you feel the stock has a likelihood of an increase in implied volatility. The short condor allows you to take advantage of these potential situations while offering a hedged position.

Profit Scenario. Maximum profit occurs when the stock closes at or above the highest of the short strikes or at or below the lowest of the short strikes. The trade will also be profitable in the event of increasing implied volatility.

Loss Scenario. Maximum loss occurs when the stock closes anywhere between the long strikes. Maximum loss is limited.

Key Concepts. Short condors are an ideal strategy for long-volatility players who seek to minimize potential losses in the event the stock moves adversely. The strategy can be viewed as two trades. In the case of a traditional condor, the position can be broken down into two conflicting vertical spreads, one long and one short. The iron condor can be broken down to a long interior strangle surrounded by a short exterior strangle. Condors are best entered into in farther-out months.

Conclusion

We began our discussion with the goal of learning about options to improve the bottom line of our financial investments. In learning to understand options, we developed a vocabulary, investigated option theory, then moved on to option strategies.

It is hoped that you can use option strategies for their intended purpose: financial gain and capital protection. As you implement options, remember to begin slowly and carefully. Paper-trade until you are comfortable using a strategy. Move from the simple to the more complicated. Look at the stocks you currently have to see if you can improve their performance using options. Keep reviewing and studying the material in this book and extend your option education.

Think gain. Use the power of options to risk a lesser amount of money to gain a higher rate of return.

Think defense. Recognize and manage risk before you enter into a trade.

Think preserve. The 2008–2009 market has shown that being able to preserve your capital puts you well ahead of the game when markets take a hit. Realize that sometimes you must sacrifice a small amount of your profit to protect and preserve your bottom line.

Think responsibility. Remember that no one cares more about your money than you do; you must be responsible for your investment decisions.

Think options! Appreciate that options can increase profits, manage risk, and provide protection for your financial future.

Five Trading Sheets

Use these five trading sheets as you read through Chapter 4, "Option Theory and the Greeks," and Chapter 5, "Synthetic Positions."

TRADING SHEET 1

QCOM. MicroHedge Trading Sheets Tuesday June 01 13:58:04 2004

QCOM.Q 06/01/04 Ini:2.0 2.0 2.0 2.0 2.0 2.0 Model:MicroHedge Type:Equity Exercise-American

Div: QCOM.Q 08/26/04 0.1 11/26/04 0.1 02/26/05 0.1 05/26/05 0.1 08/26/05 0.1 11/26/05 0.1 02/26/06 0.1 05/26/06 0.1 08/26/06 0.1 11/26/06 0.1

Days to Exp: JUN04: 18 JUL04: 46 OCT04: 137 JAN05: 235 JAN06: 599 JAN07: 963

Vol: JUN04 30.00 JUL04 30.00 OCT04 30.00 OCT04 30.00 JAN05 30.00 JAN06 30.00 JAN07 30.00

Vol	57.50	59.50	61.50	63.50	65.50	67.50	69.50	71.50	73.50	75.50	77.50			G	V
30.0	7.57 0.02	9.55 0.01	11.5 0.00	13.5 0.00	15.5 0.00	17.5 0.00	19.5 0.00	21.5 0.00	23.5 0.00	25.5 0.00	27.5 0.00	JUN	50.00	0	.000
30.0	3.11 .55	4.77 .21	6.62 .07	8.57 .02	100 0	100 -0	100 -0	100 0.00	100 0.00	100 0.00	100 0.00	JUN	55.00	.1	.000
30.0	0.63 -24	1.38 -12	2.52 .96	4.00 .44	10.5 .02	12.5 0.00	14.5 0.00	16.5 0.00	18.5 0.00	20.5 0.00	22.5 0.00	JUN	60.00	1.8	.011
30.0	0.05 7.52	0.18 5.64	3.08 1.83	5.74 .81	5.74 .18	7.62 .06	9.58 0.02	11.5 0.00	13.5 0.00	15.5 0.00	17.5 0.00	JUN	65.00	7.2	.050
30.0	-100 -0	12.5 -0	3.94 -9	1.08 .39	2.53 .34	4.35 .15	4.92 .36	6.71 .15	8.62 .05	10.5 .02	12.5 0.00	JUN	70.00	7.7	.053
30.0	-100 0.0	0.01 10.5	0.23 8.51	0.14 6.60	2.04 1.48	3.13 .72	0.85 -15	5.87 -8	7.70 -3	5.87 .30	7.70 .13	JUN	75.00	2.8	.018
30.0	-100 0.0	-100 -0	0.00 13.5	0.01 11.5	0.60 8	6.60 -82	85 -48	92 -8	97 -23	94 -13	100 -6	JUN	80.00	.4	.003
30.0	-100 0.0	-100 -0	0.00 15.5	0.00 13.5	0.03 9.51	0.12 7.57	0.31 5.76	0.70 4.14	1.35 2.78	2.31 1.74	3.59 1.0				
30.0	-100 0.0	0.00 17.5	0.00 15.5	-100 -1	-100 0	-52 -69	-48 -26	-64 -56	-23 -60	-13 -44	-6 -30				
30.0	-100 0.0	0.00 20.5	0.00 18.5	-100 0	-100 0	0.01 14.5	0.03 10.5	0.10 8.55	0.25 6.70	0.57 5.00	1.11 3.54				
30.0	-100 0.0	0.00 22.5	0.00 20.5	-100 0	-100 0	0.01 -100	0.0 -99	0.10 6	-89 -22	-44 -79	-34 -66				
30.0	7.87 0.24	9.74 0.11	11.6 0.05	13.6 0.02	15.6 0.01	17.6 0.00	19.6 0.00	21.6 0.00	23.6 0.00	25.6 0.00	27.6 0.00	JUL	50.00	.1	.001
30.0	3.93 1.30	5.42 .79	7.08 .44	8.88 .25	10.7 .12	12.7 .06	14.6 0.03	16.6 0.01	18.6 0.00	20.6 0.00	22.6 0.00	JUL	55.00	.8	.013
30.0	1.49 3.86	2.38 2.74	3.49 1.85	4.85 1.20	6.38 .74	8.09 .44	99 .25	99 .13	100 .07	15.6 .03	17.6 .02	JUL	60.00	2.8	.047
30.0	0.42 7.81	0.78 6.16	1.35 4.71	2.11 3.46	3.13 2.47	4.35 1.69	92 .71	97 1.11	88 .71	10.9 .43	12.8 .14	JUL	65.00	5.0	.087
30.0	0.15 -86	0.20 10.6	0.39 8.77	0.73 7.09	56 -56	56 -44	5.77 1.11	7.37 -25	9.09 -17	9.09 .43	10.9 .25	JUL	70.00	5.2	.092
30.0	0.09 12.5	0.04 -93	0.14 -87	0.19 11.5	1.21 5.56	1.91 4.26	81 -50	83 -50	88 -12	93 -8	95 .69	JUL	75.00	3.7	.063
30.0	0.01 17.5	0.02 15.5	0.09 13.5	0.04 16.5	0.30 -70	0.67 8.03	51 -39	51 -39	70 -30	78 -22	84 -16	JUL	80.00	1.8	.030
30.0	4 -97	2 -99	8 -97	0.01 -100	13 -88	19 -82	1.12 6.47	1.74 5.07	2.54 3.87	3.56 2.89	4.77 2.09				
30.0	0.00 22.5	0.00 20.5	0.01 18.5	4 -98	6 -94	0.19 12.5	0.27 -73	0.36 -64	46 -54	56 -45	65 -35				
30.0	-100 0.0	-100 -0	-100 -0	0.01 16.5	-99 -2	0.36 .36	0.62 12.5	0.82 6.98	1.37 7.37	1.60 5.93	2.33 4.65				
30.0								17 -89	25 -76	33 -68	42 -59				
30.0	8.97 1.21	10.6 0.87	12.3 0.62	14.2 0.44	15.6 0.01	17.6 0.30	17.9 0.21	21.8 0.10	23.8 0.06	25.8 0.04	27.8 0.03	OCT	50.00	.7	.035
30.0	81 -19	85 -15	89 -11	92 -8	99 -11	96 -4	97 -7	98 -2	99 -1	99 -0	100 -0	OCT	55.00	1.4	.076
30.0	5.67 2.88	7.02 2.23	8.50 1.71	10.1 1.28	11.7 .96	13.5 .70	15.3 .51	17.1 .36	19.0 .26	20.9 .18	22.9 .13	OCT	60.00	2.5	.123
30.0	3.31 5.50	4.29 4.48	5.43 3.60	6.70 2.87	8.09 2.25	9.59 1.76	11.1 1.35	12.8 1.03	14.6 .78	16.4 .58	18.2 .43	OCT	65.00	3.0	.156
30.0	1.77 8.97	2.43 7.61	3.23 6.39	4.16 5.31	5.22 4.37	6.42 3.56	92 -18	86 -15	91 -11	93 -7	98 -2	OCT	65.00	3.0	.156
30.0	0.89 13.1	0.97 11.4	1.79 9.96	2.42 8.57	57 -44	63 -37	7.73 2.86	9.15 2.28	10.6 1.81	12.3 1.42	13.9 1.11	OCT	70.00	3.2	.164
30.0	30 -71	37 -64	43 -57	50 -50	3.17 5.22	4.91 4.63	69 -32	74 -26	78 -22	82 -18	86 -14	OCT	70.00	3.2	.164
30.0	0.42 17.6	0.65 15.8	0.94 14.1	1.33 12.4	41 -59	47 -53	54 -47	60 -41	65 -35	70 -30	75 -25	OCT	75.00	2.9	.149
30.0	18 -83	23 -78	29 -72	1.82 10.9	1.82 10.9	3.14 8.25	3.97 7.07	4.93 6.01	5.99 5.07	7.17 4.24		OCT	75.00	2.9	.149
30.0	0.19 22.5	0.47 20.5	0.68 18	0.69 16.8	0.99 15.1	1.37 13.5	1.85 11.9	2.43 10.5	3.10 9.18	3.90 7.96	4.80 6.86	OCT	80.00	2.3	.120
30.0	12 -98	14 -95	10 -92	14 -88	18 -84	22 -80	27 -74	32 -68	37 -63	43 -58	48 -52				
30.0	10.0 2.11	11.6 1.68	13.2 1.33	13.2 1.06	16.7 0.83	18.5 0.65	20.4 0.50	22.3 0.39	24.2 0.30	26.1 0.23	28.1 0.18	JAN	50.00	.9	.080
30.0	77 -23	81 -19	84 -16	87 -13	90 -10	92 -8	93 -7	95 -5	96 -4	97 -3	97 -0	JAN	55.00	1.5	.129
30.0	6.98 4.02	8.31 3.34	9.74 2.76	11.2 2.27	12.8 1.84	14.4 1.49	16.2 1.21	17.9 0.97	19.7 0.77	21.7 0.62	23.4 0.49	JAN	55.00	1.5	.129
30.0	64 -37	69 -32	73 -27	77 -23	81 -19	84 -16	87 -13	89 -11	91 -9	94 -8	94 -6	JAN	60.00	2.0	.174
30.0	4.68 6.51	5.73 5.72	6.89 4.97	4.70 4.11	9.48 3.44	11.0 2.91	12.4 2.41	14.0 1.99	15.7 1.64	17.4 1.36	19.1 1.10	JAN	60.00	2.0	.174
30.0	50 -51	55 -45	60 -40	65 -35	70 -30	74 -27	78 -22	81 -19	84 -16	86 -14	89 -11	JAN	65.00	2.4	.205
30.0	3.02 10.0	3.60 8.77	4.70 7.65	5.53 6.63	6.63 5.67	7.56 4.91	9.30 4.21	10.6 3.57	12.1 3.02	13.6 2.57	15.2 2.15	JAN	65.00	2.4	.205
30.0	37 -64	42 -58	48 -52	53 -47	58 -43	63 -37	67 -33	71 -29	75 -25	78 -22	81 -19	JAN	70.00	2.3	.215
30.0	1.88 13.8	2.44 12.4	3.11 11.0	3.81 9.78	4.73 8.63	5.67 7.56	6.75 6.62	7.90 5.79	9.13 4.98	10.4 4.31	11.8 3.71	JAN	70.00	2.3	.215
30.0	26 -75	31 -70	37 -65	41 -60	46 -55	51 -50	56 -45	60 -40	64 -36	68 -32	72 -28	JAN	75.00	2.3	.207
30.0	1.15 18.1	1.53 16.5	1.99 14.9	2.56 13.4	3.20 12.0	4.00 10.8	4.76 9.60	5.69 8.53	6.72 7.53	7.81 6.61	9.01 5.81	JAN	75.00	2.3	.207
30.0	18 -84	22 -80	26 -75	31 -71	35 -66	40 -61	44 -56	49 -52	53 -47	58 -43	62 -39	JAN	80.00	2.1	.186
30.0	0.67 22.7	0.94 20.9	1.26 19.3	1.71 17.5	15.9	17.9	3.30 13.1	4.01 11.8	4.81 10.4	5.72 9.50	6.69 8.45	JAN	80.00	2.1	.186
30.0	12 -91	15 -87	18 -84	22 -80	15.9 26 -76	30 -71	34 -67	39 -62	43 -58	47 -53	52 -49				

TRADING SHEET 2

QCOM. MicroHedge Trading Sheets Tuesday June 01 13:57:44 2004
QCOM. 06/01/04 Int:2.0 2.0 2.0 2.0 2.0 Model:MicroHedge Type:Equity Exercise:American
Div: QCOM.Q 08/26/04 0.1 11/26/04 0.1 02/26/05 0.1 05/26/05 0.1 08/26/05 0.1 11/26/05 0.1 05/26/06 0.1 08/26/06 0.1 11/26/06 0.1
Days to Exp: JUN04: 18 JUL04: 46 OCT04: 137 JAN05: 235 JAN06: 599 JAN07: 963
Vol: JUN04 40.00 JUL04 40.00 OCT04 40.00 JAN05 40.00 JAN06 40.00 JAN07 40.00

Each stock-price column below contains a pair of values (call / put). Vol = 40.0 for all rows.

Strike	57.50	59.50	61.50	63.50	65.50	67.50	69.50	71.50	73.50	75.50	77.50	G	V
JUN 50.00	7.66 0.11	9.59 0.04	11.5 0.01	13.5 0.00	15.5 0.00	17.5 0.00	19.5 0.00	21.5 0.00	23.5 0.00	25.5 0.00	27.5 0.00	.0	.004
JUN 55.00	3.53 0.98	5.07 0.52	6.90 0.25	8.66 0.10	11.0 0.04	12.9 0.02	14.5 0.01	16.5 0.05	18.5 0.23	20.5 0.01	22.5 0.00	.4	.023
JUN 60.00	1.09 3.54	1.91 2.38	3.03 1.47	4.41 0.85	6.03 0.47	7.80 0.24	9.67 0.11	11.6 0.05	13.5 0.02	15.5 0.01	17.5 0.01	2.6	.053
JUN 65.00	0.24 7.67	0.47 5.93	0.93 4.37	1.64 3.08	2.62 2.06	3.85 1.41	5.33 0.77	6.99 0.43	8.79 0.23	10.6 0.11	12.6 0.05	5.8	.056
JUN 70.00	0.03 12.5	0.07 10.5	0.19 8.64	0.42 6.86	0.81 5.25	1.41 3.85	2.27 2.71	3.37 1.81	4.72 1.16	6.26 0.70	7.97 0.40	6.1	.032
JUN 75.00	0.00 17.5	0.01 15.5	0.03 13.5	0.07 11.5	0.17 9.63	0.37 7.82	0.71 6.15	1.24 4.68	1.98 3.41	2.97 2.41	4.19 1.62	3.6	.011
JUN 80.00	0.00 22.5	0.00 20.5	0.00 18.5	0.01 16.5	0.03 14.5	0.08 12.5	0.16 10.6	0.33 8.78	0.64 7.07	1.09 5.52	1.75 4.18	1.2	
JUL 50.00	8.26 0.63	10.0 0.39	11.8 0.24	13.7 0.14	15.7 0.08	17.6 0.05	19.6 0.02	21.6 0.01	23.6 0.01	25.6 0.04	27.6 0.00	.4	.008
JUL 55.00	4.69 2.05	6.08 1.45	7.62 0.99	9.30 0.66	11.0 0.42	12.9 0.27	14.9 0.17	16.7 0.10	18.7 0.06	20.6 0.04	22.6 0.02	1.3	.030
JUL 60.00	2.29 4.66	3.22 3.58	4.33 2.69	5.62 1.97	6.81 1.25	8.64 0.99	10.3 0.68	12.1 0.46	13.9 0.31	15.8 0.20	17.7 0.13	2.7	.063
JUL 65.00	0.96 8.34	1.47 6.83	2.16 5.61	2.69 4.37	3.39 3.39	4.64 2.36	6.59 1.93	8.07 1.41	9.68 1.02	11.3 0.71	13.1 0.50	3.8	.090
JUL 70.00	0.35 12.7	0.59 10.9	0.99 9.32	1.43 7.78	2.06 6.41	2.85 5.19	3.80 4.14	4.91 3.24	6.17 2.50	7.57 1.90	9.09 1.42	4.0	.094
JUL 75.00	0.11 17.5	0.20 15.6	0.37 13.7	0.66 11.9	0.94 10.3	1.39 8.74	1.98 7.32	2.71 6.04	3.59 4.92	4.62 3.95	5.79 3.11	3.3	.077
JUL 80.00	0.03 22.5	0.06 20.5	0.12 18.5	0.22 16.6	0.38 14.7	0.60 12.9	0.93 11.2	1.35 9.69	1.90 8.23	2.57 6.90	3.40 5.72	2.3	.052
OCT 50.00	10.0 2.24	11.5 1.80	13.2 1.44	14.9 1.15	16.6 0.91	18.4 0.71	20.3 0.56	22.2 0.44	24.1 0.34	26.0 0.26	27.9 0.20	1.0	.064
OCT 55.00	6.98 4.19	8.30 3.51	9.71 2.91	11.1 2.41	12.7 1.96	14.4 1.60	16.1 1.31	17.8 1.06	19.6 0.85	21.5 0.69	23.3 0.54	1.5	.102
OCT 60.00	4.70 6.63	5.74 5.93	6.89 5.08	7.77 4.31	9.46 3.63	10.8 3.06	12.4 2.57	13.9 2.13	15.6 1.77	17.3 1.48	19.0 1.20	2.0	.135
OCT 65.00	3.04 10.2	3.83 9.00	4.73 7.89	5.72 6.87	6.80 5.95	7.99 5.13	9.27 4.42	10.6 3.77	12.1 3.21	13.6 2.74	15.1 2.30	2.3	.157
OCT 70.00	1.92 14.1	2.48 12.6	3.14 11.2	3.90 10.0	4.76 8.89	5.69 7.82	6.75 6.87	7.90 6.01	9.11 5.22	10.4 4.53	11.8 3.92	2.4	.165
OCT 75.00	1.18 18.3	1.57 16.7	2.03 15.1	2.58 13.7	3.24 12.3	3.97 11.0	4.79 9.89	5.71 8.80	6.73 7.81	7.81 6.89	9.09 6.07	2.3	.158
OCT 80.00	0.70 22.9	0.97 21.1	1.29 19.4	1.69 17.9	2.14 16.2	2.69 14.7	3.33 13.4	4.04 12.1	4.83 10.9	5.74 9.80	6.70 8.76	2.1	.142
JAN 50.00	11.5 3.58	12.9 3.07	14.5 2.64	16.1 2.26	17.8 1.92	19.5 1.65	21.3 1.39	23.1 1.19	24.9 1.00	26.8 0.86	28.6 0.72	1.0	.114
JAN 55.00	8.73 5.77	9.77 5.07	11.3 4.41	12.6 3.87	14.3 3.36	15.9 2.93	17.5 2.54	19.1 2.20	20.9 1.91	20.5 1.65	2.6 1.42	1.3	.153
JAN 60.00	6.52 8.51	7.60 7.60	8.79 6.77	10.0 5.99	11.7 5.33	14.3 4.69	15.2 4.16	15.7 3.66	86 3.23	18.8 2.82	59 2.48	1.6	.184
JAN 65.00	4.80 11.7	5.69 10.6	6.61 9.60	7.73 8.66	6.82 7.76	10.0 6.98	14.2 6.26	17.4 5.59	14.0 4.98	15.5 4.44	17.0 3.95	1.7	.205
JAN 70.00	3.49 15.4	4.19 14.1	4.19 13.9	5.56 11.7	6.82 11.7	7.85 9.72	8.94 8.81	9.20 7.98	11.3 7.20	12.6 6.50	14.0 5.85	1.8	.215
JAN 75.00	2.49 19.4	3.07 17.9	3.31 17.9	4.31 15.2	5.20 14.0	6.03 12.8	6.99 11.8	7.97 10.7	9.06 9.87	10.1 8.98	11.4 8.20	1.8	.213
JAN 80.00	1.77 23.7	2.23 22.1	2.71 20.6	3.28 19.1	3.93 17.7	4.62 16.4	5.40 15.2	6.23 14.0	7.16 12.9	8.12 11.8	9.18 10.9	1.7	.203

QCOM. MicroHedge Trading Sheets Tuesday June 01 13:56:49 2004

QCOM. 06/01/04 Int:2.0 2.0 2.0 2.0 2.0 2.0 Model:MicroHedge Type:Equity Exercise:American

Div: QCOM.Q 08/26/04 0.1 11/26/04 0.1 02/25/05 0.1 05/26/05 0.1 08/26/05 0.1 11/26/05 0.1 02/26/06 0.1 05/26/06 0.1 08/26/06 0.1 11/26/06 0.1

Days to Exp: JUN04: 18 JUL04: 46 OCT04: 137 JAN05: 235 JAN06: 599 JAN07: 963

Vol: JUN04 50.00 JUL04 50.00 OCT04 50.00 JAN05 50.00 JAN06 50.00 JAN07 50.00

Vol 50.0		57.50	59.50	61.50	63.50	65.50	67.50	69.50	71.50	73.50	75.50	77.50	79.50			G	V
50.0	JUN 50.00	7.84 0.29	9.69 0.15	11.6 0.07	13.5 0.03	15.5 0.01	17.5 0.00		21.5 0.00	23.5 0.00	25.5 0.00	27.5 0.00	29.5 0.00	JUN 50.00	.1	.001
50.0	JUN 55.00	3.97 1.42	5.44 0.89	7.08 0.52	8.85 0.30	10.7 0.16	12.6 0.08		16.5 0.02	18.5 0.01	20.5 0.00	22.5 0.00	24.5 0.00	JUN 55.00	.9	.010
50.0	JUN 60.00	1.56 4.01	2.44 2.89	3.54 1.99	4.88 1.33	6.40 0.84	8.07 0.51	9.86 0.30	11.7 0.17	13.6 0.09	15.6 0.05	17.5 0.02	19.5 0.01	JUN 60.00	2.9	.032
50.0	JUN 65.00	0.47 7.92	0.85 6.29	1.42 4.87	2.18 3.62	3.19 2.63	4.40 1.84	5.80 1.24	7.37 0.81	9.07 0.51	10.8 0.31	12.7 0.18	14.6 0.10	JUN 65.00	4.8	.055
50.0	JUN 70.00	0.11 12.5	0.22 10.6	0.44 8.89	0.79 7.24	1.29 5.73	1.99 4.43	2.89 3.33	3.98 2.42	5.28 1.71	6.75 1.18	8.36 0.79	10.0 0.51	JUN 70.00	5.0	.058
50.0	JUN 75.00	0.02 17.5	0.05 15.5	0.11 13.5	0.22 11.6	0.42 9.87	0.74 8.18	1.19 6.63	1.82 5.25	2.63 4.06	3.64 3.07	4.83 2.26	6.19 1.62	JUN 75.00	3.6	.040
50.0	JUN 80.00	0.00 22.5	0.01 20.5	0.02 18.5	0.05 16.5	0.11 14.5	0.22 12.6	0.41 10.8	0.69 9.13	1.11 7.55	1.69 6.12	2.42 4.85	3.34 3.77	JUN 80.00	1.9	.020
50.0	JUL 50.00	8.76 1.14	10.4 0.82	12.2 0.57	14.0 0.40	15.8 0.27	17.8 0.18	19.7 0.12	21.7 0.08	23.6 0.05	25.6 0.03	27.6 0.02	29.6 0.01	JUL 50.00	.7	.019
50.0	JUL 55.00	5.44 2.81	6.79 2.15	8.25 1.62	9.84 1.20	11.5 0.89	13.2 0.64	15.1 0.47	16.9 0.32	18.8 0.22	20.8 0.16	22.7 0.11	24.7 0.07	JUL 55.00	1.5	.043
50.0	JUL 60.00	3.09 5.45	4.06 4.43	5.19 3.54	6.45 2.80	7.84 2.19	9.33 1.68	10.9 1.27	12.6 0.97	14.3 0.72	16.1 0.53	18.0 0.38	19.9 0.28	JUL 60.00	2.5	.071
50.0	JUL 65.00	1.61 8.98	2.25 7.61	3.01 6.37	3.92 5.27	4.96 4.31	6.13 3.48	7.45 2.79	8.88 2.23	10.4 1.74	12.0 1.35	13.7 1.04	15.4 0.79	JUL 65.00	3.1	.091
50.0	JUL 70.00	0.78 13.1	1.15 11.5	1.63 9.98	2.23 8.58	2.94 7.28	3.78 6.12	4.78 5.12	5.91 4.24	7.14 3.47	8.47 2.80	9.93 2.26	11.4 1.80	JUL 70.00	3.2	.095
50.0	JUL 75.00	0.34 17.7	0.55 15.9	0.82 14.1	1.18 12.5	1.64 10.9	2.20 9.54	2.89 8.22	3.70 7.04	4.64 5.97	5.68 5.01	6.85 4.17	8.14 3.46	JUL 75.00	2.9	.085
50.0	JUL 80.00	0.14 22.5	0.24 20.6	0.38 18.7	0.59 16.9	0.85 15.2	1.21 13.5	1.65 11.9	2.18 10.5	2.86 9.19	3.63 7.95	4.50 6.82	5.50 5.82	JUL 80.00	2.3	.066
50.0	OCT 50.00	11.1 3.37	12.6 2.87	14.2 2.43	15.8 2.07	17.5 1.75	19.2 1.48	21.0 1.24	22.8 1.04	24.6 0.88	26.5 0.73	28.3 0.61	30.2 0.51	OCT 50.00	1.0	.085
50.0	OCT 55.00	8.33 5.54	9.63 4.84	10.9 4.19	12.4 3.64	13.9 3.15	15.5 2.71	17.1 2.33	18.8 1.99	20.5 1.70	22.2 1.46	24.0 1.26	25.8 1.07	OCT 55.00	1.3	.116
50.0	OCT 60.00	6.11 8.30	7.18 7.37	8.35 6.53	9.57 5.75	10.9 5.08	12.2 4.45	13.7 3.90	15.2 3.42	16.8 2.94	18.4 2.60	20.0 2.25	21.8 1.97	OCT 60.00	1.6	.141
50.0	OCT 65.00	4.41 11.5	5.28 10.4	6.22 9.38	7.27 8.42	8.37 7.52	9.58 6.72	10.8 5.98	12.1 5.32	13.5 4.72	15.0 4.17	16.5 3.70	18.1 3.25	OCT 65.00	1.8	.158
50.0	OCT 70.00	3.13 15.2	3.81 13.9	4.58 12.7	5.41 11.5	6.35 10.4	7.36 9.48	8.43 8.55	9.60 7.71	10.8 6.91	12.1 6.22	13.4 5.56	14.8 4.98	OCT 70.00	1.9	.164
50.0	OCT 75.00	2.19 19.3	2.72 17.8	3.32 16.4	4.00 15.1	4.75 13.8	5.56 12.6	6.49 11.5	7.44 10.5	8.52 9.60	9.62 8.70	10.8 7.90	12.0 7.13	OCT 75.00	1.9	.162
50.0	OCT 80.00	1.52 23.6	1.93 22.0	2.38 20.5	2.92 19.0	3.51 17.6	4.19 16.2	4.93 15.0	5.73 13.8	6.63 12.6	7.57 11.6	8.61 10.6	9.68 9.73	OCT 80.00	1.8	.153
50.0	JAN 50.00	13.0 5.11	14.5 4.59	15.9 4.08	17.5 3.66	19.1 3.25	20.8 2.91	22.5 2.59	24.2 2.31	25.9 2.06	27.7 1.82	29.5 1.63	31.3 1.44	JAN 50.00	.9	.134
50.0	JAN 55.00	10.4 7.52	11.7 6.79	13.1 6.16	14.5 5.54	16.0 5.03	17.7 4.52	19.2 4.10	20.6 3.69	22.3 3.31	23.9 2.96	25.6 2.68	27.4 2.43	JAN 55.00	1.1	.164
50.0	JAN 60.00	8.36 10.3	9.47 9.47	10.6 8.66	11.9 7.91	13.0 7.22	14.6 6.59	16.0 5.98	17.5 5.47	19.0 4.96	20.5 4.53	22.1 4.12	23.7 3.72	JAN 60.00	1.3	.188
50.0	JAN 65.00	6.61 13.5	7.60 12.5	8.62 11.5	9.74 10.6	10.8 9.80	12.1 9.05	13.3 8.29	14.7 7.64	16.1 7.01	17.5 6.42	19.0 5.91	20.5 5.40	JAN 65.00	1.4	.205
50.0	JAN 70.00	5.20 17.1	6.05 15.9	6.92 14.8	7.91 13.8	8.89 12.7	10.0 11.8	11.1 10.9	12.3 10.1	13.5 9.43	14.8 8.70	16.2 8.07	17.5 7.44	JAN 70.00	1.4	.213
50.0	JAN 75.00	4.09 20.9	4.81 19.7	5.54 18.4	6.39 17.2	7.23 16.0	8.21 15.0	9.21 14.0	10.3 13.0	11.3 12.2	12.5 11.3	13.7 10.5	15.0 9.82	JAN 75.00	1.4	.215
50.0	JAN 80.00	3.20 25.0	3.80 23.6	4.43 22.2	5.15 20.9	5.87 19.6	6.72 18.5	7.57 17.3	8.52 16.3	9.51 15.2	10.5 14.3	11.6 13.4	12.7 12.5	JAN 80.00	1.4	.211

TRADING SHEET 4

QCOM, MicroHedge Trading Sheets Tuesday June 01 13:59:32 2004

QCOM, 06/01/04 Init:2.0 2.0 2.0 2.0 2.0 2.0 Model:MicroHedge Type:Equity Exercise:American

Div: QCOM.Q 08/26/04 0.1 11/26/04 0.1 02/26/05 0.1 05/26/05 0.1 08/26/05 0.1 11/26/05 0.1 02/26/06 0.1 05/26/06 0.1 08/26/06 0.1 11/26/06 0.1

Days to Exp: JUN04: 18 JUL04: 46 OCTO4: 137 JAN05: 235 JAN06: 599 JAN07: 983

Vol: JUN04 60.00 JUL04 60.00 OCT04 60.00 JAN05 60.00 JAN06 60.00 JAN07 60.00

Vol			57.50	59.50	61.50	63.50	65.50	67.50	69.50	71.50	73.50	75.50	77.50			G	V
60.0	JUN	50.00												JUN	50.00	.3	.004
60.0	JUN	55.00												JUN	55.00	1.3	.016
60.0	JUN	60.00												JUN	60.00	2.8	.038
60.0	JUN	65.00												JUN	65.00	4.1	.056
60.0	JUN	70.00												JUN	70.00	4.3	.059
60.0	JUN	75.00												JUN	75.00	3.4	.046
60.0	JUN	80.00												JUN	80.00	2.2	.029
60.0	JUL	50.00												JUL	50.00	.9	.030
60.0	JUL	55.00												JUL	55.00	1.6	.053
60.0	JUL	60.00												JUL	60.00	2.6	.076
60.0	JUL	65.00												JUL	65.00	2.6	.092
60.0	JUL	70.00												JUL	70.00	2.7	.095
60.0	JUL	75.00												JUL	75.00	2.5	.089
60.0	JUL	80.00												JUL	80.00	2.2	.076
60.0	OCT	50.00												OCT	50.00	1.0	.098
60.0	OCT	55.00												OCT	55.00	1.2	.124
60.0	OCT	60.00												OCT	60.00	1.4	.144
60.0	OCT	65.00												OCT	65.00	1.5	.157
60.0	OCT	70.00												OCT	70.00	1.6	.164
60.0	OCT	75.00												OCT	75.00	1.6	.164
60.0	OCT	80.00												OCT	80.00	1.5	.159
60.0	JAN	50.00												JAN	50.00	.8	.146
60.0	JAN	55.00												JAN	55.00	1.0	.170
60.0	JAN	60.00												JAN	60.00	1.1	.190
60.0	JAN	65.00												JAN	65.00	1.1	.203
60.0	JAN	70.00												JAN	70.00	1.2	.212
60.0	JAN	75.00												JAN	75.00	1.2	.215
60.0	JAN	80.00												JAN	80.00	1.2	.215

341

QCOM. MicroHedge Trading Sheets Tuesday June 01 14:01:37 2004
QCOM. 06/01/04 Int:2.0 2.0 2.0 2.0 2.0 2.0 Model:MicroHedge Type:Equity Exercise:American
Div:QCOM.Q 08/26/04 0.1 11/26/04 0.1 02/26/05 0.1 05/26/05 0.1 08/26/05 0.1 11/26/05 0.1 02/26/06 0.1 05/26/06 0.1 08/26/06 0.1 11/26/06 0.1
Days to Exp: JUN04: 18 JUL04: 46 OCT04:137 JAN05: 235 JAN06: 599 JAN07: 963
Vol: JUN04 70.00 JUL04 70.00 OCT04 70.00 JAN05 70.00 JAN06 70.00 JAN07 70.00

(Vol column = 70.0 for all rows. Each cell: value vega / delta theta.)

Opt	57.50	59.50	61.50	63.50	65.50	67.50	69.50	71.50	73.50	75.50	77.50	G	V
JUN 50.00	8.38 0.83/83 -17	10.1 0.55/88 -12	11.9 0.36/92 -8	13.7 0.23/94 -6	15.6 0.14/96 -4	17.6 0.08/98 -2	19.6 0.05/98 -2	21.5 0.03/99 -	23.5 0.02/99 -1	25.5 0.01/100 -	27.5 0.01/100 -0	.5	.008
JUN 55.00	4.92 2.37/64 -36	6.29 1.74/72 -28	7.80 1.24/78 -22	9.43 0.88/84 -16	11.1 0.60/88 -12	12.9 0.41/91 -9	14.8 0.27/94 -6	16.7 0.18/96 -4	18.6 0.11/97 -3	20.6 0.07/98 -2	22.6 0.04/99 -1	1.5	.022
JUN 60.00	2.56 5.01/43 -57	3.50 3.94/52 -49	4.61 3.05/60 -40	5.87 2.32/67 -33	7.29 1.73/74 -26	8.83 1.27/79 -21	10.4 0.92/83 -17	12.2 0.65/88 -12	14.0 0.46/91 -9	15.8 0.31/94 -6	17.7 0.21/95 -5	2.6	.042
JUN 65.00	1.18 8.62/25 -75	1.74 7.18/32 -68	2.45 5.69/40 -60	3.32 4.76/48 -52	4.34 3.78/57 -43	5.53 2.96/63 -37	6.84 2.16/69 -31	8.29 1.73/75 -25	9.86 1.30/79 -21	11.5 0.97/85 -15	13.0 0.70/88 -12	3.5	.057
JUN 70.00	0.43 12.9/12 -88	0.76 11.2/18 -82	1.16 9.51/24 -76	1.68 8.12/30 -70	2.35 6.79/37 -63	3.16 5.60/45 -55	4.12 4.56/53 -48	5.23 3.67/59 -41	6.47 2.91/65 -35	7.84 2.28/71 -29	9.31 1.75/77 -24	3.7	.059
JUN 75.00	0.13 17.6/4 -96	0.25 15.7/8 -87	0.51 13.9/13 -88	0.78 12.2/17 -83	1.17 10.6/23 -77	1.66 9.10/31 -71	2.29 7.73/35 -65	3.05 6.48/42 -58	3.94 5.37/49 -51	4.97 4.40/55 -45	6.12 3.55/62 -38	3.2	.050
JUN 80.00	0.06 22.5/2 -98	0.11 20.5/6 -94	0.20 18.6/9 -91	0.33 16.7/12 -88	0.53 14.9/17 -83	0.80 13.2/22 -78	1.17 11.6/27 -73	1.64 10.0/33 -67	2.23 8.66/39 -61	2.93 7.36/46 -54	3.76 6.19/54 -46	2.3	.036
JUL 50.00	9.98 2.36/75 -25	11.5 1.91/79 -21	13.1 1.52/83 -17	14.8 1.23/86 -14	16.6 0.97/88 -12	18.3 0.77/91 -9	20.2 0.62/92 -8	22.1 0.48/94 -6	24.0 0.37/95 -5	25.9 0.29/96 -4	27.8 0.23/97 -3	1.0	.039
JUL 55.00	6.99 4.36/62 -38	8.30 3.66/67 -33	9.68 3.05/72 -28	11.1 2.53/76 -24	12.7 2.09/79 -21	14.3 1.70/83 -17	16.0 1.41/85 -15	17.7 1.13/88 -12	19.5 0.92/90 -10	21.3 0.74/92 -8	23.2 0.60/93 -7	1.5	.060
JUL 60.00	4.72 7.08/49 -51	5.75 6.11/54 -46	6.89 5.25/60 -40	8.10 4.46/64 -36	9.45 3.80/69 -31	10.8 3.22/73 -27	12.3 2.70/76 -24	13.9 2.27/80 -20	15.5 1.87/83 -17	17.2 1.58/85 -15	18.9 1.29/87 -13	1.9	.079
JUL 65.00	3.09 10.4/37 -63	3.86 9.22/42 -58	4.72 8.06/47 -53	5.73 7.00/52 -48	6.80 6.15/57 -43	7.99 5.33/61 -39	9.25 4.60/66 -34	10.6 3.94/70 -30	12.0 3.39/73 -27	13.5 2.87/77 -23	15.1 2.45/80 -20	2.2	.092
JUL 70.00	1.95 14.3/27 -74	2.51 12.8/31 -69	3.18 11.5/36 -64	3.96 10.3/41 -59	4.77 9.11/46 -54	5.98 8.06/50 -50	6.75 7.09/55 -45	7.89 6.23/59 -41	9.08 5.42/63 -37	10.4 4.74/67 -33	11.7 4.08/71 -30	2.3	.096
JUL 75.00	1.20 17.4/17 -82	1.61 16.9/22 -78	2.05 14.8/26 -74	2.61 13.9/31 -69	3.27 12.6/37 -63	3.98 11.3/40 -50	4.82 10.1/47 -53	5.71 9.03/51 -49	6.73 8.06/57 -43	7.80 7.12/61 -39	8.99 6.31/68 -32	2.2	.092
JUL 80.00	0.73 23.1/13 -88	0.98 21.3/16 -85	1.30 19.6/19 -81	1.72 18.0/23 -78	2.16 16.5/28 -72	2.72 15.0/33 -67	3.38 13.6/40 -66	4.12 12.3/42 -62	4.87 11.1/47 -57	5.73 10.0/53 -47	6.72 9.04/60 -40	2.0	.082
OCT 50.00	13.4 5.74/71 -29	14.9 5.19/74 -26	16.4 4.74/76 -24	17.4 4.23/78 -22	19.5 3.82/80 -20	21.1 3.42/82 -18	22.8 3.10/84 -16	24.5 2.78/85 -15	26.2 2.52/87 -13	28.0 2.27/88 -12	29.8 2.03/89 -11	.9	.107
OCT 55.00	11.0 8.22/63 -37	12.2 7.49/66 -34	13.6 6.86/69 -31	15.0 6.23/71 -29	16.4 5.70/74 -26	17.9 5.18/77 -23	19.5 4.72/78 -22	21.1 4.31/80 -20	22.7 3.90/82 -18	24.3 3.56/83 -17	26.0 3.24/85 -15	1.1	.128
OCT 60.00	8.92 11.1/56 -44	9.88 10.0/59 -41	11.1 9.43/62 -38	12.4 8.68/64 -36	13.8 7.98/67 -33	15.1 7.35/71 -29	16.5 6.72/72 -28	18.0 6.20/75 -25	19.5 5.69/79 -21	21.0 5.22/82 -18	22.6 4.81/85 -15	1.2	.145
OCT 65.00	7.20 14.3/48 -52	8.18 13.3/52 -48	9.23 12.5/57 -43	10.3 11.5/60 -40	11.4 10.6/63 -37	12.7 9.80/67 -33	13.9 9.13/69 -31	15.3 8.47/72 -28	16.7 7.84/76 -24	18.0 7.22/78 -22	19.5 6.70/79 -21	1.3	.157
OCT 70.00	5.78 17.9/42 -58	6.65 16.7/45 -55	7.55 15.6/49 -51	8.53 14.6/53 -47	9.53 13.6/57 -43	10.6 12.7/60 -40	11.7 11.8/63 -37	12.9 11.0/65 -35	14.2 10.3/70 -30	15.4 9.59/71 -29	16.8 8.96/74 -26	1.3	.163
OCT 75.00	4.65 21.7/36 -64	5.37 20.4/40 -60	6.25 19.2/44 -56	7.10 18.1/47 -53	8.06 16.9/50 -50	8.88 15.9/54 -47	9.86 14.9/59 -41	10.9 14.0/61 -39	12.0 13.1/64 -36	13.2 12.3/66 -34	14.4 11.5/68 -32	1.4	.165
OCT 80.00	3.72 25.8/31 -70	4.31 24.4/36 -67	5.02 23.1/39 -64	5.72 22.0/43 -57	6.52 20.8/47 -53	7.37 19.4/50 -50	8.24 18.3/53 -48	9.14 17.2/51 -49	10.2 16.2/58 -48	11.2 15.3/54 -46	12.3 14.4/57 -43	1.3	.162
JAN 50.00	16.2 8.30/71 -29	17.6 7.72/75 -25	19.0 7.18/77 -23	20.6 6.71/78 -22	22.1 6.24/78 -22	23.7 5.81/80 -20	25.3 5.44/81 -19	26.9 5.07/81 -18	28.6 4.70/84 -16	30.3 4.40/85 -15	32.0 4.12/86 -14	.7	.152
JAN 55.00	13.9 10.3/65 -35	15.2 9.72/67 -33	16.5 9.02/69 -31	17.9 8.47/71 -29	19.4 7.93/73 -27	20.9 7.46/75 -25	22.4 7.00/76 -24	23.9 6.53/79 -21	25.5 6.16/82 -18	27.1 5.79/86 -15	28.7 5.79/87 -18	.8	.173
JAN 60.00	11.9 13.1/60 -40	13.1 13.1/67 -33	14.4 12.1/69 -31	15.7 11.7/71 -29	17.0 11.1/73 -27	18.4 10.3/76 -24	19.8 9.80/76 -24	21.2 9.23/73 -27	22.7 8.87/79 -21	24.2 8.20/82 -18	25.7 7.74/82 -18	.9	.189
JAN 65.00	10.3 17.2/54 -46	11.3 16.3/56 -44	12.5 15.1/59 -41	13.7 14.6/61 -39	14.9 13.6/63 -37	16.2 13.1/64 -36	17.5 12.1/67 -34	18.8 11.1/70 -30	20.2 11.1/75 -25	21.6 10.5/78 -24	23.0 9.99/78 -22	1.0	.202
JAN 70.00	8.83 20.7/49 -52	9.84 19.7/51 -49	10.8 18.7/54 -47	11.9 17.6/56 -45	13.0 16.9/58 -42	14.2 16.1/61 -39	15.4 15.3/63 -37	16.6 14.5/66 -35	17.9 13.8/70 -30	19.2 13.1/73 -28	20.6 12.4/73 -27	1.0	.210
JAN 75.00	7.61 24.4/44 -56	8.51 23.3/47 -47	9.42 22.2/49 -52	10.4 21.2/51 -49	11.4 20.3/53 -47	12.5 19.3/56 -44	13.6 18.4/57 -43	14.7 17.6/61 -39	15.9 16.6/66 -35	17.1 15.9/69 -33	18.4 15.2/69 -31	1.0	.214
JAN 80.00	6.57 28.4/40 -61	7.35 27.1/42 -58	8.20 26.0/44 -56	9.05 24.9/47 -54	10.0 23.8/49 -52	11.0 22.5/51 -50	12.0 21.8/53 -48	13.0 20.8/55 -46	14.1 19.1/57 -44	15.3 18.2/59 -42	16.5 18.2/60 -40	1.0	.215

About the Author

Ron Ianieri graduated from St. Joseph's University in Philadelphia with a degree in Finance. He started his career on the floor of the Philadelphia Stock Exchange working on the Foreign Currency Options Floor just before the crash of 1987. After two years he moved to the Equity Options Floor and was trained in option theory by well-known technical and analytical traders Cooper, Neff, and Associates.

Ron then joined TFM Investment Group, where he served as Option Specialist in Dell Computer during the early 1990s, at a time when Dell was one of the busiest option books in the United States. During this period, Ron began to develop his highly respected Option Trader and Trading Course. He later became a manager at Gateway Partners, a large, fast-growing specialist unit, where he was an integral part of the unit's expansion.

Ron was responsible for hiring and training new trader trainees and finalized the development of his Option Theory and Trading Course. He also aided in the development of the firm's proprietary trading and strategic risk management program, which featured several sophisticated pricing models and analytic tools.

During his years on the floor, Ron served on several Philadelphia Stock Exchange committees, including the Marketing Committee, the Automation Committee, and the Electronic Book Development Sub-Committee.

After a four-year stint at Gateway Partners, Ron went off the floor and joined a locally based proprietary trading desk. Since then, Ron has consulted with various mutual funds and hedge funds on investment selection protocols, risk management, and position and portfolio hedging techniques.

In 2004, Ron was approached by Brett Fogle, who had an idea to start what is now The Options University. Together they began to teach and train individual investors how to use options to enhance and protect their trades and their portfolios.

In January 2009, Ron started his own company, Ion Options (www.ionoptions.com), where he continues to teach the most dynamic, in-depth option courses available today. The courses that Ron teaches to individual investors are the same ones he taught on the floor to up-and-coming professional on-floor market makers.

Ron is a high-energy, straight-shooting, tell-it-like-it-is teacher and a highly sought-after speaker. He is regularly seen on CNBC, CNBC Asia, Fox News, Fox Business News, Bloomberg Asia, Channel News Asia, and BNN for his market commentary. Ron is also frequently quoted in financial publications and web sites, including CNBC.com, CNN.com, Dow Jones Marketwatch, Barrons, Wall Street Journal, ABC News, and countless radio talk shows.

Recently Ron has been traveling abroad, teaching option theory and strategy to professional traders and individual investors in Asia and Australia.

Index

Adaptive mesh model, 29–32
Amgen (AMGN), 172–174
Assignment, 5
At-the-money (ATM) options, 9, 125,
   127–128
  defined, 7
  effect of Greeks on, 43, 44, 45, 50

Bear spread, 209–210, 227–230,
   231–232
Bear Stearns (BSC), 273–274
Bell curve (Normal distribution),
   21–25, 31, 35
Binomial model, 26–28
Black, Fisher, 26
Black-Scholes model, 26–27
Break down, 186–187
Break-even point:
  with butterfly, 302, 313
  with call options, 15–16, 128
  with condor, 318, 328–330
  with put options, 17
  with straddles, 267–271
  with strangles, 285–288
Breakout, 171–172
Bristol Myers (BMY), 159–160
Bull spread, 209–210, 226–227,
   230–231
Butterfly, 297, 299–314
  break-even point, 302, 313
  condor compared to, 317, 321–323
  construction of, 299–301, 313, 314
  cost of, 305–306
  iron butterfly, 309–312
  key concepts of, 314

long vs. short, 299–300, 305–306,
   311, 313–314
position of Greeks with, 307–309
potential profit/loss, 301–302, 313,
   314
reasons for use, 301–303
simplifying, 303–304
synopses, 313–314
and synthetic positions, 303–305
when to use, 312–313, 314
Buy-write strategy. *See* Covered call
   (buy-write) strategy

Calendar spreads. *See* Time spreads
Call options:
  defined, 4
  intrinsic and extrinsic values of, 11
  naked, 120
  naked call, 123
  overview, 15–16
  risk involved, 16, 128–130
  synthetic, 96–106
  and volatility, 12
Call option strategies:
  butterfly, 299–314
  collar strategy, 193–205
  condor, 315–333
  covered call (buy-write) strategy,
   131–146
  diagonal spreads, 255–259
  straddles, 261–277
  strangles, 279–295
  synthetic calls, 96–106
  synthetic put (protective call)
   strategy, 106–115, 179–192

Call option strategies (*Continued*)
synthetic stock, 88–96
time (calendar) spreads, 233–253
vertical spreads, 209–231
Collar strategy, 193–205
construction of, 204
down scenario, 196
examples, 199–204
foundations of, 193–194
key concepts of, 205
leaning, 197–198
potential profit/loss, 205
stagnant scenario, 195–196
synopsis, 204–205
up scenario, 194–195
when to use, 205
Condor, 297, 315–333
break-even point, 318, 328–330
compared to butterfly, 317,
321–323
construction of, 320, 331, 332
iron condor, 326–330
key concepts of, 332, 333
long vs. short, 315–320, 328–330,
331–333
position of Greeks with, 323–326
potential profit/loss, 332, 333
reasons for use, 317–320
synopses, 331–333
when to use, 330–331, 332, 333
Contracts, 3–4
Corresponding, defined, 87
Cost of carry, 34
Covered call (buy-write) strategy,
131–146. *See also* Collar
strategy
construction of, 146
down scenario, 137, 138
examples, 141–146
foundations of, 131–135
key concepts of, 146
leaning, 138–139
potential profit/loss, 146
profit and loss curve, 133
rolling, 139–141
stagnant scenario, 136–137, 138
synopsis, 146

up scenario, 135–136, 138
when to use, 146
Covered put (sell-write) strategy,
147–163
construction of, 149–150, 163
down scenario, 151–153
effects of, 149
examples, 157–162
key concepts of, 163
leaning, 154–157
potential profit/loss, 163
process of, 150–151
rolling, 157
stagnant scenario, 153
synopsis, 163
up scenario, 153–154
when to use, 163
Credit spread, 209, 220, 225

Debit spread, 209, 220
Dell Computer (DELL), 143–144
Delta, 41, 42–52, 87. *See also* Greeks
and butterflies, 307, 311–312
of calls, 43–44
changes in, 120–123
and condors, 323
definitions for, 256
delta connection, 46–47
and diagonal spreads, 256–257
hedge ratio, 42
percent chance, 42
percent change, 42
position delta, 48–49
of puts, 44–46
relationship to strike price, 42–46, 49
and stock, 93–94
and theta, 74, 75
and time decay, 127
time effect on, 50–51
and volatility, 51–52
Delta neutral, 48–49
Diagonal spreads (stock
replacement/covered call
strategy), 255–259
overview, 259
rolling position, 259
when to use, 257–259

Directional positions *See also* Leaning
  Positions
  long/short, 5
Directional stock play, 209
Directional trading strategies, 119–123
Dividend, as input, 34–35

EBay (EBAY), 200–202
Eli Lilly (LLY), 199–200
Enbridge Energy Partners LP (EEP),
  290–291
Exhaustion models, 170, 185
Expiration date, 4
Extrinsic value, 9–11, 125–127
  in butterflies, 304, 305
  in covered call (buy-write) strategy,
    134–136, 139
  in covered put (sell-write) strategy,
    150, 153, 156
  theta and, 68–71
  in vertical spreads, 217, 220–221,
    234, 235, 246
  and volatility, 12–13
  v-theta and, 83
Exxon Mobil (XOM), 250–251

Gamma, 41, 52–56. *See also* Greeks
  and butterflies, 307–308
  and condors, 323–326
  long vs. short, 55, 56
  relationship to strike price, 53
  and stock, 95–96
  and theta, 74–79
  and time, 53–55
  and time spreads, 236
General Electric (GE), 227–228
General Motors (GM), 175–177
Goldman Sachs (GXCO), 289–290
Greeks, 41–84
  and butterflies, 307–309
  and condors, 323–326
  delta, 41, 42–52 (*See also* Delta;
    T-delta)
  front-line, 42–79
  gamma, 41, 52–56 (*See also* Gamma;
    V-gamma)
  overview, 39

second-tier, 80–84
strike-based, 87 (*See also* Gamma;
    Theta; Vega)
and synthetic calls, 99–100, 103–104
and synthetic puts, 108–110,
    113–114
T-delta, 81
T-gamma, 82–83
theta, 11, 41, 68–79 (*See also* Theta;
    Time decay)
V-delta, 80–81
vega, 41, 57–68 (*See also* Implied
    volatility; Vega; Volatility)
V-gamma, 81–82
V-theta, 83–84

Hedge ratio, 42

Imclone Systems Inc. (IMCL), 292–293
Implied volatility. *See also* Vega
  defined, 13
  in straddles, 264–265
  in strangles, 284
  in time spreads, 222, 244–246
Inputs, 32–39
  dividend, 34–35
  interest rate, 34
  kurtosis, 35–39
  skewness, 35–39
  stock price, 33
  volatility, 33
Interest rate, as input, 34
In-the-money (ITM) options, 123–124,
    125, 127–128
  defined, 8
  effect of Greeks on, 43, 72, 74–76
  and intrinsic value, 9
  risk involved, 130
Intrinsic value, 9–11, 121–122
  in butterflies, 305
  in corresponding call/put spreads,
    215–216
  in covered call (buy-write) strategy,
    139
  in covered put (sell-write) strategy,
    156
  in vertical spreads, 214–216, 217

Iron butterfly, 309–312
Iron condor, 326–330
ITT Industries (ITT), 226–227

Johnson & Johnson (JNJ), 161–162,
    228–229
J.P. Morgan (JPM), 142–143

Kurtosis, 30, 35–39

Leaning positions: *See also* Directional
    positions
    definition, 138
    in covered call (buy-write) strategy,
        138–139
    in covered put (sell-write) strategy,
        154–157
    in protective put strategy, 168–169
    in synthetic put (protective call)
        strategy, 183–184
LEAPS, 6, 62–63
Leverage, 128–130, 258, 259
Log-normal distribution, 30, 32
Long position, defined, 5

Margin trading, 148
Market perception, 122
Married put. *See* Protective put
    strategy
Martek Biosciences (MATK), 188–190
McDonald's (MCD), 141–142
Merck (MRK), 160–161
Merrill Lynch (MER), 203–204
Monte Carlo method, 26

Naked, defined, 120
Naked calls, 120, 123
Naked puts, 120, 123
Normal distributions (Bell curve),
    21–25, 35–36

Option contract, overview, 3–4
Option pricing models, 29–32
    Adaptive mesh model, 29–32
    Binomial model, 26–28

Black-Scholes model, 26–27
    fundamentals, 21–25
    inputs of, 32–39
    Monte Carlo method, 26
    outputs of, 39
    Trinomial model, 28–29
    types of, 25–32
    VSK model, 37, 38
Options. *See also* Call options; Put
    options; *specific strategies*
    defined, 3
    speed component of, 120
    terminology, 3–13
    value determination of (*See* Option
        pricing models)
Options Clearing Corporation (OCC), 4
Out-of-the-money (OTM) options,
    124–128
    defined, 8–9
    effect of Greeks on, 43, 44, 46, 50,
        74–76
    risk involved, 130
Outputs:
    Greeks, 39, 41–84
    theoretical value, 39
Over premium parity, 10–11. *See also*
    Extrinsic value

Parity, 10
Percent chance, 42
Percent change, 42
Perception of market, 122
Potential profit/loss:
    butterfly, 301–302, 313, 314
    collar strategy, 196, 205
    condor, 332, 333
    covered call (buy-write) strategy,
        146
    covered put (sell-write) strategy, 163
    diagonal spreads, 259
    protective put strategy, 168, 171,
        177–178
    straddles, 276, 277
    strangles, 294, 295
    synthetic put (protective call)
        strategy, 182, 183, 192

time spreads, 244, 246, 253
vertical spreads, 211–214, 224, 225, 231
Premium, defined, 9
Pride International (PDE), 274–275
Profit/loss potential:
butterfly, 301–302, 313, 314
collar strategy, 205
condor, 332, 333
covered call (buy-write) strategy, 146
covered put (sell-write) strategy, 163
protective put strategy, 177–178
straddles, 276, 277
strangles, 294, 295
synthetic put (protective call) strategy, 192
time spreads, 253
vertical spreads, 211–214, 231
Protective call strategy. *See* Synthetic put (protective call) strategy
Protective put strategy, 165–178.
See also Collar strategy
construction of, 177
vs. covered call (buy-write) strategy, 165
down scenario, 167–168
examples, 172–177
foundations of, 165–166
key concepts of, 178
leaning, 168–169
potential profit/loss, 177–178
stagnant scenario, 167, 168
synopsis, 177–178
up scenario, 166–167, 168
when to use, 170–171, 177
Put options:
defined, 4
intrinsic and extrinsic values of, 11
naked put, 120, 123
overview, 16–18
risk involved, 17–18, 128–130
synthetic put, 106–115
and volatility, 13
Put option strategies:
butterfly, 299–314

collar strategy, 193–205
condor, 315–333
covered put (sell-write) strategy, 147–163
diagonal spreads, 255–259
protective put strategy, 165–178
rolling put spread, 248
straddles, 261–277
strangles, 279–295
synthetic put (protective call) strategy, 106–115, 179–192
synthetic stock, 88–96
time (calendar) spreads, 233–253
vertical spreads, 209–231

Qlogic (QLGC), 187–188

Rambus (RMBS), 158–159
Random walk theory, 21–22
Raymond James Financial (RJF), 251–252
Raytheon (RTN), 252–253
Real vs. synthetic stock, 88–96
Red Hat Inc. (RHAT), 275–276
Research in Motion (RIMM), 271–272
Risk. *See also* Potential profit/loss
with call options, 16
leverage and, 128–130
with protective put strategy, 170
with put options, 17–18, 128–130
with straddles, 266–267
with strangles, 285
with synthetic calls, 103–106
with time (calendar) spreads, 244–246
Rolling positions, 139–141
in covered put (sell-write) strategy, 157
in diagonal spreads, 259
in time spreads, 246–249
in vertical spreads, 218–220

Scholes, Myron, 26
Sell-write strategy. *See* Covered put (sell-write) strategy
Short position, defined, 5

Short selling, defined, 147–148
Skewness, 30, 35–39
Spread trades:
  in butterflies, 303–305
  credit spread, 209, 220, 225
  debit spread, 209, 220, 225
  diagonal spreads, 255–259 (*See also*
    Diagonal spreads)
  imaginary scenario, 222–224
  overview, 207–208
  and rolling positions, 140–141
  rolling put spread, 248
  time (calendar) spreads, 233–253
    (*See also* Time spreads)
  and use of vega, 64–68
  vertical spreads, 209–229 (*See also*
    Vertical spreads)
Sprint (FON), 145–146
Standard deviation, 23
Stock:
  borrowed, 105
  and delta, 93–94
  real vs. synthetic, 88–96
Stock price, 8–13, 33, 52, 120–129
Straddles, 261–277
  break-even point, 267–271
  construction of, 261–262, 276,
    277
  examples, 271–276
  implied volatility and, 264–265
  key concepts of, 276, 277
  long, 272–274, 276
  overview, 271
  potential profit/loss, 276, 277
  price factors, 263–266
  process of, 262–263
  risks/rewards, 266–271
  short, 274–276, 277
  synopses, 276–277
  time decay and, 265–266
  when to use, 276, 277
Strangles, 279–295
  break-even point, 285–288
  construction of, 280–281, 294
  delta and, 283
  examples, 289–294

  implied volatility and, 283–284
  in iron condor, 326–331
  key concepts of, 294, 295
  long, 289–291, 294
  overview, 289
  potential profit/loss, 294, 295
  price factors, 282–285
  process of, 281–282
  risks/rewards, 285–288
  short, 292–295
  synopses, 294–295
  time decay and, 284–285, 287–289
  vega and, 284
  when to use, 294, 295
Strategies:
  butterfly, 299–314
  collar strategy, 193–205
  condor, 315–333
  covered call (buy-write) strategy,
    131–146
  covered put (sell-write) strategy,
    147–163
  diagonal spreads, 255–259
  protective put strategy, 165–178
  rolling put spread, 248
  straddles, 261–277
  strangles, 279–295
  synthetic calls, 96–106
  synthetic put (protective call)
    strategy, 106–115, 179–192
  synthetic stock, 88–96
  time (calendar) spreads, 233–253
  vertical spreads, 209–231
Strike price:
  defined, 5
  delta and, 42–46, 49
  gamma and, 53
  as input, 34
  symbols, 6–7
  theta and, 100
Symantec (SMYC), 229–230
Symbols, 5–7
Synopses:
  butterfly, 313–314
  collar strategy, 204–205
  condor, 331–333

covered call (buy-write) strategy, 146
covered put (sell-write) strategy, 163
protective put strategy, 177–178
straddles, 276–277
strangles, 294–295
synthetic put (protective call) strategy, 191–192
time spreads, 253
vertical spreads, 230–232
Synthetic call:
  long, 96–100
  risk involved, 98–101, 103–106
  short, 100–105
Synthetic positions, defined, 86–87
Synthetic put (protective call) strategy, 106–115, 179–192
  compared to other strategies, 180
  construction of, 191
  down scenario, 181
  examples, 187–191
  key concepts of, 192
  leaning, 183–184
  long, 106–110
  potential profit/loss, 192
  risk involved, 108–110, 113–115
  short, 110–113
  stagnant scenario, 181
  summary, 182–183
  synopsis, 191–192
  up scenario, 181–182
  when to use, 184–187, 191
Synthetic stock, 87, 88–96

T-delta, 81
Technical analysis:
  breakout, 171–172
  and synthetic put (protective call) strategy, 185
T-gamma, 82–83
Theoretical value, 19, 21, 25
  defined, 39
Theta, 68–79. *See also* Time decay
  and butterflies, 308–309
  and condors, 324–326
  defined, 11, 41

and delta, 71–74
and gamma, 74–79
key points, 79
relationship to strike price, 100
and stock, 95–96
v-theta, 83–84
Ticker symbols. *See* Symbols
Time, effect on delta, 50–51
Time decay. *See also* Theta
  and covered calls, 134
  and covered puts, 150
  defined, 11
  and delta, 127
  and straddles, 265–266
  and strangles, 284–285, 287–289
  T-gamma, 82–83
  and time spreads, 234–235
  and vertical spreads, 220–222
Time spreads, 233–253
  behavior of, 234–236
  buyer risk and reward, 244–246
  closing position, 248–249
  construction of, 233–234
  effects of volatility on, 237–244
  examples, 249–253
  implied volatility and, 222, 244–246
  key concepts of, 253
  overview, 249
  potential profit/loss, 253
  rolling position, 246–249
  synopsis, 253
  when to use, 253
Trading sheets, 338–342
Trinomial model, 28–29
Trumpification, 50–51

Ulam, Stanislaw, 26

Value. *See* Extrinsic value; Intrinsic value; Theoretical value
Value determination, 19
V-delta, 80–81
Vega, 41, 57–68. *See also* Greeks; Implied volatility; Volatility
  and butterflies, 308
  and condors, 324–326

Vega (*Continued*)
  and spread trades, 64–68
  and stock, 95–96
  and straddles, 265
  and strangles, 284
  summary of, 238
  and time, 60
  and time spreads, 239–244
  and vertical spreads, 221
  volatility smile, 60–62
  volatility tilt, 62–68
Vertical spreads. *See also* Butterfly;
    Condor
  bear spread, 209–210, 227–230,
    231–232
  bull spread, 209–210, 226–227,
    230–231
  construction of, 210–211, 230,
    231
  directional stock play, 209
  examples, 225–229
  imaginary scenario, 222–224
  intrinsic value, 214–216
  key concepts of, 231
  overview, 224–225
  potential profit/loss, 211–214,
    231
  price fluctuations, 217–218
  rolling position, 218–220
  synopses, 230–232
  time decay and, 220–222
  as volatility play, 221–222

  volatility skew, 218
  when to use, 230–231
V-gamma, 81–82
Volatility, 12–13. *See also* Implied
    volatility; Vega
  defined, 12
  and delta, 51–52
  implied (*See* Implied volatility)
  as input, 33
  key points, 57
  overview of, 238
  in straddles, 264–265, 266
  and time, 50
  in time spreads, 237–244
  V-delta, 80–81
  V-theta, 83–84
Volatility sensitivity. *See* Vega
Volatility skew, 218
Volatility smile, 29, 60–62, 330
Volatility tilt, 62–68
Volatility trading, in vertical spreads,
    221–222
VSK model, 37, 38
V-theta, 83–84

Wal-Mart (WMT), 174–175
Wynn Resorts (WYNN), 190–191

XILINX Inc. (XLNX), 293–294

Yahoo (YHOO), 202–203